D0648359

Critical Essays on Bernard Malamud

Critical Essays on Bernard Malamud

Joel Salzberg

G. K. Hall & Co. • Boston, Massachusetts

Library of Congress Cataloging-in-Publication Data

Salzberg, Joel.
   Critical essays on Bernard Malamud.

   (Critical essays on American literature)
   Includes index.
   1. Malamud, Bernard—Criticism and interpretation.
I. Title.   II. Series.
PS3563.A4Z88   1987   813'.54   87-23815
ISBN 0-8161-8881-5 (alk. paper)

This publication is printed on permanent/durable acid-free paper
MANUFACTURED IN THE UNITED STATES OF AMERICA

CRITICAL ESSAYS ON
AMERICAN LITERATURE

This series seeks to anthologize the most important criticism on a wide variety of topics and writers in American Literature. Our readers will find in various volumes not only a generous selection of reprinted articles and reviews but original essays, bibliographies, manuscript sections, and other materials brought to public attention for the first time. This volume is a collection of reviews and essays tracing the critical reputation of the career of Bernard Malamud. Of the reprinted material in the volume, there are selections by many of the most important people in American letters, among them Philip Roth, Robert Alter, Leon Edel, Robert Scholes, Harvey Swados, and Alfred Kazin. In addition to a substantial introduction by Joel Salzberg that discusses the history of critical comment on Malamud, there are original essays by Lawrence L. Langer, Guido Fink, Sidney Richman, and James M. Mellard written especially for inclusion in this volume. We are confident that this book will make a permanent and significant contribution to American literary study.

James Nagel, GENERAL EDITOR

Northeastern University

For
Adele Zelenko: 1901–1985
and
Bernard Malamud: 1914–1986

CONTENTS

INTRODUCTION   1
     Joel Salzberg

Reviews

Baseball à la Wagner: The Nibelung in the Polo Grounds
[Review of *The Natural*]   23
     Harvey Swados

Fantasist of the Ordinary [Review of *The Assistant*]   25
     Alfred Kazin

Strangers amid Ruins [Review of *The Magic Barrel*]   29
     Arthur Foff

Fantasy and Reality [Review of *A New Life*]   33
     Eugene Goodheart

The Power of Positive Sex [Review of *Idiots First*]   37
     F. W. Dupee

Yakov's Ordeal [Review of *The Fixer*]   41
     George P. Elliott

Portrait of Artist as "Escape-Goat"
[Review of *Pictures of Fidelman*]   47
     Robert Scholes

[Review of *The Tenants*]   51
     Morris Dickstein

Sliding into English [Review of *Rembrandt's Hat*]   57
     Leonard Michaels

[The Biographer in *Dubin's Lives*]   61
     Leon Edel

A Theological Fantasy [Review of *God's Grace*]   64
     Robert Alter

Sad Music [Review of *The Stories of Bernard Malamud*]   68
     Mark Shechner

Essays

The Good Man's Dilemma: *The Natural, The Assistant,*
and American Materialism 75
  Iska Alter

[From "Imagining Jews"] 98
  Philip Roth

Parody as Exorcism: "The Raven" and "The Jewbird" 108
  J. Gerald Kennedy

Malamud's Jews and the Holocaust Experience 115
  Lawrence L. Langer

Yakov Bok 125
  Lucio P. Ruotolo

The American Schlemiel Abroad: Malamud's Italian
Stories and the End of American Innocence 139
  Christof Wegelin

"Ecco la chiave!": Malamud's Italy
as the Land of Copies 151
  Guido Fink

The Tenants in the House of Fiction 165
  Steven G. Kellman

Mirrors, Windows and Peeping Toms: Women as the
Object of Voyeuristic Scrutiny in Bernard Malamud's
A New Life and *Dubin's Lives* 174
  Chiara Briganti

The "Perverse Economy" of Malamud's Art: A Lacanian
Reading of *Dubin's Lives* 186
  James M. Mellard

Malamud's Quarrel with God 203
  Sidney Richman

INDEX 223

INTRODUCTION

When Helen Bober of Bernard Malamud's *The Assistant* (1957) asks her mother why she is crying, Ida Bober's responses — " 'Why do I cry? I cry for the world. . . . I cry for you' " — are couched in the very language that Malamud was to use, shortly after the publication of the novel, in his first interview to express his identification with those who suffer.[1] In the maternal sentiments of an Ida Bober, Malamud lamented the destruction of six million Jews and the death of six to ten million Chinese during the flooding of the Yellow River: " 'Somebody had to cry — even if it's just a writer, 20 years later.' "[2] These remarks serve as a reconfirmation of the humane sensibility that Malamud's original audience discovered in *The Natural* (1952) and *The Magic Barrel* (1958), as well as in *The Assistant*. It is that sensibility, anchored in his use of the metaphorical and moral dimensions of Jewish experience,[3] and incorporated into a laconic prose free of sentimentality, which brought Malamud to national attention as an accomplished and, in his own way, a sophisticated writer who somehow withstood the corrosive influences of modern life.[4]

In the 1940s and 1950s, with the exception of *The Natural*, Malamud wrote about the lives of poor Jews and Italians with the authenticity and empathy that were the unmistakable signatures of his fiction. Moreover, his stark rendering of and his emotional response to the squalid lives of his characters compelled him, at times, to intercede on their behalf, as though he were, in some private way, attempting through them to exorcise Mankind's ancestral curse of death, suffering, and failure.[5] In his early work through such differently conceived books as *The Fixer* (1966) and *Pictures of Fidelman: An Exhibition* (1969), Malamud introduced character transformations, symbolic redemptions, and moral victories, but invariably laced with irony as a result of the exorbitant cost demanded of his characters. While Malamud's earliest critics were intrigued by his desire to wring from life a meaning in suffering, no matter how small, they also recognized an indelible sadness in his work.[6] It is not an exaggeration to say that a state of mourning is virtually the normative emotional condition that governs the behavior of a typical Malamud character: he mourns for his own wasted life or over death, suicide, or

1

alienation of family members, and he is never fully able to separate himself from the bonds of the past. This funereal quality seems to be a fitting accompaniment to an increasing philosophical pessimism culminating in what amounts to a crisis of faith in *God's Grace* (1982).[7] These foregoing observations represent a synthesis of the views generally shared by most Malamud commentators over the years.

If Malamud's humanistic themes have, in one form or another, preempted the attention of most critics over other issues, there have been some who have caught glimpses of a decidedly different Malamud. Leslie Fiedler, astutely perceived in the infancy of Malamud's career, a writer who was "a good deal blacker, more *demonic* than he is prepared to admit to himself."[8] And readers such as Nat Hentoff, Philip Roth, and Marilyn Michele Fabe have detected undercurrents of hostility in his fiction which seem directed at his own characters.[9] God himself, it might be argued, has not been exempt from such hostility. In such early stories as "Take Pity" (1958) and "Idiots First" (1963), one discovers a Malamudian anger directed at divine indifference in the face of human suffering. Indeed, subsequent works such as "Talking Horse" (1972) and, more recently, *God's Grace*, bring to the surface what seems to have been a private conflict implied in his earlier stories — Malamud's quarrel with God. And when questioned about that anger in a telephone conversation, a few months before his death on 18 March 1986, Malamud, without responding directly, suggested that it was not an unlikely reaction of a writer living in the times that we do.[10]

In the past, Malamud's thematic preoccupations — for example, the mystery of human suffering, redemption and transformation, fate and the problem of human freedom, the conflict between art and life — were also connected to innovative narrative strategies and techniques, at times revealing such modern influences as Joyce, Kafka, and Mann. And to the end, Malamud continued to push his art in new directions, as he had so often done before. In what was to be the final stage of his career, he had briefly put aside the folkloric, realistic, or allegoric narratives of his previous work in order to experiment with fictionalized biography. "In Kew Gardens" (1984) and "Alma Redeemed" (1984) were attempts to distill the complex personalities of Virginia Woolf and Alma Mahler, respectively, into a few brief pages in the manner of a William Dubin (the biographer protagonist of *Dubin's Lives* [1979]).[11] Yet Malamud's last published story, "A Lost Grave," (May 1985) attempted, in less than two pages, to evoke the tragic-comic qualities of loss and loneliness that were so successfully rendered in *The Magic Barrel*.[12] If this recent piece was merely a skeleton of Malamud's past achievements, Malamud's unfinished novel, tentatively titled *The Tribe* — a work dealing with a Russian Jewish peddler who roams the old west, and is adopted by a tribe of Indians — was his most ambitious attempt to provide a fictional new life for the exiled Jew of his earliest stories.

In scanning his career, we find that there is more than one Bernard Malamud to contend with: the benevolent humanist, sometimes approaching the mystic; the writer, reputedly nurturing an unconscious anger and aggression; the philosophical pessimist, still seeking affirmations; and, most assuredly, the literary craftsman, almost compulsively exploring new subjects, techniques, and narrative forms. If the images that have developed around Malamud and his work are various and often contradictory, the critical reaction to his fiction, past and present, has been no less diverse.

The changing character of Malamud's fiction has been registered in the critical writing on that work over the last thirty years, but biographical information of substance—letters, papers, or memoirs—is scant. Malamud had made no arrangements for an authorized biography, and he had continually avoided questions that probe more than superficially into the regions of his personal life or that attempted to make connections between his life and his fiction. One can, however, piece together the outlines of his history as man and artist through examining the short biographical chapters in such reference books as the *Dictionary of Literary Biography*, or *World Authors: 1950–1970*; the latter is an especially useful point of departure since it supplies Malamud's own concise autobiographical account of his life, with something of the colloquial style, simplicity, and directness of his fiction.[13] Malamud's introduction to *The Stories of Bernard Malamud*, a biographical *bildungsroman*, provides a backward glance at the author's development as a writer.[14] One other item of possible interest is an autobiographical memoir, *Long Work, Short Life* (1985), originally given as a lecture at Bennington College on 30 October 1984.[15] In its nineteen pages of reminiscence, it is probably the longest and most useful account of Malamud's life currently available, occasionally offering details not found in any other source.

Scholarship dealing with the revisions in Malamud's short stories or novels from manuscript to publication was not feasible while Malamud was alive since he did not permit access to his manuscripts (all in the Library of Congress), but according to Timothy Seldes, one of the executors of Malamud's estate, and president of Russell and Volkening (Malamud's literary agent), that policy is about to change. Nevertheless, it may be a while before we can expect to have a book that focuses on Malamud's imagination and literary practices comparable to Daniel Fuch's *Saul Bellow: Vision and Revision*.[16] Such investigation may well turn out to be of special interest to scholars and critics because of Malamud's acknowledged concern with the importance of revision in his own literary process: "I would write a book, or a short story, at least three times—once to understand it, the second time to improve the prose, and a third to compel it to say what it still must say."[17]

While guarded about himself and impatient with questions involving interpretation of his fiction, Malamud was exceedingly liberal in granting interviews, which now number well over thirty. Those of Leslie and Joyce Field (1975) and Daniel Stern (1975) are especially valuable, covering issues of particular interest:[18] biographical information (especially Stern), Malamud's involvement with Jewishness, with Jewish characters, literary influences, his philosophy of composition, and the relation between art and life. For those interested in chronicling Malamud's public expressions of humanism as they relate to the development of his art, Joseph Wershba's interview of 1958 is the place to begin.[19]

As Malamud continued to publish and the critical writing on his work began to accumulate, the need for primary and secondary bibliographies became apparent. Rita Natalie Kosofsky pioneered this research in her study, *Bernard Malamud: An Annotated Checklist* (1969).[20] Although Kosofsky's annotated checklist has been superseded by other secondary bibliographies, her book is still useful for citing through 1968 the original place of publication of a Malamud story or a section from a novel in progress first published in a journal. Donald Risty updated Kosofsky's citations of secondary sources in his chapter "A Comprehensive Checklist of Malamud Criticism" in *The Fiction of Bernard Malamud* (1977) with his citations of reviews, articles, chapters in books, and books through 1975.[21] Robert D. Habich supplemented Risty's research with "Bernard Malamud: A Bibliographical Survey" in *Studies in American Jewish Literature.*[22] Habich discussed the range of scholarship and criticism on Malamud's writing and concluded that "perhaps the most pressing task for contemporary scholars is the mature evaluation of Malamud's work in the hierarchy of twentieth-century American fiction."[23] Joseph Graw contributed to the ongoing research not only by listing new citations, in foreign criticism as well as in English, but also by updating Kosofsky's primary bibliography. Graw cited the original place of publication of Malamud's stories in print after 1968; in addition, he identified those stories and novels which had been translated into foreign languages and listed other stories which had been reprinted in anthologies.[24] Joel Salzberg's *Bernard Malamud: A Reference Guide* identified the patterns of Malamud criticism emerging over the last thirty years and supplied nearly nine hundred annotated citations of critical writing in English, including annotations of critical writing translated from eight foreign languages.[25] These bibliographical studies, covering three decades of critical response to Malamud's fiction, help to identify critical trends and issues that have emerged over the years.

Some of the best essays on Malamud's work in the sixties and the early seventies have been brought together in the collections of Leslie and Joyce Field. *Bernard Malamud and His Critics* (1970) reprinted twenty-one of the most important essays published in scholarly journals in the sixties.[26] The Fields offered a second collection, *Bernard Malamud: A Collection of Critical Essays* (1975), on a more modest scale, including one of the most detailed interviews of Malamud's career[27] and original essays by Sam

Bluefarb and Leslie Field. In 1976 a symposium on Malamud's fiction was held at Corvallis, Oregon, with a number of notable critics on modern American fiction, who had previously written on Malamud, participating. Papers presented by Ihab Hassan, W. J. Handy, Peter L. Hays, Leslie Field, and Ben Siegel attempted to reexamine Malamud's work in the contexts of American romanticism, modernism, and postmodernism; these were published the following year under the editorship of Richard Astro and Jackson J. Benson.[28]

A number of useful books have been written on Malamud over the last twenty years, all somewhat out of date now, since the author continued to publish new fiction until shortly before his death. Sidney Richman's *Bernard Malamud* (1966) was the first of these longer studies.[29] Richman offered a sensitive reading of Malamud's first three novels and his first two collections of stories. Although limited in scope, the book is nevertheless valuable for an overview of Malamud's work up to the mid-sixties. Sandy Cohen's *Bernard Malamud and the Trial By Love* (1974) addressed the theme of self-transcendence from Malamud's earliest work through *Pictures of Fidelman*;[30] the theme itself, however, is relevant to Malamud's subsequent fiction. In the same year Robert Ducharme's *Art and Idea in the Novels of Bernard Malamud* (1974) also examined, but with greater depth than Cohen, all of Malamud's fiction through *Pictures of Fidelman*, drawing on the psychological and anthropological perspectives of Freud, Jung, Frazer, Róheim, Joseph Campbell, and Otto Rank.[31] Sheldon Hershinow's *Bernard Malamud*, anchoring its approach in his first chapter, "The Writer as Moral Activist," presented a mainstream reading of Malamud's fiction that included *Dubin's Lives*;[32] and Iska Alter's *The Good Man's Dilemma: Social Criticism in the Fiction of Bernard Malamud* (1981) focused perceptively on the social criticism both implicit and explicit in Malamud's fiction that most American critics had generally ignored.[33] The authority of her book, however, is somewhat compromised by her failure to acknowledge the work of Cohen and Ducharme.

Prior to the longer studies, the reviews of Malamud's *The Natural* in the late 1950s introduced Malamud to the public and played their part in an important chapter in American literary history. At a time when critics like Alfred Kazin were arguing that symbolism and myth were overused by American writers, Malamud was able to draw praise because of his inventiveness in employing these conventions. Harvey Swados, Norman Podhoretz, and Leslie Fiedler were already familiar with Malamud's stories about Jews in such periodicals as *Partisan Review* and *Commentary*, and Malamud's departure from this subject matter for a narrative joining Ring Lardner with Jesse Weston brought to Leslie Fiedler, as well as other critics, both surprise and delight.[34] "If this [union] is outrageous," Fiedler observed, "it is the sort of outrage I enjoy."[35] Moreover, Fiedler had not been especially attracted to Malamud's fiction until he had read *The*

Natural, and his belated review (1955) of the book may suggest that he had initially passed it by. Others like Harvey Swados were also surprised if not wholly delighted with what Malamud had done. Swados, while cautiously wishing that Malamud had developed the vision of his short stories into a novel, nevertheless praised *The Natural* as "exciting in a way few ambitious intellectual novels are,"[36] even though he regarded it as an "honorable failure." While recognizing its unevenness in Malamud's attempt to unite elements of epic and tragedy with the popular mythos of baseball, Swados also judged that when his novel succeeded in this synthesis it was at its best.[37] Apart from the intrinsic merits of the book, the importance of *The Natural* for both Podhoretz and Fiedler must be linked to their populist sentiments as cultural critics who were unhappy with literary hierarchies. In his marriage of high-brow and low-brow art—that is, narrative employing myth and symbol with a story of American baseball—Malamud surely became an unwitting ally of their cultural and critical biases.[38]

The freshness and vigor of *The Natural* seemed to promise that in time Malamud might offer more tangible evidence of the richness of his imagination. With the publication of *The Assistant* and *The Magic Barrel* expectant critics were not disappointed, and as early as 1958, Malamud had the distinction of being regarded "as the least known writer of the first rank."[39] The early reception of *The Assistant* reflected an even greater admiration and respect than Malamud had earned for *The Natural*. Herbert Gold, typical of many writers, praised the novel for the uniqueness of its voice;[40] Robert Bowen, for its tight, economical, and colloquial prose;[41] and George [P.] Elliott, for its authoritative presentation of Jews.[42] Kazin dissented from the view that Malamud's Jews were authentic in their conception, and considered them instead as symbolic Jews in a morality tale intended as "a glorification of the Jew as a Jew."[43] His review of *The Magic Barrel* held similar reservations with regard to Malamud's use of symbolism. Although otherwise appreciative of his talent, Kazin felt that Malamud's imaginative power—"the hallucinated, the visionary, and the bizarre"—was lost when his symbolism became allegorical.[44] Fiedler found in *The Assistant* the imaginative quality that Kazin liked but regarded as insufficiently expressed, the suggestion of surrealistic absurdity.[45] If praise for *The Assistant* was qualified, *The Magic Barrel* brought Malamud almost unreserved critical acclaim, culminating in The National Book Award for 1959. Among the many perceptive reviewers recognizing Malamud's originality, Arthur Foff must be singled out for his brief but effective response to Kazin's criticism of Malamud's use of Jewish characters.[46] If Kazin felt that Malamud was too much of an allegorist and not enough of a fantasist, Philip Roth, reflecting his own priorities, suggested that Malamud's fiction was too far removed from the realities of contemporary life.[47]

Although Malamud's writing did not generate any major criticism in the late 1950s, the reviews of *The Natural*, *The Assistant*, and *The Magic*

Barrel dealt with a number of topics that were to become the basis of important articles in the 1960s, perhaps the most productive decade in Malamud criticism. These reviews eventually nurtured some of the richest discussion of Malamud's work, embracing myth and archetype, religious, psychological, oneiric, and existential themes, and intertextuality.

Earl Rovit initiated this mature phase of Malamud study in discussing Malamud's connection to the Jewish literary tradition. While he acknowledged Malamud's general success in fusing the Jewish experience, past and present, with modern fictional techniques, Rovit was disappointed at the deflation of tragic vision through comic or grotesque characterization, a position that seems overly prescriptive.[48] Next Robert Alter explored Malamud's work through *The Fixer*, and claimed that he was "the first important American writer to shape out of his early experiences in the immigrant milieu a whole distinctive style of imagination and, to a lesser degree, a distinctive technique of fiction as well."[49] Complementing Alter's piece, Sam Bluefarb's insightful essay found in Malamud's work one of its central tensions, "the syncretism of Hebraism and Hellenism," as well as a synthesis of Judaic motifs with the themes of western literature.[50] Sheldon Norman Grebstein's essay, "Bernard Malamud and the Jewish Movement," is of interest more for what it has to say about the richness of Malamud's style and literary idiom than for its reflections on Malamud's place among contemporary Jewish American writers.[51] Despite its brevity, Leonard Michaels's review of *Rembrandt's Hat* makes significant additions to Grebstein's analysis of Malamud's style and is especially sensitive to the rich interplay of Yiddish and English in Malamud's stories.[52]

Various commentators had recognized the influences of such Eastern European Jewish writers as I. L. Peretz, Mendele Moyker-Sforim, and Sholom Aleichem on Malamud's fiction, but no serious discussion had emerged until books by Ruth Wisse and Sanford Pinsker simultaneously appeared in 1971.[53] Both critics knowledgeably explored the Jewish as well as the non-Jewish origins of the schlemiel figure in folklore and literature. While there is some inevitable overlapping in their historical overview, there are also some noticeable differences in their treatment of Malamud's schlemiel hero. Wisse observed that one of the major characteristics of all schlemiel literature is the need of the figure to protect his inner self at all costs, reflected in Malamud's fiction as his schlemiel's need "for recognizing himself as, alas, only himself."[54] Pinsker's discussion of Malamud's schlemiel tended to focus on his inevitable bungling in his frustrated attempts to change his life. Shiv P. Kumar extended Wisse and Pinkser's discussion of the schlemiel to include the folk figures they had omitted in their studies—the *schnorrer,* the *luftmenschen,* and the *shadkhyn.*[55]

The moral and religious sensibility governing Malamud's fiction has always accounted for a signficant portion of the criticism on his work. Glen Meeter's early comparative study of the religious dimensions of Malamud and Roth's fiction still furnishes useful insights;[56] Giles B. Gunn observed in Malamud's fiction unique combinations of the sacred and profane reminiscent of a Whitmanesque vision.[57] And Robert Kegan claimed for Malamud (and Saul Bellow) the influence of Martin Buber's Chasidic vision.[58] Ita Sheres has persuasively argued that the key to an understanding of Malamud's fiction is the story of the "Akedah," complemented by the legend of the "Lamed Vov" and the mysticism of Isaac Luria.[59] Focusing on *The Natural, The Assistant, The Fixer,* and *The Tenants,* Sheres examined, in the context of these biblical themes, the exile and alienation of Malamud's protagonists from their origins as the basis for their subsequent insights into the nature of existence. In what may well be the most important essay in recent years on Malamud as a "religious" writer, Sidney Richman argues in "Malamud's Quarrel with God" that *God's Grace* "tests as never before the resources of the redemptive spirit one finds at work in most of his earlier fiction" and, despite much critical comment to the contrary, Richman discovers in Malamud's harrowing conclusion "an unconditional mark of God's mercy."[60]

Thirteen years passed before the mythical allusiveness of *The Natural* was fully discussed in a major article, and in that span of time Malamud had completed *The Assistant* and *A New Life.* Earl Wasserman's "*The Natural*: Malamud's World Ceres" broke new ground in its examination of Jungian archetypes, along with Malamud's use of the Grail and vegetation myths.[61] Wasserman judged that *The Natural* was "the necessary reference text" for an understanding of the "subsequent fiction."[62] James Mellard's "Malamud's Novels: Four Versions of Pastoral" was a logical sequel to Wasserman's mythic and archetypal study.[63] Discussing *The Natural, The Assistant, A New life,* and *The Fixer,* Mellard pursued Malamud's use of the pastoral mode and demonstrated its shaping influence on the types of characters in his novels. While continuing to work with myth, Max F. Schulz added a new dimension to this approach by revealing how Malamud fused Marxian assumptions and mythic patterns in his plots, ultimately creating proletarian heroes who also function as mythic saviors.[64] In essence, these mythically oriented critics were impressed by Malamud's skillful development of ordinary and fallible characters within the framework of highly stylized literary conventions.

By the end of the sixties, however, the mythical and archetypal approaches to Malamud's fiction had essentially run their course, but in this decade, and beyond, other critics pursued themes that were closer to home. Some drew attention to Malamud's connection to the American romance tradition, as well as his adaptation of themes central to nineteenth century American writing in general. Jonathan Baumbach, for example, observed in Malamud the moral fabler and fantasist.[65] And Thomas Alva Hoyt's comment that Malamud's protagonists, in typical romantic fashion, reject old evidence in favor of new solutions, has been a commonplace view in Malamud criticism over the years.[66] Malamud's affinities with nineteenth century American writing began to crystallize more fully after the publication of *A New Life*. David Burrows recognized in Malamud's S. Levin an indebtedness to Emersonian self-reliance and to the moral vision of Thoreau and James.[67] In the first in a series of intertextual approaches, Samuel Bellman went on to demonstrate how James's "The Madonna of the Future" inspired Malamud's "Still Life" (originally published in *Partisan Review* and collected in *Idiots First*).[68] Christof Wegelin, however, took a major step forward in Malamud studies in his illuminating discussion of Malamud's appropriation of James's international theme. In examining Malamud's Italian stories, Wegelin revealed the shrinking differences between Italians and Americans and the final loss of American innocence.[69] Guido Fink, bringing an Italian (and Jewish) perspective to the international theme, discussed Malamud's protean imagination in his creation of Jews and Italians. Fink observed that Malamud's imaginative conversion of Jews into Italians and Italians into Jews through the medium of suffering allowed both groups to compete for the dubious honor of representing the suffering human condition.[70] Applying the most rigorous intertextual approach to a Malamud work thus far, J. Gerald Kennedy explored Poe's "The Raven" and Malamud's "The Jewbird" and perceived not only satire on Jewish anti-Semitism but also a parody through which Malamud exorcised the authority of his literary predecessor on his imagination.[71] The essays of Wegelin, Fink, and Kennedy rival some of the best work of the sixties in their depth and originality.

Among the various critical approaches to Malamud's work emerging in the seventies, the psychological and oneiric and, to some degree, the existential, contributed their share of insights, sometimes provocative. Norman Lear, following the leads of those who had recognized Dostoevskian elements in Malamud's fiction, discussed the double theme in *The Assistant* and *Crime and Punishment*, and determined that the pattern of inner conflict in Malamud's novel is rendered ironically.[72] Addressing a different psychological issue, a small body of critics, uncomfortable with the severity of suffering involved in Malamud's moral vision, ascribed a subliminal motivation to his characters, if not to Malamud himself. Philip Roth's "Imagining Jews," while predominantly concerned with exploring the use of Jewish and gentile stereotypes in the fiction of Jewish authors, declared that "*The Assistant* is a manifestation of ethical Jewhood with a vengeance. Beneath the austerity and the pathos, Malamud . . . has a fury all his own."[73] Indeed, as far back as 1963, Nat Hentoff had suggested in a review of *Idiots First* that a disjunction existed between Malamud's benevolent public pronouncements about man and a latent hostility that seems to engulf his characters.[74] Marilyn Michele Fabe made this issue the central concern of her dissertation, and applied modern psychological theory to a study of Malamud's guilt ridden characters.[75] According to

Fabe, most critics casually accept the proposition that Malamud's protagonists achieve moral and spiritual "success" only through suffering, but they fail to explore the possible implications of that suffering. Fabe argued that "the self abnegation of Malamud's characters has an obsessional quality about it," a condition "compelled by a dark inner necessity."[76] Finally, in bringing the post-Freudian poetics of Jacques Lacan to a reading of *Dubin's Lives*, James Mellard uncovered the patterns of repetition and doubling associated with William Dubin's unconscious quest for identity.[77]

The psychological approaches to Malamud's fiction have far outweighed the existential in number and substance, even though much of Malamud's fiction with its Kafkaesque and absurdist elements, and with its concern with man's freedom, surely invites existentialist interpretation. William J. Handy's "The Malamud Hero: A Quest for Existence" often flirts with existential issues.[78] Lucio P. Ruotolo, however, observing points of contact between Malamud and Kierkegaard, confronts these issues directly in his reading of *The Fixer*.[79] Questions pertaining either to the absence or the nature of God in Malamud's fiction, and the nature of the self in works other than *The Fixer*, persist and still need to be probed and discussed.

The remoteness of Malamud's earlier fiction from the actual world was, for some critics, a flaw in his art to be reckoned with. Philip Roth asserted in 1961 that Malamud had "not shown specific interest in the anxieties and the dilemmas and corruptions of the contemporary American Jew."[80] The appearance of *The Fixer* in 1966 and *The Tenants* in 1971, however, brought Malamud closer to a mimetic representation of life than did his earlier fiction. Even though, as *Time* magazine complained, *The Fixer* is not anchored in the American scene, according to Malamud it originated in his concern with social injustice in American life.[81] *The Tenants*, more than any other Malamud novel, registered Malamud's involvement in one of the major social conflicts of the sixties — the racial tensions involving urban Jews and blacks. Morris Dickstein felt that Malamud's handling of the black writer, Willie Spearmint, never got beyond external stereotypes; but Dickstein also remarked that Malamud's black and white confrontation "at its best depicts a range of real human interaction."[82] Essays by Cynthia Ozick and Steven G. Kellman, radically differing in their approaches and arriving at different estimates of the novel, extended the range of the controversy.[83] In contrast to Dickstein, Ozick argued that Malamud did not create the stereotype of Willie Spearmint, but rather "mimicked him — from the literature and politics of the black movement," which Malamud held up to scrutiny at the risk of his own art. Kellman, departing from both Dickstein and Ozick, asserted that in *The Tenants*, a self-reflexive novel, "realistic allusion is shattered by literary allusion." Although finally judging the novel harshly because of its escape from contemporary life, Kellman, nevertheless, seemed fascinated with its connection to other novels within the reflexive tradition. Finally,

Evelyn Gross Avery's *Rebels and Victims: The Fiction of Richard Wright and Bernard Malamud* should be consulted for its comparative study of the black rebel and the Jewish victim in the urban setting.[84]

A critical issue related to Malamud's treatment of society that has surfaced only in recent years involves Malamud's representation of the Holocaust experience. Malamud himself was reticent if not ambivalent in discussing the subject. In an interview with Phyliss Meras concerning *The Fixer*, Malamud remarked that, apart from its actual subject, a man accused of ritual murder in Tsarist Russia, "It is also concerned with the fate of the Jews under the Nazis. . . ."[85] At a later date, Malamud, when asked to comment on the extent to which the Holocaust influenced his writing, replied: "I am compelled to think about it as a man rather than as a writer. Someone like Elie Wiesel who had a first hand knowledge of the experience is in a better position to write about it than I."[86] In a fairly recent article Michael Brown argued that Malamud indeed has introduced the subject into some of his fiction, but only allusively, through symbol and metaphor, in *The Assistant*, *The Fixer*, and "Lady of the Lake."[87] Lawrence Langer, however, takes issue with Brown, particularly the attempt to universalize the Holocaust experience by perceiving in Morris Bober a symbolic Holocaust victim.[88] As Langer goes on to survey Malamud's fiction, he concludes that its representation of suffering belongs to literary tragedy, a dimension of experience that is in an altogether different category from Holocaust suffering.

If for Philip Roth, Malamud had not been sufficiently engaged in exploring the problems of contemporary Jews in his fiction of the fifties and early sixties, for Charles Thomas Samuels the appearance of *The Fixer* revealed that Malamud had been unduly influenced by critics to become a socially conscious writer.[89] The criticism is finally irrelevant to the central issue facing the reader — that is, whether a Malamud novel, regardless of its matter or its manner, is successful on its own artistic terms. Nevertheless, the parties to this debate may have stimulated, in some measure, the next wave, small though it might be, of a Malamud criticism concerned with social issues in fiction other than *The Fixer* and *The Tenants*.

Some European critics of Malamud, especially German critics, have read Malamud's fiction with an eye to his indictment of American life. Eva Manske in reviewing *The Assistant* observed that Malamud presents a nightmare inversion of the American dream, but stops short of offering any alternative.[90] In a similar vein, Tobias Hergt suggested that Malamud's fiction exposes the sickness of American society.[91] Iska Alter, in her book-length study of Malamud's fiction, undertook a full exploration of Malamud's "social criticism" from *The Natural* through *The Tenants*, and indeed her book underscores issues that had been set aside by earlier Malamud critics. Alter asserted that Malamud "is not only interested in describing actual social structures . . . [but] is also concerned with defining and dramatizing the underlining forces which form the bases upon which a given community is built."[92]

While Malamud's fiction has given priority to addressing the value of human life—Malamud rejected the Robbe-Grillet theory that fiction should record rather than interpret life, and even went so far as to criticize Joyce for becoming overly concerned with linguistic technique at the expense of content[93]—his own work has been characterized nevertheless by various kinds of innovation. In this connection Tony Tanner has suggested that Malamud's vitality seemed to be expressed through his ability to write in a variety of fictional modes.[94] If in one moment Malamud could assert that ultimately art tends toward morality, in the next he could value a writer, morality or content aside, for sheer artistic daring. "I'm glad," he remarked in an interview, "Virginia Woolf did *Orlando*, although it isn't my favorite work."[95]

With the publication of the experimental *Pictures of Fidelman* and *The Tenants*, Malamud's earlier flirtation with myth, or his mixing of fantasy with realism, seemed tame. The result of Malamud's radical departure from the conventional narrative forms of his previous work was, as might be expected, disappointing for some critics and impressive for others. The anonymous reviewer in the *Times Literary Supplement* faulted *Pictures of Fidelman* for its excessive ingenuity.[96] Katherine Gaus Jackson considered Arthur Fidelman's endless predicaments tedious.[97] Martin Tucker judged that Malamud's themes of suffering and loss had become nothing more than fictional ploys.[98] Josh Greenfeld, however, considered the work the most underrated novel of the year.[99] And Robert Scholes called it Malamud's most successful work, and perceptively noted that "its panel of pictures is reminiscent of Hogarth."[100] Robert Ducharme's examination of the form as well as the dominant themes of the work remains the most comprehensive study to date.[101]

The Tenants was also marked by similar critical disagreement. Mordecai Richler regarded the book as muddled and careless, and Roger Sale found the plot strategy unclear.[102] On the other hand, Pearl K. Bell considered the novel Malamud's best work, and Anatole Broyard, while acknowledging Malamud's artistic lapses, perceived that Malamud had taken risks in attempting to communicate his deeply felt human concerns.[103] Jacob Korg briefly alluded to the experimental quality of the novel, observing that it was "the first of Malamud's novels to employ post modern techniques of the kind attributable to the influence of Joyce, Gide, Kafka and experimental poetry."[104] "In Kew Garden" and "Alma Redeemed" appear to be exceptions to Malamud's experiments in form and technique in behalf of theme and content, but Malamud himself, dissented from this view. For him Virginia Woolf and Alma Mahler were connected to his past work, for in their brief portrayal he hoped to capture glimpses into the essence of their lives, both as complex human beings and as women.[105]

The persistency of Malamud's artistic innovations have something of

Ahab's obsessiveness, insofar as Malamud has used them as much to force illumination of the mystery of human experience as to avoid repeating himself. Apropos of Davidov's remark to Rosen in "Take Pity" regarding the cryptic writing in the census taker's notebook — "It's an old-fashioned language that they don't use it nowadays" — Malamud, like Jacob wrestling with an Angel of God for a blessing, attempted to wring from his narrative art some form of redemptive grace: that is, "to compel it to say what it still must say"[106] in behalf of what is human. In the vein of his own character Beppo in *Pictures of Fidelman*, Malamud had virtually willed himself to invent not only art but also reinvent meaning for human life which so many of his contemporaries had exiled from their fiction.

If even Malamud's most sympathetic critics were dubious about the artistic success of *The Tenants*, the publication of a third collection of Malamud stories, *Rembrandt's Hat* (1973), elicited praise from almost all reviewers. Charles Deemer, for example, considered Malamud's collection superior to the works of Cheever, E. M. Forster, and Nabokov which were evaluated in the same review.[107] The anonymous review of *Rembrandt's Hat* in the *New Republic* also gave Malamud high praise, judging him the best of contemporary short story writers, and drawing special attention to "Man in the Drawer" and "Talking Horse."[108] These strong endorsements merely register a wide consensus that Malamud's skill and profundity as a writer have been largely sustained in the genre of the short story rather than the novel. Thus the appearance of *Dubin's Lives* (1979) six years after the very mixed reviews of *The Tenants* was, in some ways, a more important event than the publication of *Rembrandt's Hat* insofar as it was to be measured against *The Tenants*, as well as Malamud's previously published novels.

Both in style and content *Dubin's Lives* represented a departure from Malamud's past work. Anchored in the realistic and ruminating style of much nineteenth century fiction, and at some distance from the didacticism and ethnicity of his earlier novels, *Dubin's Lives* was indeed a different Malamud. The response of a fair number of early reviews was respectful caution rather than a sense of certainty. For Richard Gilman, *Dubin's Lives* embodied typical Malamudian flaws and virtues. Possessed of a somewhat rambling narrative, the novel nevertheless carried for this critic a "Jewish expressiveness" and Jamesian nuances of tone.[109] Commentators like Pearl K. Bell and Tom Landress seemed particularly disappointed that the novel reflected a reduction of Malamudian humanism and Jewish ethos.[110] For other critics, Malamud's handling of the art of writing biography held a special appeal, apart from other artistic considerations. Both Leon Edel and Katherine Frank considered Malamud unusually insightful in his general grasp of the biographer's art.[111] A small number of early reviews, however, claimed for *Dubin's Lives* a virtually unqualified excellence not achieved since *The Assistant*. Douglas Hill observed that it might well be his richest novel.[112] Christopher Lehmann-

Haupt judged it similarly, regarding the sustained tension between intellect and instinct one of its major strengths.[113] Roger Sale, who had only qualified praise for *The Tenants*, felt that Malamud's treatment of a man's confrontation with his own mortality may have been one of his greatest accomplishments.[114] Melvin J. Friedman also suggested that *Dubin's Lives* might be Malamud's best novel since *The Assistant* and considered his handling of Jewish and Christian motifs especially skillful.[115]

Beyond these reviews, a number of recent longer studies are of special interest, particularly in connection with Malamud's treatment of women, a topic that was generally neglected until the publication of *Dubin's Lives*. Iska Alter devoted a chapter in her book to Malamud's women and observed that they evolve from icons to various levels of complexity.[116] Barbara Koenig Quart concluded that Malamud's characterization of women is generally weak, yet they play an important part in the dreams, fantasies, and yearnings of his men.[117] Chiara Briganti discussed women as objects of voyeurism in *A New Life* and in *Dubin's Lives*.[118] On a closely related topic, Malamud's handling of sexuality, Rita K. Golin asserted that *Dubin's Lives* provided the fullest expression thus far of the relation between desire and morality, and Rafael Cancel-Ortiz offered illuminating observations on Malamud's use of Lawrentian themes regarding love and sex.[119]

In *God's Grace* Malamud's return to allegory, animal fable, and ethnic characterization, with an added touch of science fiction, was once again indicative of his need to breath new life into genres that had served him well in the past, as well as to confront new subjects. Because this last Malamud novel is still relatively new, reviews provide the only critical discussion of it, with the important exception of Sidney Richman's original contribution to this collection. Robert Alter observed that Malamud used the narrative as a platform to confront the inscrutability of God. While Alter found the theological argument intellectually thin, the modulation of tone and humor in the fantasy were characteristically Malamud at his best.[120] Alter's generally very receptive review also called to attention what a few critics had addressed in earlier Malamud works only in passing, the intensity of aggression found in the fable: "Even without pursuing psychoanalytic conjecture, we may note that there is a palpable gap between such unleashing of aggression against characters and readers, and the moral claims made for the fictional expression of all that rage."[121] Critical judgment of *God's Grace* remains polarized, and on the question of whether there is finally a meaningful expression of optimism embodied in the mysterious interplay of character and events in Malamud's apocalyptic narrative, only Sidney Richman has yet to supply a satisfactory answer.

Richman persuasively argues that the nature of Malamud's faith is ultimately the central subject of *God's Grace* and that the murder of Cohn which concludes the novel is a first step in a process of atonement involving the abnegation of rationality for the sake of a total reverence and love of God. In his lucid exposition of the novel, Richman will surely force critics, both those who have already admired and those who have found serious fault with it, to return for another reading. Richman's essay may offer the most convincing illustration thus far of the tenacity and integrity of Malamud's imagination.

With the long-sustained and extensive critical discussion of Malamud's novels over the years—some of it unfortunately repetitious—the student is amply provided with a variety of stimulating perspectives. One area of criticism that remains sketchy, however, is the explication of Malamud's short stories, a good number of them with sufficient richness, complexity, and ambiguity to justify further investigation. In addition, criticism has totally ignored Malamud's uncollected stories, largely because they are not easily accessible. They are nonetheless worth examining at a time when Malamud is likely to be the subject of a general reassessment.

The greatest need in Malamud studies is for a critical biography that would bridge Malamud's personal life with his fiction so that one might illuminate the other. Students of Malamud who have sampled the available biographical materials have already some awareness of the extent to which Malamud's fictional world was born out of the author's experiences with death, separation, poverty, loneliness, and his unyielding struggle to become a writer. The early death of his mother, the loss of a brother, his relations with his father, the thin family life with a stepmother, to name just a few crucial events, constitute Malamud's formative experiences which he refused to discuss in any detail; they are the distilled human dynamics of his fiction, with their attendant urban and, sometimes, cosmic sense of gratuitous suffering.

Given the fragments of information we have about Malamud's personal life, together with his public statements concerning art and the role of the artist in society, only readers unfamilar with Malamud's past, or critics theoretically uncomfortable with relating author biography to fictional texts, would tend to read Malamud's characters as autonomous fictions, detached from the strong emotional and imaginative ties with their author. While Malamud has acknowledged the impact of familial history on his work and his own personality in the creation of his characters, he has nevertheless attempted to discourage readers from identifying him with them, arguing, for example, that William Dubin is ultimately a product of invention and that "biographical details remain merely strings of uncooked spaghetti."[122] Yet for all of his cautioning, and despite his often ironic fictional portraits of his protagonists, Malamud appears to be a self-referential writer—especially in his treatment of the artist manqué—at some deeper level, innocent that he is actually encouraging the reader to discover a bonding between himself and them. Indeed, phraseology from a Malamud character occasionally echoes as a motif in

Malamud's own nonfictional voice without any premeditated allusion to his own fiction.[123]

Surely, Malamud's own dogged commitment to his art, which as one commentator has observed, kept him pounding away like a shoemaker even through mortal illness, is reflected in the determination of his own characters who, by sheer acts of will, attempt to transform their lives and occasionally even the laws of the universe.[124] In *A New Life*, S. Levin's reply to Gerald Gilley's question regarding Levin's ability to assume the burdens of Pauline Gilley—"Because I can, you son of a bitch"—defines that characteristic Malamudian stance. If Malamud's Ginzburg of "Idiots First" was not in the anthropomorphic business, the essential Bernard Malamud was. And the extent to which Malamud used his art as an investment in that business is in itself a story that still needs to be told in the full context of his biography.

I am grateful to the Lucius N. Littauer Foundation for a grant that helped to bring this book to completion. Thanks are also due to Professors Herbert Eldridge and Rex Burns of the University of Colorado at Denver for their useful editorial suggestions, and to Carolyn Dameron and Ann Underwood for putting their typing skills at my disposal on short notice. To my wife, Kathleen Salzberg, I owe special thanks for both tangible and intangible assistance.

JOEL SALZBERG

University of Colorado at Denver

Notes

1. Joseph Wershba, "Not Horror but 'Sadness,'" *New York Post*, 14 September 1958, M2.

2. Ibid., M2.

3. Malamud's controversial statement, "All men are Jews except they don't know it," was, according to Malamud, a way of figuratively suggesting the vulnerability of all men in history. See Leslie and Joyce Field, "An Interview with Bernard Malamud," in *Bernard Malamud: A Collection of Critical Essays*, ed. Leslie Field and Joyce Field (Englewood Cliffs, N.J.: Prentice-Hall, 1975), 11. Morris Bober's sense of obligation and responsibility toward his fellow man has long been regarded as a model of the essential Malamudian morality exemplified in his earliest work. See also Josephine Zadovsky Knopp's "The Code of *Mentshlekhkayt* and the Trial of Judaism" in *The Trial of Judaism in Contemporary Jewish Writing* (Urbana: University of Illinois Press, 1975), 6–29 as an illuminating perspective on the Judaic sources of Malamud's moral vision.

4. See Norman Podhoretz, "The New Nihilism and the Novel," *Partisan Review* 25, no. 4 (1958):589–90

5. As suggested in the conclusion of this introduction, Malamud's fiction is based, to a large degree, on his own familial experience with suffering, as well as an acknowledged empathy with the human family. Whether Malamud has always been able to translate his own preoccupations with these emotionally laden themes into effective art, or whether his obsession with them occasionally overwhelms a work to the extent that it fails to have appropriate "objective correlatives" for these themes, is an unsettled issue that should invite

further discussion. From an ethical perspective, Malamud's treatment of his characters is rooted in the Jewish convenental relationship with God. If God is derelict in his obligations to man, and allows him to suffer gratuitously, "then it is man's responsibility to take God's duty upon himself." See Knopp, "The Code of Mentshlekhkayt and the Trial of Judaism," 12–13.

6. Ihab Hassan's section on Malamud in *Radical Innocence: The Contemporary American Novel* (New York: Harper & Row, 1966), 161–68 is an example of some of early Malamud criticism at its best.

7. See Sidney Richman's essay, which was written especially for this collection.

8. See Leslie [A.] Fiedler, *The Jew in the American Novel*, Pamphlet no. 1 (New York: Herzl Institute, 1959), 57–58.

9. See Nat Hentoff, "Bernard Malamud," *Commonweal* 79 (6 December 1963):328–29; Philip Roth, "Imagining Jews," *New York Review of Books* 21 (3 October 1974):22–28; Michele Marilyn Fabe, "Successful Failures: Guilt and Morality in the Novels of Bernard Malamud," Ph.D. diss., University of California, Berkeley, 1975.

10. Bernard Malamud, telephone interview with Joel Salzberg, 27 January 1986. For what may be the earliest fictional expression of Malamud's own anger, surely at odds with his theme of redemptive suffering, see Joel Salzberg's "Irremediable Suffering: A Reading of Malamud's 'Take Pity,' " *Studies in Short Fiction* 23, no. 1 (Winter, 1986): 19–24.

11. Malamud recalled (see note 10) that his interest in Virginia Woolf as a subject for a short story was stimulated by a course that he had taught at Bennington College. As a result of his readings for it, he became increasingly fascinated by Woolf as a human being, a writer, and a genius. Moreover, he felt that his insight into Woolf might be increased by his own attempt to distill the life of this complex woman into a very brief narrative.

12. Bernard Malamud, "A Lost Grave," *Esquire* 103 (May 1985):204, 206.

13. See Jeffrey Helterman, "Bernard Malamud," in *Dictionary of Literary Biography*, vol. 2, *American Novelists since World War II*, ed. Jeffrey Helterman and Richard Layman (Detroit: Gale Research, 1978) 291–304; and "Bernard Malamud," in *World Authors, 1950–1970: A Companion Volume to Twentieth Century Authors*, ed. John Wakeman (New York: H. H. Wilson, 1975), 917–20.

14. *The Stories of Bernard Malamud* (New York: Farrar Straus Giroux, 1983), vii–xiii.

15. Bernard Malamud, *Long Work, Short Life*, The Bennington Chapbooks in Literature (Bennington, Vt.: Bennington College, 1985), 1–19.

16. Daniel Fuchs, *Saul Bellow: Vision and Revision* (Durham, N.C.: Duke University Press, 1984).

17. Malamud, *Long Work, Short Life*, 19.

18. See Field, "An Interview with Bernard Malamud," *Bernard Malamud: A Collection of Critical Essays*, 8–17; and Daniel Stern, "The Art of Fiction: Bernard Malamud," *Paris Review*, no. 61 (Spring 1975):40–64.

19. Wershba, "Not Horror but 'Sadness,' " M2; see also Malamud's rationale for his fiction in his acceptance address for the National Book Award (1959), quoted in Granville Hicks, "His Hopes on the Human Heart," *Saturday Review* 46, no. 41 (12 October 1963):32.

20. Rita Natalie Kosofsky, *Bernard Malamud: An Annotated Checklist*, The Serif Series, Bibliographies and Checklists, ed. William White, no. 7 (Kent, Ohio: Kent State University Press, 1969).

21. Donald Risty, "A Checklist of Malamud Criticism," in *The Fiction of Bernard Malamud*, eds. Richard Astro and Jackson J. Benson (Corvallis: Oregon State University Press, 1969), 163–90.

22. Robert D. Habich, "Bernard Malamud: A Bibliographical Survey," *Studies in American Jewish Literature* 4 (Spring 1978):78–84.

23. Ibid., 84.

24. Joseph A. Grau, "Bernard Malamud: A Bibliographical Addendum," *Bulletin of*

Bibliography 37, no. 4 (December, 1980):157–66; and Joseph A. Grau, "Bernard Malamud: A Further Bibliographical Addendum," *Bulletin of Bibliography* 38, no. 2 (April–June 1981):101–4.

25. Joel Salzberg, *Bernard Malamud: A Reference Guide* (Boston: G. K. Hall, 1985).

26. Leslie and Joyce Field, eds., *Bernard Malamud and the Critics* (New York: New York University Press, 1970).

27. Field, *Bernard Malamud: A Collection of Critical Essays.*

28. Richard Astro and Jackson J. Benson, eds., *The Fiction of Bernard Malamud* (Corvallis: Oregon State University Press, 1977).

29. Sidney Richman, *Bernard Malamud* (New York: Twayne, 1966).

30. Sandy Cohen, *Bernard Malamud and the Trial by Love*, Melville Studies in American Literature, ed. Robert Brainard Pearsall (Amsterdam: Rodopi, N.V., 1974).

31. Robert [E.] Ducharme, *Art and Idea in the Novels of Bernard Malamud: Toward "The Fixer"* (The Hague: Mouton, 1974).

32. Sheldon J. Hershinow, *Bernard Malamud*, Modern Literature Monographs (New York: Frederick Ungar, 1980).

33. Iska [Sheila] Alter, *The Good Man's Dilemma: Social Criticism in the Fiction of Bernard Malamud*, AMS Studies in Modern Literature, No. 5 (New York; AMS Press, 1981).

34. See Leslie [A.] Fiedler, "In the Interest of Surprise and Delight," *Folio* 20, no. 3 (Summer 1955):17–20. Reprinted in *No! In Thunder: Essays on Myth and Literature* (Boston: Beacon Press, 1960).

35. Fiedler, "In the Interest of Surprise and Delight," 20.

36. Harvey Swados, "Baseball à la Wagner: The Nibelung in the Polo Grounds," *American Mercury* 75, no. 346 (October 1952):106, reprinted in this volume.

37. Norman Podhoretz, "Achilles in Left Field," *Commentary* 15, no. 3 (March 1953):323

38. Podhoretz, "Achilles in Left Field," 326. Regarding high-brow versus low-brow art, see also Leslie Fiedler, "Leslie Fiedler Reintroduces Himself," *New York Times Book Review*, 27 May 1971, 20.

39. Wershba, "Not Horror but 'Sadness,' " M2.

40. Herbert Gold, "Dream to be Good," *Nation* 184 (20 April 1957):350.

41. Robert Bowen, "Bagels, Sour Cream and the Heart of the Current Novel," *Northwest Review* 1, no. 1 (Spring 1957):350.

42. George [P.] Elliott, "Fiction Chronicle," *Hudson Review* 10, no. 2 (Summer 1957):288–95.

43. Alfred Kazin, "Fantasist of the Ordinary," *Commentary* 24, no. 1 (July 1957), 89–92, reprinted in this volume.

44. Alfred Kazin, "Bernard Malamud: The Magic and the Dread," *Reporter* (29 May 1958):202–7; reprinted in *Contemporaries* (Boston: Little, Brown, 1962); and *On Contemporary Literature*, ed. Richard Kostelanetz (New York: Avon, 1964).

45. Leslie Fiedler, "The Commonplace as Absurd," *Reconstructionist* 24 (21 February 1958); reprinted in *No! In Thunder: Essays on Myth and Literature* (Boston: Beacon Press, 1960).

46. Arthur Foff, "Strangers amid Ruins," *Northwest Review* 2, no. 1 (Fall-Winter 1958):63–67, reprinted in this volume.

47. Philip Roth, "Writing American Fiction," *Commentary* 31, no. 3 (March 1961):223–33; reprinted in *The American Novel Since World War II*, ed. Marcus Klein (Greenwich, Conn.: Fawcett, 1969); and Philip Roth, *Reading Myself and Others* (New York: Penguin Books, 1985).

48. Earl Rovit, "Bernard Malamud and the Jewish Literary Tradition," *Critique* 3, no. 2 (Winter-Spring):3–10; reprinted in Leslie [A.] Field, *Bernard Malamud and the Critics* (New York: New York University Press; London: University of London Press, 1970).

49. Robert Alter, "Malamud as Jewish Writer," *Commentary* 42, no. 3 (September 1966):71–76; reprinted as "Bernard Malamud: Jewishness as Metaphor," in *After the Tradition: Essays on Modern Jewish Writing* (New York: E. P. Dutton, 1969) and in Field, *Bernard Malamud and the Critics*.

50. Sam Bluefarb, "Bernard Malamud: The Scope of Caricature," *English Journal* 53, no. 5 (May 1964):319–26, 335; reprinted in Field, *Bernard Malamud and the Critics*.

51. Sheldon Norman Grebstein, "Bernard Malamud and the Jev 'sh Movement," *Contemporary American Jewish Literature: Critical Essays*, ed. Irving Malin (Bloomington: Indiana University Press, 1973), 175–212; reprinted in Field, *Bernard Malamud: A Collection of Critical Essays*.

52. Leonard Michaels, "Sliding into English," *New York Review of Books* 20 (20 September 1973):37–40, reprinted in this volume.

53. See Ruth Wisse, *The Schlemiel as Modern Hero* (Chicago: University of Chicago Press, 1971), 39, 82–83, 110–18; and Sanford Pinkser, "The Schlemiel as Moral Bungler: Bernard Malamud's Ironic Heroes," in *The Schlemiel as Metaphor: Studies in the Yiddish and American Jewish Novel* (Carbondale: Southern Illinois University Press, 1971), 87–124.

54. Wisse, *Schlemiel as Modern Hero*, 111.

55. Shiv P. Kumar, "Marionettes in Taleysim: Yiddish Folkfigures in Two Malamud Stories," *Indian Journal of American Studies* 8, no. 1 (July 1977):18–24.

56. Glen Meeter, "Bernard Malamud and Philip Roth: A Critical Essay," *Contemporary Writers in Christian Perspective*, ed. Roderick Jellema (Grand Rapids, Mich.: William B. Eerdmans, 1968).

57. Giles B. Gunn, "Bernard Malamud and the High Cost of Living," in *Adversity and Grace: Studies in Recent American Literature*, ed. Nathan A. Scott, Jr. (Chicago: University of Chicago Press, 1968), 59–85.

58. Robert Kegan, *The Sweeter Welcome, Voices for a Vision of Affirmation: Bellow, Malamud and Martin Buber* (Needham Heights, Mass.: Humanitas Press, 1976).

59. Ita Sheres, "The Alienated Sufferer: Malamud's Novels from the Perspective of Old Testament and Jewish Mystical Thought," *Studies in American Jewish Literature* 4, no. 1 (Spring 1978):68–76.

60. See note 7.

61. Earl R. Wasserman, "*The Natural*: Malamud's World Ceres," *Centennial Review* 9 (Fall 1965):438–60; reprinted in *Bernard Malamud and the Critics*.

62. Ibid., 460.

63. James M. Mellard, "Malamud's Novels: Four Versions of Pastoral," *Critique* 9, no. 2 (1967):5–19; reprinted in *Bernard Malamud and the Critics*.

64. Max F. Schulz, "Bernard Malamud's Mythic Proletarians," in *Radical Sophistication: Studies in Contemporary Jewish American Novelists* (Athens: Ohio University Press, 1969), 56–58; reprinted in *Bernard Malamud and the Critics*.

65. Jonathan Baumbach, "All Men Are Jews: *The Assistant* by Bernard Malamud," in *The Landscape of Nightmare: Studies in the Contemporary American Novel* (New York: New York University Press, 1965), 102.

66. Thomas Alva Hoyt, "Bernard Malamud and the New Romanticism," *Contemporary American Novelists*, ed. Harry Thornton Moore (Carbondale: Southern Illinois University Press, 1964), 65–79; reprinted in *Bernard Malamud and the Critics*.

67. David Burrows, "The American Past in Malamud's *A New Life*," in *Private Dealings: Eight American Writers* (Stockholm: Almqvist & Wiksell, 1969), 86–94.

68. Samuel Irving Bellman, "Henry James's 'The Madonna of the Future' and Two Modern Parallels," *California English Journal* 1, no. 3 (1965):47–53.

69. Christof Wegelin, "The American Schlemiel Abroad: Malamud's Italian Stories and the End of American Innocence," *Twentieth Century American Literature* 19 (April 1973):77–88, reprinted in this volume.

70. Guido Fink's essay was written especially for this collection.

71. J. Gerald Kennedy, "Parody as Exorcism: 'The Raven' and 'The Jewbird,' " *Genre* 13 (Summer 1980):161–69, reprinted in this volume.

72. Norman Leer, "The Double Theme in Malamud's *The Assistant*: Dostoevsky with Irony," *Mosaic* 4 (Spring 1971):89–102.

73. Philip Roth, "Imagining Jews," *New York Review of Books* 21 (3 October 1974):26, reprinted in this volume.

74. Hentoff, "Bernard Malamud," 79.

75. Fabe, "Successful Failures."

76. Ibid., 5

77. James Mellard's essay was written especially for this collection.

78. W[illiam] J. Handy, "The Malamud Hero: A Quest for Existence," in *The Fiction of Bernard Malamud*, ed. Richard Astro and Jackson J. Benson, 65–86.

79. Lucio P. Ruotolo, "Yakov Bok," in *Six Existential Heroes: The Politics of Faith* (Cambridge, Mass.: Harvard University Press), 121–39, reprinted in this volume.

80. Roth, "Writing American Fiction," 229.

81. "The Outsider," *Time* 88 (9 September 1966):106, 108.

82. Morris Dickstein, Review of *The Tenants*, *New York Times Book Review* 76 (3 October 1971):18, reprinted in this volume.

83. Cynthia Ozick, "Literary Blacks and Jews," *Midstream* 18, no. 6 (June-July 1972):21; reprinted in Field, *Bernard Malamud: A Collection of Critical Essays*; Cynthia Ozick, *Art and Ardor: Essays by Cynthia Ozick* (New York: Alfred A. Knopf, 1983); and Steven G. Kellman, "*The Tenants* in the House of Fiction," *Studies in The Novel* (Winter 1976):458–67.

84. Eveyln Gross Avery, *Rebels and Victims: The Fiction of Richard Wright and Bernard Malamud*: (Port Washington, N.Y.: National University Publications, Kennikat Press, 1979).

85. Phyliss Meras, ". . . An Interview with Its Author," *Providence Sunday Journal*, 11 September 1966, H-9.

86. Quoted in Salzberg, *Bernard Malamud: A Reference Guide*, xiv.

87. Michael Brown, "Metaphor for Holocaust and Holocaust for Metaphor: *The Assistant* and *The Fixer* of Bernard Malamud Reexamined," *Judaism* 29, no. 4 (Fall):479–88.

88. Lawrence Langer's essay was written especially for this collection.

89. Charles Thomas Samuels, "The Career of Bernard Malamud," *New Republic* 155 (10 September 1966):19–21.

90. Eva Manske, Review of *Der Gehilfe* [*The Assistant*], *Zeitschrift für Anglistik and Amerikanistik* 25, no. 3 (1977):272–73.

91. Tobias Hergt, "Bernard Malamud's 'A Choice of Profession': Interpretation einer Kurzgeschichte mit Anregungen zu ihrer Behandlung in Oberstufenunterricht," *Die Neueren Sprachen* 24 (October 1975):443–53

92. Alter, *The Good Man's Dilemma*, 2–3.

93. Vida E. Markovic, "S Bernardom Malamudom" [An Interview], *Savremenik* [Belgrade] 17, no. 33 (1971):282–86.

94. Tony Tanner, "A New Life," in *City of Words: American Fiction 1950–1970* (New York: Harper & Row, 1971) 322–43.

95. Stern, "The Art of Fiction: Bernard Malamud," 51.

96. "I Paint with My Paint," *Times Literary Supplement*, no. 3529 (16 October 1969):1177.

97. Katherine Gaus Jackson, Review of *Pictures of Fidelman, Harpers* 238, no. 1428 (June 1969):92–93.

98. Martin Tucker, Review of *Pictures of Fidelman, Commonweal* 90 (27 June 1969):420–21.

99. Josh Greenfeld, Review of *Pictures of Fidelman, Commonweal* 91 (5 December 1969):314–15.

100. Robert Scholes, "Portrait of Artist as 'Escape-Goat,' " *Saturday Review* 52 (10 May 1969):33; reprinted in *Fabulation and Metafiction* (Urbana: University of Illinois Press, 1979), reprinted in this volume.

101. Robert Ducharme, *Art and Irony in the Novels of Bernard Malamud: Toward the Fixer* (The Hague: Mouton, 1973).

102. See Mordecai Richler, "Malamud's Race War," *Life* 67 (22 October 1971):10; and Roger Sale, "What Went Wrong?" *New York Review of Books* 17, no. 6 (21 October 1971):3–6.

103. See Pearl K. Bell, "Morality Tale without Mercy," *New Leader* 54 (18 October 1971):17–18; and Anatole Broyard, "The View from the Tenement I," *New York Times*, 20 September 1971, 23.

104. Jacob Korg, "Ishmael and Israel," *Commentary* 53, no. 5 (May 1972):82–84.

105. Malamud, telephone interview with Joel Salzberg.

106. Malamud, *Long Work, Short Life*, 19.

107. Charles Deemer, "Old Masters' New Stories," *New Leader* 56 (17 September 1973):19–20.

108. Review of *Rembrandt's Hat, New Republic* 168 (9 June 1973):32.

109. Richard Gilman, Review of *Dubin's Lives, New Republic* 180 (24 March 1979):28–30.

110. See Pearl K. Bell, "Heller & Malamud, Then & Now," *Commentary* 67, no. 6 (June 1979):71–75; and Tom Landess, "Sense and Sensuality," *D. Magazine (Magazine of Dallas)* 6 (1979):81–88.

111. See Katherine Frank, "Writing Lives: Theory and Practice in Literary Biography," *Genre* 14, no. 4 (Winter):499–516; and Leon Edel, "Narcissists Need Not Apply," *American Scholar* 49 (Winter 1979):130–32.

112. Douglas Hill, "The Examined Life," *Books in Canada* 8 (April 1979):6–7.

113. Christopher Lehmann-Haupt, Review of *Dubin's Lives, New York Times*, 2 February 1979, C23.

114. Roger Sale, *"Dubin's Lives." New York Review of Books* 26 (22 February 1979):19–20.

115. Melvin J. Friedman, "The American Jewish Literary Scene, 1979: A Review Essay," *Studies in American Fiction* 8, no. 2 (Autumn 1980):19–20.

116. Alter, *The Good Man's Dilemma*, 83–113.

117. Barbara Koenig Quart, "Women in Bernard Malamud's Fiction," *Studies in American Jewish Literature*, no. 3 (1983):138–50.

118. Chiara Briganti, "Mirrors, Windows and Peeping Toms: Women as the Object of Voyeuristic Scrutiny in Bernard Malamud's *A New Life* and *Dubin's Lives*," *Studies in American Jewish Literature*, no. 3 (1983):151–65, reprinted in this volume.

119. Rafael Cancel-Ortiz, "The Passion of William Dubin: D. H. Lawrence's Themes in Bernard Malamud's *Dubin's Lives*," *D. H. Lawrence Review* 16, no. 1 (Spring 1983):83–97.

120. Robert Alter, "A Theological Fantasy," *New Republic*, 187 (20–27 September 1982):38–40, reprinted in this volume.

121. Ibid., 70.

122. Anatole Broyard, "Being a Character," *New York Times Book Review*, 22 November 1981, 55; on the problem of aesthetic distance between author and character, see Morris Dickstein, "The World in a Mirror: Problems of Distance in Recent American Fiction," *Sewanee Review* 89, no. 3 (Summer 1981):386–400 passim.

123. The title of Malamud's memoir, for example, *Long Work, Short Life*, as well as its very tenor, is a slight variation of the fortune teller's remark to Arthur Fidelman, "Art is long, inspiration, short" in "A Pimp's Revenge," *Pictures of Fidelman* (New York: New American Library, 1985), 98.

124. Perhaps the most poignant account of Malamud's own determination to overcome the immutable laws governing his own life is to be found in Philip Roth's memoir, "Pictures of Malamud," *New York Times Book Review*, 20 April 1986, 1, 40, 41.

Reviews

Baseball à la Wagner: The Nibelung in the Polo Grounds

Harvey Swados*

Bernard Malamud is the author of a number of short stories of unusual power and stubborn originality. They are impressive because they all read as though they were written by Bernard Malamud and no one else, because there is no indication that they have been trimmed to fit the sails of different magazines, and because they have in the main dealt with the Great Depression's effect upon small shopkeepers, mostly Jewish, without the least self-consciousness that they are covering ground that has presumably been worked to exhaustion. On the contrary, they derive their impact, as does all good non-intellectual art, precisely from the deliberate use of material that is already a part of the common body of experience.

I was eager to see what Mr. Malamud's first novel would be like. And I was surprised to discover that he had chosen not the world of the doomed little businessman but the world of baseball. "The Natural" is Roy Hobbs, a ballplayer of such phenomenal skill that he can come from nowhere at the age of thirty-four and in one incredible season establish himself as one of the game's immortal figures. He is, together with his golden bat Wonderboy, which he has carved from the heart of a tree split by lightning, the Wagnerian hero of a mythic drama that draws on folk legend, newspaper headlines, and the stylistic manner of the pulps to achieve its effects.

Mr. Malamud has not hesitated to incorporate materials familiar to every baseball fan: Babe Ruth's gargantuan appetite, Branch Rickey's reputed miserliness, Casey Stengel's encounter with the ball flung from the top of the Washington Monument, Eddie Waitkus' shooting by a crazed girl, Shoeless Joe Jackson's tragic downfall. . . . But his hero, although he partakes of many of the more memorable aspects of baseball's gods, is a "natural" in even more meanings of the term than those assigned to it by those professional sentimentalists, the baseball writers.

When Roy Hobbs actually knocks the cover off the ball in his first

*Review of *The Natural*. Reprinted from *American Mercury* 75, no. 346 (October 1952): 104–6.

time at bat, in response to his manager's fervent appeal, he not only sets the semicomic tone of the fantasy that is to follow, he not only establishes himself immediately as a superhuman athlete: he reveals himself as a natural man, as yet uncorrupted by his employers, his audiences, or his chroniclers.

But there is a fatal flaw in Roy Hobbs as there must be in all tragic heroes. In his case it has been implanted at the age of nineteen by the silver bullet fired at him by an unbalanced girl, a highly charged symbolic figure, who travels about the country slaughtering athletes. The fifteen years that elapse between the wound and his one dazzling year of triumph in the major leagues have infected him with a fanatic sense of urgency to recapture his lost youth by smashing all records and finding the love of which he had been cheated by the bullet. The impossibility of realizing his immense dream betrays him into betraying himself and forfeiting the love of an honest woman for the treacherous embrace of a villainness who is in love with the memory of his dead predecessor.

Mr. Malamud utilizes Roy's feverish year of achievement to develop the uneven and delicately balanced relationship between the hero and his worshippers, in whose frenzied admiration there is always an element of hatred not unrelated to self-hatred—for they want the impossible, they expect it, they demand it, and they turn on him like wolves when he fails them even temporarily in a batting slump.

The story is carried forward with remarkable swiftness by a style that alternates between tough-romantic, rather elliptic prose, and sports-fiction lingo that comes straight from *Dime Sports* magazine. The lingo is much more disturbing than such minor distractions as awkward shifts in point of view, which are not unexpected in first novels; for the considerable gains in employing a language and a plot that are ready to hand and attractive to a potentially enormous audience ranging from lowbrows to highbrows (if for different reasons) are more than outweighed by the disadvantages.

The principal gain in utilizing pulp terminology is that the style of the epic is congruous with its substance: we are reading about a baseball god in terms of what the sports pages have trained us to think about our heroes; we are driven and bullied from page to page, and we have to find out whether Roy can catch the towering fly, or whether his Wonderboy can smash the essential bases-loaded homer.

But after the last out has been made we are left wondering, like a bunch of second-guessers, what would have happened if Roy had behaved just a little differently. Tragedy is never inevitable in the pulps; happy and sad endings are interchangeable parts, and the very manner in which Roy's downfall is described must rob it of the pathos, the grandeur, and the inevitability which Mr. Malamud surely intended.

Besides, we are reminded from time to time that the pulp style, which implies a literal belief in fabulous events, is only a front, a convenient satirical device for conveying the author's real message.

What is the message? That is where the book breaks down. I don't think Mr. Malamud is quite sure himself what the worship of unseen athlete-heroes means, what the price is that the natural man must pay for being transformed from country boy into god, or what is the actual symbolic weight of baseball in America. I am not referring to "answers" which we cannot legitimately request of novelists, but rather to attitudes, which may make the difference between sharply defined, memorable writing, and diverting fiction, meaningful only during the hours that it is read.

What is big-time baseball as a specifically American phenomenon? Is it funny? Exciting? Pathetic? Horrible? Yes, Mr. Malamud says, it is all of these and more. But his rapid oscillations of style and plot from fantasy to wish-fulfilment to melodrama to pulp-realism to broad satire fragmentalize the American myth and destroy the cohesiveness of the allegory.

Maybe baseball, which Scott Fitzgerald once called a children's game played by adults, is simply not susceptible of any more weighty literary translation than that given it by Ring Lardner. I am not sure about that, but in any case Mr. Malamud has not succeeded even in fully establishing the possibility. Nevertheless, his failure is more than merely honorable — it is exciting in a way that few ambitious intellectual novels are nowadays, principally because Mr. Malamud is neither ashamed of being a storyteller nor afraid of the narrow boundaries separating pathos from bathos and sentiment from sentimentality.

One is always tempted to prescribe the path that a writer should take, and it would be particularly easy in the case of Mr. Malamud to regret that he has not seen fit to write a novel that would enlarge the vision of his beautiful short stories. But he has earned the right to claim our attention on his own terms, and it is on his own terms that his future work will have to be evaluated.

Fantasist of the Ordinary Alfred Kazin*

Bernard Malamud's second novel has been getting extremely friendly reviews, for he is a talented writer, has a particularly intense sympathy for his Jewish material, and — what doesn't always accompany sympathy — an utterly objective ear for the harsh and plaintive American Yiddish speech. But none of the reviews that I have seen has suggested that Malamud's

*Review of *The Assistant*. Reprinted, with permission, from *Commentary* 24, no. 1 (July 1957):89–92.

seemingly modest and "warm" little tale about a Jewish grocer in Brooklyn and his Italian assistant is really a hymn to a symbolic Jew as he is confronted by a hostile, baffled, and finally envious Gentile. And it is because I think that Malamud's book tries for so much more, in symbol, than what he actually gives us as fiction that I find myself regretfully dissenting from the other reviews.

Like most second-generation American Jewish novelists, Malamud's problem is to form a creative synthesis out of the Yiddish world of his childhood and his natural sophistication and heretical training as a modern writer. As one can see in his highly surrealistic baseball novel, *The Natural*, and in his eery *Partisan Review* story of a Jewish marriage broker, "The Magic Barrel," Malamud is naturally a fantasist of the ordinary, the commonplace, the average. He writes, a little, the way Chagall paints — except that the natural course of Malamud's imagination is to seek not the open and the lyrical but symbols of the highly involuted personal life of Jews. He loves what he himself calls "violins and candles" in the sky, old-clothes-men who masquerade something sinister yet unnamable; he has a natural sense of the humdrum transposed to the extreme, of the symbolic and the highly colored. He tends to the bizarre, the contorted, the verge of things that makes you shiver, not laugh. Although his dialogue in *The Assistant* is marvelously faithful to Yiddish-American, he makes you think not that Jews really talk this way but how violent, fear-fraught, always on the edge, Jewish talk can be. In the superb "The Magic Barrel," Malamud really caught the accents of the hallucinated, the visionary, and the bizarre that belong to a people whose images are as much of the next world, and of other worlds, as they are of this one.

Now the trouble with *The Assistant*, from my point of view, is that Malamud's natural taste for abstraction, his gift for symbolic representation, has gone to make up a morality story which is essentially a glorification of the Jew as Jew. My objection is that his understandable allegiance to this theme has been made the overriding motive of the book despite the fact that Malamud's talent is inherently too subtle to serve what I would call an emotional motive. Malamud is an extremely sympathetic and feeling writer, and I don't mean to suggest that he is a surrealist pure; his hold on reality is too strong, and he is, as I admiringly feel about him, very "Jewish," very much of this world. But in "The Magic Barrel" his sympathy with suffering and his deliberately distorted perspective — that sense of "magic" which seems to me the strongest element in his work — worked to represent things that could not be moralized; the character of the marriage broker was revealed entirely by technique, rendered exclusively by the use of incongruities rarely employed to describe Jewish life. The final effect was "strange" and true — there was nothing left over to paraphrase, to moralize.

In *The Assistant*, however, just the opposite is true. For what he is getting at in the life of the Jewish grocer, Morris Bober, is precisely what, after Bober's death, a rabbi—who never knew him—can say over his coffin:

"Yes, Morris Bober was to me a true Jew because he lived in the Jewish experience, which he remembered, and with the Jewish heart. Maybe not to our formal tradition . . . but he was true to the spirit of our life—to want for others that which he wants also for himself. . . . For such reasons he was a Jew. What more does our sweet God ask his poor people?"

Morris Bober is a Jew in exile, exiled even from most of his own formal traditions: in short, he is *the* Jew. But he opens his grocery at six each morning, groaning, in order to give a Polish woman a three-cent roll. When the Irish detective's bummer son, Ward Minogue, holds up Morris, Minogue curses him as a "Jew liar." When, in a fit of conscience, Frank Alpine, the other robber, forces himself on Morris as an "assistant," insists on working for spending money, he explains to Morris that "I always liked Jews." And watching Morris's miserable existence reveal itself all day long in the shabby little grocery, Frank reflects—"What kind of a man did you have to be to shut yourself up in an overgrown coffin and never once during the day, so help you, outside of going for your Jewish newspaper, poke your head out of the door for a snootful of air? The answer wasn't very hard to say—you had to be a Jew. They were born prisoners." When Frank, increasingly moved by Morris's virtuous and threadbare existence, decides to confess his part in the robbery, it turns out that originally it was *because* Morris was a Jew that Ward Minogue planned to rob him, "so Frank agreed to go with him."

But as for Morris Bober himself—"he was Morris Bober and could be nobody more fortunate. With that name you had no sure sense of property, as if it were in your blood and history not to possess, or if by some miracle to own something, to do so on the verge of loss." He is *the* Jew in everything and to everyone. His grocery is devouring him; his wife, Ida, who never gives him a moment's tenderness, but loves him harshly, cries bitterly when she sees her daughter kissing the *goy*: "Why do I cry? I cry for the world. I cry for my life that it went away wasted. I cry for you." His unmarried daughter, Helen, is twenty-three and getting anxious, but she will not compromise in her demand for love. So that into this Jewish circle, this archetype family, the dark outsider, Frank Alpine, the "assistant," comes as another symbol. And the whole story turns on the fact that he learns from Morris not, as the jacket delicately puts it, "the beauty of morality," but the beauty of the Jews. Morris recounts his life to the assistant during the many dull stretches in the store, tells him how he ran away from the Czar's conscription to America. When Frank asks Morris what it is to be a Jew and taunts him with not obeying the dietary laws, Morris answers him—"Nobody will tell me that I am not Jewish because I put in my mouth once in a while, when my tongue is dry, a piece of ham. But they will tell me, and I will believe them, if I forget the Law. This means to do what is right, to be honest, to be good. . . . For everybody should be the best, not only for you or me. We ain't animals. This is why we need the Law. This is what a Jew believes." Frank persists: "But tell me why it is that the Jews suffer so damn much, Morris? It seems to me that they like to suffer, don't they. . . . What do you suffer for, Morris?" "I suffer for you."

At the end of the story, Helen is raped by Ward Minogue, and Frank, after rescuing her, forgets himself and hysterically forces himself upon her, too: to which symbol Helen replies by naming it. She calls him "Dog— uncircumcised dog!" Frank can expiate his guilt only by taking Morris's place, after Morris dies from the effects of shoveling snow from in front of his store so that people can pass. The point of the novel is made at the end: Morris has been cheated by his fellow Jews as well as robbed and assaulted by Ward Minogue. But Frank himself becomes Morris Bober, sends Helen to N.Y.U., and on the last page, is circumcised and converted to Judaism. The point, as he says, is not merely that for the Jews "Suffering is like a piece of goods. I bet the Jews could make a suit of [it]. . . ." but: "The funny thing is that there are more of them [Jews] around than anybody knows about."

All these sentiments are unexceptionable, but the novel as constituted doesn't bear them out. The detail, while marvelously faithful, is always too clear in outline, the moral is too pointed, to convince me. And touching and utterly authentic as Morris is, there is a peculiarly unempha- sized quality about him, as if Malamud were writing entirely from memory, were trying to get a beloved figure right rather than to create, with the needed sharp edges, the character demanded by the imagination. Bober himself remains too generalized a Jew, as Frank Alpine is too shadowy and unvisualized the Gentile, to make their symbolic relation- ship simply felt.

Where Malamud's very real talent comes through best in this book, it seems to me, is in figures of suffering — his natural element — who are not average but extreme figures. Malamud is the poet of the desperately clownish, not of the good who shall inherit the earth — and this unusual gift of his comes through in two wonderful little portraits of Jews. One is of Breitbart, a bankrupt, deserted by his wife, who took to peddling. "He bought electric bulbs at wholesale and carried two cartons of them slung, with clothesline rope, over his shoulder. Every day, in his crooked shoes, he walked miles, looking into stores and calling out in a mournful voice, 'Lights for sale.' " The other is of a professional arsonist, "a skinny man in an old hat and a dark overcoat down to his ankles. His nose was long, throat gaunt, and he wore a wisp of red beard on his bony chin." The "scarecrow" comes in saying "a gut shabos," though "shabos" is a day away and looking around the Bober grocery, remarks, "It smells here like an open grave." He wets his lips and whispers, "Insurinks you got — fire insurinks?" and taking out a piece of "celluloy," shows how he does his work. "Magic," he hoarsely announced. "No ashes. This is why we use celluloy, not paper, not rags." The word "magic" naturally occurs in Malamud's best work—or when he is at his best. And then, as befits a writer who has lived "in the Jewish experience," it serves to clarify and intensify our sense of what that experience really is.

Strangers amid Ruins   Arthur Foff*

Although Bernard Malamud has been one of our most scrupulous and rewarding prose writers for a number of years, he never received wide, public recognition until the publication of his second novel, *The Assistant*, in 1957. Now that thirteen of his best short stories have been collected in *The Magic Barrel*, that recognition is certainly secure. Even book dealers and daily reviewers know his name, and I can think of few more obvious seals of approval. Of course, Malamud has not and likely will not ever get the hushed adulation of a Cozzens or the daffy notoriety of a Kerouac because he is as incapable of boring his readers into admiration as he is of capturing them with sophomoric phoniness. He owns both talent and discipline: properties that disqualify him from best sellership, easy contentment, and public office. Yet, in his own sober, dedicated, and humane way he has arrived. Since his arrival marks for all discerning readers the gain of a terse and unique sensibility manifesting itself in exciting and authentic literary terms, he deserves our fullest gratitude.

As every silver lining has its little cloud, however, so do certain conditions of Malamud's critical success beckon worry. He is, for example, frequently compared to Doestoevsky although his affinity in style and structure to Chekhov is far greater. Dim fuddlers like Granville Hicks and W.G. Rogers champion him—enough to dismay any artist. Herbert Gold and Leslie Fiedler laud him for his surrealistic use of myth without noting the extent of his removal from Tristan Tzara, André Breton, and all the little Henry Millers, or the fact that he has employed symbolic literary patterns only twice—in *The Natural* and "The Lady of the Lake." In both instances, the patterns have been derived from the Matter of Britain and have been superimposed upon rather than indigenous to the original materials.

More importantly, what these and other critics who have addressed themselves to his writing hold in common is an insistence upon his value as a Jewish writer. While it is true enough that Malamud is preoccupied with the figure of the Jew, it is equally true that to see him only as the portrayer of a single group or the pleader of a special case is to limit the largeness of

*Review of *The Magic Barrel*. Reprinted, with permission, from *Northwest Review* 2, no. 1 (Fall–Winter 1958):63–67.

his accomplishment. Alfred Kazin, free-associating in the May, 1958, issue of *The Reporter*, remarked the overeagerness of "minority" authors to "be freed of certain painful experiences through the ritualistic catharsis of modern symbolism." Aside from the clinical inaccuracy of a statement which confuses compulsion neurosis with catharsis, and in so doing completely misses the obsessional character of Malamud's vision, it is even more damaging in that it guesses about the writer's life instead of dealing with his work. Before a critic delivers himself of oracles on an author's motives, he had better examine his stories as closely as possible. The biographical problem of why something was said must wait on an accurate literary knowledge of what was said.

Now, the stories which make up *The Magic Barrel* do share and explore an archetypal pattern. Out of a world of dispossessed strangers, two characters, often an older person and a younger man, meet. The scene is stark and unpromising: a cheap and barren room in a rachitic tenement; a deserted city street under frozen powerlines; a run-down beat-up grocery that smells like a graveyard. The physical background, in short, is as skeletal and yet as inescapable as the gutted ground of a concentration camp or the high, narrow barriers of a ghetto. Yet, once a cosmic accidentalism has crossed these two lives, the characters are transfixed in a long and agonizing moment. The irrelevant, chance meeting becomes the necessary relationship. The impossible demand becomes the imperative debt. Rosen, the hopelessly ill salesman in "Take Pity," is bound to offer both life and hope to the destitute widow Eva and her two children, Fega and Surale. In "The Bill," Willy Schlegel, a janitor dusty and gray from the ash cans of poverty and personal loss, is visited with an endless trial of shame because of his failure to pay his bill of eighty-three dollars and some cents to the proprietors of a "small, dark delicatessen . . . really a hole in the wall." And Lieb, the baker of one of Malamud's finest lyrics of despair, "The Loan," finds that his tear-sweetened loaves of bread have turned to "charred corpses," like so many bodies in the ovens of Birkenau, when he fails to give an old friend money for a grave stone for his wife.

The world which Bernard Malamud creates for us is a bitched-up, zero-at-the-bone world. His characters are poor past poverty; beaten past defeat. They drag their weary heels along cracked pavements that lead from one hell to another; indeed, the misery and bleakness of their surroundings and their journey are not only real in themselves, but are also the objective correlatives of their spiritual dilemma. Other writers may advertise the surface decorum of a society where money signifies decency and where wives are more properly pals than lovers. But Malamud will have none of this. No old lies, no hollow pretensions, no inflated oratory. Where Hemingway envisioned a botched civilization, Malamud envisions no civilization at all, only ghostly ruins where disinherited strangers pass in a feverish night.

This is not nihilism. To the contrary, Malamud's search is for value and here he belongs squarely in the great line of moral realists which stretches from Hawthorne to Henry James, Stephen Crane, F. Scott Fitzgerald, and Hemingway himself. Hemingway's *nada* was never so much pure negation as assertion of the necessity for a value system in a day where conventional morals and manners had perished. The ethic he found for living when all else had gone to pot was what Edmund Wilson has so keenly termed "the principle of sportsmanship." Although Hemingway's heroes must suffer because they have a sharply defined code, they rise to a sort of grandeur in meeting betrayal and defeat on their own terms. Malamud's central characters also have an ethic, but their struggle is to discover it in themselves as well as to apply it. Hemingway's heroes must "feel good." Malamud's must do good.

And it is the wrenching difficulty of doing good when one is sick or aged or poor — and sometimes all three — which furnishes Malamud's characters with their spiritual crises. When Willy's wife suggests that he pay the Panessas, in "The Bill," he replies with frightening desperation: "What have I got that I can pay? With what? With the meat off my bones? With the ashes in my eyes. With the piss I mop up on the floors. With the cold in my lungs when I sleep." Nevertheless, Willy eventually recognizes the stringency of his obligation "because after all what was credit but the fact that people were human beings, and if you were really a human being you gave credit to somebody else and he gave credit to you."

In these stories, the characters are forever laboring under the burden of debt. While the debt is frequently a literal one, it is always more than this. In a world of permanent depression where the moral terrain is uncharted, money becomes a counter for the measurement of good and evil. The tragedy of Willy and of Lieb, as of Fidelman in "The Last Mohican" and Rosen in "Take Pity," is that they cannot discharge the debts that would guarantee their humanity. Malamud's characters care compassionately, but when they are unwilling to bear the consequences of their caring they learn that the cost of material salvation is the expense of spiritual damnation. Rosen is tormented by the apparition of his failure even after death. Fidelman, lost in the moral ghetto of a triumphant but belated insight, must stand by as Susskind, his potential savior, flees through the streets of eternity.

Although human indebtedness, its circumstances and its complexity, is basic to Bernard Malamud's artistic preoccupation, not all of his characters are doomed. It is this capacity to envisage resurrection as well as self-crucifixion, along with the rare ability to love his characters who fail as much as those who succeed, that helps to make the world of *The Magic Barrel* (and *The Assistant*) so compellingly immediate and significant.

In "A Summer's Reading," George Stoyonovich, an ignorant neighborhood boy, is able to fulfill an inner imperative to attain knowledge and a sense of identity only after acknowledging his external obligation to an older man. In "The Mourners," old Kessler, once an egg candler, and his landlord, Gruber, have sinned against the past and poisoned the present; however, when they realize this and become mourners together, they are visited by a moment of fragrant and sunlit grace.

"Angel Levine," one of the most central stories in the Malamud canon, poses the problem of faith and salvation with sharp brilliance. Manischevitz, a tailor who has suffered excruciating losses, is now faced with the impending death of his wife, Fanny. Appears in his flat a Jewish Negro, Levine, who claims that he is on probation as a "bona fide angel of God . . . not to be confused with the members of any particular sect, order, or organization. . . ." If Manischevitz can believe, the condition of Levine's probation will be satisfied and Fanny will be spared. But herein lies the catch, for the tailor finds faith almost impossible.

"So if God sends to me an angel, why a black? Why not a white that there are so many of them?"

His doubt grows when he travels to Harlem in search of Levine and finds the Negro dancing in a shabby cabaret. Fanny is at death's door. Manischevitz visits a synagogue, but though he speaks to God he receives no reply. That afternoon in troubled sleep he envisions Levine preening tiny and fragile wings. The dream is not a surrealistic illumination; it is a Freudian confirmation. Manischevitz interprets the dream more directly and accurately than most of Malamud's critics. "This means," he tells himself, "that it is possible he could be an angel." The dream thus brings to light the belief which the tailor, beset by reverses and common-sense logic, has hidden from himself.

Once again he seeks out Levine. This time he wanders into a crude synagogue where four Negroes in skullcaps are pondering the riddle of the soul as immaterial substance. Although the Negroes are unable to resolve the apparent dichotomy of the theological axiom, they conclude with a triumphant hallelujah of faith. "Praise Lawd and utter loud His speechless name." "Blow de bugle till it bust the sky."

Heartened, Manischevitz limps across the street, finds Levine in the cabaret, and confesses to him his faith. This declaration saves both the Negro and the tailor, for when Manischevitz gets home his wife has recovered and is mopping the flat. "A wonderful thing, Fanny," he cries. "Believe me, there are Jews everywhere."

This, as well as any single line, conveys the essence of Malamud's vision and art. We, all of us, live in a world of loss, ghettos, and darkness. We are all of us strangers, scapegoats, refugees. Yet, if we can realize this, can realize that we owe still our human debt of humanity to others, that encroaching darkness may be stayed a little. The Jew is a typical figure in *The Magic Barrel* not because Malamud is exclusively interested in a given religion or race, but because the Jew is for him, as for all of us, a perduring symbol of him who would preserve the spirit despite his own absolute loneliness and defeat. Every man is a minority group of one. By his insistence upon the universality of such isolation, Malamud has given us not only an allegory of our common predicament, but also a clue to our redemption. To appreciate fully Bernard Malamud's contribution to contemporary letters we must understand that the body of his work forms a covenant of grace. We must understand, like Manischevitz, that although salvation may assume strange shapes in unlikely places, it is as simple and yet splendid as our deepest and most abiding impulse — as love itself.

Fantasy and Reality   Eugene Goodheart*

In a recent issue of *Commentary*, Philip Roth delivers a long complaint against "the American reality" from the point of view of the writer. "The American writer in the middle of the 20th century has his hands full in trying to understand, and then describe, and then make *credible* much of the American reality." Roth is understandably appalled by the extravagance of a culture that has produced Charles Van Doren, Roy Cohn, David Shine, Sherman Adams, Bernard Goldfine and Dwight David Eisenhower. He speaks ironically of the American reality as "a kind of embarrassment to one's own meager imagination," and what he means, I suppose, is that the writer cannot expect from his world a center or poise that will make it possible for him to see his world whole. The point Roth is making has been made in a somewhat different form by Mary McCarthy in an article in which she examines the failure of the modern novelist to contain a whole society in his imagination.[1] The achievement of a Balzac or a Tolstoy no longer seems possible. The self enclosed discreteness of modern experiences has broken the chain of being which enabled the nineteenth century novelist to see the whole world (or nation) in the individual destiny. So that no contemporary writer seems able to produce, for instance, the resonance of the Tolstoyan sentence: "The previous history of Ivan Ilych was the simplest, the most ordinary and therefore the most terrible."

Bernard Malamud is an interesting case in point, for his novels and stories are especially moving in the modest and natural way in which they apparently open out from the local and temporal fact into the larger spaces of myth and history. Yet despite the reverberations and resonances of Malamud's fiction, one is still puzzled by what they signify. Has Malamud been able to find in the baseball player (*The Natural*) or the Jewish grocer (*The Assistant*) or the assorted characters that inhabit his short stories (see *The Magic Barrel and other stories*) successful instances of

*Review of *A New Life*. Reprinted, with permission, from *Midstream* 7, no. 4 (Autumn 1961):102–5.

the American (let alone the human) destiny in its latest stage? Are the resonances of his fiction signs that Malamud has done what none of his contemporaries has been able to do: to sustain authentically in the immediate fact the imaginative power for those larger spaces of myth and history? Or are those resonances simply the product of extraordinary gifts of rhetoric and fantasy? *A New Life* perhaps more than his earlier work, provokes these questions.

The hero of Malamud's new novel is Seymour Levin, who arrives in the mythical western town of Marathon, Cascadia with suitcase and valise, an immigrant from an alcoholic life in New York City. With his wonderful ear for the Yiddish idiom, Malamud recalls the Yiddish immigrant tale. "Bearded, fatigued, lonely, Levin set down a valise and suitcase and looked around in a strange land for welcome." Levin is greeted at the station by Gerald Gilley, Director of Freshman Composition at Cascadia College where Levin will teach as an instructor in English, and Gilley's wife. Cascadia College, a science and technology school (much to Levin's dismay), is an obvious opportunity for the kind of satire on the academy that has become fashionable in recent years.

The main academic drama that is enacted is a rivalry for departmental chairmanship between C. D. Fabrikant, a somewhat dryasdust scholar with integrity, and Gilley, the amiable mediocrity, whose concern with the pleasure of the State Legislature far exceeds his concern with literature. The retiring chairman, Professor Fairchild, whose textbook *Elements of Grammar* is in its thirteenth edition, is one of those oppressive presences in American academic life, friendly to mediocrity and hostile to intellect, and yet redeemed by the complex ironic sympathy in which Malamud envelops him. His passion for grammar genuine, Professor Fairchild utters his dying words in Levin's arms, "the mysteries of the infinitive." Levin, one of the few friends of intellect at Cascadia, discovers what is now merely a painful truism, that the life of the academy has little to do with either intellect or moral courage. The Fairchilds, the Gilleys, the Bullocks (George Bullock, a handsome athletic type has special sympathy for athletes, and together with the coaches steers his boys through gut-courses): they constitute the provincial academy.

Malamud is knowledgeable about American college life. He has caught perfectly the traditional speech of the departmental chairman (or the College President) at the beginning of the term, welcoming a new faculty member whom he hopes will "enrich us from his experience in the East," or a returning faculty member who has completed his dissertation on *Piers Plowman.* ("The Ph.D. is our *conditio sine qua non*, and everyone who has not acquired the degree should be working for it, no matter how rigorous the course.") Malamud knows that a new instructor is likely to have an affair with one of his students and that the chances are good that he will have an affair with one of the faculty wives. He knows too that courage and genuineness are as rare in the academy as elsewhere in the world.

The ultimate effect of Malamud's scenes of academic life, however, is neither satire nor sociology. The provincial academy, set in nature, the latest version of America's "manifest destiny," becomes the arena for a kind of Tolstoyan exploration of LIFE and the pursuit of happiness. It is certainly no accident that the hero's name is Levin, for like his namesake in *Anna Karenina*, he demands nothing less than the meaning of life and the full measure of human happiness. Clumsy in the social world (in his adventures and responses he resembles the Yiddish *schlemiel*), Malamud's Levin, like Tolstoy's, is a worshipper of nature.

> The sight of the expectant earth raised a hunger in Levin's throat. He yearned for the return of spring, a terrifying habit he strongly resisted: the season was not yet officially autumn. He was now dead set against the destruction of unlived time. As he walked, he enjoyed surprises of landscape: the variety of green, yellow, brown and black fields, compositions with distant trees, the poetry of perspective.

Like that of the elegy, the rhythm of *A New Life* is determined by the seasonal changes. And in "the open forest," Levin finds his fulfillment with Pauline Gilley, the wife of the Director of Freshman Composition. Malamud has done a rare thing in modern literature: he has written a pastoral romance. His hero and heroine live in an earlier time of romantic hope, free of the corrosive modern cynicism about love. Neither the pain nor the absurdity can dim the glow of their expectation of renewal. In order to protect his romantic imagination from the eye of satire, Malamud has rejected the realistic mode. The fantastic complication of plot and event, the charmingly whimsical lyricism of style sustain the atmosphere of romance. Counterpointed to Fairchild's sterile musings on "the mysteries of the infinitive" are the conjugations of Levin and Pauline.

> He hung his trousers over the branch of a fir. When he knelt she received him, with outstretched arms, gently smoothed his beard, then embraced with passion as she fixed her rhythm to his.
> He was throughout conscious of the marvel of it — in the open forest, nothing less, what triumph!

The little academic drama is complicated by Levin's affair with Pauline and by a strange, poignant memory which all the characters share of an irrepressibly rebellious Leo Duffy, Levin's predecessor, who was fired and subsequently committed suicide. Duffy is the specter from the East. Radical and explosive, he exemplifies the virtues of an earlier time: intellect, courage, erotic fulfillment. (And like Frank Alpine, the "assistant" of the earlier novel, Duffy is the kind of *goy* that serves Malamud's demonstration that all men are Jews.) Even after his death, his memory threatens the philistine repose of Cascadia's English faculty. The test of a character is his attitude toward Duffy, and most of the people in the novel fail the test. Fabrikant, who supported Duffy for a while, proves a last minute failure. Pauline, it turns out, was Duffy's soul-mate and she relives her love for Duffy in her affair with Levin. Levin, as expected, reenacts Duffy's career, is fired, but leaves his Arcadia with Pauline to renew is *Vita Nuova.*

What significance are we to find in the little academic drama? If Duffy is the ghost to Levin's Hamlet, then it is clear that the bitter and tormented past that Levin is trying to forget must be bravely remembered and faced. Early in the novel, Levin tells Fabrikant that he has left New York, "seeking, you might say, my manifest destiny." Fabrikant replies:

> This corner of the country was come upon by explorers searching for the mythical Northwest Passage, and it was opened by traders and trappers in their canoes trying to find the Great River of the West, the second Mississippi they had heard of. Then the settlers came, fighting the Indians, clearing the land, and building their homes out of their guts and bone . . . "There were giants in those days." Their descendants are playing a defensive game. Their great fear is that tomorrow will be different from today. I've never seen so many pygmies in my life.

The novel opens outs from time to time to this kind of vision of the American past. The past is at once irony and possibility, for if the present appears filled with "so many pygmies" in the ironic light of the past, there is nevertheless the reminder of the possibility for renewal to anyone with the capacity and courage to remember.

The Utopian impulse in *A New Life* is very strong, and it accounts for the pastoral romance, the extravagances of whimsy and plot. And how else could Malamud have saved the immediate fact from triviality and inconsequence, if he had not abandoned the realistic mode? The squalor of contemporary fact does come through when at moments Malamud adopts the naturalistic manner (e.g. Levin's introduction to the Gilley household), and we can then perceive graphically the plight of the contemporary novelist. It is as if the novelist has to work *against* reality, to perform through fantasy, pastoral dream and mythic recreation of the past the acts of faith that make the celebration of life still possible. (Even in *The Assistant* in which the miserably gray life of the Jewish grocer is so *brilliantly* depicted, Malamud needs all the fantasy he can muster to elicit significance, and, indeed, one wonders whether for all his inventiveness, he has succeeded in realizing the full significance of his story. His stories sometimes fail to yield even when his fantasy works overtime as in "Lady of the Lake.") And it is for this reason that the novelist who chooses the mode of celebration and affirmation does not finally convince, for he expects us, despite the overwhelming presence of the actual, to believe in his fantasy. When Levin and Pauline drive off to their happiness, we read in disbelief. Having gazed at the immediate fact, Malamud, unlike the nineteenth century novelist, has found the absurd and the trivial, and has tried to redeem the fact through the *grace* of his art. For a moment we are enchanted by the gossamer loveliness of Malamud's dream, but when the actual world comes to us again, the dream becomes a kind of irony in our lives.

Notes

1. Mary McCarthy, "The Fact in Fiction," *Partisan Review*, xvii (Summer, 1960), pp. 438–458.

The Power of Positive Sex   F. W. Dupee*

Looking up Malamud in Leslie Fiedler's capacious *Love and Death in the American Novel* I find that the treatment of him there is surprisingly brief and unenthusiastic. Given Mr. Fiedler's prepossessions I should have expected him to award Malamud high marks. Fiedler is carrying the torch for "mature genital sexuality" — something that he finds deplorably lacking in the erotic life of the American novel. I have myself just read, not only the recent *Idiots First*, but all of Malamud's work that I can find in print; and my conviction is that the sexual norm of his world is eminently normal, as in fact it would have to be since his people are mostly too busy establishing themselves and their families in an elementally hostile world to feel desire in excessive or distorted forms.

True, they often suffer mildly from an *insufficiency* of sex, especially when they are young. But this suffering is apt to seek relief in the simpler forms of action, namely in going to bed with the opposite sex, or trying to. At worst, the sense of deprivation manifests itself in a sexual curiosity so candid as scarcely to deserve the fancy term "voyeurism." In no other author, surely, are so many pretty girls so sweetly obliging about getting undressed in front of their boy friends. "Would you mind if I peeled and went in for a dip?" the girl student asks her teacher in "A Choice of Profession," a story in *Idiots First*. "Go ahead," the teacher says happily, and she does. But "A Choice of Profession" is not one of those steamy romances with a campus setting. The student turns out to have been a call girl in her past life; and the teacher, on her telling him this, recoils from her in fear and disgust even though he himself is so far from being a lily himself that he has been entertaining furtive designs on her. But he is only

*Review of *Idiots First*. Reprinted from *Partisan Review* 31, no. 3 (Summer 1964): 425–30.

a prig, not a creep; and the point as finally voiced by him is that "It's hard to be moral."

In Mr. Malamud's novel, *The Assistant*, to be sure, we have in the Italian youth, Frank Alpine, a bad case of distorted sexuality. He is a thief, a peeping Tom and, just once, a rapist. But Frank is by definition an outsider, especially in the Jewish family that shelters him. Even so, he finally atones for everything. He settles down, marries the girl he raped,[1] has himself circumcized and becomes a Jew. The lesson is as clear as the lesson is in *The Golden Bowl*, where James's Anglo-Saxon girl succeeds in reforming *her* beloved Italian, the adulterous American. Essentially the lesson is the same in both authors. Mature sexuality culminating in marriage is the norm. And so potent a force is the norm that it accomplishes not only the regeneration of the erring ones but their actual or virtual assimilation to another culture. Indeed "assimilation," but with the Jew seeking the moral assimilation of the non-Jew, is a basic principle of Malamud's work. And as concerns sex, the power of the Jew is reinforced by his or her relative normality.

If Mr. Fiedler fails to credit Malamud with his own sexual values it is because he has other values which Malamud's work fails to meet. Fiedler is carrying a second torch: for the "Gothic" strain in American fiction. Gothic fantasy, he believes, "provides a way into not only the magic world of the baseball fan . . . but also into certain areas of our social life where nightmare violence and guilt actually exist." The reference here is to Malamud's first novel, *The Natural*, which is about the heroics and horrors of professional baseball. Influenced, apparently, by Nathanael West's mordant dealings with American folklore, *The Natural*, true to its Westian prototypes, explodes at one point into bloody fantasy. This is what Mr. Fiedler means by "Gothic" and it is what he likes about *The Natural*. And so, while praising that book for its "lovely, absurd madness" he reproaches its author for the "denial of the marvellous" implicit in much of his later work, where, says Fiedler, "he turns back to the muted, drab world of the Depression as remembered two decades later." For Fiedler, "the denial of the marvellous" seems to be the gravest of apostasies, a dereliction of one's duty to be Gothic. But as I see it, the "marvellous" requires of its user the rarest of talents. The mode of it established by one writer seldom survives imitation by another (consider the fate of Kafka's imitators). And the presence of standardized Gothic equipment in a novel — for example the secret staircases and come-alive portraits in Hawthorne — often substitutes for true literary invention. In any case, so irrelevant are Gothic fancies to Malamud's sturdy characters, so little can they afford the luxury of a "lovely, absurd madness," that they are easily imagined as retorting: "So what's lovely about madness that we should play Ophelia?"

All this by way not so much of quizzing Mr. Fiedler, who has his better moments, but of trying to define Malamud, especially his differences from the "Gothic" or "wacky" strain in contemporary novels from *Catch 22* to *Naked Lunch* to *V*. The differences are notable and tend to align Malamud with such a writer as J. F. Powers rather than with most of the Jewish novelists of today to whom he is generally compared. Like J. F. Powers, Malamud is a mildly conservative force in writing at present, a fact which he, like Powers, perhaps owes in part to his interest in the short story, with its necessary economy and — in the old-fashioned parlance — its highly "conscious art." Not for Powers or Malamud, in any case, those specialities of the modern Gothic, or wacky novel: the "sick" hero, the stateless setting, the general effect of improvised narrative, the marathon sentence which, in its attempt to deliver instantaneously a total physical experience, leaves the reader feeling as if he had been frisked all over by a peculiarly assiduous cop. For the people of Malamud and Powers, Bellevue is out of bounds; they are not *that* sick. Moreover, a distinct localism rules their choice of settings; even when foreign, they are never stateless in the sense given to that word by Mary McCarthy in her account of *Naked Lunch*. In addition, neat patterns are traced on the reader's mind by the movement of the "story lines" of a Malamud or a Powers narrative; there is no effect of improvisation. And their prose avails itself of the special authority, so beautifully exploited by the early Joyce, that is inherent in the short declarative sentence. Norman Podhoretz has noted Malamud's genius for getting the maximum authenticity from the maximum economy of such a statement as, "And there were days when he was sick to death of everything." Here are familiar words and a familiar rhythm for one who is "sick," presumably, in the sadly familiar way of hard-pressed people.

Malamud's ability to persuade us of the reality of his characters — their emotions, deeds, words, surroundings — remains astonishing. In most of the twelve stories that make up *Idiots First*, that ability is quite as evident as it was in *The Magic Barrel*, his earlier short story collection, and in those long stories we call his novels. There is no accounting for this elusive gift except by terms so trite as to seem like abstractions. His identification with his people tends to be perfect; and it is perfect because, on the one hand, they are mostly Jews of a certain class, as he is, and on the other (to quote Mr. Podhoretz further), they are "copied not from any models on earth but from an idea in the mind of Bernard Malamud." The idea brings about a grand simplification, or specialization, of historical reality. For one thing, Malamud's Jewish community is chiefly composed of people of East European origin. For another, they tend to retain, morally speaking, their immigrant status. Life is centered in the home and the workshop and remains tough and full of threats. The atmosphere is not that of the 1930's Depression alone, as Fiedler says, but that of the hard times ever immanent in the nature of things. Prosper his people may for a while and within limits. But memories and connections continue to bind them to the Old World, in some cases to the world of the Old Testament where Jacob labors for Laban and Job suffers for everyone. Some, it is true, progress to the point of acquiring ineffably Anglo-Saxon first names ("Arthur Fidelman," for example). Some are found claiming that all-American privilege of the post-war period, "a year in Italy." But in Italy they become, or fear to become, immigrants all over again, and the old American theme of innocents abroad is updated. Golden Italy so confounds the professor of "The Maid's Shoes" that he dares open his heart to it not at all. The art student Arthur Fidelman is made of different stuff but not of stuff good enough to prevail against the glorious menace of golden Italy. In the story about him in *The Magic Barrel*, his first days in Rome were shown to be haunted by a crafty alter ego (a "refugee from Israel") and Fidelman lost his notes on Giotto, the "Christian artist." In the two stories about him in *Idiots First* he is still being badly hustled in Italy and his few victories are painfully Pyrrhic.

The Fidelman stories are beautifully done and very funny. Something about them, however, suggest the rigors of a punitive expedition on the part of the author and possibly at his own expense. One remembers his earlier tales of would-be artists and intellectuals—those dreary youths who lie all day on their rooming house beds trying to concentrate on the reading of *Madame Bovary* or on writing novels themselves. And one suspects that in these cases Malamud's identification with his world is carried beyond the point of perfection, to a certain guilt and fear. His people seem to be watching him rather than he them. And then there is the story ("Black Is My Favorite Color") in which Mr. Malamud tries to motivate the love of a Jewish liquor dealer for a Negro woman by giving him a good deal of wry sensibility. "That was the night she wore a purple dress and I thought to myself, My God, what colors. Who paints that picture paints a masterpiece." This strikes my not wholly unpracticed ear as a mere stereotype of Second Avenue folksiness. Nor are the author's powers of invention quite equal to the demands of the metaphysical fantasy which serves this volume as title story. Here an old man is pursued by Death until he acquires the courage to look Death squarely in the eye, thus winning the desired extension of his borrowed time. Meanwhile each has clarified his position to the other in the artificially racy speech of what seems a kind of bull session. Challenged to explain his lack of "responsibility," Death says, "I ain't in the anthropomorphic business." And the old man yells, "You bastard, don't you know what it means human?" Nor does it help that Malamud, humorizing, calls Death "Ginzburg." He sets out, perhaps, to disinfect Kafka's universe of its total tragedy and ends up approximating the whimsical affirmations of Paddy Chayefsky. Such are the occasional failures of a first rate talent bent upon maintaining his "commitment" to his own people and trying to be as positive as possible. In these cases, commitment, that necessary stage in the development towards freedom of self and imagination, seems to have become an end in itself.

Among the many fine stories in *Idiots First*, two are very fine. One,

"The German Refugee," simulates reportage rather than fable — perhaps it *is* reportage — and is the most profound version of the refugee theme I know. The other, "The Death of Me," is the epitome of the author's whole matter and manner — his fabling manner. Marcus, a former tailor, has risen to the level of clothier only to be harassed to death by the furious quarrels of his present tailor, a thin bitter hysterical Sicilian, and his presser, a beefy beery sobbing Pole. Their fury flows from their consciousness of old unhappy far off things in their lives. And the prose in which Malamud renders their deliberate squalor and pain-wrung cries makes their troubles sound like all the troubles that ever were in the world.

To Malamud, Mr. Podhoretz says, "the Jew is humanity seen under the twin aspects of suffering and moral aspiration. Therefore any man who suffers greatly and also longs to be better than he is can be called a Jew." True, and the special appeal of "The Death of Me" comes from its giving the thumbscrew of this theme a decisive turn. Here are two men whose sufferings exceed those of Marcus the Jew until, realizing that they are beyond assimilation by his own ethos, he experiences the supreme suffering of despair and gives up the ghost. There is real "madness" in this story — the madness not of Fiedler but, as Henry James would have said, of great art.

Notes

1. Dupee is incorrect in stating that Frank Alpine and Helen Bober actually marry. [Editor's note.]

Yakov's Ordeal   George P. Elliott*

For quite a few years it has been clear that Bernard Malamud would be able to tell his story when he found it. The best of the tales he has already told (*The Assistant*, short stories like "The Magic Barrel") have elements in common which the failures (led by "The Lady of the Lake") lack; so it has been possible to guess at the contours of the story he would tell when the time came.

Its central character would surely be a money-worried, East European, not particularly religious Jew who respects learning and whose thought is full of Yiddish turns. He is busily trying to get through a risky world which he never made but has partly chosen — not Italy, not Oregon, probably New York City. The story will of course be told gracefully, with

*Review of *The Fixer*. Reprinted by permission from *New York Times Book Review* 71 (4 September 1966):1, 25, 26. © 1966 by The New York Times Company.

the economy and assurance of a thorough professional, and in tone it will be humane, at once funny and painful. Less easy to guess was what balance the story would strike between the meticulously realistic and the fabulously fantastic. One would certainly be asking: What does the hero's being a Jew stand for? Above all, it was clear that both Jewishness and what Jewishness stands for are apparently at the heart of the Malamud story.

Occasionally in Malamud's previous books, the hero's Jewishness has been no more symbolic than his Americanness; he grew up in it as he grew up in the 20th century. But often it has been a great concern to him, and more often to his author. The test case has been the hero of *The Assistant*. Born a Catholic, he becomes a Jew in the last sentence of the book. From what has gone before, we know that this becoming is more than religious conversion; and from experience of the world, we know that by and large Jews are born, not made, that Jewishness, whatever it may be, is not something one is naturalized into. For Malamud, Jewishness has evidently symbolized some sort of exalted condition of the humanistic spirit which might be summed up in the formula: "to suffer is to be Jewish." Historically, this is nonsense; nearly all men suffer and very few are Jews. Metaphorically, it is no better; though the Jewish people may have done better than most peoples at putting suffering to spiritual use, there is nothing exclusively Jewish about doing so.

Like many literary intellectual American Jews, Malamud has at best employed "Jewishness" as an ill-defined, pseudo-mystical quality latent in all men but manifest in Jews: a vague, irreligious substitute for the concept of the chosen people." At worst, he has employed it as a contemporary, secular equivalent to the most arrogant Christianity. "To be Jewish is to be human" offends and invites attack by non-Jews in the same way as "to be saved you must be Christian" offends and invites attack by non-Christians.

Nevertheless, if the uncertain meaning of the special "Jewishness" has prevented Malamud from satisfactorily handling the issues he has raised, he has been dealing with some great ones: justice, degradation, suffering. And his fiction has always been open to imaginative life; by not treating these issues as solvable problems, his world remains marvelous and his characters have souls, not psyches. They look for salvation in this world, not the next, and they discover that love and good works are not good enough. What is enough? Malamud's answer, insofar as he has tried to give one, has been "Jewishness." Few non-Jews, and not all Jews, find this answer acceptable. Indeed, from the near-flippancy of tone with which Malamud has tossed it in, he has not been satisfied with it either.

Now, in *The Fixer*, Malamud has found most of his story, and the publication of the book is a matter for some public rejoicing. The basic ingredients one had expected are here — with two exceptions: the setting is not contemporary New York but Kiev in the years before World War I, and the story, though it centers on the persecution of a Jew by anti-Semites, is not about "Jewishness." Both surprises prove altogether fortunate.

In that alien, familiar world, Malamud the realist is at one with Malamud the tale-teller, for the real Russian anti-Semitism of that era was a fantasy outrageous enough for the wildest fable. Of course New York is now fantastic (as Irvin Faust's stories show) but it is not suitable to the purpose—few New Yorkers believe in exterminating Jews, our Government opposes such belief, we have no pogroms. And in history, our slaughtering the Indians and enslaving the Negroes had nothing in common, ideologically or religiously, with full-blown anti-Semitism.

Or Nazi Germany might have seemed Malamud's best setting for this story. Many generations hence it may serve for some appalling fable; now it is unusable. Realistic fiction cannot center on an absolute victim. It especially cannot center on one who, like a Jew in Belsen, is given no opportunity to act outside his victimization; his every character trait is forced to subserve a horror which is so strong as to obliterate our other emotions and the character himself. In story-telling, an absolute victim serves his circumstances. But we already knew about these from history. A story about a pure victim is—must be—propaganda. Such propaganda has its uses; they are not the uses of art. In Czarist Russia, Malamud found a society far enough from him to look fabulous, but close enough for its ordinary side to be clear.

The Russian state approved anti-Semitism, if often surreptitiously (it was almost certainly the Czar's secret police who forged that bible of modern Jew-killers, "The Protocols of the Elders of Zion"); yet the state also contained powerful elements that opposed such persecution. It was Christianity, of course, which ages ago invented anti-Semitism in the first place, and restraining but giving supernatural sanction to everybody's natural impulse to find scapegoats. At the time of Malamud's story there was a strong faction in the Russian churches, both Orthodox and Catholic, which still fed the popular superstition; yet again, powerful church elements opposed it. Jews were degraded and oppressed, especially in the Ukraine, most especially in Kiev, that holy city; but they were not threatened with genocide: in the eyes of the law they were not to be in Nazi Germany. Russia, however perverted, no matter how much madness and dissolution it was rotten with, was still recognizably a civilized state, not a monstrous parody of one.

Malamud's Yakov the fixer (or handyman) can, then, be at the bottom of society but still of it. He may be destroyed, but he will not be officially denied as a person. Most important to fiction, he can contribute to his own downfall—perhaps not more than Oedipus at the crossroad did by killing his attacker, ignorant that it was his father, but just enough to make a good story possible. Yakov is framed and worse; the anti-Semitic laws he violates are stupid and crazy; and most of the legal officers he faces are wicked and brutal. All the same, we know and he knows that if he had obeyed the law he would not have suffered as he does.

The bones of the story are these. Yakov is thirty or so, a poor man in a poor *shtetl*. When his wife runs off with another man, Yakov, who is not a believer and who has a few vague humanistic ideas he has picked up here and there, mostly from reading a little Spinoza, goes to the nearest city, Kiev, with some notion of making money to get to America. Friendless, jobless, nearly penniless, one cold night he rescues a drunken Russian who has collapsed face-down in the snow. For reward, this man, who wears the button of the Black Hundreds (a society of virulent anti-Semites), offers him a good job as general manager in his small brick factory. Yakov does not say he is a Jew, and though the factory is in a quarter of the city in which Jews are forbidden to dwell, he lives in the plant both because it is rent-free and also to discover who has been stealing the owner's bricks.

The thieves turn out to be the foreman of the plant and his assistants, who hate Yakov for doing his job well. One day a boy whom Yakov has chased out of the yard a couple of times is found dead in a cave not far away, the body stabbed in dozens of places. Rumor declares this a Jewish ritual murder, that the Christian boy's blood has been used to make matzos. Before long, Yakov is accused of the crime and arrested. Circumstantial evidence feeds popular anti-Semitism, and the case becomes a cause célèbre. Police, priests, the Czar himself, and masses of Russians demand that this atrocity be punished. There is danger the case will be used to provoke a pogrom.

The bulk of the story details Yakov's more than two years in prison, most of this time in solitary confinement. The machinery of the state is trying to break him down — guards, prison officials, state attorneys, above all the secret police. However, the investigating magistrate is convinced Yakov is being framed, both by the murdered boy's depraved mother and by the state itself, and he gathers evidence for an acquittal. Before long he is himself imprisoned and hangs himself. Through terrible deprivation, degradation, and pain, Yakov refuses to confess. This section of the story is perhaps over-extended. Of necessity, it recalls all the other accounts of political imprisonment and torture with which the literature of our century is graced, from Alexander Berkman's autobiographical *Prison Memoirs of an Anarchist* through Koestler's half-journalistic *Darkness at Noon* to Orwell's fantastic *1984* and the recent *Lazarus* by James Hartenfels. Malamud's version stands up to the best of them; but even at its best, the genre is literarily thin, the theme now nearly exhausted; if *The Fixer* were not so well told, this part would invite a good deal of skipping.

Legally, Yakov cannot be helped until he is indicted, and his persecutors delay the indictment intolerably. When it becomes clear that he will die before breaking (they do not use the extremest forms of torture), a public indictment is arranged. Meanwhile, the Jews of Kiev have hired a lawyer — a former anti-Semite — for the defense. The book closes with Yakov riding in a police carriage through crowd-lined streets, on his way to the court where he will be indicted, very likely convicted — though perhaps acquitted. At the least, evidence in support of his innocence will be publicly presented; all who are not blind with anti-Semitism will know that the trial is itself a crime.

We have seen Yakov offend the law (pretending to be a Christian and living in a prescribed section of Kiev) in full knowledge that he is doing so: he is punished by men and the state; his prolonged suffering cannot be taken as an atonement for sin. Yet Malamud tells Yakov's story so well that he obliges us to a play of reflection on some ultimate matters — justice, freedom, power, the law. He does this both by the very structure of the story and also by authorial nudges. "Freedom exists in the cracks of the state," says a Jew who thinks Yakov may win. And on the last page, Yakov thinks: "One thing I've learned, there's no such thing as an unpolitical man, especially a Jew. You can't be one without the other, that's clear enough." In both places, as in many others, <u>the character is almost blatantly speaking for the auth</u>or.

But this is not an allegory, *this* equaling *that*. The story is dense with local history: such things really happened in Russia in those years. Moreover, it casts light upon a number of matters which are neither narrative particularities nor ultimate abstractions: the nature of modern anti-Semitism; how politics swells as religion shrinks; how the ideal of individualism is conditioned by the reality of politics; why secret police are so reactionary; the need for decent men both to take political action and also to oppose governmental efficiency; Nazi Germany; white America. . . .

"Jewishness," thank God, is not one of the issues in the story. "Jewishness" in a lot of recent American fiction seems to be neither Judaism nor Jewry, neither a definable religion nor an historical people, but a vague quality pretending to mystical virtue but delivering little more than sentimental smugness — tradition deteriorated into props. As presented by many writers, especially by Malamud in his previous books, "Jewishness" has become what is left when Jews are no longer sure who chose them or for what (although they agree it has something to do with unjust persecution and a lot to do with suffering) but continue nevertheless to act as though they have been chosen for a superior destiny. One quality that survives intact is the famous Jewish humor, verbal, self-deprecating, aggressive, understating, oblique; this irony serves the needs of anxiety and ambivalence now as well as it used to serve the mortal dread that generated it.

In *The Fixer* there are Jews but not this sentimental "Jewishness." And they are Jews in the way of the actual world. Yakov is a Jew because he is born one and everybody agrees he is one, and his attitude toward being a Jew is that it is a nuisance which he'd like to be shed of but which, being stuck with it, he had better make the best of it—like actual Jews who are non-believers, Malamud does not make him seem in some inexplicable fashion persecuted because he is better, or better because he is persecuted. Yakov is a good man, but, from what we learn, no better than the investigating magistrate. The deputy warden is a vile man, but no viler than a Jewish prisoner who to serve himself bears false witness against Yakov.

And very wisely, Malamud reminds us of how Spinoza's fellow-Jews persecuted him, that gentle, humane man, and cast him out for a scapegoat. Anti-Semitism in the book is a social madness which encourages ordinary sane people to accede to the dreadful acts of brutal sane people; so does anti-Semitism do this in the actual world. In sum, Malamud does not attempt the impossible task of identifying "Jewishness" nor does he use it for ambiguous ends. *The Fixer* is not a Jewish story primarily, but a political story, ultimately about all men.

It is not a psychological novel: it does not set out to illuminate the obscure workings of certain characters' minds and Yakov, whom we know much the best, is a normal man. It is not an esthetic novel, dazzling the reader with form and surface. But to the extent that it forces one to contemplate some ultimate matters, it transcends the political and becomes philosophical or metaphysical. Metaphysically, it has a weakness.

The story ends on a note of hope—but where does the hope come from? Yakov's moral strength in resisting his evil enemies could quite plausibly have led him to stoic resignation. For a long stretch, he has no external reason to think that the injustice done him will be remedied or even known, and only the vaguest reason to hope that he will be so much as legally indicted. It is true that in Russia historically there was reason for some minimal hope for a victim in his plight. But Malamud keeps this actual cause for hope out of the story for so long after the death of the investigating magistrate that when he reintroduces it toward the end, it functions almost like a *deus ex machina*; it is in this last section of the novel that Malamud begins to "teach" the reader too much.

For much of the story, Yakov is stripped and pressed for none but a destructive end—despairing madness, honorable suicide, unjust execution. Any hope of a political deliverance pales before a doom as bitter as his. The emotions and expectations aroused in the reader are too ferocious to be assuaged much less satisfied, by due process of law; for they are outside the law, above any statutes or courts. Malamud has not finished tragically the tragic story he was telling. Maybe he has two fine stories to tell, one political, the other metaphysical. Maybe the political and metaphysical are two aspects of his one supreme story. In any case, at the end of *The Fixer* he lets the two modes get in each other's way. If our only hope for redemption in this world is through political means, we have no hope; metaphysically, at the deepest passional level, this is what the story means, though not what it says on the surface.

Portrait of Artist as "Escape-Goat"

Robert Scholes*

Bernard Malamud's *Pictures of Fidelman* is his Portrait of the Artist. In each of its six pictures (or stories) Arthur Fidelman is caught, frozen in some crucial posture, on his way to an esthetic Calvary. The stories are, in a sense, six comic Stations of the Cross. We can trace Fidelman's progress through these Stations, as he plays the roles of both Judas and Jesus, betrayer and betrayed, until the ultimate betrayal, which is his salvation. It is safe to say these rather ponderous and academic things about Malamud because his readership is established and knows that he never fails to communicate in a simple and humane manner. In this respect he resembles that quite different novelist Kurt Vonnegut, Jr. Both men have tried to write really serious and modern fiction for a broader audience than that reached by some of their contemporaries. It may be no accident that they also share a comic and compassionate vision of the world, although Vonnegut is primarily, like John Barth and John Leonard, a novelist of ideas, whereas Malamud is primarily, like Saul Bellow and Philip Roth, a more traditional novelist of social and psychological behavior. And, like the Bellow of *Herzog* and the Roth of *Portnoy*, Malamud is forthrightly and gratefully a Jewish novelist. However, it seems to me (and I write from a *goyische* perspective) that Malamud is the best of these Jewish novelists, that he has been more successful than the others in universalizing his Jewishness.

The recent waspish parody of *Portnoy* in the *New York Times Book Review* — a mock review of "Peabody's Complaint" — was possible because *Portnoy* is ostensibly so exclusively Jewish. (As if only Jews have Jewish mothers!) But Malamud's Arthur Fidelman, who also has a mother and a sister whom he spies and sponges on, passes through as universal a rendition of the artist's progress as the Catholic Stephen Dedalus or the Protestant Gulley Jimson.

Three of the six Fidelman stories appeared in Malamud's two published collections of short fiction: "Last Mohican" in *The Magic Barrel* (1958), "Still Life" and "Naked Nude" in *Idiots First* (1963). Since they were among the strongest stories in those two remarkable collections, the completion of the Fidelman saga is an important literary event. Though "Still Life" remains, in my opinion, the best individual story in the group, the new ones are worthy companion to the old, and the comic catastrophe narrated in them is an entirely satisfying conclusion to the history of this sad artist. *Pictures of Fidelman*, then, by its nature and its title, seems to invite a kind of retrospective consideration of Malamud's own work,

---

*Review of *Pictures of Fidelman*. Reprinted by permission from *Saturday Review* 52 (10 May 1969):32–34. © 1969 *Saturday Review* magazine.

beginning with the publication of his brilliant baseball fantasy, *The Natural*, in 1952.

In the sixteen years since it appeared, *The Natural* has been rivaled only by Robert Coover's *Universal Baseball Association* (1968) as an example of American sporting mythology transmuted into literary art. Combining legend and history, Malamud created in Roy Hobbs a character who reverberated with virtually every baseball echo from Casey at the Bat to Shoeless Joe Jackson — a fabulous archetype of hero and goat, savior and scapegoat.

This startling achievement in fantasy was followed by Malamud's most intense novel, *The Assistant* (1957). In this somber and bittersweet story he found the theme that has been at the center of all his later novels. Though telling of a gentile who becomes a Jew, the story is not about Jewishness or Judaism. None of the Malamud books are. It is about the possibility of change in man. If we are all locked in ourselves, we start doomed and there is no hope for us. But if we can change ourselves, remake ourselves in some good image, we can indeed save our souls. In *The Assistant* Frank Alpine climbs out of evil into good. From a life of petty crimes and graceless lusts, by stages too gradual to summarize, he struggles through to honesty, responsibility, and love. As Helen, whose love he has lost because he forced his lust upon her, sees his regeneration:

> It was a strange thing about people — they could look the same but be different. He had been one thing, low, dirty, but because of something in himself, something she couldn't define, a memory perhaps, an ideal he might have forgotten and then remembered — he had changed into somebody else, no longer what he had been.

The theme of regeneration is made explicit in the title of Malamud's next book, *A New Life* (1961), a comic treatment of academic pettiness and erotic foibles. In it Seymour Levin, "formerly a drunkard," progresses — not like Frank Alpine from evil to good, but from weakness and fear to strength and courage. An instructor at an agricultural college, Levin fumbles his way through sex and into love, through teaching and into understanding. After the impact of *The Assistant* this lighter book seemed to many a disappointment. In some ways it is. The surface particulars of life at Cascadia College simply refuse to take on the typicality and luminosity that comic detail requires. Academic routine is hardly interesting enough to support comic scrutiny without being exaggerated into caricature. And Malamud's essential gentleness seems to bar him from satiric postures.

For most readers *The Fixer* (1966) erased any disappointment in *A New Life* and challenged *The Assistant* as the *chef d'oeuvre* of the Malamudic canon. Again he had refused to repeat his earlier work but essayed a new mode and a new subject matter. As *The Natural* was mythic, *The Assistant* problematic, and *A New Life* comic, *The Fixer* was historical, a novel based upon the actual trial of the Jew Mendel Beiliss for alleged ritual murder of a Christian child. *The Natural* had been set in a fabulous world of baseball legend, *The Assistant* in the moody actuality of a New York Jewish neighborhood, and *A New Life* amidst the bright tackiness of the American Northwest. But *The Fixer* was located in Kiev, Russia, half a century ago. To an extent its materials had to be researched rather than experienced, and this showed in the book's construction. Most readers and critics seem to have admired it greatly. For myself and some others, it was rather disappointing.

Those who liked it, I believe, did so because they approved of its morality and took the good will for the good deed. The title character, Yakov Bok, learned through his suffering that every man lives in history and must be ready to engage in the great continuing struggle between freedom and oppression. This is not only a worthy moral; it is also a fashionable one: "One thing I've learned, he thought, there's no such thing as an unpolitical man, especially a Jew." Or, as we might appropriately add, especially a black, or a draft-bait young man. It is a relevant message. But my feeling is that in so far as *The Fixer* is a political and historical novel it oversimplifies the politics and history on which the narrative is based. And yet as a personal story it is complicated by intrusions of undigested historical and political data. For some writers *The Fixer* would be an achievement. For Malamud the book is merely a success.

Pictures of Fidelman, an allegory of the artistic and moral life, is clearly an achievement. I hope it will have the success it deserves as Malamud's finest comic work and a proper rival to *The Assistant*. The story in its panel of pictures is reminiscent of Hogarth but whereas Hogarth's Rake and Harlot progress downward to destruction, Fidelman progresses down and out — to salvation. He becomes (to coin formally an expression I have seen on high-school English themes) an "escape-goat."

When we first see Fidelman in "Last Mohican" he is making a false start on his career — the first of many. He plans to be an art critic and has come to Italy with the opening chapter of a book on Giotto already completed. In Rome he encounters the *schnorrer* Shimon Susskind, who steals his manuscript and finally burns it, offering in defense the statement: "I did you a favor. . . . The words were there but the spirit was missing." Saved by the grace of Susskind from the hideous fate of becoming a critic, Fidelman seems on his way. After all, how could an artist fall lower than to repudiate art for criticism? Fidelman could and does. In the second picture, "Still Life," he rents part of a woman artist's studio in Rome, only to pursue her more assiduously than his work. After a sequence of bizarre misadventures, he unlocks the young *pittrice*'s heart and door inadvertently by donning a priest's garb to attempt a self-portrait "of the Artist as a Priest." Annamaria confesses to him what she cannot tell her confessor, and he finally makes love to her, still wearing, at her request, part of his costume:

> "Not the cassock, too clumsy."
> "At least the biretta."
> He agreed to that.
> Annamaria undressed in a swoop. Her body was extraordinarily lovely, the flesh glowing. In her bed they tightly embraced. She clasped his buttocks, he cupped hers. Pumping slowly he nailed her to her cross.

In the next picture, "Naked Nude," Fidelman has "progressed" from false priest and lover to janitor of a whore house. Here he forges a Titian nude in order to escape from his despicable position. As a forger he paints his best work, and he ratifies this criminal deed by stealing his copy instead of the original when he has the chance. In "A Pimp's Revenge" Fidelman does not merely sink to pandering. The subject of his one continuing painting-in-progress sinks from "Mother and Son," to "Brother and Sister," to "Prostitute and Procurer." (Alexander Portnoy would understand.) Even the artist's name in this tale dwindles from Fidelman to F. When he completes this new and truer portrait of himself, the artist as pimp, he cannot let it alone and finally ruins the picture by trying to make it "truer to life."

The fifth picture presents, in a mosaic of fragmented episodes, Fidelman's descent to the underworld: the artist as huckster peddling holes in the ground as sculpture with a pseudo-esthetic pitch about form being the content of art; the artist as Judas, trying to win fame by painting Christ-Susskind's portrait, then spending his traitor's reward of silver on "paints, brushes, canvas"; and finally the artist as a brother too preoccupied with his work to speak to his dying sister. Through a comic miracle, Fidelman finally says "hello" to Bessie on her deathbed, preparing the way for his salvation in the sixth picture.

Salvation works in queer ways. In "The Glass Blower of Venice" Fidelman has given up painting and lives by performing menial errands. Then he seduces—or is seduced by—the wife of Beppo, a glass-blower. One day Beppo, who prefers men to women anyway, catches Fidelman in the act of adultery and gently sodomizes him. "Think of love," the glass-blower murmurs. "You've run from it all your life." Apprenticed to Beppo, Fidelman learns to invent life instead of art. He discovers love, and he becomes a glass-worker. Ultimately he returns home. "In America he worked as a craftsman in glass and loved men and women."

This sometime critic, impostor, forger, pimp, and Judas is saved by giving love rather than taking it, and by abandoning the pretenses of art for the honesty of craftsmanship. Salvation through sodomy sounds like an outrageous and almost blasphemous notion. But as presented by Malamud it is only sufficiently shocking to wake us into awareness. Malamud is writing about love; and love, which is never "normal," is not an automatic thing like heterosexuality. In the iconography of these pictures, Fidelman's submission to Beppo symbolizes his acceptance of imperfection in existence. Craft, not art; love of men and women, not Love. This wise and kindly vision concludes a work in which we find Malamud the craftsman at his wry and comic best.

[Review of *The Tenants*]   Morris Dickstein*

Out of the torrent of Jewish novels published in the last 20 years, which for a time became the central current of our literature, it seems now that three books — all flawed but all more or less justly celebrated — stand out as having added something inalienable to the stock of American self-knowledge: Malamud's *The Assistant*, which (along with the related stories in *The Magic Barrel*) turned the first-generation immigrant experience into timeless Jewish parable of suffering and redemption, Bellow's *Herzog*, his best book, a manically buoyant epic of Jewish intellectuality, and *Portnoy's Complaint*, Philip Roth's raunchy *summa* of the Jewish family romance.

I sometimes think there is a fourth (unwritten) masterpiece of Jewish lust and love, shards of which glisten intermittently in all three writers, especially in the strong sensuality of Malamud's later writing. But on the whole, sharpened by centuries of dispersion and persecution, mitigated only by the sometimes suffocating closeness of the family, the Jewish literary sensibility has shown greater familiarity with suffering than with pleasure, a shuddering intimacy with physical anguish, mental anguish, and all the consequent anguish of the moral life.

This is why Malamud's books deserve a special place even in so selective a constellation. Though *The Assistant* and *The Magic Barrel* boast no character like Portnoy or Herzog monomaniacal enough to become a cultural byword, they have claims to being the purest expression of the Jewish imagination in American literature. They resemble the best books by contemporary black writers in their authenticity of setting and feeling, and their sense of the ironies life perpetrates on those who live too close to the margin.

I first read these two books some dozen years ago as an undergraduate, not long after they appeared, and they had on me a very special impact. Speaking at once in the charged, fabulistic vein of Hawthorne and in the precise rhythms of the Yiddish-American characters among whom I had grown up, they helped bridge the gap between an intense parochial upbringing and the newer charms of the Western Tradition which had solicited and assaulted me from my first day in college.

*Reprinted by permission from *New York Times Book Review* 76 (3 October 1971):1, 4, 16, 18, 20. ©1971 by the New York Times Company.

The stifling little store in *The Assistant*, which some may have taken for an emblem of the human condition, had for me as a child been an everyday reality, too painful to be much pondered, too banal to be significant. Into such settings, not exactly my world but too close for the consoling distance of Literature, Malamud had distilled what seemed like the emotional essence of first-generation Eastern European Jews, stoic, self-abnegating, mildly hysterical, passionately familial — all done with a sureness of touch that makes Bellow and Roth seem assimilated, and whose only peer, it seems clear today, is that anachronistic survivor I. B. Singer.

Rereading these two books recently in connection with Malamud's new novel *The Tenants*, I was surprised at how well they held up after the great ferment of literary style in the sixties, and after so many years of imitation and, finally, glut in Jewish writing. I was also struck by how closely the new book returned to the basic pattern if not the style of the earlier work. Malamud's is not exactly an expansive talent, but he tried hard during the sixties to shift the deep but narrow channel he had cut for himself, to avoid repeating old successes.

A New Life (1961) *was* an expansive book, alternately lyrical, satiric and resolutely realistic, and it represented a bold if uneven departure from the tight parabolic manner which had won him such critical praise. Set at a college in the Pacific Northwest but with an antihero very much out of Malamud's New York Jewish gallery, the book is the best of the academic novels, but it is more nearly about the discovery of America, a country not much in evidence in the shadowy New York sub-world of the earlier books.

Other variations in mood and manner could be found in the miscellaneous stories of *Idiots First* (1963), but Malamud's later divagations were to prove increasingly less happy. I suppose *The Fixer* (1966), a painstaking re-creation of anti-Semitic viciousness in Czarist Russia, deserved some of its critical and commercial success, on grounds of assiduity alone, and of belated justice to a writer whose work had been intensely but not widely appreciated. It was the Jewish version of a black protest novel, but its remote and bizarre historical circumstances attenuated its force.

It was in truth an unbearably flat book. The poetic power that had enabled Malamud in *The Assistant* to turn a grocery store into a prison, and a metaphor for all that is pinched and constraining in our lives, foundered in a catalogue of the endless torments of actual prison life; and the Malamud *shlemiel* character, who was not Peretz's holy fool but the normal man with a rare talent for catastrophe, proved meaningless when all his trials were inflicted arbitrarily from without. In stories like "The Last Mohican" and "The Magic Barrel" Malamud had shown a genius for moral ambiguity which evaporated in the black-and-white persecution pattern of *The Fixer*.

But if *The Fixer* proved disappointing, his last book, a linked collection of stories called *Pictures of Fidelman* (1969), can only be called a dud. I don't know what possessed Malamud to transplant the hero of "The Last Mohican," an art student and "self-confessed failure as a painter," into a black comedy of wild misadventures in the Italian art underworld, but the result, passed off as a semi-novel but actually spanning over ten years of Malamud's career, might simply be graphed as downhill all the way. It also involved something decidedly offensive, a masochistic comedy of humiliation that was a close counterpart to the more ghastly — but, in a literary sense, equally pointless humiliations that made up the whole of the fixer's prison experiences.

So I came to *The Tenants* with a certain grim foreboding, anticipating new tricks and wondering whether Malamud had completely exhausted the best of his talent. Such fears proved groundless, for *The Tenants*, though a mixture of new and older devices, is a welcome recovery for the writer. It is not on a level with *The Assistant* and *The Magic Barrel*, its ruminative manner is thin and portentously symbolic compared to the rich narrative specificity of the earlier books, but it is his best book in years.

The newer elements strike one first. Malamud long ago wrote two stories partly about blacks, but no outsider has as yet ventured to take the measure of what is obviously one of the great subjects of our time, the cultural and psychological upheaval caused by the insurgence of nationalism, separatism and racial pride among blacks today, which has affected the lives of all of us. Malamud is an ideal if unexpected candidate, for he has always been as much interested in ethnicity in general as in Jews, in those passions and perversities that make men behave like characters in folk stories and operas, fabulistic in their very essence. If his Russians were too literary, dwarfed by the shades of their Dostoevskian originals, his Italians have always been as remarkable as his Jews. But the blacks present a unique problem, for they resist outsiders at the moment, they show only their hard shell, even as they lay claims and hurl charges that are too serious and desperate to be subsumed by any sort of folkloric approach.

As it happens though, blacks have more and more been revealing themselves deeply in their own writing, and Malamud's chief black character is an aspiring but clumsy writer named Willie Spearmint, who gets intricately involved with another writer, Jewish, who bears the perfectly Malamudian name of Lesser, Harry Lesser. Their interaction, and that of the books they are trying to write, forms the core of this novel. By chance I came to *The Tenants* after two or three months of immersion in contemporary black writing, and while delighted at how neatly Malamud had caught the contours of the literature and the new cultural attitudes, I was distressed that he had not been able to resist the folkloric impulse, as evidenced even by Willie's name, by his speech, and most of all by his writings, which figure significantly in the book.

As Malamud constructs them his literary efforts are a gross pastiche of all black confessional writers since Richard Wright. We are told, for example, that the chapter titles of his book progress from "Downsouth Boy" to "Black Writer," by way of "Upsouth," "Harlem Nights," "Prison Education," with a short last chapter, "I Write for Black Freedom." The writing itself, almost entirely summarized rather than quoted, has the same quality of pastiche and superficiality. There's a serious problem of tone for Malamud. He intends this all to be mildly funny, but also serious, whereas in fact it is neither very funny nor very real.

Malamud has made a genuine effort of sympathy and tact, but in his hands the black experience suffers a mildly whimsical trivialization, emerging neither exaggerated enough to be satiric nor yet inward enough to express the full human reality. I'm reminded by contrast of the subtly shifting narrative viewpoint which so humanized one character after another in *The Assistant*, eventually transposing the whole book from the perspective of the old Jewish storekeeper, Morris Bober, to that of his anti-type, the young Italian assistant, Frank Alpine. Willie Spearmint, on the other hand, is never done from within: we see him and his work entirely through Lesser's eyes. From his first irritated line — "Man, can't you see me writing on my book?" — even when he is angry, we are meant mainly to savor him for his piquancy. As the demon-refugee Susskind of "The Last Mohican" says to the distraught Fidelman, whose manuscript on Giotto he has just destroyed: "The words were there but the spirit was missing."

This brings me to the more familiar elements of *The Tenants*, most obviously Malamud's return, for the first time in nearly a decade, to the somewhat allegorized and spectral New York milieu that formed a setting for his best work. The nearly abandoned tenement, where Lesser hangs in to finish his novel and Willie squats to write his, has much of the symbolic force and grisly urban reality of the grocery store in *The Assistant*. Both are metaphors of solitude and constraint, of the failure to live, of men bound down to their work — which in Lesser's case is a novel already ten years in the making, symbolically coterminous with his life, for which he cannot in any sense "find the end."

In other words the more important similarity is what actually happens in these settings, for *The Tenants* goes back to the basic plot of the best of Malamud's early stories: the confrontation of the insulated self with the *acher*, its repressed "other," the anti-self which irresistibly breaks down its defenses against experience, often catastrophically but usually also redemptively. The stiff-necked, obsessively honest storekeeper and the drifter and petty thief he hires in *The Assistant*, the rabbinical student and the marriage broker in *The Magic Barrel*, Fidelman and Susskind, assimilated Jew and ghetto sprite of "The Last Mohican" — link up in a way that illustrates the Christian and tragic principle that only he who loses his life can find it.

Harry Lesser fits this pattern perfectly. Prematurely old at 36, isolated from all human connection, he is a model of discipline, craft and devotion to art. As he writes on doggedly in a nearly dead house, he becomes a quietly apocalyptic (but also self-limited) embodiment of the last vestiges of art and civilization in a world overrun. Next door a jungle sprouts, full of obscene sexual imagery, on walls only recently belonging to a Mr. Holzheimer, "a German-born gentleman, originally from Karls-ruhe." Here Willie Spearmint, himself presented as a kind of jungle apparition, establishes his own very different palace of art. Willie's writing and life style have a raw intensity that Lesser has refined out of both his life and work, and the gradual interweaving of their two fates is the most effective thing in Malamud's novel.

Lesser provides criticism of the black man's writing, improves his sense of form, but also instills in him something of his own capacity for unpleasure — his dedication to work, his self-abnegation. "You've bitched up and whammied all my pleasure that I used to enjoy out of my writing," he shouts at Lesser. Meanwhile, as Willie labors to write "better and better. Black but better," Lesser's own compulsiveness ebbs; he is reawak-ened sexually, first by a black girl, then by Willie's own white girl friend, whom he steals away, in revenge for which the black destroys the manuscript of his almost completed novel. Unfortunately, rather than undermining the stereotypes about black sexuality, this plot simply re-verses them; the black girl, for example, turns out to be frigid, despite Lesser's manful best. Malamud is letting his own fantasies run loose, as blacks themselves often do when they are not writing very well.

The role of the woman is a familiar part of Malamud's pattern — the third point of a triangle, overshadowed by the two men — for what he calls "the self occluded" can often be reached only through sexual need. Also, the device of the ruined manuscript we have encountered before in "The Last Mohican." Indeed though *The Tenants* is Malamud's first extended portrayal of a writer, and yields some rare insight into his view of his own work, what we get are mostly reverential mutterings about the lambent flame of art and a 1950's cant about craft and technique, "though I know it's not stylish," says Lesser. More shopworn still is the whole motif of art versus experience already conventional when Henry James exploited it for his marvelous fables about artists and writers, some eighty or more years ago.

The partly symbolic treatment of the black man has an interesting parallel in Bellow's Negro pickpocket in *Mr. Sammler's Planet*, whom Bellow presents, without irony or qualification, as an elemental, amoral force that threatens "civilization," an embodiment of the spirit of a barbarous age. But Malamud's apocalypse is humanly very different from Bellow's. Where the latter's version is a paranoid manipulation of stereo-types and racial fantasies, Malamud's novel at its best depicts a range of real human interaction. Though Willie appears on the scene as a kind of primitive, though he barbarously destroys Lesser's manuscript, he has a genuine grievance, he has been callously injured, and he is himself an artist trying to make sense of his experience, to grow and change.

Bellow's black can't change because he is a mere emblem, a criminal who speaks wordless threats by brandishing his genitals, a force of insurgent primitivism and animality in whom Bellow summarizes all the sins of the sixties: sex, youth, women, blacks, crime in the streets. Bellow yearns to be Sammler, the old sage contemplating Meister Eckhardt, but Malamud's novel is directed against the very withdrawal that Bellow finally apotheosizes. Lesser, somewhat unconvincingly, is two decades younger than his creator, a man still in the middle of the journey, still able to make choices, to will to live again.

But Lesser goes back on his own redemption; the choice he eventually makes indicates a new level of pessimism in Malamud's work. Many critics have commented on the movement of rebirth and renewal that concludes almost all of his books. After his manuscript on Giotto is destroyed, Fidelman becomes a painter again, and by the last line of the book he has returned to America "as a craftsman in glass and loved men and women." But with Lesser's novel gone he falls away from the resolve of a new life, neglects and loses the girl as he tries obsessively to recreate his lost work, though he proves no more able to find an end than before. To do so would be to come to terms with time, aging and dying, which his long effort has come to represent, to find humanity and love — the subject of his book — through writing rather than living, as the character in his unfinished novel tries to do.

Lesser's book (like Malamud's) is about a writer who is blocked as a human being and who instead seeks love through the characters he creates. The moral is corny ("if you have to make a journey to track down love maybe you're lost to begin with"), and the Chinese-box effect is not endearing, but it inevitably points backward to Malamud himself, the outer box, the primary writer. The book has a strong personal resonance. Malamud's protagonists are always roughly the same person, lesser versions of himself, himself seen under the aspect of frustration and failure, and Lesser's particular failure arises out of his profound but desiccating devotion to art. In *his* book, *The Tenants*, Malamud too is unable to make an end, to resolve his meditation on time. "Each book I write nudges me that much closer to death," muses Lesser.

Malamud ends *The Tenants* on a frozen scream, a cry for mercy from the Dickensian owner of the tenement, who wants to tear the whole building down. That is preceded by the last and most real of Lesser's reveries, in which the black and the Jew, both at a dead end, square off in savage combat in the now-enveloping jungle, mutilating each other head and sex in a ghastly symbiosis of failure and irresolution. Each has at last overcome his isolation; that is the only redemptive note.

As Malamud puts it in an ingenious sentence, "Each, thought the writer, feels the anguish of the other." Reality and reverie, anguish and anguish, black and Jew, writer and writer, interanimate each other in a community of pain. But "the writer" is also Malamud, projecting this ending which is not an ending, straining to salvage, in one desperate verbal touch, out of the community of pain a brief communion of sympathy, but one with no conceivable issue in love.

Sliding into English   Leonard Michaels*

Meet Rifkele:

> . . . she looks thirty and probably has the mentality of age ten. Her skin glowed, face wet, fleshy, the small mouth open and would be forever; eyes set wide apart on the broad unfocused face, either washed-out green or brown, or one of each — he wasn't sure. She seemed not to mind his appraisal, gurgled faintly.

Rifkele is the rabbi's daughter. She runs down a corridor in a dingy apartment; her body bumps the walls. She eats bananas. She exudes a prurience unbearable to consider. Nothing is more natural, or unnatural, than this holy beast. Rifkele would be an ideal bride for Faulkner's Benjele, but, as it happens, she is running, noshing, moaning in Malamud's "The Silver Crown," a story of sentimental — magical, brutal, stoical — irony.

Rifkele is like the very language in which she is realized. Both are full of energy and — in so far as language is a way of seeing the world — both have differently colored eyes. Malamud forbids us to look precisely at Rifkele's eyes — "green or brown, or one of each" — but his sentences are available. In the opening passage English and Yiddish focus on the failing condition of this world:

> Gans, the father, lay dying in a hospital bed. Different doctors said different things, held different theories. There was talk of an exploratory operation but they thought it might kill him. One doctor said cancer.
>
> "Of the heart," the old man said bitterly.
>
> "It wouldn't be impossible."

"Held different theories" shrugs, against the burden, toward vacancy. Theories at a time like this. "One doctor said cancer" shrugs similarly for the paragraph. The mysterious scene — operate where? — concludes in a threat which seems to come not from the doctor who said cancer, but from the big doctor in the sky.

*Review of *Rembrandt's Hat*. Reprinted with permission from the *New York Review of Books* 20 (20 September 1973):37–40. © 1973 Nyrev, Inc.

I am mixing my metaphors, going from eyes to ears to kinesthetic signals, but, in Malamud's language, there is a way to see in listening, and both kinds of apprehension seem connected to a sort of muscular activity in his syntax. Perhaps this variety of expressive powers is what allows for his remarkable compression of meaning; in the six lines above, for example, he reviews a convention of inaccessible, disapproving, dying fathers that is familiar to us in the novels of Saul Bellow and the stories of Kafka. At the end of "The Silver Crown," Malamud kills both the convention and the fathers. When old Gans's son loses his temper and says, "He hates me, the son of a bitch, I hope he croaks," old Gans drops dead. Thus, in more than one sense, a story is finished — as if to say, in a stroke of exasperation, "Enough already!" Or as if, by his art, Malamud abolishes one of its major subjects — fathers — and the oppressive feelings associated with this subject.

In the language we hear — before it actually happens — that Gans is essentially dead. God is dead. Read "a" as in mamma and Gans becomes Yiddish for "all." The conflation of English and Yiddish is funny, but, if Malamud is making a joke, he is also exploiting a significant tension within his bivalent language. He is closer to Wordsworth than to Milton Berle. The conflation of languages and the joke-making seem to become a subject of the story called "Talking Horse," which Yiddish wiggles in and out of English, making its peculiar subtle qualifications. In brief the story goes like this:

A Yiddish-English speaking horse named Abramowitz discovers himself in "a sideshow full of freaks . . . and then in center ring . . . with his deaf-mute master — Goldberg himself." Abramowitz is forced to participate in a comedy routine. Goldberg asks questions and the amazing talking horse gives funny answers.

Abramowitz says: "All I know is I've been here for years and still don't understand the nature of my fate; in short if I'm Abramowitz, a horse; or a horse *including* Abramowitz." At last the horse-head is torn off; "Amid the stench of blood and bowel a man's pale head popped out of the hole in the horse." He pulls himself out up to the navel, and thus, in his new condition, Abramowitz has a physical form appropriate to his conflation of languages. "Departing the circus grounds he cantered across a grassy soft field into a dark wood, a free centaur."

In the heart of this horse lives a Yiddish human, a sad, semitranscendent clown, whose fictional language is self-consciously freakish and yet irrepressible. Abramowitz therefore must no longer be seen, by his critics, as part of a comedy act with Goldberg. That stereotypical name belongs to a grotesque deaf-mute. The name Abramowitz has complexity.

The differences among characters in the stories in *Rembrandt's Hat* are less important than their similarities. Their capacity to be foolish and miserable, to get into sticky relationships with one another, remains consistent. What does change, more than the particular characters, is the ubiquitous character we might call Malamud's language, modulating toward English or Yiddish, sometimes within a story, mostly from one story to another. In the passage where Gans lies dying, Yiddish is evident throughout if one listens for Malamud's fiddle making phrases, the length and pressure of his strokes signifying as much as the notes.

Other Jewish writers make this music too. In its rhythms and intonations there is an appeal that is prior to, deeper than, one's individualistic, "New World" discriminations. It is an appeal — to all who hear it, and all who hear themselves in it — for solidarity: a united Jewish appeal. However, Malamud represents rather than solicits feeling, turning his language according to the requirements of human temperature and natural force. In a story called "Notes From a Lady at a Dinner Party," where the characters are New World types, Malamud uses swift, orderly English. The story is about depraved egocentricity and the giddy sexual betrayal of — I think — civilization.

The most general implications of the stories in this collection are as relevant to Malamud's idea of his art as to his subjects. He seems to indicate, in various ways, that he is concerned to represent feeling, not extraordinary allegiances, however profound, however well justified. Perhaps for this reason Malamud offers two epigraphs for this book which express a kind of pain in his artistic heart. One epigraph is from T. S. Eliot, not remarkable for any allegiance to Jewish things (excepting banks, books, publishing, the Bible, and God). It reads: "And an old white horse galloped away in the meadow." I am not sure what this means in "The Journey of the Magi," which is about the *qvech* of death in life, but, through Eliot, his cultural antithesis, Malamud apparently intimates himself as an artist; Eliot's spiritual brother. At least three of the stories in this collection are about artists in relation to their art.

A second epigraph, from a letter by the genteel James T. Fields to Henry James, complicates the suggestion in the first: "What we want is short cheerful stories." Given Malamud's stories, the quotation seems chosen with ironic deliberation. In being inconsistent with these stories, it is not inconsistent with Malamud's masochistic clown side, where feeling is in constant consultation with anxiety, its worst friend. Between them the epigraphs evoke the spirit of Malamud, the artist, as if he were himself attending this exhibition of his art.

A man half-pops out of a horse, or, in another story, "Man in the Drawer," half-pops out of a drawer; a language is half-English, half-Yiddish; a cretinous energetic girl has differently colored eyes; the character who wears Rembrandt's hat, in the title story, actually turns out to be wearing something like a chef's hat, which is the hat of an artisan (not Rembrandt) who is more committed than any artist should be to real-life kinds of natural stimulation. One begins to perceive how Malamud's astonishing centaur, half-man, half-beast, gallops in theme, plot, and language. "My Son the Murderer," possibly the best story in the collection, most clearly exhibits this centaur quality. It begins:

> He wakes feeling his father is in the hallway, listening. He listens to him sleep and dream. Listening to him get up and fumble for his pants. He won't put on his shoes. To him not going to the kitchen to eat. Staring with shut eyes in the mirror. Sitting an hour on the toilet. Flipping the pages of a book he can't read. To his anguish, loneliness. The father stands in the hall. The son hears him listen.

Yiddish slides into English: "Sitting an hour on the toilet." This is not pretty. It is in fact lugubrious. Also accurate, appropriate. More interesting, who is thinking this sentence? It is like the others in grammatical form, but it is, apparently, the narrator's own Yiddish-English idiom, offered in a rush of feeling which embraces both characters, and then recedes at the next word, "Flipping." The passage is like a weird, dull, broken lullaby, heard on the verge of dream when it is impossible to tell rocking from singing. The echoing, a-transitional sentences stand as far apart as the father and the son are intimate, which is immensely. Their anguish and loneliness are simultaneous, magnetic, equivalent, and reciprocally intensifying. The father listens and the son listens to him listen. This relationship extends, finally, to its place in the natural inhumanity of things.

Relationship, which is what we have when we have nothing better, is a modern word meaning isolation, especially in those groups — the family, for example — which once generated illusions of unselfconscious, natural, human coherence. The family, in Malamud's story and elsewhere, is perhaps now understood, in the manner of the father and the son, as being at once related and unrelated to such modern phenomena as the war in Southeast Asia. When news films of the war appear on TV the son, who is waiting to be drafted, presses his hand to the glass and waits for his hand to die. His father, trying to remind him of humane feelings and an earlier idea of life, says in plaintive, hopelessly inadequate Yiddish-English:

> When you were a little boy, every night when I came home you used to run to me. I picked you up and lifted you up to the ceiling. You liked to touch it with your small hand.

The timing of this statement in the story, which cannot be reproduced here, makes the joke exquisite, and, if considered simply for its icy artistry, it has demoniacal power. In the world right now, with no traditional-natural sustaining illusions of human feeling, the son finds continuation of life problematic. He goes out of the apartment and seeks nature. Coney Island. His father, helplessly reduced by fear and loss, follows him.

> Harry, what can I say to you? All I can say to you is who says life is easy? Since when? It wasn't for me and it isn't for you. It's life, that's the

way it is— what more can I say? But if a person don't want to live what
can he do if he's dead? Nothing. Nothing is nothing, it's better to live.

Come home, Harry, he said. It's cold here. You'll catch a cold with
your feet in the water.

Harry stood motionless in the water and after a while his father
left. As he was leaving, the wind plucked his hat off his head and sent it
rolling along the shore.

My father listens in the hallway. He follows me in the street. We
meet at the edge of the water.

He runs after his hat.

My son stands with his feet in the ocean.

The scene reminds me of the moment when Bellow's Herzog, peeking
through a window, sees his little daughter being bathed by the hideous
Gersbach. He decides not to shoot Gersbach. Turning from the bathtub
Herzog considers the stars and then swells into reflection on the inhumanity of human multiplication. This scene, like Malamud's, is in the mode of
the bathetic sublime, so to speak. But Malamud simply fashions a
metaphor: the father contemplates the son lost to him in the water.
Ethnically, I can see no absolute distinction between a bathtub and the
Atlantic Ocean. Water is water.

Here, says the witty Malamud, in this water, in this Coney Island
pastoral, comes a wind that blows off your head. (I remember the hero of
A New Life, struck by a vista of natural beauty, tipping his hat.) The
feeling heart is obliged to run, in Malamud's language, after the Yiddish
head, along the English shore. "My Son the Murderer," in the way of
Malamud, is an ode on intimations of mortality. In the variety of their art,
in the delicate and shocking juxtapositions of the personal and impersonal,
the stories in this collection seem to me terrific.

[The Biographer in *Dubin's Lives*]   Leon Edel*

So far as I know, Bernard Malamud is the first novelist to devote an
entire novel to a biographer.[1] That particular walk of life has never had
much appeal to novelists, although novels have pretended to be biographies (*Tristram Shandy* or *David Copperfield*), and in modern times
Virginia Woolf, encouraged by Lytton Strachey, wrote a mock biography,
Orlando, which was almost a treatise on the art. But biographers as
characters are rare indeed compared with scholars and professors or
novelists and poets. Perhaps the biographer is not a very good subject for
fiction. He tends to lead a mysterious double life; one can't be sure

*Reprinted from *The American Scholar* 49 (Winter 1979):130–32. © by The United
Chapter of Phi Beta Kappa. By permission of the publishers.

whether he is himself or his subject. This makes many biographers seem insubstantial or invisible, for they hide in another's skin. Such, at any rate, is the received opinion of the descendants of Plutarch. And then too, like critics, biographers tend to be incomplete. A critic completes himself with the work of another; a biographer (some say) completes himself with the life of another. We are dealing, it would seem, with cannibals. Of a biographer it might be said that he is perhaps most interesting when he plays the essential role of sleuth; he does attract attention by discovering a batch of Shelley's letters in a national archive where one would least expect to find it, or by revealing some ancient bit of scandal, or by solving the murder of Marlowe—if indeed it was solved. Otherwise I think biographers are no different than their fellow writers, save that their special branch of history leads them into entire cemeteries of the dead, a world of phantoms whose dress has to be language.

Malamud's biographer lives with his own ghosts, not the ghosts of his subject. Lincoln seems to have been the interest of his youth, then Thoreau, and we find him at work on D. H. Lawrence. He is so absorbed in his work and in himself—and especially the latter—that one wonders how he is able to be interested in anyone else. Such a lack makes him a failed husband, a failed father, and a vacillating lover; we discover him submerged in general impotence, a crisis of middle age. Is he a failed biographer as well? Certainly we are justified to ask, What kind of a biographer is William Dubin? Malamud does not tell us; he treats him as he would any writer, although he refers to him as "the biographer" as if it were a special rank.

There are many kinds of biographers. There are the hacks who will sign a contract for writing any life. There are the publish-or-perish biographers, who write not out of vocation but to hold down a job. There are biographers whose subjects are a front for ego failure; one acquires importance by writing of great historical figures. The committed biographer, on the other hand, writing with a sense of art and vocation, is at once more extrovert, more in touch with people and life, less obsessed than a narcissist like Dubin. A professional biographer embraces his way of expression through human sympathy and the gift of empathy; he is as committed to his subject as a novelist is to his novel or a poet to his poem. He lives for the doing—an ideal of perfection, of shape, and of form. Above all, he possesses a sufficiency of self to be able to see his work as something outside himself and as related to a continuing order of reality.

Malamud's Dubin fits none of these categories, although he is clearly not a hack. However, he is so busy looking at others' lives that he fails to look at himself. He converts these lives continually into mirrors of the self. This suggests that his Thoreau is a very Dubinesque Thoreau, and he is so involved with Lawrence that he cannot disentangle his own inability to love from Lawrence's sexual passions. One of the characters in the novel, a psychoanalyst, interrogates the obsessive-compulsive biographer: "I could never figure out why a man of your disposition and temperament would want to get so many years of his life involved with a tormented semi-narcissistic figure like D. H. Lawrence. Thoreau I can understand for you, but not this fellow." I would suggest that Thoreau seems right for Dubin as a fellow narcissist, and Walden Pond had a splendid mirrorlike surface for them both. Lawrence is partly right because of his sexual narcissism. I know of no narcissist who has ever written a useful or successful biography, although narcissists are capable of writing excellent works about themselves.

"I write to know the next room of my fate," Dubin says in one of his more poetic moments. Most biographers write for other reasons: to tell a real-life story, to capture a personality, a character, a vessel of experience. Dubin has "given up life to write lives," and this suggests that he has absorbed lives to replace a life of his own. He puts it in a more enigmatic way: "Everybody's life is mine unlived"; he is saying once again that his own unlived life is in the lives of others. Dubin is thus a seeker of masks and mirrors. I can think of only one real-life biographer in recent American literary history who bears a curious resemblance to him. The late Van Wyck Brooks, a man in search of himself, chose to find his identity in a series of American biographies — Mark Twain, Emerson, Henry James, Howells — and I rather think he found himself in Howells. He was for years in and out of sanitariums; he had terrible depressions; his life continually crumbled. He tried to justify his sense of failure in the "failures" of Mark Twain and Henry James. Instead of accepting the life dilemmas of his subjects, he sought answers to his own dilemma. Without expanding on this fascinating "case," I feel that Dubin is a kind of Jewish Van Wyck Brooks — but also much less of an artist than Brooks, who had a feeling for the salty American character and a poetic style.

Dubin, then, must be judged a rum sort of biographer; he illustrates Freud's repeated warning to biographers against identification with their subjects. Indeed at one point Dubin is "devastated" to read in Freud, "Anyone turning biographer has committed himself to lies, to conceal-ment, to hypocrisy, to flattery and even to hiding his own lack of understanding: for biographical truth is not to be had, and even if it were, it couldn't be useful." Dubin, in his self-absorption, cannot appreciate this. Freud's warning is against the biographer's blocking his own work. He explains this in his essay on Leonardo: all biographers choose subjects close to themselves, and the natural desire then is to remold the subject into the likeness of some agreeable figure in the biographer's deepest memories. Freud, however, also was aware that he had to face this problem in listening to the oral biographies of his patients. He demanded that psychoanalysts first be analyzed themselves so as to learn to analyze others. The lesson for biographers is obvious. The most successful modern biographers have been those who knew themselves before they embarked upon the knowing of others. Some come to this because they are intuitive

Menschenkenner; others achieve biographical wisdom by accepting the modern therapies for "Know thyself." It is to be noted that Freud, in spite of his belief that few biographies can be "useful," singled out Strachey's *Elizabeth and Essex* and wrote to him, "As a historian, you show that you are steeped in the spirit of psychoanalysis."

Critics have already dwelled on the many fascinations of Malamud's richly humane novel. With certain shortcomings, it describes an atypical biographer, but in doing so it provides insights into the biographical art and craft. Malamud's instinctive grasp of the general nature of biography is never better than in a parable he may have placed in his book unconsciously to illustrate the biographer's dilemma. Dubin, shaving by a sunlit window, watches his wife in the garden suddenly performing a dance. It seems strange; he has never seen her swoop, dive, hop in this way. Has she been studying dancing? Is she performing a fertility rite? Is she imitating the swoop and dive of the birds? Dubin's mind ranges over many possibilities, but not the one closest to reality: she is trying to get rid of a bee which has flown into her blouse. The dance has been an act of panic. Malamud's fable is close to the experience of most biographers. How often do we speculate about motives, and find innumerable reasons for them, only to discover that the explanation is simple beyond words — a change of weather, a secret impulse, a sudden whim, a bee in a blouse! A poem is definitive, a concrete act; the novelist rules over his novel; but biography is a constant quest, a never-ending speculation and inquiry.

Notes

1. At the request of Leon Edel, the original title of this article, "Narcissists Need Not Apply," was changed.

A Theological Fantasy   Robert Alter*

Bernard Malamud is a writer who early on established an emphatic paradigm for his fictional world and who ever since has been struggling in a variety of ways to escape its confines. His latest novel is his most strenuous strategem of escape, moving beyond the urban horizon of his formative work into an entirely new mode of postapocalyptic fantasy — with intriguing though somewhat problematic results.

When I say "paradigm," I am not referring to the explicit Jewish themes or to the morally floundering Jewish protagonists that have been trademarks of Malamud's fiction, with the exception of his first novel, *The*

*Review of *God's Grace*. Reprinted by permission of the *New Republic*, from the *New Republic* 187 (20–27 September 1982):38–40. © 1982; The New Republic, Inc.

Natural. In fact, *God's Grace* is the most self-consciously Jewish of all his books. Its hero, Calvin (née Seymour) Cohn, the son of a rabbi and himself a former rabbinic student, carries his dog-eared copy of the Pentateuch into the strange new world in which he finds himself, tries to transfer its ethical teaching to the new reality, conducts inward arguments with God, sometimes even alluding to rabbinic texts, and, above all, broods over the awesome story of the Binding of Isaac and wonders what it might suggest about God's real intentions toward humanity. What I mean by "paradigm" is, in essence, the phenomenological substructure of Malamud's fictional world — its constant tilting of its protagonists into narrow enclosures, preferably cluttered and dirty, and ultimately with no real exits. The novelist has repeatedly sought to give his own claustrophobic sensibility a moral as well as thematic justification by intimating that these sundry traps, prisons, and living graves in which he places his protagonists (Morris Bober's grocery store, Yakov Bok's cell, Harry Lesser's condemned tenement) are the harsh limits within which a true moral life of commitment is realized. But, as I have had occasion to argue elsewhere, this is precisely the least convincing aspect of Malamud's work.

God's Grace, as a future fiction, sets to one side — without, however, entirely suppressing — the Malamudian vision of cluttered incarceration by sweeping the global slate clean. Calvin Cohn, a gentle-souled, rabbinically learned oceanographer, happens to be in a bathosphere at the bottom of the Pacific when a nuclear war is launched that in a few minutes destroys all animal life on earth, down to the last creeping things and the last fish swarming in the sea. By an absurd oversight of God — or is it, Cohn wonders, a new twist of His inscrutable design? — Cohn alone of all humanity is saved in the insulated roundness of of his deep-sea submersible. Up to this point, the plot follows a familiar enough route of reasonably plausible science fiction, but by rapid stages, uninhibited fantasy takes over. Summary is bound to be a little unfair to the novel because Malamud makes it far more engaging than will be suggested by the bare fictional data.

Cohn discovers that another living creature has somehow survived with him on the oceanographic vessel, a young male chimpanzee named Buz, who has been extraordinarily trained by his late scientist-owner: as the story emerges, Buz has been given both the capacity for perfectly articulate speech and a stubborn adherence to the tenets of Christianity. Cohn assumes toward the chimp a benign Crusoe-to-Friday relationship of mentor and friend, though this eventually turns into something utterly different from what first appears. Meanwhile, once Cohn and Buz have established themselves on a blessedly fruit-bearing tropical island, other simian survivors of the devastation enter the scene: a huge melancholy gorilla who reveals a fondness for cantorial singing, a small group of chimps who under Cohn's tutelage prove as wonderfully educable as Buz, and a family of luckless baboons.

Cohn's island might of course be construed as another version of the Malamudian prison, but it has a spaciousness, a paradisiacal sense of benign nature, absent from the characteristic roach-ridden cells, literal and figurative, of Malamud's previous fiction. Even the Crusoesque cave that Cohn makes into his home, complete with rough-hewn furniture, shelves, and a rolling wooden barrier at the mouth, is more cosy womb than tomb. This mode of fantasy, moreover, releases an element of exuberance in Malamud's writing that was exhibited in some of his most attractive early stories, like "Angel Levine" and "Idiots First." The opening chapter, in which Cohn, in his dripping wet suit, discovers that, despite the promise recorded in Genesis, the Flood has come again, and then finds himself addressed from above by an impatient Lord of Hosts, is a bravura performance. Many of the pages that follow are informed by a winning zaniness of invention. Modulations of tone are always essential when Malamud's writing is working well, and the quality of wry bemusement, hovering between sad reflection and self-ironic laughter, lends a certain emotional authority to the fantasy. "Maybe this island was Paradise," Cohn wonders,

> although where was everybody who had been rumored to be rentless in eternity? No visible living creature moved through the outsize vegetation, only a lone Jewish gentleman and a defenseless orphaned chimp, befriended on a doomed oceanography vessel.

The muted comic effect of such writing seems just right, avoiding mawkishness or the melodrama that Cohn's post-deluvian plight might invite through quietly witty formulations like the characterization of the blessed as "rentless in eternity" or the image of "a lone Jewish gentleman" (only five foot six) peering into the outsize vegetation.

Malamud has described his own novel as "a visionary tale with a prophetic warning." Some of his efforts, I fear, to convey a visionary argument through the story betray an underlying weakness, and the prophetic warning at the end, though it may seem to the author to serve a moral purpose, is a painful illustration of how Malamud's materials can go wildly out of control. Let me first address the visionary argument. Given the calamitous state to which humankind has brought the world, and, if you are a believer, to which God has permitted humankind to bring the world, Malamud not only questions human nature but also the nature of the God who allows His own handiwork such a cruel genius for self-annihilation. This theological inquiry is focused chiefly through a confrontation between Jewish and Christian views (in the persons of Cohn and Buz) of the story of the Binding of Isaac, the compelling and baffling parable of how God might seem to require the slaughter of His human sons. Christian tradition calls the story the Sacrifice of Isaac because it is taken as the typological intimation of the Crucifixion; Judaism calls it the Binding because the actual denouement of the story is stressed, in which the angel's voice stays the sacrificial knife just before it plunges. Cohn is led to speculate, considering what has happened to his own century from the Holocaust through Hiroshima to the ultimate devastation, that the Lord who oversees this world might in fact want an actual immolation of humanity.

Struggling to perpetuate a humane Jewish ethics, Cohn promulgates to his fellow primates what he calls the Seven Admonitions (in deference to his Mosaic predecessor, he avoids the term commandment), which reflect a cautiously hopeful, pragmatic view of the necessity for altruism and of man's small but real potential for good. The Second Admonition reads: "Note: God is not love. God is God. Remember Him." This Jewish theological emphasis, it might be observed, reverses certain subterranean Christian motifs that can be detected in the earlier Malamud. (The most apposite contrast is the story "The Magic Barrel" where the rabbinic student Finkle is led by the plot, according to sound Pauline doctrine, to turn away from the law, to which he has been devoted, for the sake of love.) Late in the book, at a point when Cohn's hoped-for new covenant is manifestly disintegrating, Buz, who has played a shadowy role in the process of disintegration, makes bold to erase the word "not" from the Second Admonition. The theological assertion, thus Christianized, that God is love, might seem benign enough, but in view of what is afterward perpetrated by the hand that has revised the Admonition, an anti-Christian polemic is clearly implied. Those who make such an ideal claim about God, we may infer, are the most likely to slip into the abyss of the anti-ideal; or, alternately, a God who is supposed to be love in a world where so little of it is in evidence may also enact the outrageous paradox of sacrificing mankind, His only-begotten beloved son, in the most ghastly way to demonstrate that He is love.

Malamud's theological argument, unlike the tonality and humor of his fantasy, is not misrepresented by summary. It is, in other words, schematic, sketchy, lacking weight of experience and density of intellectual texture. One symptom of this lack of anchorage is that Cohn's abundant references to Jewish tradition are patently secondhand and in some instances misinformed. More serious is the fact that this polemic with Christianity in the end contradictorily reimagines a doctrine of Original Sin, the plot concluding with an irresistible assertion of the Old Adam. There is an ambiguity here that is confused rather than fruitful: a reader, contemplating the conclusion, could easily turn the whole book around, something I doubt the author intends, and claim that Cohn's guarded Jewish optimism about humanity was all along a superficial view and, worse, an abysmal delusion.

The denouement involves a horrific orgy of infanticide and cannibalism and then dire consequences of a rather strained symbolic character for Cohn himself. Malamud wants this to be taken as prophetic warning, but it seems far more like sheer punishment inflicted by the author on his protagonist and thus implicitly on the reader as well. Punishing his incarcerated characters has been a temptation to which Malamud has of course succumbed again and again. The feel of the ending here is unfortunately very like that of the ghastly ending of *The Tenants*, when Harry Lesser sinks an ax into the skull of Willie Spearmint at the exact moment his black rival lashes off his testicles with a razor-sharp knife. Even without pursuing psychoanalytic conjecture, we may note that there is a palpable gap between such unleashing of aggression against characters and readers, and the moral claims made for the fictional expression of all that rage.

In just this regard, Gore Vidal's *Kalki* (1978) provides an instructive contrast to *God's Grace*. It is also a post-apocalyptic fantasy, though the bulk of the novel is devoted to a brilliantly suspenseful account of the plot to bring about the apocalypse. Here, too, the relentless egoism of some of the survivors ends by subverting the possibility of survival. There is, however, a kind of purity of witty misanthropy in Vidal's treatment of this whole subject. No "prophetic" or moralistic claims are made for the story; it is an end-of-the-world thriller that reveals the essential nastiness of the ingenious human animal, something about which the author has never been seriously in doubt. This is probably too glib and too limited a view of mankind to generate anything like major fiction, but it does give the work in question a certain consistency, even a kind of circumscribed integrity. *God's Grace*, by contrast, invites us to take it as an impassioned plea for kindness and pity for all living creatures in the face of man's enormous capacity for murderous destruction. The moral message is unexceptionable, but the vehemence with which the brutish counterforce to kindness and pity is imagined at the end is disquieting. Instead of holding a prophetic mirror to the contorted face of mankind, the novelist—at least so it seems to this reader—has once again taken his lovingly fashioned creatures, bound them hand and foot, and begun to play with axes, knives, tearing incisors, and other instruments of dismemberment.

Sad Music   Mark Shechner*

Any doubts we may have had about Bernard Malamud's stature as a modern master should be dispelled by this collection of his stories. This personal selection of twenty-five stories presents Malamud at his best—as a writer of eloquent and poignant vignettes. Though Malamud has published seven novels, each one touched with his distinctive laconic grace, the short story remains the purest distillation of his abiding

*Review of *The Stories of Bernard Malamud*. Reprinted, with permission, from *Partisan Review* 51, no. 3 (1984):451–58.

leitmotif: the still, sad music of humanity. Typically, the Malamud story is an epiphany of disappointment and failure, a document of the half-life — the shabby region of mediocre existence just a notch above pure disaster — bathed in the melodies of despair, in the taut, concise adagios of woe. By and large, however, Malamud's range of characters and situations has been too narrow to sustain longer constructions. Lacking variety and any feel for the architecture of sustained fiction, his novels hold the note of sorrow too long, until what had begun as a lamentation ends as a *kvetch*. But in the short story, Malamud achieves an almost psalmlike compression. He has been called the Jewish Hawthorne, but he might just as well be thought a Jewish Chopin, a prose composer of preludes and nocturnes.

The Malamud character is one we've long since come to recognize: the underground man transposed into a small merchant or retiree or pensioner. He is commonly alone, or beset by family, creditors, or customers (he seldom has friends). He runs a grocery, a deli, a candy store where the cash register is always empty and the accounts receivable book full. His sons, if he has sons, avoid him; his daughters, like Lear's, are ungrateful, and there is no Cordelia to love him in spite of himself. He may have a heart condition, like Mendel in "Idiot's First," or Marcus the tailor in "The Death of Me," or Mr. Panessa in "The Loan," or he may take his own life, like Rosen the ex-coffee salesman in "Take Pity," or Oskar Gassner in "The Jewish Refugee." At his most wretched he is a Jewbird, black as a caftan, fishy as a herring, and cursed/blessed with the powers of flight, though he longs only for the comforts of a home. With few exceptions, he is miserable, without hope, and waiting for death. Indeed, not only does the typical Malamud story end with death, but the keynote store in this collection, "Take Pity," begins with death, one that releases the character into a chamber of heaven that looks remarkably like a furnished room. Even death, it seems, brings no elevation.

This makes for anything but happy reading, and we might well ask why anyone would bother with a writer so insistently depressive, who peoples his stories with characters who exist for most of us only in memory and nightmare. That is not a simple question to answer, but we might begin with Malamud's own words. In one of the stories in this collection, "Man in the Drawer," Levitansky, a Russian-Jewish writer whose work cannot be published in the Soviet Union, entices an American journalist, Howard Harvitz, who is touring Russia, to read some of his stories. Harvitz, after much shilly-shallying, reads them and renders an approving judgment: "I like the primary, close-to-the-bone quality of the writing. The stories impress me as strong if simply wrought; I appreciate your feeling for the people and at the same time the objectivity with which you render them. It's sort of Chekhovian in quality, but more compressed, sinewy, direct, if you know what I mean." Levitansky, it appears, is a portrait of what Malamud himself might have been and have suffered had fate seen fit to send his grandparents east to Russia rather than west to

America, and these terms of praise are Malamud's own terms for what is strong in his art.

Sinewy, direct, simply wrought, close to the bone — Malamud's writing is all that, but an apprehension of his simplicity takes us only so far toward a definition of his appeal, which has, I think, two other sources: an apprehension that touches some core of panic in all of us and his music. "Man in the Drawer" exhibits a dimension of the Malamud world that powerfully draws us in. Levitansky is the nightmare Jew, but he is also Harvitz's semblable, his alter ego, the victim who, but for an accident of fortune, might be himself. Plainly, he is *our* other self. Malamud's tenement Jews, his Russian-Jewish writers, his lonely pensioners, his forsaken fathers and embittered children are all stained by that tincture of possibility. Even in the midst of plenty, in this best of all possible diasporas, a portion of every Jew stands poised for flight and expecting the worst. It is Malamud, more than any other Jewish writer, who retains that imagination of disaster and speaks the old dialects of loneliness, confinement, and exile.

The music of Malamud's writing is a curious one — dark and brooding but not overly abundant or reliably melodic. One comes repeatedly upon passages that are just plain clumsy, as though Malamud had forgotten the syntax of English or pieced together his own upon Yiddish syntactical patterns. He is no Bellow or Roth or Updike with an endless fund of bright phrases at his elbow; his idiom is a limited one that has not noticeably grown in the thirty-four years he has been writing. He writes in what might be called basic English, now lyrical, now stumbling, reminding us more than a little of Isaac Babel in his regard for simple truths and his studied neglect of ornamentation.

Within that limited budget of words, however, Malamud achieves in his stories a *Kleine Nachtmusik*, a simple melodic weariness that envelops his characters like a syrup.

> Davidov, the Census-taker, opened the door without knocking, limped into the room, and sat wearily down. Out came his notebook and he was on the job. Rosen, the ex-coffee salesman, wasted, eyes despairing, sat motionless, cross-legged, on his cot. The square, clean but cold room, lit by a dim globe, was sparsely furnished: the cot, a folding chair, small table, old unpainted chests — no closets but who needed them? — and a small sink with a rough piece of green, institutional soap on its holder — you could smell it across the room. The worn black shade over the single narrow window was drawn to the ledge, surprising Davidov.

It takes us a while to comprehend that Rosen is dead and that death is no release, just a pane of one-way glass between himself and the living. The green institutional soap, the worn shade, the cot are the furniture of his life and of his heart, which has all the color and warmth of a cold-water flat. Alfred Kazin speaks of Malamud's poverty as "an aesthetic medium

. . . coloring everything with its woebegone utensils, its stubborn immi-grant English, its all-circulating despair." One might want to say that defeat, not just poverty, is the enveloping medium, but Kazin's general point stands: some depletion of the spirit — call it poverty, call it defeat — not only commands the situation but choreographs every act, every speech, every word on the page. Through seas of sadness, Malamud's characters swim like fish.

The initial impression Malamud gave in the 1950s, with his early stories in *The Magic Barrel* and the novels *The Natural* and *The Assistant*, was that of being a purveyor of Jewish admonitions. The novels in particular cast long, didactic shadows and ask us to judge some of their characters as deserving of their trials. Moreover, *The Natural* and *The Assistant*, as well as stories like "The Lady of the Lake," "Girl of My Dreams," and "The Magic Barrel," broadcast suggestions of a sexual moralism as well, though its exact nature is never spelled out. The sexual moralist in Malamud has been largely excluded from this collection, and where sex turns up in a moral equation, as it does in "God's Wrath" and "The Magic Barrel," it posits mysteries rather than precepts.

And yet Malamud *is* a moralist and an insistent one, though the law to which he binds his characters has little in it of noticeably Jewish content. It is the law of simple charity and compassion. Most of his characters either earn their misery through hardheartedness or are the victims of others'. Kessler, the former egg candler of "The Mourners," is quarrelsome and a troublemaker and is self-isolated in his tenement apartment. Rosen, the ex-coffee salesman in "Take Pity," has been driven to the grave by a widow who, out of misplaced pride, rejects his charity. Glasser, the retired shamus in "God's Wrath," has had poor luck with his children, and we may guess without being told that they had had no better luck with him. In story after story coldness is returned for love, a warm heart is battered by a cold one. The word "no" is the most powerful and bitter word in all of Malamud.

Malamud is quintessentially a Jewish writer, though there is nothing of religious belief and only the shards of ritual to be found in his writing and only *shmatas* of Jewish culture or history. Yet, for all that, his writing is so impregnated with Jewishness — as distinct from Judaism — that there can be no mistaking it. Sometimes it is the spectral Jewishness of Singer and Chagall, but more commonly it is the melancholy Jewishness of Roman Vishniac's photos of the old country in its last hours. In his modest and laconic style of narrative, Malamud has found the exact prose equivalent of the dull light and gray tones of Vishniac's world, a world exhausted by siege and conscious of its defeat.

Perhaps Malamud's Jewishness is best understood in terms of Mat-thew Arnold's definition of Hebraism, "strictness of conscience." By such a definition, Malamud is our leading Hebraist of letters, for strictness of conscience is as much his abiding theme as sorrow is his abiding disposition. But though Malamud treats it as a requirement of civilized existence, he often renders it as a curse, a habit of withholding that interdicts the normal flow of human feelings. Many of Malamud's characters treat others with a rabbinical harshness, though one detached from any conception of a sacramental life or, for that matter, a clear moral intention. They habitually ward off intimacy and often give the appearance of performing archaic rites that they have long since ceased to understand. A textbook approach to their "problem" might call them compulsive-neurotics, for they are case studies of conscience gone haywire.

In a Malamud story, conscience beyond an individual's need or capacity or right to do good propels the argument. In "Take Pity," Rosen recites to a census-taker in heaven the tale of his failures at charity toward the wife of a grocery store owner. She would not heed his advice to liquidate the store; she refused his offer of a place to stay when the store went bankrupt; she recoiled at his proposal of marriage; she returned money anonymously given, knowing it was from Rosen. But, determined Rosen, *"I will give."*

> "I went then to my lawyer and we made out a will that everything I had — all my investments, my two houses that I owned, also furniture, my car, the checking account — every cent would go to her, and when she died, the rest would be left for the two girls. The same with my insurance. They would be my beneficiaries. Then I signed and went home. In the kitchen I turned on the gas and put my head in the stove."
> "Let her say no now."

This is charity unto death. By what right does Rosen impose these unwanted gifts upon the unwilling widow? And by what law of self-reliance does she so obdurately decline what is offered her solely out of love? Both Rosen and the Widow Kalish are stark examples of a Hebraism so advanced, so unleavened by reflection or sweetness and light as to be the literal death of one and the spiritual death of the other.

> Davidov, scratching his stubbled cheek, nodded. . . . He got up and, before Rosen could cry no, idly raised the window shade.
> It was twilight in space but a woman stood before the window.
> Rosen with a bound was off his cot to see.
> It was Eva, staring at him with haunted beseeching eyes. She raised her arms to him.
> Infuriated, the ex-salesman shook his fist.
> "Whore, bastard, bitch," he shouted at her. "Go 'way from here. Go home to your children."
> Davidov made no move to hinder him as Rosen rammed down the window shade.

Strictness of conscience has proven to be a moral cul-de-sac for both. Malamud's Jewish characters, one often feels, are automatons of conscience and fanatics. It is a commonplace of criticism that they are ruined by circumstance, but it is less often observed that those circumstances are helped along by their own narrowness and rigidity.

So deeply ingrained is this woe that it seems virtually biological — a mourning bound in helixes within every cell. But in the first postwar decade, it had the full sanction of the times and was well-nigh universal among Jewish writers and intellectuals. The sorrow that penetrates to the bone in Malamud was the mood of a generation of Jewish writers who had been raised on immigrant poverty and worldwide depression and brought abruptly to adulthood by the holocaust. Low spirits came as naturally to them as hunger or ambition or breath.

But for some of those writers sorrow was a transient mood and a burden, and they were glad to be relieved of it in the 1950s when the prevailing conditions of life would no longer sustain their Dostoevskian migraines. As a character in an unfinished novel by Saul Bellow announced in 1950, "You heard me tell my old aunt a while back when she asked me what I wanted, that I didn't want to be sad any more." Bellow, his stethoscope pressed to the bosom of the *zeitgeist*, had uttered that sentence on behalf of a new mood which held that "being sad is being disfigured," and while in 1950 he was still tentative enough to put those sentiments in the mouth of a mental patient in a novel he could not complete, three years later he would confirm them in a full-blown festival of high spirits, *The Adventures of Augie March*.

Throughout the fifties and the sixties, Malamud stood aside from the cavalcade of cheerfulness and let it pass unapplauded. Though he *would* take detours into sunnier climes and endeavor to compose in a more robust key, most notably in *Pictures of Fidelman*, he never strayed far from his sorrow. Throughout the fifties, while other writers in the *Partisan Review* orbit were spreading the good news about "Our Country and Our Culture," Malamud was prowling the tenements of the imagination for vistas of misfortune, scenes of Old World pathos in New World ghettos. His major novel of that decade was *The Assistant*, his story of Jewish and Italian self-immolation in a failing grocery store. If the Kennedy era and the years of the counter-cultural revolution made any impression on his mood, it is not visible in his stories of the sixties. One single note sounds long and uninterrupted through the stories of three decades: the note of mourning.

Collected Stories is a book of mourning, an anthology, one might say, of elegies. Even where there is no death, characters cloak themselves in talliths and recite Kaddishes for the living, as Salzman the matchmaker does for his client, Leo Finkle, in "The Magic Barrel" and Kessler the egg candler and Gruber the landlord do for themselves at the end of "The Mourners." Malamud has written stories of other kinds but has selected these for reissue, as if to honor that region of his imagination that is most accustomed to grief. The singularity of this grieving marks the book as a testament, a memorial, we may suppose, to the world that disappeared into the crematoria of Auschwitz, the memory hole of Russia, the suburbs of America. This book, then, is an act of Yiskor, an admonition to remember.

But such a reading leaves certain things unexplained: the broken bonds between children and parents and the resounding NO that frustrates every desire, every generous act. This sorrow, appended to history though it may be, is also unmistakably personal and was planted in the heart before it ever found its image in the world; we may be certain of that. But this heartache, whatever the source, has led Malamud to a deep identification with the tears of the Jewish past and an affection, to the point of love, for a world that his father's generation fled as best it could: the tenement, the candy store, the hand-to-mouth hardships of immigrant life. All Jewish writers respond in some degree to this undertow of ghetto misery — but only Malamud has canonized it.

This steady allegiance to a single grief, despite all the vicissitudes of personal fortune and historical change, calls to mind Isaac Rosenfeld's words about Abraham Cahan's David Levinsky, a man who in *The Rise of David Levinsky* courts a singular aridity of spirit that he himself does not comprehend.

> Because hunger is strong in him, he must always strive to relieve it; but precisely because it is strong, it has to be preserved. It owes its strength to the fact that for so many years everything that influenced Levinsky most deeply — say, piety and mother love — was inseparable from it. For hunger, in this broader, rather metaphysical sense of the term that I have been using, is not only the state of tension out of which the desires for relief and betterment spring; precisely because the desires are formed under its sign, they become assimilated to it, and convert it into the prime source of all value, so that the man, in his pursuit of whatever he considers pleasurable and good, seeks to return to his yearning as much as he does to escape it.

Like Levinsky, Malamud's characters preserve the hunger and court the downside of life out of hidden motives that they mistake for principles. They reach for their cup of sorrow.

I'm told by Japanese friends that Malamud translates better than other Jewish writers and has a larger audience in Japan than Bellow. I can't testify to the truth of that but I think it plausible. So much of Bellow's power springs from his linguistic virtuosity, whereas Malamud's is rather subterranean and prelinguistic and pressed into images rather than words, Jewbirds rather than Herzogs. As that suggests, these stories are, at their best, symbols of hidden things which have the power, much like myth, to spread wide ripples from very small disturbances. To paraphrase Gide, we should not understand them too quickly.

Essays

The Good Man's Dilemma:
The Natural, The Assistant, and
American Materialism

Iska Alter*

In the explosion of Jewish-American fiction that has characterized this country's literary history since the Second World War, Bernard Malamud's work retains a certain singularity in both subject matter and form. Without the exuberant self-promotion of Norman Mailer, the black and bitter humor of Joseph Heller, the increasing self-absorption of Philip Roth, or, more significantly, the moral comedy of Saul Bellow, Malamud has continued to be a humanistic spokesman, albeit a frequently disappointed one in recent years, for responsibility, compassion, and goodness in a world spinning out of control with frightening speed. To embody his concerns as a Jew, an artist, and a moral man, Malamud has evolved a style that is uniquely his. Its fusion of the fabulous and the factual, called "lyrical realism" by the Yiddish critic Mayer Shticker,[1] is the fictive analogue to the Chasidic belief that the mystical connection to God is to be found not in ascetic isolation, but through man's participation in the ordinary activities and mundane events of daily existence.[2]

Given Malamud's not-quite-fashionable content[3] and his paradoxical technique, it should not be surprising that the critical response to his fiction has been varied, and sometimes contradictory. On the one hand, he is condemned by Philip Roth[4] for his distance from an actual, firmly presented social environment; on the other, he is praised by Tony Tanner[5] for this very same quality. Within this range of opposites, several distinct orientations are apparent. For example, Alfred Kazin denigrates *The Natural* because it is rooted in fantasy, preferring those novels and short stories that seem to be a more naturalistic portrayal of the Jew's experiential reality,[6] while Marcus Klein notes Malamud's variations on the accommodationist spirit that Klein perceives as the major force in post-World War II literature. Like Kazin, Klein is not entirely comfortable with what he believes to be Malamud's intense, parochial exoticism. But he recognizes that the characters in Malamud's fiction are driven "to be

*Reprinted from *The Good Man's Dilemma: Social Critisim in the Fiction of Bernard Malamud*, AMS Studies in Modern Literature, No. 5 (New York: AMS Press, Inc. 1981), 1–26. © 1981 AMS Press, Inc.

out of this world and in a more certainly felt reality. . . . And their adventure is precisely their frustration; the end of straining and the beginning of heroism, if achieved, is the beginning of acceptance. . . . His hero's heroism is his hero's loss."[7]

There are critics such as Leslie Fielder,[8] Stanley Edgar Hyman,[9] and Earl Wasserman,[10] who view Malamud only in his mythic context, counting as most worthy those works with an explicitly archetypal content, esteeming *The Natural*, in particular, for its lively sense of mythic play. Others belonging to this school are more interested in tracing the continuity of archetypal patterns from novel to novel.[11] Of course, and with good reason, there are those who consider Malamud primarily as a Jewish-American writer mindful only of his use of Jewish motifs. Mayer Shticker has noted that with *The Assistant* Bernard Malamud "has brought into American literature . . . the emotional sensibility of the heart [*herzlekhayt*] that reminds us so strongly of the great masters of Jewish writing, Sholem Aleichem, Peretz, and David Bergelson."[12] Robert Alter, however, believes that all but *The Fixer* are a vulgarization of that illustrious Yiddish tradition.[13] For Josephine Zadovsky Knopp, the concept of *mentshlekhayt* is at the core of Malamud's work and is the source of its strength.[14]

It would be foolish to deny or minimize the validity of much that the critics have observed and written about Bernard Malamud; yet there is one whole area of the author's fiction, his social criticism, that has been neglected, ignored, or even declared nonexistent.[15] Indeed, the later novels, whose judgments about society are more pronounced, have usually been accorded less value than *The Assistant* or *The Magic Barrel*. But Malamud has, in fact, shown a constant awareness of the societies in which his fictions take place. He is not only interested in describing actual social structures, or the human interactions that sustain them; he is also concerned with defining and dramatizing the underlying forces which form the bases upon which a given community is built. This study will attempt to show that from the myth of *The Natural* to the apocalyptic design of *The Tenants*, Malamud has fictively presented the decline of the American dream into the nightmare of an entire civilization in decay, a surprising theme, perhaps, from an author supposedly unconcerned with the difficult realities of society and the problems of a disintegrating culture.

It is with *The Natural* (1952), his first novel, that Malamud begins to suggest and depict the frauds perpetrated on men by an established order, particularly the bogus values and the fakery that seem to be as much a part of the American dream as its hopes and promises. The American dream: a paradox to be sure, one that embodies both the idealism of the nation and the corrosive materialism that appears to be its tangible outgrowth. This democratic dream speaks of a society that welcomes another's exiles; where the barriers against individual fulfillment are absent and the self can flourish, releasing the vitality of future possibilities; where the *I* can expand to encompass the universe.

However, those very elements that constitute the culture's visionary potential are also the source of its terror: alienation, loneliness, transience, the psychological and geographical movement from roots and tradition. It is also a civilization that defines achievement externally and success acquisitively, making failure a punishment, poverty a sin, and love a purchasable commodity. And it is an increasingly firm axiom of Malamud's fiction that to succeed in such an environment is to lose one's soul; to fail is to preserve one's moral integrity.

Utilizing this series of assumptions to shape his version of the democratic dilemma, Malamud in *The Natural* offers a variant of the Horatio Alger archetype wherein the hero must choose between two opposing concepts of success. Roy Hobbs can be a true democratic hero, self-created, faithful to his natural talent and individual possibility, believing in and accepting the power of the middle class version of the good life: "a house they had bought, with a redheaded baby on her lap, and himself going fishing in a way that made it satisfying to fish, knowing that everything was all right behind him, and the home-cooked meal would be hot and plentiful, and the kid would carry the name of Roy Hobbs into generations his old man would never know. With this in mind he fished the stream in peace. . . ."[16]

Or Roy Hobbs, succumbing to his status as celebrated cultural product, can betray his true capacities as one of Nature's noblemen in order to obtain the outward signs of socially approved success: money, power, things, which are represented not by the fruitful Iris Lemon, but by the barren Memo Paris, the boss's niece, failed movie starlet of Miss America perfection. Her siren's song is that of a typically American Lorelei, whose chant is the dream turned rapacious:

> I am afraid to be poor. . . . Maybe I am weak or spoiled, but I am the type who has to have somebody who can support her in a decent way. I'm sick of living like a slave. I got to have a house of my own, a maid to help me with the hard work, a decent car to shop with and a fur coat for winter time when it's cold. I don't want to have to worry every time a can of beans jumps a nickel. I suppose it's wrong to want all of that but I can't help it. I've been around too long and seen too much. I saw how my mother lived and I know it killed her. I made up my mind to have certain things. . . . You're thirty-five now and that don't give you much time left as a ball player. . . . I'm sorry to say this, Roy, but I have to be practical. Suppose the next one is your last season, or that you will have one more after that? Sure, you'll probably get a good contract till then but it costs money to live, and then what'll we do for the rest of our lives?" [199–200]

The source of decay in the mythic American landscape of *The Natural* is money, poisoning even the pure idealism of the country's symbolic national pastime (hence the verbal echoes of the 1919 Black Sox scandal that close the book).[17] Wealth is obviously important in any social system, but in a democratic one such as America, predicated on the premise of human equality, the possession of money as a major external token denoting difference, separation, and inequity becomes a more ambiguous force, perhaps threatening to the fabric of the national community. On the one hand, the acquisition of money is proof that an open society still operates, that money is the just reward for living the letter of the American dream. On the other hand, the possession of money bears witness to the destruction of traditional values, beliefs, and commitments, an indication not of continued vitality but of the nation's flaws, the disintegration of its promise. For Malamud, the need for money, and therefore power, becomes the concrete emblem of popular, superficial notions of success and accomplishment, ultimately corrupting all facets of the national experience—moral, economic, and sensual.

Goodwill Banner (a suitably ironic name for a notoriously bad-tempered individual) is the embodiment of a morally corrupt, exploitative America. He instinctively recognizes that this society not only prefers things to people, but also that its materialistic ethic rationalizes the transformation of people into things, objects to be manipulated. His wealth, obtained illegally, through the exercise of established capitalistic virtues based on the management of human weakness and greed, is put at the service of this awareness, thereby justifying his appetite for control. The crowds who come to his stadium are merely coins, Pop Fisher is an obstruction to be bought out by any means, and Roy Hobbs is a life-sized toy to be used in order to acquire *more*. Fittingly, the trophy in his tower office is a stuffed shark.

As a judge, Banner also dispenses dark wisdom, parables and aphorisms which punctuate his conversation, making him seem a cynical Poor Richard: "The dog is turned to his vomit again" [96]. "The love of money is the root of all evil" [99]. "He that maketh haste to be rich shall not be innocent" [101]. "Put a knife to thy throat if thou be a man given to appetite" [101]. "Resist all evil" [102]. He is, in fact, enamoured of darkness, planning to write a disquisition on the subject entitled "On the Harmony of Darkness; Can Evil Exist in Harmony?" (echoing, no doubt, Melville's "On the Whiteness of the Whale"): "There is in the darkness a unity, if you will, that cannot be achieved in any other environment, a blending of the self with what the self perceives. . ." [100]. And like a perverse and pessimistic Ben Franklin or Jay Gatsby, the Judge is, in a very American way, self-invented: "As a youngster I was frightened of the dark—used to wake up sobbing in it, as if it were water and I were drowning—but you will observe that I have so disciplined myself thoroughly against that fear, that I much prefer a dark to a lit room, and water is my favorite beverage" [100].

Goodwill Banner has decided against the vision of a sunny, jovial

America; and in his treatment of fellow human beings, he has passed judgment on American innocence and found it suitable for purchase. Working in collusion with Judge Banner is Gus Sands, the one-eyed Supreme Bookie, a representation of economic corruption and the decline of American capitalism.

To be sure, the original impetus of the American economic system had been to insure growth, progress, and the pursuit of happiness. Capitalism is, indeed, the financial analogue to the psychic and political freedoms on which the country was founded. It reinforced the idea of individual ability as the way to true achievement; it exalted the willingness to risk, the capacity to take a chance, and the readiness to seize the moment; it made real the national rags-to-riches mythology; it allowed more people to have a share in society's affluence. But for Malamud these factors no longer work as theorized. The economic system that was once the hope of the shopkeeper, the small farmer, the businessman with little capital and much ability, has become the servant of the rich who use it to drain and profit from those who have less.

Gus Sands, partially blind, seeing the individual only as an expendable commodity, is one such exploiter. Like the Judge, Sands has amassed a fortune by trading in human frailty, in this case the impulse bred into the American to get rich quick, to reach for the fast buck, no matter how. For if money is that necessary icon, the indispensable sign of acceptance, approval, goodness, wisdom, and power, then the means by which it is to be procured is irrelevant. Gus, secure in his knowledge of the secret heart of his countrymen, is, like the serpent in Eden (Roy Hobbs even calls him "wormy"), a masterful tempter.

He is also more than simply the Supreme Bookie. As a gambler, he is the epitome of the risk-taker, the speculative capitalist whose product, in this instance, just happens to be money:

> "Didn't know you bet on any special player."
> "On anybody or anything. We bet on strikes, balls, hits, runs, innings, and full games. If a good team plays a lousy team we will bet on the spread of runs. We cover anything anyone wants to bet on. Once in a Series games I bet a hundred grand on three pitched balls."
> "How'd you make out on that?"
> "Guess."
> "I guess you didn't.
> "Right, I didn't. . . . But it don't matter. The next week I ruined the guy in a different deal. Sometimes we win, sometimes we don't but the percentage is for us. Today we lost on you, some other time we will clean up double." [108]

And though dependent on luck and accident, like a good entrepreneur he controls luck and minimizes accident through bribery ("Say the word, slugger, and you can make yourself a nice pile of dough quick" [174]), seduction, dishonesty, and the chicanery that has become an established part of American business practice.

Memo Paris (whose name—a memory of Paris—may suggest the treacherous Helen of Troy or that sensual, erotic, tempting City of Lights), seductive agent of Judge Banner and Gus Sands, is clearly an exponent of the business of commercial sensuality. That she may be a national symbol of sorts is indicated by Roy's seeing her "as a truly beautiful doll with a form like Miss America" [166]. She is, indeed, a doll, an object, all surface prettiness with little emotional depth or internal integrity. And as a beauty contest winner, value has necessarily been placed on those superficial qualities that guarantee victory. Just as Roy Hobbs attempts to succeed in a particular area of mass entertainment, so too does Memo Paris. But she chooses the Hollywood dream factory, where success is contingent upon appearance far more than it is dependent upon talent. She fails, however, not because she lacks outward beauty, but because she lacks talent. She has no inner resources to draw on; she possesses a limited, closed self that has been determined by her external attractiveness:

> "I won a beauty contest where they picked a winner from each state and she was sent to Hollywood to be a starlet. For a few weeks I felt like the Queen of May, then they took a screen test and though I had the looks and figure my test did not come out so good in acting and they practically told me to go home. . . . I stayed there for three more years, doing night club work and going to an acting school besides, hoping that I would some day be a good enough actress, but it didn't take. I knew what *I was supposed to do but I couldn't make myself, in my thoughts, into somebody else.* You're supposed to forget who you are." [119–120][18]

As we have already seen, Memo's wants are not only conditioned by her fear of poverty, but also by what society has legitimized as essential for happiness: maids, fur coats, houses, cars. And she has been taught by that society that it is perfectly appropriate to sell herself in order to secure those things. Marketing her sensuality, however, corrupts the buyer as well. Memo Paris is, in fact, negotiable merchandise to be bought at the right price—a man's soul.

Into this knotty web of societal decay comes Roy Hobbs, a natural man, whose notable American innocence has prevented his education through experience; this difficult process has never been a popular American ideal, much to Malamud's disappointment. Roy is to be the authentic American hero whose adventures take place on the field of mass ritual—baseball—not in the realm of elite diversion to please the few. There is no question that he has great talent, the kind of native ability meant to be nurtured in a democracy. But his ambition is narrow and unchanging. It is expressed in the same language at the outset of his career at the age of nineteen—"Sometimes when I walk down the street I bet people will say there goes Roy Hobbs, the best there ever was in the game"

[33] — and then at its resumption, age thirty-five: "Maybe I might break my back while I am at it, . . . but I will do my best — the best I am able — to the greatest there ever was in the game" [114].

And his desires are at the mercy of social and cultural influences that stress money, possessions, acquisitiveness:

> It had to be something big or it wouldn't pay back enough. And if it was a big company he could take it a little easy. . . . He pondered where to get another twenty-five thousand, and it had to be before the start of the next baseball season because as soon as everybody saw he wasn't playing, it wouldn't be easy to cash in on his name. . . . He thought of other means to earn money fast — selling the story of his life to the papers, barnstorming a bit this fall and winter. . . . But neither of these things added up to much — not twenty-five grand. [201]

Because he does not grasp the meaning of the heroic beyond its simplest definition; because his society has deceived him about what is to be truly valued in life; because he accepts the tokens of success rather than actual accomplishment, he chooses fidelity to his genius too late, after he has already betrayed it for cash. Roy is therefore doomed to repeat his suffering without understanding its significance: "I never did learn anything out of my past life, now I have to suffer again" [236].

If *The Natural* presents a simplified definition of the American experience where villainy is easily identifiable and the pattern of right action obvious, *The Assistant* offers complex, perhaps perplexing, ambiguities. The world of *The Assistant* seems closed, rigid, without opportunity or economic progress, where the traditional values of honesty, thrift, and hard work go unrewarded, and may, in fact, even be meaningless. It is an America inhabited by the marginal, the frustrated, the luckless, whom a hungry, active, pushing civilization has discarded as useless: immigrant Jews left behind in the rush toward assimilation and the good life; would-be criminals successful only in their failure; the trapped, who are caught forever in a net of unfulfilled expectations.[19]

In this society of the powerless, so unlike that of *The Natural*, evil is neither predatory, nor sinister, nor particularly threatening. It is, rather, clumsy, slightly comical, and "Karping." Yet in such a defeatist environment, characters seem nevertheless capable of moral choice; positive human change can occur. Ultimately, however, though choices are undoubtedly made and changes certainly do occur, they are equivocal and claustrophobic, imprisoning rather than liberating. Perhaps this paradox is an indication that such virtues as honor, duty, responsibility, and goodness are a hindrance in an aggressive society addicted to the pursuit of externally determined success, not its internal reality; that morality and ethical behavior are signs marking only the failed, the lost.

Walter Shear has rightly perceived *The Assistant* to be a dramatization of the never-quite-resolved conflict between two cultures — the Jewish tradition of the Bobers, Pearls, and Karps and the American heritage, the wisdom of the old world versus the utilitarianism of the new.[20] This analysis is true as far as it goes. But the encounter as presented in the novel is more subtly ironic. The Jewish tradition, as Malamud depicts it, may be morally admirable; but it is essentially heterodox and secular, divorced from its sources in orthodox Judaism and the European situation that conditioned it, and no longer appropriate in an open, liberal social system.[21] Morris Bober may have brought with him his own entombment but without sufficient spiritual consolation to sustain him. And the American heritage, vital and promising as it may be, stands not only as a mockery of hopes betrayed, or as a series of poisoned expectations, but as a sardonic tribute to the hypocrisy that is also a part of the American dream. Karp succeeds in the financially approved way, but it is without joy and without love.

We begin with the only Jewish families who inhabit, resentfully, uncomfortably, an impoverished, decaying, non-Jewish neighborhood in New York — the Karps, the Pearls, the Bobers: "She [Ida Bober] had waked that morning resenting the grocer for having dragged her, so many years ago, out of a Jewish neighborhood into this. She missed to this day their old friends and landsleit — lost for parnusseh unrealized."[22] Each represents, in some way, a facet of the Jewish experience in this *goldene medinah*, this golden land. While these families do have those aspirations common to American imagination, they are Jews who have, for the most part, been unable to enter the mainstream of middle-class life and acceptability. They are reminders of the immigrant past for whom the promise of *better* has not been kept. Fulfillment is for their children — Louis, Nat, and Helen. They are the generation who will belong. Although the patriarchs are entrepreneurs, self-employed businessmen — ironic exemplars of the classic American prescription for success — the isolated condition of these three Jewish families makes them vulnerable, susceptible to paralyzing memories of their ghetto history. Although these families are still anxious to participate in the flawed American dream, they are viewed by many of the Gentiles in the community as seeming embodiments of the anti-semite's stereotypical Jew, and therefore as legitimate targets for robbery and violence.

Julius Karp is the wealthy exception among the three families. At the end of Prohibition, good businessman that he was, Karp astutely (by society's valuation of such things) acquired the necessary license to transform cheap shoes into expensive bottles. The liquor store, not surprisingly, did well in so poor a neighborhood, and Karp flourished. But for Malamud, Karp's success had been bought at dehumanizing cost. After all, his wealth, like Judge Banner's or Gus Sands's, is based on the exploitation of human frailty. "A business for drunken bums" [9], says Morris Bober, the novel's moral voice, judging with disapproval and contempt. Karp, in an act that signifies the breaking of the human connections that have tied him to his fellow Jews, has also moved out of the neighborhood into "a big house on the Parkway . . . complete with two-car garage and Mercury" [16], the middle-class American's vision of accomplishment. It is worth noting here how often success, in this country, is measured by the geographical distance one has moved from his origins and roots — the further one goes, the more one has achieved. This fact has allowed Karp to become an absentee exploiter, using the neighborhood for his own, as property, then leaving it to die from his poison, a singular example of the abdication of moral responsibility in favor of personal financial satisfaction.

But Julius Karp's deficiencies as a human being are more extensive. Having become the kind of success society values, he is now free to exercise the power conferred by money: the ability to transform human beings into commodities to be manipulated for gain. Because he has attained position, Julis Karp assumes also that he has been given wisdom. In this culture, the ability to acquire money attests to sagacity; therefore Karp is free to "run down the store and spout unwanted advice" [22]. After all, since Morris Bober is a poor man, a failure by anyone's estimation, what can he possibly know that is worth anything? And Karp, assuming that the world, as he knows, dances only to the tune of cash, even converts love into a business proposition with Helen Bober an object to be traded for financial security:

> Karp felt he could ease his son's way to Helen by making Morris a proposition he had had in the back of his head for almost a year. He would describe Louis' prospects after marriage in terms of cold cash and other advantages, and suggest that Morris speak to Helen on the subject of going with him seriously. If they went together a couple of months — Louis would give her an extravagant good time — and the combination worked out, it would benefit not only the daughter, but the grocer as well, for then Karp would take over Morris's sad gesheft and renovate and enlarge it into a self-service market with the latest fixtures and goods. . . . With himself as the silent partner giving practical advice, it would take a marvelous catastrophe to keep the grocer from earning a decent living. . . . [151]

Finally, and perhaps most significantly, Karp betrays friendship, loyalty, and his own humanity for a mercenary reward by allowing into the neighborhood another grocery store to compete with the unfortunate Morris for business, since competition is the essence of the American way. Karp does this first at the beginning of the novel when, rejecting Morris's pleas, he sells the empty tailor shop to Schmitz: "Morris ran to Karp. 'What did you do to me?' The liquor dealer said with a one-shouldered shrug, 'You saw how long stayed empty the store. Who will pay my taxes? But don't worry,' he added, 'he'll sell more delicatessen but you'll sell more groceries. Wait, you'll see he'll bring you in customers' " [11]. And he resells to Taast and Pederson, knowing full well that such competition will be destructive:

> "What happened to Schmitz?"
> "He has a bad blood disease and lays now in the hospital."
> "Poor man," the grocer sighed. . . . "Will he give the store in auction?"
> Karp was devastating, "What do you mean give in auction? It's a good store. He sold it Wednesday to two up-to-date Norwegian partners and they will open next week a modern fancy grocery and delicatessen. You will see where your business will go. . . . What could I do? I couldn't tell him to go in auction if he had a chance to sell." [155]

That Karp chooses, in both instances, to sell to *goyim* is a further betrayal of Morris, who is portrayed as the essence of Jewishness.

Yet in Karp there exists a vague, ineffable, dissatisfaction, an unconscious recognition that perhaps his kind of achievement is incomplete, a suspicion that something is indeed more vital than dollars. For, like the crooked Charlie Sobeloff, Morris's former partner made rich at the expense of Bober's trusting innocence, Karp finds it necessary to have Morris's approval and acceptance: "For some reason that was not clear to him Karp liked Morris to like him. . ." [149]. True wisdom makes itself known even to the most hardened.

As for the next generation, Louis Karp is the son of such a father. And it is hardly surprising that his ambitions are narrow, limited to those obtainable by purchase:

> "Louis," she [Helen Bober] said, watching a far-off light on the water, "what do you want out of your life?"
> He kept his arm around her. "The same thing I got — plus."
> "Plus what?"
> "Plus more, so my wife and family can have also." [43]

However, in this version of America, unlike the landscape of *The Natural*, there is retribution for those who have made their pact with the American serpent, who have been seduced by the force and potency of economic materialism. Karp's liquor store, feeding on itself, is burnt to the ground by Ward Minogue, an ironic avenging angel. Karp himself has a heart attack, and he can no longer continue those activities that have given justification to his existence. And Louis, interested in immediate gain, goes to work as a salesman for a liquor concern, rather than rebuild his father's business. Perhaps punishment is possible because in *The Assistant* Malamud has chosen to portray a society of the helpless where there is only minimal power to be exercised, rather than the omnipotence of Judge Banner and Gus Sands.

The Pearls are also foils for the values represented by Morris. Sam, in spite of his poor candy store, is an entrepreneurial success after a fashion, although not within the *legitimate* economic structure employed by Karp.

While he "neglected the store . . . Sam's luck with the nags was exceptional and he had nicely supported Nat in college until the scholarships started rolling in" [15]. Like any good risk-taking capitalist, he spends his days brooding over the dope sheets in much the same way a broker studies stock quotations and Dow Jones averages — and to much the same end. And such an occupation requires a fierce dedication to the study of the main chance in order that every possible money-making opportunity be exploited. However, this commitment, according to Malamud, narrows one's encounters with the world and with humanity, a weakness that once again only Morris recognizes for what it is: "Morris took the *Forward* from the newsstand and dropped a nickel into the cigar box. Sam Pearl, working over a green racing sheet, gave him a wave of his hammy hand. They never bothered to talk. What did he know about race horses? And what did the other know of the tragic quality of life? Wisdom flew over his hard head" [17–18].

More relevant for the novel's antipathy to America's driving materialism is the character of Nat Pearl, "magna cum laude, Columbia, now in his second year at law school" [14], and, as Helen observes, a soon-to-be professional "with first-rate prospects, also rich friends he had never bothered to introduce her to" [14]. By virtue of his education, his job choice, and those values inherited from his father and the culture at large, Nat ultimately will become part of society's controlling machinery. That Nat has chosen the law is obviously significant, for, as a profession, it provides easy access to real wealth and power, temptation enough for anyone, let alone the son of immigrants: "Nat Pearl wanted to be 'somebody,' but to him this mean making money to lead the life of some of his well-to-do friends at law school" [133]. How unlike Morris, for whom the Law (always capitalized in Morris's usage) is seen as a mode of ethical behavior and right conduct.

It is important to understand how Nat's acceptance (and perhaps America's as well) of the law as a tool, simply a pragmatic device whose function is to wheedle, to manipulate, to justify, and to excuse wrong action, shapes his dealings with Helen Bober. First, however, it is necessary to acknowledge how much that relationship has been conditioned by the very fact of Nat's promise rather than his beliefs. This recognition is particularly fitting considering that America has always been the civilization symbolized by a commitment to a better future for all its inhabitants. Helen is acutely aware that the society's respect for Nat's possibilities has allowed her to act against her own personally developed moral sense: "Nat Pearl, handsome, cleft-chinned, gifted, ambitious, had wanted without too much trouble a lay and she, half in love, had obliged and regretted. Not the loving, but that it had taken her so long to realize how little he wanted" [14]. Nat, like Louis Karp, regards Helen as an object to be acquired and used. Louis offers money and fails. Nat, more sophisticated, knowing that he stands, in some way, for entry into that culture that has labelled the Bobers outsiders, offers possibilities and succeeds. But when Helen, recognizing the nature of her seduction, develops scruples, Nat does not hesitate to use a kind of legal chop-logic to defend his behavior and to demean her conscience—that is what being a lawyer means:

> "Helen, I honestly want to know how somebody's supposed to defend himself when he hasn't any idea what's in the indictment against him? What kind of crime have I committed? . . ."
> "I'm not a lawyer—I don't make indictments. . . ."
> "You're a funny kid," Nat was saying. "You've got some old-fashioned values about some things. I always told you you punish yourself too much. Why should anybody have such a hot and heavy conscience in these times? People are freer in the twentieth century. . . . What," Nat argued, "would peoples' lives be like if everybody regretted every beautiful minute of all that happened? Where's the poetry of living?" [109]

When Helen finally rejects Nat and what he represents, she becomes for him only "You bitch." And Nat, because of an allegiance to a philosophy which turns people into things—a kind of transformational materialism endemic in American society—must suffer the loss of wisdom; hardly much of a loss, he would suspect, if it is to be defined by Morris Bober.

The Bobers are clearly failures, at least as society would judge them. They have neither money, nor power, nor the intense drive to belong that is characteristic of so many immigrants. And they lack that seemingly national trait, crucial if one is to succeed in America, the ability to create their own destiny. They do not control fate; it controls them. The Bobers are, in fact, frightened and disappointed in the country they have escaped to. They take no risks; they do not gamble (except on the grocery store—a losing proposition if there ever was one); they cannot hear opportunity's knock. And they are immobile, stationary, afraid to venture beyond the block. To a large degree, they are responsible for their entombment in that grave of a business, for their attitudes are unsuitable to achievement and accomplishment in American terms. Finally, Ida and Morris have, in the worst betrayal of the American dream, deprived their child of a future in this new golden land. Yet the Bobers, as a family, seem to represent a source of strength, goodness, wisdom, and morality unavailable to the rest of society, and perhaps unattainable if the price be social and economic failure.

Ida Bober, however, is considerably less willing to accept moral virtue if it is unaccompanied by sufficient financial rewards. In fact, Ida is obsessed by her need for monetary security to a degree that often dehumanizes her. She is suspicious of anyone who may attack what little position and self-respect she has acquired. She is therefore hostile to the newcomer Frank Alpine on two counts: as a stranger, he may steal money; and, as a non-Jew, he might steal a more valuable piece of property, a key to the future, her daughter. And because Ida is wise in the ways of the American world, her Cassandra-like prophecies of doom have much accuracy. Unlike Morris, she believes "a business is a business" [9] even if the money is made at the expense of another's weakness. She clearly resents her husband's claims to superior moral sensitivity, "everybody is a stupe but not Morris Bober" [10], especially if it means a loss in dollars. She nags if Morris trusts enough to give credit. Her measurement of human worth is material possessions. And significantly it is only Ida who respects and even admires Julius Karp for his foresight and his success, though it be to her husband's cost:

> "Why does he bring me buyers? Why didn't he keep out the German around the corner?"
> She sighed. "He tries to help you now because he feels sorry for you."
> "Who needs his sorrow?" Morris said. "Who needs him?"
> "So why *you* didn't have the sense to make out of your grocery a wine and liquor store when came out the licenses?"
> "Who had cash for stock?"
> "So if you don't have, don't talk."
> "A business for drunken bums."
> "A business is a business. What Julius Karp takes in next door in a day we don't take in in two weeks." [9]

Ida is perfectly capable, even anxious, to use the deceptive techniques of the good (in a monetary, if not a moral, sense) businessperson in order to cheat the naive refugee Podolsky if it means ridding herself of the millstone the store has become. That she might be imprisoning Podolsky, who had come to America for the mythical new life as Morris had so many years ago, is not her concern. Nor can she comprehend Frank's willingness to work for nothing in order to pay a symbolic debt to Morris and redeem his own soul.

But the most important factor, for Malamud, in Ida's adherence to this American version of reductive materialism is that it diminishes the value of love. Such an unpredictable emotion threatens the business of marriage, an arrangement, as perceived by Ida, to escape poverty, the only way that a woman can achieve status, wealth, and power. This view of matrimony is her only way of protecting and insuring what future Helen might have: " 'Helen,' she said, holding back her tears, 'the only thing I want for you is the best. Don't make my mistake. Don't make worse and spoil your whole life, with a poor man that he is only a grocery clerk which we don't know about him nothing. Marry somebody who can give you a better life, a nice professional boy with a college education. Don't mix up now with a stranger. Helen, I know what I'm talking. Believe me, I know' " [146].

Ida, therefore, measures potential husbands not by their inherent value as human beings, not by their ability to love, but by the money they have or might have: Nat Pearl will be "someday a rich lawyer" [4]; even "the stupe" Louis Karp is acceptable since he can offer financial security. And any quality in Helen, particularly her intelligence—"Some people want their children to read more. I want you to read less." [115]—that reduces her marketability is to be decried and condemned.

What has so embittered Ida is not simple nagging dissatisfaction but guilt, "her guilt that she had talked him into a grocery store when he was in the first year of evening high school, preparing, he had said, for pharmacy" [8]. She had settled for the immediate gratification of ownership and possession rather than wait for long-range possibilities, withheld fulfillment, and postponed satisfaction. It is only when Morris is dead (living he was a constant reminder of that guilt) and she no longer fears starving because of Frank's rent and Helen's salary and Rubin's job that she softens into humanity.

Helen Bober is a more complex character, a mass of American and old-country contradictions, whose perceptions, ambitions, and desires have been conditioned by the hard American materialism of her mother and the otherworldly, inappropriate wisdom of her father. Helen tends to see herself, as do Ida, the Karps, Nat Pearl, and even Frank Alpine initially, as merchandise upon whom a price has been set. Although she is concerned with abstract goals and impractical notions of morality, preoccupied with philosophy, an idealist believing in the something more beyond the material that gives life its meaning (symbolized by her addiction to literature), she nevertheless thinks of Helen Bober as a commodity to be judged by some sort of externally devised concept of worth. And that standard is a social one contingent on her lack of prospects, "as poor as her name sounded, with little promise of a better future" [14]. Therefore, in spite of her obvious intelligence, sensitivity, and capacity for love, she is constantly worried at being valued under her expectations, certain that she is worthless even to a man like Nat Pearl, whose ambitions she derides and suspects. As she says, she loves before she is loved, perhaps inviting the expected rejection because of her fear she is not worth the loving. Perhaps that is one of the reasons why Helen chooses Frank, so clearly less than she, an alien, a wanderer, a non-Jew, without position or stability.

As a true child of her parents, Helen romanticizes the power of education, placing her faith in it as the key to realizing her sense of potential, becoming American in the best sense of the word. She does not wish to use education simply to acquire a marketable skill, because such is not the true function of learning. To be educated according to Helen (and to Malamud, no doubt) is to possess wisdom and understanding of life. Helen desires education so that she may become a better person, hardly a useful talent, much less an appropriate one for the national economy. It is this deprivation that Helen feels most strongly, and Frank Alpine ultimately recognizes that it is the one gift he can offer that Helen cannot return.

At this point, we must examine Helen's curious ambivalence toward the act of gift-giving, a persistent motif throughout the novel. She is able to give *things* — her salary to her parents, for example — as an expression of her feelings, but she cannot, in the course of the novel, give her body because it is the concrete form taken by the self, the physical essence of the soul. To offer so precious a gift and to have it rejected or misvalued is to destroy the integrity of the person that is Helen Bober. Even Helen, in a subtle fashion, uses the external, the physical, the concrete, as a source and standard of individual worth. However, Helen is most reluctant to accept gifts for a number of reasons. First, to accept a gift is to acknowledge another's judgment on Helen-as-object, whose value is instantly visible by the quality of the gift: "Nat, at his best, had produced a half-dozen small pink roses" [112], while Frank had given her an expensive scarf and a leather-bound copy of Shakespeare. Second, to accept a gift is to incur debt and obligation, is to become a human IOU, a particularly uncomfortable situation for the insecure. Says Helen, "for gifts you pay" [112]. And finally, to accept a gift is to put a price on love, to admit that affection can be bought for things, an idea that Helen instinctively knows to be false in spite of a culture that has made it a truth. Although Helen wants no part of Nat Pearl's materialism, admiring instead the intangible and impractical qualities of sensitivity, perception, and depth, and resents her treatment as a commodity, she nevertheless chooses to treat Frank Alpine as such a vehicle for the realization of a future.

Yet it is only when Helen realizes that gifts are merely an outward sign, an honest expression of true emotion, when she learns to take gracefully as well as to give generously, when she can thank Frank for his unselfish help, that Helen can become truly loving.

Because of the limitations placed on her needs and ambitions by economics and her own psychology, Frank, who has traveled, moved, *lived*, is transformed into the embodiment of her unfulfilled possibilities. Since she resents her loss — "The world has shrunk for me. . . . I want a larger and better life. I want the return of my possibilities" [43] — she makes Frank the *tabula rasa* on which to write her dreams:

> And if she married Frank, her first job would be to help him realize his wish to be somebody. . . . Frank . . . was struggling to realize himself as a person, a more worthwhile ambition. Though Nat had an excellent formal education, Frank knew more about life and gave the impression of greater potential depth. She wanted him to become what he might, and conceived a plan to support him through college. Maybe she could even see him through a master's degree, once he knew what he wanted to do. She realized this would mean the end of her own vague plans for going to day college, but that was really lost long ago,

> and she thought she would at last accept the fact once Frank had got
> what she hadn't. [133]

When she discovers that Frank is anything but a paragon, a mere man
with considerably more than his share of human weaknesses (as thief and
rapist), she hates him for being less than her fantasy of him, a deception
using her body as a possession; and she hates herself for so radical a
misjudgment and for once again being valued under her expectations.
Helen can only accept her own flawed humanity when she recognizes the
real humanity in Frank, acknowledging that he has in fact changed, that
he has become that better person, not through a college education but
through suffering. Hardly the American dream, Malamud believes, but it
will do.

But it is in the creation of Morris Bober and his encounters with the
world that Malamud offers his disapproval of aspects of the American
dream: the expectations and promise defined, the defeats and loss explored. Morris's immigrant history may be seen as disappointment. First
there is an escape from tyranny and persecution which was life in the old
country. "They were poor and there were pogroms. So when he was about
to be conscripted into the czar's army his father said, 'Run to America' "
[81]. Then comes a taste of freedom, the opening of possibilities. "After I
came here I wanted to be a druggist. . . . I went for a year in night
school. I took algebra, also German and English. 'Come,' said the wind to
the leaves one day, 'come over the meadow with me and play.' This is a
poem I learned. But I didn't have the patience to stay in night school, so
when I met my wife I gave up my chances" [83]. And finally, immobiliz-
ing entrapment in a dying economic venture, "He had escaped out of the
Russian Army to the U.S.A., but once in a store he was like a fish fried in
deep fat" [83]. Why then did a man who risked the wrath of the czar's
sergeant fail when confronted with America's multiple opportunities?
What spoiled the hope? And how could such a failure, with so many lost
chances in a society that offered so many futures, become the moral center
of *The Assistant?*

Josephine Zadovsky Knopp defines Morris's ethical beliefs as the
concept of *mentshlekhkayt* which

> has as its fundamental premise the innocence of man, man free of the
> sins of the Fall. It recognizes that within man run opposing tendencies
> toward good and evil, and that within this context man is completely
> free to choose. It rests its ultimate faith in man's basic goodness and the
> implicit assumption that, in the final analysis, he will always choose
> what is morally and ethically right. It believes in action as the path
> toward moral redemption. . . . It is an ethic concerned with improving
> man's lot in this world. . . . To those who accept, perhaps even uncon-
> sciously, the ethical code of *mentshlekhkayt*, the concept of an "absurd"
> universe is foreign; to them the universe has a definite structure and
> meaning. . . . At least a part of this meaning resides in the code's

implicit faith in the moral significance of man's action, . . . and that he has the obligation to apply this power in the cause of good.

Mentshlekhkayt also encompasses the very strong sense of community that has traditionally been a feature of Jewish life. The paramount characteristic of this community feeling is the moral imperative of man's responsibility to his fellow man. . . .

The code . . . is an order, a Law in a world of chaos and suffering, and thereby brings sanity and significance to life.[23]

While this clearly describes elements of Morris's credo, Knopp does not appear to appreciate the irony of assigning such an ethical system to a man who inhabits a society that makes adherence to such values a sure sign of failure. Given American culture as it is portrayed in *The Assistant*, this admirable moral structure appears to be a source of passive endurance, rather than an active commitment for change.

Morris collapses into prisoner and victim because the national community that Morris has chosen as refuge and affirmation no longer uses or finds valuable the virtues of a truly good man. And while it is true that even Karp keeps returning to Morris for approval and spiritual sustenance, it does the liquor store owner no good, for he continues to denigrate, mock, and betray the values Morris subscribes to. In Morris's decline, embodied in his inability and unwillingness to adapt to an increasingly opportunistic culture, we witness the triumph of the dream as nightmare. The memories that haunt Morris throughout the novel are not, ironically, of an American paradise but of an Eastern European one: "No, not for an age had he lived a whole day in the open. As a boy, always running in the muddy, rutted streets of the village, or across the fields, or bathing with the other boys in the river; but as a man, in America, he rarely saw the sky. In the early days when he drove a horse and wagon, yes, but not since his first store. In a store you were entombed" [5–6]. The world of persecution has become a remembered Eden of open spaces, while America, the new land, is a closed box, a coffin.

In an environment where every penny is important and money an icon (notice how carefully Malamud accounts for the store's income before the robbery), Morris trusts and gives trust:

> "My mother says . . . can you trust her till tomorrow for a pound of butter, a loaf of rye bread and a small bottle of cider vinegar?"
> He knew the mother. "No more trust."
> The girl burst into tears.
> Morris gave her. . . . The total now came to $2.03, which he never hoped to see. But Ida would nag, . . . so he reduced the amount. . . . His peace — the little he lived with — was worth forty-two cents." [4]

A Lincolnesque figure, his honesty is only the stuff of legends and eulogies, and about as relevant in this civilization: "Helen, his dear daughter, remembers from when she was a small girl that her father ran two blocks in the snow to give back to a poor Italian lady a nickel that she forgot on the counter" [228]. He is a man of responsibility in a culture of the irresponsible, who wakes early, morning after morning, to insure that the Poilisheh gets her three-cent roll.

In a society that elevates transcience and prizes mobility, Morris, especially after the death of his son and future, remains frozen and immobile, actually as well as metaphorically *going nowhere*. He does not cheat. He will not steal, even in a business situation where such behavior is not only commonplace and justified but also necessary to insure that magic word — profit.

> "It's easy to fool people," said Morris.
> "Why don't you try a couple of those tricks yourself, Morris? Your amount of profit is small."
> Morris looked at him in surprise. "Why should I steal from my customers? Do they steal from me?"
> "They would if they could."
> "When a man is honest he don't worry when he sleeps. This is more important than a nickel." [84]

And in spite of his admiration for the greater efficiency and practicality of the modern, Morris is, not surprisingly, attached to the old ways. He teaches Frank the skills he possesses with a mixture of pride and embarrassment, remembering when it required real ability to be a grocer: "As if ashamed somebody could learn the business so easily, Morris explained to him how different it had been to be a grocer only a few years ago. In those days one was more of a macher, a craftsman. Who was ever called on nowadays to slice up a loaf of bread . . . or ladle out a quart of milk?" [83–84]. But since "the chain store kills the small man" [33], of what significance are those abilities in a packaged culture valuing speed not technique, convenience not aptitude, and the plastic rather than the authentic: "Now is everything in containers, jars, or packages. Even hard cheeses that they cut them for hundreds of years by hand now come sliced up in cellophane packages. Nobody has to know anything any more" [84].

As that traditional but impossible American paradigm — the small business where "at least you're your own boss" [33] — Morris is a failure. Perhaps the ideal has become mendacious — "To be a boss of nothing" [33]. Certainly Ida and even Helen, trapped in a civilization that has divorced success from human worth, ethical conduct, and morality, condemn or minimize the quality of Morris's true achievement.

> I said Papa was honest but what was the good of such honesty if he couldn't exist in the world? . . . Poor Papa; being naturally honest, he didn't believe that others come by their dishonesty naturally. And he couldn't hold onto those things he had worked so hard to get. He gave away, in a sense, more than he owned. . . . He knew, at least, what was good. . . . People liked him, but who can admire a man passing his life

in such a store? He buried himself in it; he didn't have the imagination
to know what he was missing. He made himself a victim. He could, with
a little more courage, have been more than he was. [230]

Morris's final judgment is also one of regret, loss, and disappointment: "He
thought of his life with sadness. . . . His mood was one of regret. I gave
away my life for nothing. It was the thunderous truth" [226].

Ida, Helen, and Morris are to a limited degree correct in their
assessment of Morris's accomplishments or lack of them. Unfortunately,
the paradox (according to Malamud) is that, given the kind of man Morris
Bober was, his future in America was inevitable. The essential characteristics that one must acknowledge and admire in him are those very
characteristics that made financial success in the world impossible.

The America that has diminished and defeated Morris Bober accords
respect, admiration, and power to the insensitive Karp who seizes the
main chance at the expense of honor, loyalty, and friendship, and rewards
with success and wealth the corrupt Charlie Sobeloff, "a cross-eyed but
clever conniver" [204] who cheated and defrauded the innocent and
trusting Morris.

> Arriving at Sobeloff's Self-Service Market, Morris . . . was amazed
> at its size. Charlie had tripled the original space. . . . The result was a
> huge market with a large number of stalls and shelved sections loaded
> with groceries. The supermarket was so crowded with people that to
> Morris . . . it looked like a department store. He felt a pang, thinking
> that part of this might now be his if he had taken care of what he had
> once owned. He would not envy Charlie Sobeloff his dishonest wealth,
> but when he thought of what he could do for Helen with a little money
> his regret deepened that he had nothing. [207]

As Morris joins that "silent knot of men who drifted along Sixth
Avenue stopping at the employment agency doors to read impassively the
list of jobs chalked up on the blackboard signs" [208], he sees an America
that has discarded the poor, the old, the sick, the uneducated, and has
rendered them useless, unfit for participation in a society that popularly
believes that "God loves the poor people but he helps the rich" [211].

It is an America that has betrayed its symbolic promise and traditional ideals. For Morris, "America had become too complicated. One
man counted for nothing. There were too many stores, depressions,
anxieties. What had he escaped to here?" [206]. A good man can retain his
soul only at the expense of a freedom too easily become opportunism, and
an opportunism too easily become deceit, trickery, corruption.

Frank Alpine enters the story like a dingy American Lochinvar "lately
come from the West, looking for a better opportunity" [29]. Like Helen,
Frank is a divided personality, one who steals yet yearns for goodness, who
wanders yet yearns for stability, who rapes yet yearns for love. He wants
"money, nightclubs, babes" [92], and at the same time wishes to be like St.

Francis, for whom "poverty was a queen" [31]: "Every time I read about somebody like him I get a feeling inside of me I have to fight to keep from crying. He was born good, which is a talent if you have it" [31]. Frank is a man ensnared by the corruption of his culture, as well as by his own inner drives and compulsions; he is looking for a model to provide an alternative mode of being. Not finding St. Francis, he discovers the next best thing in contemporary America — Morris Bober — and becomes his surrogate son, and spiritual heir, giving up the opportunities of the world, the flesh, and the devil for the ascetic discipline of the imprisoning grocery store.

Frank is that not uncommon American phenomenon, the wanderer, the mover, the man without roots who leaves when things do not work out or disappears when responsibility weighs too heavily and commitments become too demanding. "I am too restless — six months in any one place is too much for me. Also I grab at everything too quick — too impatient. I don't do what I have to. . . . The result is I move into a place with nothing, and I move out with nothing" [37]. And like so many of his fellow citizens, he rationalizes this particularly American brand of irresponsibility as the testing of freedom, a trying of opportunities, the correct use of his country's promise. It is hardly surprising that Helen, who longs for such motion and such possibilities, is seduced by Frank's words:

> "The way I figure, anything is possible. I always think about the different kinds of chances I have. This has stuck in my mind — don't get yourself trapped in one thing, because maybe you can do something else a whole lot better. That's why I guess I never settled down so far. I've been exploring conditions. I still have some very good ambitions which I would like to see come true. The first step to that, I know for sure now, is to get a good education. I didn't use to think like that, but the more I live the more I do." [98]

An excellent statement of the national credo. That he may be using this pronouncement to seduce Helen does not obviate the fact that a portion of Frank's personality believes it.

Frank wants to be better than he is in both the financial and moral spheres of the American experience without perceiving that he cannot achieve both ambitions in the kind of driven, materialistic culture America has in fact become. He is particularly concerned with the acquisition of wealth, power, and importance; he is possessed by the sense that "he was meant for something a whole lot better — to do something big, different" [91–92]. Daniel Bell has indicated in his essay "Crime as an American Way of Life" that for a man with no skills, the American dream may be achieved through crime.[24] Thus Frank thinks that:

> At crime he would change his luck, make adventure, live like a prince. He shivered with pleasure as he conceived robberies, assaults — murders if it had to be — each violent act helping to satisfy a craving that somebody suffer as his own fortune improved. He felt infinitely relieved,

believing that if a person figured for himself something big, something different in his life, he had a better chance to get it than some poor jerk who couldn't think that high up. [92]

Frank's dream is only partially influenced by its Dostoevskian counterparts. The Russian's protagonists are, in fact, concerned with the metaphysics of power while Frank wants the external accoutrements of success that can be acquired by crime.

But crime is taking, the way Frank takes from Morris by theft, from Helen by rape. It is simply another variant of the culture's dominating materialism that defines people as things for use, manipulation, exploitation, or expropriation. However, it is only when Frank can learn to give unselfishly, without hope for return or need of payment, that he can achieve moral success. And this education begins when he willingly attaches himself to the Bobers and to the enclosing confinement of the grocery store.

Initially Frank brings into the store the values of the American universe outside. Though improvements are made in the best sense of American business, Frank steals, exploits, uses. He robs Morris, defending his actions as the cause of the store's improvement. He (and Ida) are willing to make changes that the conservative Morris has resisted as a sign of integrity — the change from milk bottles to containers. He suggests, to Morris's horror, that they cheat customers. And perhaps most significantly, Frank is a salesman, a "supersalesman" [67] one of the customers calls him, capable of utilizing all the manipulative techniques of salesmanship Morris disdains: "The customers seemed to like him. . . . He somehow drew in people she had never before seen in the neighborhood. . . . Frank tired things that Morris and she could never do, such as attempting to sell people more than they asked for, and usually he succeeded" [67]. Even the practical Ida wonders if she and Morris had been "really suited to the grocery business. They had never been salesmen" [67].

We can clearly see that use of exploitation in Frank's treatment of Helen as well. Because he wants something from her and not Helen herself, he tells her what he senses she wants to hear. In fact, all of Frank's actions at the beginning of the novel are for an ulterior purpose, not for the doing of the actions themselves: either to alleviate guilt, or to seduce Helen, or to charm his way past Ida's suspicions. It is only when Frank ceases to act within the manipulative behavioral conventions approved by his society, when he can act unselfishly, with no thought of return or repayment, that the alterations he makes in both the store and his life are valuable and permanent.

But the reader is not meant to forget the ambiguous, uncomfortable price of Frank's commitments — isolation, entombment, and an emblematic castration. By enduring circumcision in order to become a Jew, that final echoing choice in *The Assistant*,[25] Frank Alpine elects to assume what was Morris Bober's inevitable fate, moving out of the materialistic mainstream of his own culture, rejecting the values that had brought him to rob the grocer in the first place. For Malamud in this novel, to be a Jew is to be the moral man, a perpetual alien, an unacceptable phenomenon in a social system that defines success by the extent to which human beings have been devalued and transformed into exploitable toys, and calls the responsible, honest individual a failure.

That Malamud's characters are complex human beings, individuals whose flaws are often the source of their pain and their predicament is obvious enough. What has not been made sufficiently apparent, and therefore is the reason for this study, is the extent to which Malamud portrays and comments upon a culture that exacerbates the difficulties created by personality and ego. In the first novels, published in the quiescent fifties, this concern is implied, the criticism muted and obliquely stated. But as the social situation alters, as dissolution and chaos appear the preeminent threats of the nineteen sixties and early seventies, Malamud's ambivalent hostilities toward civilization are presented more overtly and purposefully. What must be emphasized, however, is that Malamud is no Rousseauistic idealist for whom individual and societal perfection are legitimate goals to be desired. Rather, the author believes that though a given society may be self-deceiving and exploitative, or an entire civilization corrupt and decaying, there can be no escape from or evasion of responsibility. These are a child's responses. Imperfect man living in an imperfect world must still attempt goodness, even if the results of his efforts are ambiguous, or incomplete, or futile.

It begins to seem clear then that Malamud's first two novels are more than fable, more than fantasy, more than folklore. The author is making a significant statement about the effects of an aggressive materialism on the principles that purportedly govern the American commonwealth. In *The Natural* Roy Hobbs chooses money, irresponsibility, and betrayal, and becomes more than simply a failure as a man—he loses that power which might have regenerated and ennobled his civilization, a true hero's function.[26] Frank Alpine, in *The Assistant*, makes the correct moral choice, only to become an imprisoned victim because he has learned goodness. In Malamud's America, the attempt to liberate others is to confine oneself. . . .

Notes

1. "The Blossoming Epoch of Jewish-American Creativity," trans. Sylvia Protter and Iska Alter, *The Forward*, 16 January 1977, 6.

2. An excellent, if somewhat dramatized, account of the significance of Chasidism is the subject of Elie Wiesel's *Souls on Fire* (New York: Random House, 1972).

3. Saul Bellow in his Nobel Prize acceptance speech asks for a *return* to precisely the

kind of fiction Bernard Malamud has always written. *The New York Times*, 13 December 1976, 9.

4. "Writing American Fiction," *Commentary* (March, 1961), 228–231.

5. *City of Words* (New York: Harper and Row, 1971).

6. "Fantasist of the Ordinary," *Commentary* (July, 1957), 89–92, and *Bright Book of Life* (New York: Delta Books, 1973), pp. 138–144.

7. *After Alienation* (Cleveland and New York: Meridian Books, 1964), pp. 251, 253.

8. "In the Interest of Surprise and Delight," *Folio 20* (Summer, 1955), 17–20, and *Love and Death in the American Novel* (New York: Dell Books, 1969), 499–500.

9. *Standards* (New York: Horizon Press, 1966).

10. Wasserman has written the complete archetypical analysis of *The Natural* in the brilliant essay, "*The Natural*: Malamud's World Ceres" (*The Centennial Review of Arts and Science*, 9 [1965], 438–460).

11. James Mellard writes such an analysis in "Malamud's Novels: Four Versions of the Pastoral," (*Critique*, 9 [1967], ii, 5–19) as does Edwin Eigner in "Malamud's Use of the Quest Romance," (*Genre*, 1 [1968], 55–75).

12. "The Blossoming Epoch of Jewish-American Creativity," 6.

13. *After the Tradition* (New York: E. P. Dutton, 1969).

14. *The Trial of Judaism in Contemporary Jewish Writing* (Urbana: University of Illinois Press, 1975).

15. There are exceptions to this observation, but they are few: Max Schulz, *Radical Sophistication* (Athens, Ohio: Ohio University Press, 1969); John Barsness, "*A New Life*: The Frontier Myth in Perspective," *Western American Literature*, 3 (Winter, 1969), 297–302; Walter Shear, "Culture Conflict in *The Assistant*," *Midwest Quarterly*, 7 (1966), 367–380.

16. Bernard Malamud, *The Natural* (New York: Farrar, Straus and Giroux, 1952), p. 179. All citations are from this edition, and further page references will appear in brackets in the text.

17. "Say it ain't true, Roy" does indeed echo "Say it ain't so, Joe," reportedly asked of Shoeless Joe Jackson after the 1919 Black Sox Scandal exploded. For additional information, see Harold Seymour, *Baseball: The Golden Age* (New York: Oxford University Press, 1971), 294–310, and Eliot Asinof, *Eight Men Out* (New York: Holt, Rinehart and Winston, 1963). As Asinof's book indicates, a number of parallels can be drawn between the events of *The Natural* and the actual scandal: the character of Shoeless Joe Jackson who was himself considered the greatest *natural* hitter of his day; the epic cheapness of Charles Comiskey, owner of the White Sox which echoes that quality in Judge Goodwill Banner; the phenomenal luck of the gambler Arnold Rothstein which resembles Gus Sands's good luck.

18. Italics mine.

19. For an accurate, poignant, and complete account of the various phases of Eastern European Jewish immigration to New York City, see Irving Howe's *World of Our Fathers* (New York: Harcourt, Brace, Jovanovich, 1976).

20. "Culture Conflict in *The Assistant*."

21. Robert Alter considers this version of Judaism both sentimental and a falsification of religious traditionalism in his essay "Sentimentalizing the Jews," in *After the Tradition*, pp. 35–45.

22. Bernard Malamud, *The Assistant* (New York: Farrar, Straus and Giroux, 1957), p. 8. All citations are from this edition, and further page references will appear in brackets in the text.

23. *The Trial of Judaism in Contemporary Jewish Writing*, pp. 6–7.

24. Daniel Bell, "Crime as an American Way of Life: A Queer Ladder of Social

Mobility," in *An End to Ideology: On the Exhaustion of the Political Ideas of the Fifties* (New York: Collier Books, 1961), pp. 127–150. Bell clearly perceives that crime is the underside of the American dream, and that criminals represent a dark, violent version of the Horatio Alger myth.

25. This ambiguous imprisonment, at once a sign of moral stature and societal failure, is symbolized by an equally ambiguous gesture, that of circumcision which is both an entry into the community of suffering and a castration, the loss of manhood, as observed by Ihab Hassan in *Radical Innocence* (Princeton: Princeton University Press, 1961), p. 168.

26. This sense of community responsibility is very much a part of the heroic paradigm, according to Joseph Campbell in *The Hero with a Thousand Faces* (Cleveland and New York: Meridian Books, 1970).

[From "Imagining Jews"]   Philip Roth*

If Saul Bellow's longer works[1] tend generally to associate the Jewish Jew with the struggles of ethical Jewhood and the non-Jewish Jew and the Gentile with the release of appetite and aggression (Gersbach, the Buber booster and wife-stealer, is really no great exception, since he is a *spurious* Jewish Jew, who can't even pronounce his Yiddish right; and Madeleine, that Magdalene, has of course worn a cross and worked at Fordham), in the work of Bernard Malamud these tendencies are so sharply and schematically present as to give Malamud's novels the lineaments of moral allegory. For Malamud, generally speaking, the Jew is innocent, passive, virtuous, and this to the degree that he defines himself or is defined by others as a Jew; the Gentile, on the other hand, is characteristically corrupt, violent, and lustful, particularly when he enters a room or a store or a cell with a Jew in it.

Now on the face of it, it would seem that a writer could not get very far with such evangelistic simplifications. And yet that is not at all the case with Malamud (as it isn't with Jerzy Kosinski in *The Painted Bird*), for so instinctively do the figures of a good Jew and a bad goy emerge from an imagination essentially folkloric and didactic that his fiction is actually most convincing the more strictly he adheres to these simplifications, and diminishes in moral conviction and narrative drive to the extent that he surrenders them, or tries, however slyly, to undo their hold on him.

The best book—containing as it does the classic Malamudian moral arrangement—is still *The Assistant*, which proposes that an entombed and impoverished grocer named Morris Bober shall by the example of his passive suffering and his goodness of heart transform a young thieving Italian drifter named Frank Alpine into another entombed, impoverished, suffering Jewish grocer, and that this shall constitute an act of *assistance*,

*Reprinted with permission from the *New York Review of Books* 21 (3 October 1974):22–28. © 1974 Nyrev, Inc.

and set Alpine on the road to redemption — or so the stern morality of the book suggests.

Redemption from what? Crimes of violence and deceit against a good Jewish father, crimes of lust against the father's virginal daughter, whom the goy has spied upon naked and then raped. But oh how punitive is this redemption! We might almost take what happens to the bad goy when he falls into the hands of the good Jew as an act of enraged Old Testament retribution visited upon him by the wrathful Jewish author — if it weren't for the moral pathos and the gentle religious coloration with which Malamud invests the tale of conversion; and also the emphasis that is clear to the author throughout — that it is the good Jews who have fallen into the hands of the bad goy. It has occurred to me that a less hopeful Jewish writer than Malamud — Kosinski, say, whose novels don't put much stock in the capacity for redemption, but concentrate rather determinedly on the persistence of brutality and malice — might not have understood Alpine's transformation into Jewish grocer and Jewish father (with all those roles entail in this book) as a sign of moral improvement, but as the cruel realization of Bober's revenge. "Now suffer, you goy bastard, the way I did."

To see how still another sort of Jewish writer, Norman Mailer, might have registered the implications of a story like *The Assistant*, we can look to his famous essay, "The White Negro," published first in *Dissent* magazine in 1957, the very year Malamud's novel appeared. Imagining all of this independently of Malamud, Mailer nonetheless comes up with a startlingly similar scenario to the one with which *The Assistant* begins. In Mailer's version there are also two hoodlums who beat a defenseless shopkeeper over the head and take his money; however, quite characteristically for Mailer — and it is this that invariably distinguishes his concerns from Malamud's or Bellow's — he appraises the vicious act as it effects the well-being of the violator rather than the violated.

"It can of course be suggested," writes Mailer parenthetically about "encourag[ing] the psychopath in oneself," "that it takes little courage for two eighteen-year-old hoodlums, let us say, to beat in the brains of a candy-store keeper, and indeed the act — even by the logic of the psychopath — is not likely to prove very therapeutic, for the victim is not an immediate equal. Still, courage of a sort is necessary, for one murders not only a weak fifty-year-old man but an institution as well, one violates private property, one enters into a new relation with the police, and introduces a dangerous element into one's life. The hoodlum is therefore daring the unknown, and so no matter how brutal the act, it is not altogether cowardly."

These few lines on the positive value homicide has for the psychopath should make it clear why Jewish cultural audiences, which are generally pleased to hear Saul Bellow and Bernard Malamud identified by critics as Jewish writers, are perfectly content that by and large Norman Mailer, with all his considerable influence and stature, should go forth onto the lecture platform and the television talk shows as a writer *period*. This is obviously okay too with the author of *The Deer Park* and *An American Dream*, to name just two of his books with heroes he chooses not to call Cohen. It is pointless to wonder what Jews (or Gentiles) would have made of those two books if the author had had other than an O'Shaugnessy as the libidinous voyager or a Rojack as the wife-murderer and spade-whipper in his American Gomorrah, for that an identifiably Jewish hero would perpetrate such spectacular transgressions with so much gusto and so little self-doubt or ethical disorientation turns out to be as inconceivable to Norman Mailer as it is to Bernard Malamud. And maybe for the same reason: it is just the Jew in one that says "No, no, *restrain* yourself" to such grandiose lusts and drives. To which prohibition Malamud adds, "Amen," but to which Mailer replies, "Then I'll see ya' around."

I cannot imagine Mailer having much patience with the conclusion of the violent hoodlum-defenseless shopkeeper scenario as Malamud realizes it in *The Assistant*. Some other lines from "The White Negro" might in fact stand as Mailer's description of just what is happening to Frank Alpine, who dons Morris Bober's apron, installs himself for eighteen hours a day behind his cash register, and from the tomb of a dying grocery store takes responsibility for the college education (rather than the orgasmic, no holes barred, time-of-her-timish education) of Morris's Jewish daughter: "new kinds of victories," Mailer writes, "increase one's power for new kinds of perception; and defeats, the wrong kind of defeats, attack the body and imprison one's energy until one is jailed in the prison air of other people's habits, other people's defeats, boredom, quiet desperation, and muted, icy, self-destroying rage. . . ."

It is precisely with an "attack" upon the body — upon the very organ with which Alpine had attacked Bober's daughter — that Malamud concludes *The Assistant*. Whether Malamud himself sees it as an attack, as something more like cruel and unusual punishment than poetic justice, is another matter; given the novel's own signposts, it appears that the reader is expected to take the last paragraph in the book as describing the conclusive act of Frank's *redemption*, the final solution to his Gentile problem.

> One day in April Frank went to the hospital and had himself circumcised. For a couple of days he dragged himself around with a pain between his legs. The pain enraged and inspired him. After Passover he became a Jew.

So penance for the criminal penis has been done. No cautionary folk tale on the dangers of self-abuse could be any more vivid or pointed than this, nor could those connections that I have tried to trace in Bellow's novels be more glaringly apparent than they are here: Renunciation is Jewish and renunciation is All. By comparison to the tyrannical Yahweh who rules over *The Assistant*, the Bellow of *Mr. Sammler's Planet* seems like a doting parent who asks only for contraceptive common sense and no hard drugs. *The Assistant* is a manifestation of ethical Jewhood with what one might legitimately call a vengeance. Beneath the austerity and the pathos, Malamud, as we shall see again, has a fury all his own.

The Fixer, page 69: "The fixer readily confessed he was a Jew. Otherwise he was innocent." Page 80: "I'm an innocent man . . . I've had little in life." Page 98: "I swear to you, I am innocent of any serious crime. . . . It's not in my nature." *What* isn't in his nature? Ritual murder and sexual assault — vengeful aggression and brutal lust. So it is for the crimes of Frank Alpine and Ward Minogue, the two hoodlum goyim who prey upon the innocent helpless Jewish family of *The Assistant*, that Yakov Bok, the helpless innocent Russian Jewish handyman of *The Fixer*, is arrested and imprisoned, and in something far worse even than a dungeon of a grocery store. In fact, I know of no serious authors who have chronicled physical brutality and fleshly mortification in such detail and at such length, and who likewise have taken a single defenseless innocent and constructed almost an entire book out of the relentless violations suffered by that character at the hands of cruel and perverse captors, other than Malamud, the Marquis de Sade, and the pseudonymous author of *The Story of O. The Fixer*, the opening of Chapter V:

> The days were passing and the Russian officials were waiting impatiently for his menstrual period to begin. Grubeshov and the army general often consulted the calendar. If it didn't start soon they threatened to pump blood out of his penis with a machine they had for that purpose. The machine was a pump made of iron with a red indicator to show how much blood was being drained out. The danger of it was that it didn't always work right and sometimes sucked every drop of blood out of the body. It was used exclusively on Jews; only their penises fitted it.

The careful social and historical documentation of *The Fixer* — which Malamud's instinctive feel for folk material is generally able to transform from fiction researched into fiction imagined — envelops what is at its center a relentless work of violent pornography, in which the pure and innocent Jew, whose queasiness at the sight of blood is at the outset almost maidenly, is ravished by the sadistic goyim, "men," a knowledgeable ghost informs him, "who [are] without morality."

Four paragraphs from the end of the book, the defenseless Jew who has been falsely accused of murdering a twelve-year-old boy and drinking his blood, and has been unjustly brutalized for that crime for almost three hundred pages, has his revenge offered him suddenly on a silver platter — and he takes it. If it's murder they want, it's murder they'll get. With his revolver he shoots the Czar! "Yakov pressed the trigger. Nicholas" — the italics are mine — "*in the act of crossing himself*, overturned his chair, and fell, to his surprise, to the floor, the stain spreading on his breast." And there is no remorse or guilt in Yakov, not after what he has been through at the hands of Czar Nicholas's henchmen. "Better him than us," he thinks, dismissing with a commonplace idiom of four simple words the crime of crimes: regicide, the murder of the Goyische King.

Only it happens that all of this takes place in Yakov's imagination. It is a vengeful and heroic daydream that he is having on the way to the trial at which it would seem he is surely doomed. Which is as it must be in Malamud's world: for it is not in Yakov's nature, any more than it is in Morris Bober's (or Moses Herzog's) to press a real trigger and shed real blood. Remember Herzog with his pistol? "It's not everyone who gets the opportunity to kill with a clear conscience. They had," Herzog tells himself, "opened the way to justifiable murder." But at the bathroom window, peering in at his enemy Gersbach bathing his daughter Junie, he cannot pull the trigger. "Firing the pistol," writes Bellow in *Herzog* (though it could as well be Malamud at the conclusion of *The Fixer*), "was nothing but a thought." Vengeance then must come in other forms for these victimized Jewish men, if it comes at all. That vengeance isn't in his nature is a large part of what makes him heroic to the author himself.

In *Pictures of Fidelman* Malamud sets out to turn the tables on himself and, gamely, to take a holiday from his own obsessive mythology: here he imagines as the hero a Jewish man living without shame and even with a kind of virile, if schlemielish, forcefulness in a world of Italian gangsters, thieves, pimps, whores, and bohemians, and a man who eventually finds love face-down with a Venetian glassblower who is the husband of his own mistress — and most of it has no more impact than the bullet that Yakov Bok fired in his imagination had on the real Czar of Russia. And largely because it has been conceived as a similar kind of compensatory daydream; in *Fidelman*, unfortunately, natural repugnance and constraints, and a genuine sense of what conversions cost, are by and large dissolved in rhetorical flourishes rather than through the sort of human struggle that Malamud's own deeply held sense of things calls forth in *The Assistant* and *The Fixer*. It's no accident that this of all the longer works generates virtually no internal narrative tension (a means whereby it might seek to test its own assumptions) and is without the continuous sequential development that comes to this kind of storyteller so naturally and acts in him as a necessary counterforce against runaway fantasy. This playful daydream of waywardness, criminality, transgression, lust, and sexual perversion could not have stood up against that kind of opposition.

There are of course winning and amusing pages along the way — there is a conversation between Fidelman and a talking light bulb in the section called "Pictures of the Artist" that is Malamud the folk comic at his best — but after the first section, "The Last Mohican," the book has an air of unchecked and unfocused indulgence, which is freewheeling about a libidinous and disordered life more or less to the extent that nothing much is at stake or seriously challenged. What distinguishes "The Last Mohican" from all that comes after is that *its* Fidelman, so meticulous about himself, so very cautious and constrained, is not at all the same fellow who turns up later cleaning out toilets in a whorehouse, shacking up with prostitutes, and dealing one-on-one with a pimp; the author may have convinced himself that it was the experience with Susskind he undergoes in "The Last Mohican" that, as it were, frees Fidelman for what follows, but, if so, that comes under the category, as a little too much does here, of magical thinking. Wherever the unconstraining processes, the struggles toward release, might appropriately be dramatized, there is a chapter break, and when the narrative resumes the freedom is a *fait accompli.*

Of "The Last Mohican" 's Fidelman it is written: "He was, at odd hours, in certain streets, several times solicited by prostitutes, some heartbreakingly pretty, one a slender unhappy-looking girl with bags under her eyes whom he desired mightily, but Fidelman feared for his health." *This* Fidelman desires unhappy-looking girls bearing signs of wear and tear. *This* Fidelman fears for his health. And that isn't all he fears for. But then this Fidelman is not a Jew in name only. "To be unmasked as a hidden Jew," which is what frightens Yakov Bok in the early stages of *The Fixer,* could in fact serve to describe what happens to "The Last Mohican" 's Fidelman, with the assistance of his own Bober, the wily schnorring refugee Susskind.

"The Last Mohican" is a tale of conscience tried and human sympathy unclotted, arising out of very different interests from the fiction that comes after — and it abounds with references, humble, comic, and solemn, to Jewish history and life. But that is it, by and large, for the Jews: enter sex in chapter two, called "Still Life," and exit Susskind and Fidelman the unmasked Jew. What is henceforth to be unmasked in Fidelman in this book — which would, if it could, be a kind of counter-*Assistant* — is the hidden goy, a man whose appetites are associated elsewhere with the lust-ridden "uncircumcised dog" Alpine.

And if there should be any doubt as to how fierce and reflexive is the identification in Malamud's imagination between renunciation and Jew and appetite and goy, one need only compare the pathetic air of self-surrender that marks the ending of "The Last Mohican" —

> "Susskind, come back," he shouted, half sobbing. "The suit is yours. All is forgiven."
>
> He came to a dead halt but the refugee ran on. When last seen he was still running.

to the comic and triumphant ending of "Still Life." The second chapter concludes with Fidelman's first successful penetration, which he is able, after much frustration, to accomplish upon a strong-minded Italian *pittrice* by inadvertently disguising himself in a priest's vestments. There is both more and less to this scene than Malamud may have intended:

> She grabbed his knees. "Help me, Father, for Christ's sake."
>
> Fidelman, after a short tormented time, said in a quavering voice, "I forgive you, my child."
>
> "The penance," she wailed, "first the penance."
>
> After reflecting, he replied, "Say one hundred times each, Our Father and Hail Mary."
>
> "More," Annamaria wept. "More, more. Much more."
>
> Gripping his knees so hard they shook she burrowed her head into his black-buttoned lap. He felt the surprised beginnings of an erection.

But really it should not have come as such a surprise, this erection that arrives in priest's clothing. What would have been surprising is if Fidelman had disguised himself as a Susskind, say, and found *that* working like an aphrodisiac, maybe even on a Jewish girl like Helen Bober. Then would something have been at stake, then would something have been challenged. But as it is written, with Fidelman copulating in a priest's biretta rather than a skullcap, the scene moves the novel nowhere, particularly as the final line seems to me to get entirely backward the implications of the joke that is being played here. "Pumping slowly," the chapter ends, "he nailed her to her cross." But isn't it rather the Jew in the biretta who is being nailed, if not to his cross, to the structure of his inhibitions?

The trouble with lines like the last one in that chapter is that they settle an issue with a crisp rhetorical flourish before it has even been allowed to have much of a life. At the moment that the writer appears to be most forceful and candid, he is in fact shying away from his own subject and suppressing whatever is psychologically rich or morally troublesome with a clever, but essentially evasive, figure of speech. Here, for instance, is Fidelman's detumescence described earlier on. Premature ejaculation has just finished him off, much to the *pittrice*'s dismay, and though he hasn't as yet stumbled unwittingly upon the clerical disguise that will make him fully potent and desirable, we note that the figure for erotic revitalization is, as usual, Christian; also noteworthy is that generally speaking in *Fidelman*, where the sex act is, there shall whimsical metaphor be. "Although he mightily willed resurrection, his wilted flower bit the dust." And here is the hero discovering himself to be a homosexual. "Fidelman had never in his life said 'I love you' without reservation to anyone. He said it to Beppo. If that's the way it works, that's the way it works." But that isn't the way it works at all. That is a dream of the way it works, and all of it neatly koshered with the superego and other defense agencies, with that reassuring word "love."

"Think of love," says Beppo, as he leaps on naked Fidelman from behind, "you've run from it all your life." And, magically, one might say, just by *thinking* of it, Fidelman instantaneously loves, so that between the homosexual act of anal intercourse — an act which society still generally considers a disgusting transgression indeed—and its transformation into ideal behavior, there is not even time for the reader to say ouch. Or for Fidelman to think whatever perplexing thoughts might well accompany entry into the world of the taboo by the tight-assed fellow who at the outset, in the marvelous "The Last Mohican" chapter, would barely give the refugee Susskind the time of day.

One wonders why the taboo must be idealized quite so fast. Why must Fidelman dress up as a priest merely to get himself laid right, and not only think of love, but *fall* in love, the first time he gets buggered? Why not think of lust, of base and unseemly desire? And surrender himself to *that?* People, after all, have been known to run from it too all their lives, just as fast and far. And when last seen were still running. "In America," the book concludes, "he worked as a craftsman in glass and loved men and women."

Recall the last lines of *The Assistant*. Frank Alpine should have it so easy with *his* appetites. But whereas in *The Assistant* the lusting goy's passionate and aggressive act of *genuinely* loving desire for the Jewish girl takes the form of rape, and requires penance (or retribution) of the harshest kind, in *Pictures of Fidelman*, the Jew's most wayward (albeit comfortingly passive) sexual act is, without anything faintly resembling Alpine's enormous personal struggle, converted on the spot into love. And if this is still insufficiently reassuring about a Jew and sexual appetite, the book manages by the end to have severed the bisexual Fidelman as thoroughly from things Jewish as *The Assistant*, by its conclusion, has marked the sexually constrained, if not desexed, Alpine as a Jew forevermore. Of all of Malamud's Jewish heroes is there any who is by comparison so strikingly *un*-Jewish (after chapter one is out of the way, that is), who insists upon it so little and is so little reminded of it by the Gentile world? And is there any who, at the conclusion, is happier?

In short Fidelman is Malamud's Henderson, Italy his Africa, and "love" is the name that Malamud, for reasons that by now should be apparent, gives in this book to getting finally what you want the way you want it. Suggesting precisely the disjunction between act and self-knowledge that accounts for the lightheaded dreaminess of *Fidelman*, and that differentiates it so sharply from those wholly convincing novels, *The Assistant* and *The Fixer*, where no beclouding ambivalence stands between the author's imagination and the objects of his fury.

And now to return to *Portnoy's Complaint* and the hero imagined by this Jewish writer. Obviously the problem for Alexander Portnoy is that, unlike Arthur Fidelman, nothing *inflames* his Jewish self-consciousness so much as setting forth on a wayward libidinous adventure—that is, nothing makes it seem quite so wayward than that a Jewish man like himself should be wanting the things that he wants. The hidden Jew is unmasked in *him* by the sight of his own erection. He cannot suppress the one in the interests of the other, nor can he imagine them living happily ever after in peaceful coexistence. Like the rest of us, he too has read Saul Bellow, Bernard Malamud, and Norman Mailer.

His condition might be compared to Frank Alpine's, if, after his painful circumcision — with all that means to him about virtuous renunci- ation — Alpine had all at once found his old disreputable self, the uncir- cumcised dog and Maileresque hoodlum of the forbidden lusts and desires, emerging from solitary confinement to engage his freshly circumcised and circumscribed self in hand-to-hand combat. In Portnoy the disapproving moralist who says "I am horrified" will not disappear when the libidinous slob shows up screaming "I want!" Nor will the coarse, anti-social Alpine in him be permanently subdued by whatever of Morris Bober, or of his own hard-working, well-intentioned Boberish father, there may be in his nature. This imaginary Jew also drags himself around with a pain between his legs, only it inspires him to acts of frenzied and embarrassing lust.

A lusting Jew. A Jew as a sexual defiler. An odd type, as it turns out, in recent Jewish fiction, where it is usually the goy who does the sexual defiling; also, it has been alleged, one of the "crudest and most venerable stereotypes of anti-Semitic lore." I am quoting from a letter written by Marie Syrkin — a well-known American Zionist leader and daughter of one of Socialist Zionism's outstanding organizers and polemicists in the first quarter of the century — and published in *Commentary* in March, 1973. The letter constituted her improvement on two separate attacks that had appeared several months earlier in *Commentary*, one by Irving Howe directed at my work (most specifically *Goodbye, Columbus* and *Portnoy's Complaint*) and the other by the magazine's editor, Norman Podhoretz, directed at what is assumed by him to be my cultural position and reputation. (*Commentary* associate editor Peter Shaw had already at- tacked *Portnoy's Complaint* for "fanaticism in the hatred of things Jewish" in the review he wrote when the novel first appeared and which somehow turned up in *Commentary* too.)

The historical references Syrkin employs to identify what is repug- nant to her about *Portnoy's Complaint* suggest that to some I had gone beyond the odd or eccentric in this book, exceeded even the reductive "vulgarity" which Howe said "deeply marred" my fiction here as else- where, and had entered into the realm of the pathological. Here is Syrkin's characterization of Portnoy's lustful, even *vengefully* lustful, designs upon a rich and pretty Wasp girl, a *shiksa* whom he would have perform fellatio upon him, if only she could master the skill without asphyxiating herself. It is of no interest to Syrkin that Portnoy goes about tutoring his "tender young countess" in techniques of breathing rather more like a patient swimming instructor with a timid ten-year-old at a summer camp than in the manner of the Marquis de Sade or even Sergius O'Shaugnessy, nor does she give any indication that oral intercourse may not necessarily constitute the last word in human degradation, even for the participants themselves:

"a classic description," writes Syrkin, "of what the Nazis called *rassen-schande* (racial defilement)"; "straight out of the Goebbels-Streicher script"; "the anti-Semitic indictment straight through Hitler is that the Jew is the defiler and destroyer of the Gentile world."

Hitler, Goebbels, Streicher. Had she not been constrained by limitations of space, Syrkin might eventually have had me in the dock with the entire roster of Nuremberg defendants. On the other hand it does not seem to occur to her that sexual entanglements between Jewish men and Gentile women might themselves be marked, in any number of instances, by the history of anti-Semitism that so obviously determines her own rhetoric and point of view, at least in this letter. Nor is she about to allow the most obvious point of all: that this Portnoy can no more enter into an erotic relationship unconscious of his Jewishness and his victim's or, if you will, his assistant's Gentileness, than Bober could enter into a relationship on terms less charged than those with Alpine, or Levanthal with Allbee. Rather, to Syrkin, for a Jew to have the kind of sexual desires Alexander Portnoy has (conflict-laden and self-defeating as they frequently are) is unimaginable to anyone but a Nazi.

Now arguing as she does for what a Jew is not and could not be, other than to a pathological Nazi racist, Syrkin leaves little doubt that she herself has strongly held ideas of what a Jew in fact is or certainly ought to be. As did Theodor Herzl; as did Weizmann, Jabotinsky, and Nahman Syrkin; as did Hitler, Goebbels, and Streicher; as do Jean-Paul Sartre, Moshe Dayan, Meir Kahane, Leonid Brezhnev, and the Union of American Hebrew Congregations . . . not to mention lesser historical personages and institutions such as were designated at the outset of the standard bar mitzvah speech of my childhood as "My dear grandparents, parents, assembled relatives, friends, and members of the congregation." In an era which has seen the avid and, as it were, brilliant Americanization of millions of uprooted Jewish immigrants and refugees, the annihilation as human trash of millions of Europeanized Jews, and the establishment and survival in the ancient holy land of a spirited, defiant modern Jewish state, it can safely be said that imagining what Jews are and ought to be has been anything but the marginal activity of a few American-Jewish novelists. The writer's enterprise—particularly in books like *The Victim*, *The Assistant*, and *Portnoy's Complaint*—might itself be described as imagining Jews being imagined, by themselves and by others; given all those projections, fantasies, illusions, programs, dreams, and solutions that the existence of the Jews has given rise to, it is no wonder that these three books, whatever may be their differences in literary merit and approach, are largely nightmares of bondage, each informed in its way by a mood of baffled, claustrophobic struggle.

For the Jewish novelist, then, it has not been a matter of going forth to forge in the smithy of his soul the *un*created conscience of his race, but of finding his inspiration in that conscience that has been created and undone a hundred times over in this century alone . . . and out of which the solitary being who has been designated "Jew" by whomever has had to imagine what *he* is and is not, must and must not be.

If he would imagine himself to be such a thing at all. For as the most serious of American-Jewish novelists seem to indicate in those choices of subject and emphasis that lead to the heart of what a writer thinks, there are ways of living, many having to do with the least tame of our passions, that not even spirits as unfettered as theirs are able to attribute to the character who is forthrightly presented as a Jew.

Notes

1. I say "longer works" because the hard and ugly facts of life in a short story like "The Old System," published first in *Playboy* in 1967, are of the sort that have been known to set the phones ringing at the Anti-Defamation League. Baldly put (which is how these things tend to be put when the lines are drawn) it is a story of rich Jews and their money: first, how they make it big in the world with under-the-table payoffs (a hundred thousand delivered to an elegant old Wasp for lucrative country club acreage and delivered by a Jew Bellow depicts as an orthodox religious man); and then it is about how Jews cheat and finagle one another out of the Almighty Dollar: a dying Jewish woman, with a dirty mouth no less, demands twenty thousand in cash from her businessman brother for the privilege of seeing her before she expires in her hospital bed. This scene of sibling hatred and financial cunning in a Jewish family is in fact the astonishing climax to which the story moves.

One wonders about the reception the defense agencies would have given to this story, especially appearing as it did in *Playboy* magazine, had it been the work of some unknown Schwartz or Levy, instead of the author of *Herzog*. Indeed, in the aftermath of Sixties political radicalism and the traumatic shock upon Jews of the October 1973 war, one wonders what position the Jewish press and cultural journals would take if a first novel like *Dangling Man* was suddenly to be published, wherein the thoroughly deracinated and depressive hero seems to dislike no one quite so much as his Jewish brother's bourgeois family, or if out of the blue a book like *The Victim* was now to appear, in which the hero's Jewishness is at times made to resemble a species of psychopathology.

Parody as Exorcism: "The Raven" and "The Jewbird"   J. Gerald Kennedy*

Unlike other literary modes, parody describes not an intrinsic structure or quality in a work but rather a condition of relationship to another text or set of texts. Parody creates a theoretical juxtaposition in which the more recent work ironically re-presents selected elements of its antecedent, usually through mocking exaggeration. As Jonathan Culler has noted, parody typically places in tension two authorial perspectives: "the order of the original and the point of view which undermines it."[1] This subversive

*Reprinted, with permission, from *Genre* 13 (Summer 1980):161–69.

process resists easy explanation, however, since it resides in the play of differences and similarities between texts. In order for parody to occur, there must be a patent resemblance — usually in style or theme — between the second text and the first. Yet the element of parody emerges only when we perceive the disparities lodged in this network of correspondences: the verbal deviations, contextual changes, and transformations of familiar narrative patterns. Though parody typically employs overt distortion (and can be said to fail when its target is not immediately recognizable), it may, like other forms of irony, possess a complexity of purpose and implication. In a single work, the parodist may undertake to satirize the content of an earlier text, the affectations of its author, the formal conventions he utilized, or the cultural values projected in his writing. The parodist may (like Jane Austen in *Northanger Abbey*) aim to lampoon a specific genre or aesthetic tradition. Or he may be engaged in a more private enterprise: to exorcise a secret demon and thus rid himself of an earlier writer's perplexing and undesired influence.

Among the multiple uses of parody, this last strategy seems both more interesting and, because it involves an esoteric intention, less susceptible to analysis. An initial clarification comes, however, from Proust, who in acknowledging the entrancing effect of Flaubert's writing declared:

> Concerning Flaubertian intoxication, I wouldn't know how to recommend too highly to writers the purgative, exorcising force of parody. When one has just finished a book, he not only wishes to continue to live with its characters, . . . but also our inner voice, which has been conditioned during the entire reading to follow the rhythm of a Balzac or a Flaubert, wants to continue to speak like them. One must let it have its way a moment, let the pedal prolong the sound; that is, create a deliberate parody, so that afterward one can again recover his originality and not create involuntary parody all of his life.[2]

Proust suggests that this method of regaining one's authorial voice entails a willful, temporary surrender to the language of the earlier text. By sustaining the sound of this "rhythme obsesseur," the writer frees himself from the repetition mechanism which produces inadvertent parody. Proust's formulation describes a purgative impulse present to some extent, perhaps, in all parody, since mockery tacitly expresses (as Harold Bloom might say) an anxiety about the influence of an earlier work and a desire to break its hold. Yet it seems equally apparent that self-conscious exorcism must produce a form of parody unlike the transparent derision of Fielding's *Shamela* or Hemingway's *The Torrents of Spring*. The difference will be one of kind rather than degree, inasmuch as the Proustian "pastiche volontaire" develops not from a sense of the foolishness of the earlier work but rather from an awareness of its haunting insistence. Since in this scheme ironic emulation reflects both the avowal and displacement of an influence, we should anticipate in literary exorcism a quality antithetical to conventional parody: ambivalence.

This is precisely the condition which obscures the filiation between Bernard Malamud's story "The Jewbird" (From *The Magic Barrel*) and Poe's famous poem, "The Raven." To gain further insight into the phenomenon Proust has adumbrated, I wish to treat these works as a provisional model of the complex linkage produced by exorcism. I assume at the outset that a parodic relationship exists; that the purpose of this ironic representation is unclear; and that this ambiguity signals the unfolding of an exorcistic project. To explain: it seems almost self-evident that Malamud's tale consciously exploits the dramatic situation of "The Raven," for in both works a black bird of mysterious origin and seemingly magical intelligence flies in an open window and takes up residence in the protagonist's apartment. We see both birds perched above a doorway, uttering words that torment the human listener; gradually we realize that the bird objectifies some aspect of the protagonist's experience with which he has failed to come to terms. The man is oppressed by the bird's presence and tries to learn its ultimate purpose, but failing to do so, he implores the bird to leave. Presented so starkly, these parallels seem obvious, and it is a matter of some astonishment that critics have barely mentioned the connection.[3] Yet this neglect illustrates one of the odd features of exorcistic parody: it is simultaneously overt and discreet, unmistakably present yet playfully elusive.

Of course thematic parallels do not in themselves constitute parody; the effect of sly imitation emerges rather through the comic variations worked upon "The Raven." Such disparities lend ironic resonance to verbal echoes: Poe's persona commands the bird, "Tell me what thy lordly name is on the Night's Plutonian shore!" But Malamud's Harry Cohen, a frozen food salesman, snarls less poetically: "So what's your name, if you don't mind saying?" Poe's speaker expresses his fears about the raven's hellish origins: " 'Prophet!' said I, 'thing of evil! — prophet still if bird or devil! —' " The same uncertainty afflicts Cohen, who asks the Jewbird, "You sure you're not some kind of ghost or dybbuk?" Later he repeats the question, using the exact contraries of Poe's speaker: "But how do I know you're a bird and not some kind of a goddamn devil?" The vulgarity epitomizes Malamud's transformation of the Poe material; Cohen's modern slang and the banal details of his world create an indirect contrast to the formal elegance of "The Raven."

Closer attention to dramatic parallels further sharpens our sense of potential parody in "The Jewbird." The initiatory event in each work is the appearance of a mysterious bird, and in "The Raven" this moment suggests the advent of nobility: "In there stepped a stately Raven of the saintly days of yore; / Not the least obeisance made he; not a minute stopped or stayed he; / But, with mien of lord or lady, perched above my chamber door." When the Jewbird arrives, however, there is a conspicuous lack of decorum: "The bird wearily flapped through the open kitchen window of Harry Cohen's top-floor apartment on First Avenue near the lower East River. . . . This black-type longbeaked bird — its ruffled head and dull eyes, crossed a little, making it look like a dissipated crow — landed if not smack on Cohen's thick lamb chop, at least on the table, close by." After Cohen takes a swat at him, the Jewbird shifts to a more familiar position: "The bird cawed hoarsely and with a flap of its bedraggled wings — feathers tufted this way and that — rose heavily to the top of the open kitchen door, where it perched staring down." Malamud's caricature of Poe's raven possesses some critical justification: we recall that the bird initially provokes a smile from Poe's narrator; that its crest is "shorn and shaven"; that its appearance is laughably described as "grim, ungainly, ghastly, gaunt." Malamud further distorts these qualities to make the Jewbird "bedraggled," "scrawny," and malodorous; at one point Cohen explodes, "For Christ sake, why don't you wash yourself sometimes? Why must you always stink like a dead fish?"

Whether ominous or merely offensive, the bird's presence at last becomes so aggravating that the protagonist commands his visitor to leave. Poe's persona beseeches the raven: "Get the back into the tempest and the Night's Plutonian shore!" Less grandiosely Cohen warns the Jewbird, "Time to hit flyways. . . . Now scat or it's open war." Here, however, Malamud's story departs from its analogical relationship to the poem. Whereas Poe's character ultimately realizes that he will never escape from the raven's influence, Cohen indeed declares war on Schwartz the Jewbird; reversing the nemesis relationship, he buys a cat and permits it to stalk the feathered intruder. Hence near the end of the tale we see Schwartz perching "terror-stricken closer to the ceiling than the floor, as the cat, his tale flicking, endlessly watched him."

But despite these entertaining parallels, made to seem all the more glaringly by selective emphasis, Malamud's evocation of "The Raven" does not produce the effect of conventional parody — mockery through distortion. Indeed, although he appropriates Poe's central concept (a visitation by a mysterious talking bird), reduces it to comic terms, and develops a set of verbal and dramatic similarities laced with ironic disparities, Malamud refrains from anything like overt ridicule of Poe's poem. Instead, he submerges the parody and directs his satire at an aspect of the Americanized Jew personified by Cohen: a contempt for the customs and manners of Old-World Jews. As Robert Alter has pointed out, these traditional ways are embodied in Schwartz, the wandering Jewbird, whose chutzpah and fondness for herring and schnapps disgust the "assimilated" Cohen. As Alter explains, the bird represents for Cohen "the stigmatized stereotype of a kind of Jew that he emphatically wants to leave behind. Cohen is really attacking part of himself in his hostility toward Schwartz."[4] The essential truth about the frozen-food salesman emerges at the story's end when Cohen's son finds the remains of Schwartz's body and asks who killed him;

his mother answers, "Anti-Semeets." In this sense, the tale dramatizes a familiar theme in recent Jewish fiction: the Jew's complicated and sometimes scornful attitude about his own cultural roots.[5]

Understandably, critical attention to "The Jewbird" has dealt almost exclusively with this issue; in satirizing Jewish anti-Semitism, Malamud attacks a problem of social, ethnic, and political significance. His decision not to lampoon "The Raven" seems therefore understandable, since blatant parody would have compromised the satirical assault and diminished its effect. Yet the verbal echoes and dramatic parallels remain; the poem lingers as an ironic, ghostly presence in "The Jewbird," seemingly unrelated to the surface narrative and its satirical objectives. What do these traces then signify? It would be possible to argue that Malamud conjures up elements of the poem to remind us of Poe's notorious anti-Semitism; however, this reading depends more upon external information about Poe than upon textual evidence. One could also argue that the bluntness of Cohen's language and the banality of his ordeal are designed to mock through parodic inversion the ornate rhetoric and Romantic melancholy upon which the effect of "The Raven" depends; but this analysis seems tenuous at best, since "The Jewbird" displays neither explicit scorn for the poem nor visible hostility toward the Romantic sensibility.

And so we return to the original paradox: the poem obtrudes as a palpable yet phantasmic influence, which dominates the foreground of "The Jewbird" while remaining nearly invisible — a kind of purloined letter. And the more intently we seek the function of this allusion / illusion along the plane of satirical meaning (in relation to the attack on Jewish anti-Semitism), the less certain we become of its instrumentality. Aside from the curious fact that, as in "The Raven," the appearance of the Jewbird coincides with the death of a woman (here, Cohen's mother), the overlapping between the two texts seems almost gratuitous. But it does not occur by chance: at the very least, these parallels imply a sustained imaginative engagement with the poem. And if we are willing to move from the level of overt satire to consider Cohen's struggle with Schwartz figuratively, as the reflection of Malamud's reflection on "The Raven" — that is, as metaphor — quite a different understanding of the action emerges. From this perspective, the relationship between Cohen and the bird seems analogically to represent the author's effort to free himself from the persistent, improbable influence of "The Raven." Ludicrous but inescapable, the bird (poem) torments Cohen (Malamud) by insinuating itself into his private world. For a time, Cohen accepts its presence and allows it to have its way, but to reassert his authority, he finally attacks the bird and flings it out the window. Thus the literal events mirror the key stages in Malamud's presumed ordeal with the poem; the narrative becomes a metatext on its own composition. This oblique view of "The Jewbird" also reveals an absolute disjunction — perhaps symptomatic of literary exorcism — between public and private implication. Cohen's final gesture (the destruction of Schwartz) clarifies the incommensurability of satirical and parodic meaning: while on one level this pogrom illustrates the shameful anti-Semitism that Malamud obviously disparages, on another it conversely represents a necessary, purgative process — the writer's effort to cast out a literary bête noire, the influence of "The Raven."

Such a theory of composition enables us to come to terms with the ambiguous evocation of Poe which informs "The Jewbird." Apparently "The Raven" epitomized those aspects of Poe's writing which constituted for Malamud its imaginative contagion; to break its hold, Malamud indulged in authorial play, allowing the idea of the poem to express itself in idiomatic Yiddish humor, in a comic form possessing its own integrity and purpose. While Harry Cohen is said to receive a "permanent scar" from his bout with the Jewbird, the evidence of Malamud's fiction seems to indicate that through this ironic transformation of "The Raven," he effectually liberated his work from Poe's influence. Despite his fascination with magic and the supernatural, for example, Malamud appears not to have drawn upon the Gothic fantasies of his predecessor; as Professor Alter has shown, he derives this occult interest principally from the motifs of Jewish folklore.[6] Yet critical emphasis on ethnic, Jewish elements in his fiction has perhaps obscured Malamud's response to goyish American literature. That this dimension will assume greater interpretive importance seems inevitable in the wake of *Dubin's Lives*, a 1979 novel depicting the troubled love life of a Jewish biographer whose literary obsessions include Thoreau, Emerson, and Twain. A passing reference to "the miserable youth of Edgar Allen Poe" reminds us of the obsession Malamud had already displaced in writing "The Jewbird."

Although the foregoing discussion offers only a preliminary inquiry into the exorcistic process described by Proust, it nevertheless suggests some of its characteristic features. Further study in this direction will, I think, reveal the surprising extent to which this mechanism underlies significant contemporary fiction. Its wide currency seems, upon consideration, predictable enough; Emerson's remark that genius is "the enemy of genius by over-influence" gets at the crux of a pervasive authorial problem which exorcism seeks to resolve. Precisely because great writing weighs upon subsequent writers, exacting the tribute of conscious or unconscious emulation, any author who wishes to establish his own voice must come to terms with the "enemy" — the genius of his predecessors. The purposeful strategies of exorcism (not to be confused with Professor Bloom's subliminal conflicts) can be discerned in a number of familiar modern texts: Alter has observed, for instance, that *Henderson the Rain King* involves a "composite parody" of the twentieth-century "personal or mythic quest into dark regions." Noting a doubleness of ambiguity similar to the effect for exorcism, Alter calls Bellow's novel almost a "perfect parody, catching the outlandishness of its literary models and at the same time putting them to serious new uses that make it an independent imaginative entity."[7] A comparable ironic mimesis occurs in the fiction of Nabokov, where Tony Tanner has recently uncovered the very tactics described by Proust: "This game, like many games, is also a form of defense; it is a way of distancing an influence and reducing its potency. Proust said that a writer might parody another writer to become free of his spell and thus able to write his own novels. Just so we could see Nabokov keeping at bay, for example, Poe and Dostoievsky in *Lolita*."[8]

Insofar as the "over-influence" of genius upon genius implies that imaginative tension at the heart of parody, it seems probable that the most revealing cases of exorcism will prove to be those in which an important writer simultaneously acknowledges and subverts the influence of an earlier master: Bellow overthrowing Conrad; Nabokov confronting Poe; Thomas Wolfe in *Look Homeward, Angel* fending off Joyce's *Portrait of the Artist*; William Styron in *Lie Down in Darkness* grappling with *The Sound and the Fury*; or Hemingway in *The Old Man and the Sea* reducing *Moby-Dick* to a mutilated fragment. Moreover, highly influential works should be expected to generate more exorcistic parody than other works; it seems entirely possible to construct a history of ambiguously parodic response to certain classic texts. Thus a novel like *The Scarlet Letter* might be examined in terms of its ironic evocation in works like Faulkner's *As I Lay Dying* and Updike's *A Month of Sundays*. Comparative studies of this kind would shed light not only upon the distinctive imaginative order created by each writer but also upon the psychology of literary influence, raising such questions as why certain prominent features induce parodic response. Such approaches are made possible by the recognition central to this discussion — that the desire to break the spell of an earlier writer produces a peculiar form of parody indicative of the parodist's uneasy relationship to the predecessor and his work.

By its nature, all parody involves a systematic play of similarity and difference; but in literary exorcism this process functions as a kind of therapeutic game, a conscious and controlled manipulation of those elements in another author's writing which have exerted a persistent and perhaps inexplicable effect. By appropriating and transforming these materials, by marking them as his own and subordinating them to his own imaginative ends, the parodist effects a psychological release and completes the demystification (or detoxification) of the prior text. Restraint governs the procedure; while the transposition of borrowed elements to a new environment provides ironic overtones and implications, the earlier text never becomes the explicit object of ridicule: the name of the demon cannot be spoken. Indeed, as we discover in "The Jewbird," these transposed elements are sometimes so fully subsumed by the narrative in which they occur that they acquire a phantasmic quality. This paradoxical phenomenon of visibility / invisibility can thus be understood finally as a function of the contradictory process described by Proust as exorcism. One regains his authorial voice by losing it: the obsessive material assumes a tangible form as the parodist allows it to have its way for a while; yet the whole enterprise depends upon his ability to reassert control, to subordinate this material to his own creative purposes, and at last to slide it beneath the surface of the liberating text. Only through this arcane ritual, it would seem, can he free himself from the literary influence which haunts him like an ominous bird of yore.

Notes

1. *Structuralist Poetics* (Ithaca: Cornell University Press, 1975), p. 152.

2. *Chroniques* (Paris: Gallimard, 1927), p. 204. Translation mine.

3. Two essays mention the Poe connection briefly, without exploring its significance. See Samuel Irving Bellman, "Women, Children, and Idiots First," in *Bernard Malamud and the Critics*, ed. Leslie A. Field and Joyce W. Field (New York: New York University Press 1970), p. 25; Jackson J. Benson, "An Introduction: Bernard Malamud and the Haunting of America," in *The Fiction of Bernard Malamud*," ed. Richard Astro and Jackson J. Benson (Corvallis, Ore.: Oregon State University Press 1977), p. 24.

4. "Jewish Humor and the Domestication of Myth," in *Veins of Humor*, ed. Harry Levin (Cambridge: Harvard University Press, 1972), p. 262.

5. Sheldon Norman Grebstein has written that Jewish humor often "delivers ironic observations about itself and its practitioners, the chosen people. Frequently it verges on self-hatred, . . . or conveys the desperation of a wisdom about moral conduct which is impossible to practice." See "Bernard Malamud and the Jewish Movement," in *Contemporary American-Jewish Literature*, ed. Irving Malin (Bloomington: Indiana University Press, 1973), p. 106.

6. "Bernard Malamud: Jewishness as Metaphor," *After the Tradition* (New York: E. P. Dutton, 1971), p. 117.

7. "Saul Bellow: A Dissent from Modernism," *After the Tradition*, p. 105.

8. *City of Words: American Fiction 1950–1970* (New York: Harper and Row, 1971), p. 38.

Malamud's Jews and the Holocaust Experience

Lawrence L. Langer*

How much of world literature, from Job and Oedipus through Tolstoy and Dostoevsky to Saul Bellow and Bernard Malamud, embraces the principle that suffering kindles a moral advantage, an inner discipline, a spiritual strength? The capacity to suffer, with its accompanying cleansing and sanctifying of consciousness, distinguishes us from the beasts. It makes us more human. It helps us — theoretically, as lighted by the prism of literature — to bear with dignity the burdens of living and dying. Despite

*This essay was written specifically for this volume and is published here for the first time by permission of the author.

the formulaic tone of these sentiments, they have served the literary imagination as irreducible havens of the human in the midst of the unfolding and expanding oppressions and atrocities of history, especially in our own time. Even a resolute secularist like Camus embraced the disciplinary value of suffering. Undismayed by the spectacle of man adrift in a universe without a master, he could conclude of his Sisyphus that the "struggle itself toward the heights is enough to fill a man's heart,"[1] and of his threatened population in *The Plague* that in time of pestilence "There are more things to admire in men than to despise."[2] Contrary to expectation, and perhaps even experience, we have been taught to believe by the vision of our writers that physical anguish or deprivation inspires the soul and nourishes the quality of our inner lives.

It is not surprising to find that an American writer like Bernard Malamud, concerned with Jewish character and Jewish themes, should fall easily (and admirably) into the pattern of this vision. No matter how bleak the lives of figures like Morris Bober (*The Assistant*) and Yakov Bok (*The Fixer*), no matter how helpless their natures and hopeless their situations, they retain the gift of suffering, and this keeps their minimal existences from dissolving into despair. Moreover, the gift is transferable and transformational, since Bok's stubborn humanity in the midst of misery infiltrates the sensibilities of one of his jailors, while Bober's finally provides a model of being for his wayward assistant's undisciplined nature. Suffering thus has an exemplary as well as a personal value, and the idea lends literature a resonance that formalists might not applaud but which Malamud has affirmed in novel and story throughout his career.

In an address accepting the National Book Award for *The Magic Barrel*, Malamud was unequivocal about his own humanist position: "I am quite tired of the colossally deceitful devaluation of man in this day. . . ." No one could question the sincerity of this benign view, which is not just speech-rhetoric, since a belief in fundamental human dignity pervades Malamud's writing. But it represents a point of view, not a truth, and Malamud's weariness with somber visions that devaluate man cannot validate (though it certainly does much to explain) his truculent use of "deceitful." In a century abounding in war, assassination, mass-murder, and acts of terrorism, we are surrounded and almost engulfed by an obvious loss of reverence for the human, at least on the part of the human agents of and participants in these acts. Malamud's conclusion that "The devaluation exists because [man] accepts it without protest"[3] may have some foundation in experience, but it rather naively oversimplifies an enormously complicated issue. Charging the enemy with bayonets of verbal dissent does little to illuminate this issue.

Why has a writer like Malamud, in whose work the themes of suffering and dignity are so closely allied, touched so peripherally on the matter of the Holocaust? And how, when he has approached it, has he reconciled its atrocities with his determination to illuminate the human?

How does his personal vision accord with the remarkable exclamation of a deathcamp survivor in a videotaped interview: "I saw the sun in Auschwitz, and the sun was black—the sun was destruction"? The extraordinary inversion of imagery, reminding us of Milton's "darkness visible," illuminates not the human but *in*human, and I suspect that even Malamud would find it difficult to declare this implicit devaluation "deceitful." The experience of the deathcamps has transformed many other sources of warmth and light—family bonding, friendship, culture, trust, hope, belief in progress—into perilously vulnerable consolations, an uncongenial possibility that devalues the human whether men protest or not. Such conclusions would naturally appear deceitful to a writer whose characters are snared by their own mistakes, errors of judgment, stubbornness, determination to resist the corruption of their moral nature. But this is no more than confessing that most of Malamud's characters inhabit a universe alien to the premises on which the Holocaust universe are built.

In a fine essay on Malamud's work, devoted chiefly to *The Fixer*, Robert Alter suggests that for Malamud in this novel "1911 is 1943 in small compass and sharp focus," that the Beiliss Case gives him "a way of approaching the European Holocaust on a scale that is imaginable, susceptible of fictional representation." But by reducing the scale of that event from the extermination of a people to the persecution of a person, Malamud does more than make that momentous atrocity manageable; he transforms it into a story of the affirmation of private dignity that elevates the ordeal to tragic dimensions. Alter's very language echoes a vision and a tradition that fall comfortably into a familiar literary stance, but settle uneasily on the circumstantial dilemmas confronting the Holocaust victim. Of Malamud's protagonist in *The Fixer* he says: forced "to summon up all his inner resources of survival in order to stay sane and alive in solitary confinement, Bok in his cell recapitulates the darkest, most heroic aspects of Jewish existence in the diaspora."[4] But how could we use such language to describe that final expression of diaspora in Europe called deportation to the deathcamps?

Alter lucidly describes Malamud's protagonists as "futilely aware of their own limitations . . . 'self-confessed failures' caught in the trap of themselves and rankling over their predicament, though just a little amused by it too."[5] Now imagine writing about protagonists in Holocaust fiction, after the ordeal of the camps, engaging in a self-confrontation resembling this one. Such confrontations are luxuries reserved for sensibilities in situations, painful as they may be, which permit meaningful moral resistance. Bok, for example, will not sign a confession. But who could speak of Treblinka as a "predicament"? Who could be "rankled" by finding oneself in proximity to the gas chamber? What have one's human limitations to do with such a doom? And what constitutes success in such an environment—survival as a starving corpse? And how could one be even a little amused by such a scenario? The critical vocabulary relevant to

Malamud's vision can do little to illuminate the problems of character and fate, choice and chance, moral vision and moral failure in a Holocaust setting, since atrocity provides for the writer a perplexing barrage of abnormalities undreamt of in the worst nightmares of a Morris Bober or a Jakov Bok. Death in a place like Auschwitz was neither "human" nor "fate," and though Bober's demise is pitiful, he is in his generosity and folly very much the agent of his own end. Bok's ordeal is a celebration of character over circumstance; fiction about survival in a deathcamp is not a celebration but a concession to a more modest goal: nurturing irreducible needs, minimal gestures to keep the body physically alive.

Despite the ignorant anti-Semitism of the boatman who ferries Yakov Bok from the shtetl to the city, with his augury of the total destruction of the Jews, Malamud's fiction does not anticipate or evoke the horrors of the Holocaust. His ancestry in this novel, beside the pogrom mentality of nineteenth century Russia, is the prison literature of a Dostoevsky, a Koestler, a Solzhenitsyn, the story of an individual whose moral sensibilities are assaulted by an external oppression which breeds internal resistance in the potential victim. Bok's resolve to flee the shtetl-prison to try his life elsewhere resounds with a deafening irony, but it is a self-chosen flight, and even the arrest and bizarre "justice" he careens toward is an imaginable if painful future, consistent with the atmosphere of pogrom and Tsarist oppression. His discourses with himself in prison, his imaginary dialogues at the end with the Tsar, also remain in the realm of imaginative possibility. But how would such discourse, private or public in its thrust, shed light on the dilemmas of the concentration camp victim? How would Bok's descendants in the camps carry on with Hitler the kind of conversation that Bok indulges in with the Tsar? Would they say to Hitler, as Bok does to Nicholas, that he is lacking "the sort of insight . . . that creates in man charity, respect for the most miserable"? The very vocabulary blushes at its own insolence. What in Holocaust literature could replace the Tsar's self-pitying defense: "I am — I can truthfully say — a kind person and love my people. Though the Jews cause me a great deal of trouble, and we must sometimes suppress them to maintain order, believe me, I wish them well."[6] Malamud makes this confrontation the culmination of his novel, imagining the encounter with little difficulty. But how could we imagine Adolf Hitler addressing one of his victims in comparably appropriate tones? George Steiner (in *The Portage to San Cristobal of A. H.*) seems to be the sole contemporary writer to attempt such a feat, and his achievement represents a triumph of rhetoric, not literary art (so did, one might argue, Hitler's). The dilemma of the Jew in Malamud's fiction, in any event, does not foreshadow future artistic challenges, but reflects earlier traditions. The conversation with the Tsar in *The Fixer* is not so far removed from Sholom Aleichem's Tevye the milkman's effort to engage his God in dialogue, and his wittily critical tone spills over into the voice of Yakov Bok.

Oppression, suffering, misery, humiliation are *tests* of Jewish character and Jewish dignity in novels like *The Fixer* and *The Assistant*. Life may
be a prison for Malamud's Jews, in real jail or in a grocery store from
which Morris Bober rarely ventures, but within those limitations much
space remains to choose one's future — not only one's attitude, but one's
deeds. When Yakov Bok fears that his jailors are poisoning his food, he
refuses to eat; his refusal leads to permission to inspect the food in the
kitchen and receive his portion there. Equivalent options are unavailable
in the imagined world of Holocaust prisons, where starvation was part of
the persecutor's design. The premises controlling Jewish existence in each
arena are entirely different; and so would be one's treatment of character.
By making a specific choice crucial to the remembered action of *Sophie's
Choice*, William Styron melodramatizes without illuminating the moral
discontinuity representative of the Holocaust experience; by attributing
the choice to a Christian prisoner, he skews that experience even further.
Christians, whether the Black Hundreds or Ward Minogue and Frankie
Alpine, play vital roles in the destiny of Malamud's Jews. But their anti-
Semitism afflicts only private fates, providing a mere flickering prelude to
the incomprehensible fiery doom that consumed European Jewry decades
later.

Circumstances in Malamud always permit moral concern. His Jews
are sooner heedless of physical consequences than of this stabilizing and
dignifying feature of their inner being. Bok steadfastly refuses to sign a
false confession, even if it might lead to his release, because this would
implicate his innocent fellow Jews in his alleged crime and impose on him
a complicity that would pollute his nature. In his imagined dialogue with
the Tsar, Bok has his royal disputant sentimentally conclude that suffering
has at least taught the prisoner mercy, but Bok promptly rebuts this cliche:
"Excuse me, Your Majesty, but what suffering has taught me is the
uselessness of suffering." Bok here refers to *unjust* suffering, since his self-
imposed suffering, the suffering resulting from his casual indifference to
his identity or responsibility as a Jew, has helped to involve him in his
present dilemma. His agony has supplemented and clarified Spinoza:
"One thing I've learned, he thought," on the novel's final page, "there's no
such thing as an unpolitical man, especially a Jew."[7]

Malamud is committed to verifying human identity even in the midst
of chaos, which for Yakov Bok signifies amplifying and ultimately affirming the meaning of being a Jew. Living illegally outside the Pale with an
assumed Christian name has made him suspect to more than the police.
Wrong choices have made him vulnerable. But — to pursue our analogy —
wrong choices by the Jew during the Holocaust were meaningless if one
was detected, while concealing one's identity successfully was one of the
surest means of survival. These circumstances had nothing to do with
moral concern, since even the minimal justice available to a Yakov Bok
was inaccessible to the Holocaust victim. If the old terminology lingers in

discussions of fictional treatments of that event, it may be because as readers we have been trained to view literature through its predecessors and their moral assumptions. For these assert continuity in moral vision despite the disruptions of the Holocaust. Quick to trust, slow to condemn, unwilling to hate, Morris Bober in *The Assistant* pays with his life even during his life for his belief in the value of suffering. And he becomes thereby a shining example of goodness to his assistant, former hoodlum, former anti-Semite, finally a convert to the Judaism of mutual responsibility that Morris clings to in his world of diminished possibilities.

Once again, the vocabulary is appropriate to Malamud's moral vision; but can *The Assistant*, any more than *The Fixer*, cast a light on the shrunken human possibilities of the Holocaust experience? At least one reader has insisted that Malamud means the book "in part, to be a metaphor for the Holocaust experience." In an essay on Malamud called "Metaphor for Holocaust and Holocaust as Metaphor," Michael Brown follows Robert Alter in arguing that the Holocaust is symbolic of the modern condition. He goes further: the Holocaust is the ultimate means "that modernity has invented to destroy man by making his environment inhuman and by degrading his person." Universalizing the event leads to the conclusion, as Brown says approvingly, that there is a connection "between the struggles of American blacks, Russian Jews, and many others for the right to be themselves, and the sufferings of Holocaust Jews because of what they were." But whose advantage do we serve by likening inferior housing and job prejudice among minorities in America, or government hostility to religious practices and refusal of permission to emigrate in the Soviet Union to the ordeal of Jews in Auschwitz and Maidanek? Or by suggesting, as Brown does, that the gas radiator which nearly killed Morris Bober, whether through accident or intention, is "surely a reference to the fate of Jews in Auschwitz and other camps"?[8]

The Assistant, written before *The Fixer* but set chronologically after its time period, during the very years, in fact, when Hitler was consolidating his power, is an obvious quarry for anyone determined to mine the Holocaust from its pages. Morris Bober, that island of Jewish stolidity amidst reefs of anti-Semitic assaults, is a natural candidate for the prototypical representative of the Holocaust victim. Such a view, however, deflects us from Malamud's own central concern, which is Frankie Alpine's efforts to understand what makes Morris "tick," as man and Jew. The novel, after all, is called *The Assistant*, not *The Grocer*, and the main character conflict, between desire and love, force and friendship, guilt and repentance, pilfering and honesty, consistency and self-contradiction, is embodied in Frankie, not Morris. Morris we pity, Morris we admire; but Frankie we need to understand, as he needs to understand himself. Malamud is unequivocal here: Morris the Jew need learn nothing about the fraternal impulse, which he possesses as a birthright. He suffers for others. It is his fate; it is also, ironically, his undoing.

If *The Fixer* dramatizes the dilemma of the Jew as a result of nineteenth century pogrom mentalities, *The Assistant* presents the Jew as victim in the twentieth century of different forms of anti-Semitism, unconnected to judicial procedures, however phony. Against Ward Minogue's brutal, ignorant, open violence Morris is defenseless; the few glimpses we have of this familiar but frightening figure of the terrorist without conscience makes us wish that Malamud had not dispensed with him so conveniently. We will never understand the Holocaust until we understand its Ward Minogues. But Frankie Alpine's anti-Semitism is more subtle, though no less familiar, than Ward's; it is, however, complicated by twitches of remorse that occasionally awaken echoes of a conscience smothered or stillborn. Frankie simply cannot penetrate the motives for Morris's way of life, and this breeds contempt: "What kind of man did you have to be born to shut yourself up in an overgrown coffin. . . . The answer wasn't hard to say—you had to be a Jew. They were born prisoners."[9] There is neither need nor justification for finding in Frankie Alpine's attitude here the mentality of the latent SS man, nor for seeing in "prisoners" and "coffin" antecedents of deathcamp and crematorium. Here if anywhere Malamud universalizes the predicament of the dispossessed like Frankie, searching for a core of goodness while rationalizing his failures through hatred and exploitation of others. The one place where Malamud possibly *does* shed some light on Holocaust themes is in his representation of those who use the Jew to conceal their own limitations as human beings.

Morris may be overwhelmed at the end by the waste that has been his life; but we are touched by the consideration that has been his heart. What happens next is that many readers, guided by an instinctive desire to transform the Holocaust ordeal into a heroic challenge, supported by critical enthusiasm for the same end, accept Morris Bober's behavior as a kind of existence exemplary of the camp experience. When Michael Brown writes of Morris that he "suffers honorably and quietly in order to maintain his Jewishness, his *menschlichkeit*, in a world that seeks to obliterate everything Judaism stands for," he transgresses the bounds of Morris's moral vision, and perhaps even Malamud's. Morris did not inhabit such a world, though European Jewry did. But by speaking of Morris as a victim "who knows what he suffers for and accepts the burden,"[10] the critic furnishes us with an easily assimilable, admirable profile of the Holocaust victim too, who bore his burden with honor and dignity and like Morris Bober may have paid for them with his life but never left in question that he was worthy of his sufferings and his sufferings worthy of him.

But literary tragedy, however modified (as in *The Assistant*) by a character's restraint, is not simply transferable to historical atrocity. Whatever Morris's burdens, he does not face slow starvation, exhaustion, daily beatings, untreated disease, he does not spend his nights picking lice from his scalp and the crevices of his clothing, he does not live in proximity to gas chamber and crematorium, redolent of extermination. How can we consider this kind of agony exemplary? To convert the focus or the scope of suffering in a Tsarist prison or a failing Brooklyn grocery store into metaphors of the Jewish experience of atrocity in the concentration camps is to abuse metaphor and to distort one half of the comparison. Certainly it is consoling for most of us to make inhuman conditions (and, often, less than "human" responses to them) appear more human; but that is an expression of our needs, not of the conditions we recoil from. Only a search for such consolation could lead someone to describe the Holocaust, as Brown does, as "a potent symbol of the dangers posed by the modern world to any person who would be different, to anyone who would insist on being a man."[11] Most Holocaust victims simply hoped to remain alive, nor did they see anything symbolic in what threatened to consume them.

Malamud himself is not guilty of such abstract assertions, though his conventional moral vision may unintentionally encourage them. There are terrible griefs, he knows, and there are inexpressible ones, and he does not confuse them. When he uses metaphors for the Holocaust, which he does more rarely than some of his critics insist, he keeps his distinctions clear. In the brief tale "The Loan" from *The Magic Barrel*, Lieb, his friend Kobotsky, and his wife Bessie all have their lost youths to mourn, with equal legitimacy. Jews have had a hard life in the twentieth century. But the miseries of Malamud's triumvirate are set into grim context when Bessie suddenly sniffs the burning bread, wrenches open the oven, and is greeted by a "metaphor" that reminds us unforgettably of the relativity of woe: "A cloud of smoke billowed out at her. The loaves in the trays were blackened bricks — charred corpses."[12] Does Malamud use this metaphor as a warning against Bessie's stifled charity, as an invitation to the rebirth of fraternal feeling from the ashes of Auschwitz? Or does he suggest that Bessie's Holocaust background has altered in her the spirit of charity that comes so easily to a Morris Bober? The didactic reading would neutralize the impact of the tale; the gloomier one finds some support from the two longer stories in *The Magic Barrel* that use authentic Holocaust survivors to dramatize their themes.

"The Lady of the Lake" *is* a warning, one so transparent that it diminishes the story's effect. Henry Levin, who has repudiated his Jewish identity and assumed the name of Henry R. Freeman, is tired of the limitations imposed on him by the past. This sentiment from the opening paragraph meets its mirror image in the closing lines when the Italian girl whom Levin wants to marry turns out to be a Jewish survivor of Buchenwald, who declares: "I can't marry you. We are Jews. My past is meaningful to me. I treasure what I suffered for."[13] Levin, who has denied to the girl that he is Jewish, is trapped by his own lie, and loses the girl. But we have here only the confrontation of two attitudes, not two human beings, since Levin's boredom with ancient history (including, presumably, the Holocaust) is as brittle and unconvincing as Isabella's survivor status, confirmed by numbers tattoed on the unlikely, not to say impossible area of her breasts. Her pitiful emblem, certainly not metaphor, of her Holocaust experience, cannot adequately project that experience, which remains locked behind the barriers of mere verbal assertion.

Malamud realizes more fully the dilemma of confrontation between Holocaust survivor and the vain, insensitive American Jew in his finest story using the Holocaust theme, "The Last Mohican." But even here, the focus is not on the survivor, Susskind, whose past is important in the fiction only as it impinges on the sensibilities of Fidelman, the American. And once again, unlike other Holocaust writers, Malamud is not concerned with evoking particular atrocities but with the failure or inability to imagine a kind of suffering that might penetrate and undermine our pompous facades of self-assurance. "Imagine all that history" exclaims Fidelman as he arrives in Rome and contemplates the Baths of Diocletian. But he has a more recent history to "imagine," the history that has reduced Susskind to an impoverished conman without funds, homeland, passport, or even meaningful identity. And this, for Malamud, is the fundamental challenge of the Holocaust, distinct from the romantic appeal that inspires Fidelman and insulates him from unpleasant truths: "History was mysterious, the remembrance of things unknown, in a way burdensome, in a way a sensuous experience. It uplifted and depressed, why he did not know, except that it excited his thoughts more than he thought good for him."[14] Fidelman lacks a language for understanding Susskind's past, and hence his own. As long as he depends on such conventional formulas, history, the past, his Jewish heritage, and the Holocaust experience will remain mysteries to him that have nothing to do with his obscure definitions. His search for Susskind through the ghetto, in the synagogue, to the Jewish cemetery, is a voyage of discovery, but until the very end he does not comprehend the signs that attempt to guide him. When the beadle in the synagogue mentions to the inquiring Fidelman "My own son — killed in the Ardeatine Caves," Fidelman murmurs his regrets, but surely has never heard of the place or of the famous Nazi atrocity that occurred there. And when his search takes him to the Jewish section of the cemetery, where Susskind sometimes works, Fidelman gazes at a monument inscribed "For my beloved father / . . . Murdered at Auschwitz by the barbarous Nazis / " but concludes with disappointment: "But no Susskind."[15] An adequate response, a true insight, would have been "But *yes* Susskind," since in this testament to Holocaust victims lay the history of his antagonist which would explain his behavior and in turn mirror the insufficiencies of Fidelman's life. But he is still blind to the necessity for such insight.

A dream vision leads to the transformative experience in Fidelman, a vision combining Christian and Jewish heritage with the fundamental question of Fidelman's vocation and Malamud's career: "Why is art?" He dreams of a Giotto fresco of St. Francis giving his garment to a poor knight, and intuitively learns what he must do—surrender to Susskind the suit that the survivor needs more than he does. Whether the waking "triumphant insight" that Fidelman arrives at corresponds exactly to the dream vision of charity, of the basic human gesture, the reader is left to interpret, since Fidelman's last words to Susskind, "All is forgiven," remain ambivalent. But Susskind's final words to Fidelman—"The words were there, but the spirit was missing,"[16]—are less ambiguous, and they lead directly to a final evaluation of Malamud's encounter with the Holocaust theme and some of the meanings that have been imposed on that encounter.

Malamud's involvement with the Holocaust has been minimal, possibly because he realized how uncongenial its atrocities were with his impatience at the modern devaluation of man. Facing the difficulty of translating such inhumanity into artistic vision, the writer exposes himself to the charge that the words are there but the spirit is missing, though not necessarily with the derogatory intent of Susskind's accusation. Holocaust atrocity is often not commensurate with spirit of any kind. Malamud critics like Michael Brown, however, noting accurately Malamud's desire to portray men in circumstances allowing them to achieve their potential humanity to the full, extend Malamud's limited ambitions toward the Holocaust beyond verifiable frontiers, ones certainly unverifiable in Malamud's fiction: "The inhumanity of the modern condition can be defeated, as the Jews defeated the Holocaust through their survival."[17] I suspect that Malamud himself would be astounded to find this principle deduced from his novels and stories about particular Jews affirming dignity despite their suffering. Immodest claims like these aggrandize his achievement without illuminating it. Malamud's indirect, tentative, circumscribed inroads on Holocaust reality leave untouched vast areas of harsh and unbearable experience that require fresh explorations of the conventional bond linking the word and the spirit. The results may be more frightening than Malamud's, but no less responsive and significant than his own to the cogent question which he himself raises: "Why is art?"

Notes

1. Albert Camus, *The Myth of Sisyphus and Other Essays*, trans. Justin O'Brien (New York: Vintage Books, 1955), 91.

2. Albert Camus, *The Plague*, trans. Stuart Gilbert (New York: Vintage Books, 1972), 287.

3. Quotes in Granville Hicks, "Literary Horizons," *Saturday Review* 46, No. 3 (12 Oct. 1963):32.

4. Robert Alter, "Bernard Malamud: Jewishness as Metaphor," in *After the Tradition: Essays on Modern Jewish Writing* (New York: E. P. Dutton, 1969), 125, 128.

5. Ibid., 118.

6. Bernard Malamud, *The Fixer* (New York: Farrar, Straus and Giroux, 1966), 333.

7. Ibid., 335.

8. Michael Brown, "Metaphor for Holocaust and Holocaust as Metaphor: *The Assistant* and *The Fixer* of Bernard Malamud Reexamined," *Judaism* 29 (Fall 1980):484, 487.

9. Bernard Malamud, *The Assistant* (New York: Avon Books, 1980), 102.

10. Brown, "Metaphor," 484.

11. Ibid., 487.

12. Bernard Malamud, *The Magic Barrel* (New York: Avon Books, 1980), 171.

13. Ibid., 120.

14. Ibid., 144.

15. Ibid., 157.

16. Ibid., 162.

17. Brown, "Metaphor," 488.

Yakov Bok   Lucio P. Ruotolo*

Whether it is because Bernard Malamud is a Jew or simply because he is sensitive to the changes in American life that distinguished the sixties, *The Fixer* illustrates a growing political emphasis in the existential novel. Yakov Bok, like the heroes previously discussed, discovers himself by resisting the temptation to submit to the impositional intentions of others. He too chooses to endure suffering in the apocalyptic faith that his ordeal will prove meaningful. At the end of the book, however, he reflects on the most important insight his suffering has won: "One thing I've learned, he thought, there's no such thing as an unpolitical man, especially a Jew. You can't be one without the other, that's clear enough."[1]

Whereas *Lord of the Flies* might be set at almost any time in the course of Western civilization, the locale of *The Fixer*, Russia just prior to the first world war, is the precondition for Yakov Bok's emergence as a hero. Georg Lukács would surely approve. And yet, while the social environment of Kiev and the shtetl is central to Malamud's artistic intention, his novel invites a critique of Lukács's thesis that existentially oriented writers move necessarily toward an ahistorical form of romanticism.

Paul Tillich perhaps best describes the quality of existential historicity that Lukács finds objectionable. He clarifies the distinction between existentialism and essentialism in his *Systematic Theology*: "Existence is estrangement and not reconciliation; it is dehumanization and not the expression of essential humanity. It is the process in which man becomes a thing and ceases to be a person. History is not the divine self-manifestation

*Reprinted by permission of the publishers from *Six Existential Heroes: The Politics of Faith* (Cambridge, Mass.: Harvard University Press, 1973), 121–39, 152–54. Copyright © 1973, President and Fellows of Harvard College.

but a series of unreconciled conflicts, threatening man with self-destruction. The existence of the individual is filled with anxiety and threatened by meaninglessness. With this description of man's predicament all existentialists agree and are therefore opposed to Hegel's essentialism. They feel that it is an attempt to hide the truth about man's actual state."[2] Tillich's words, as I shall suggest, illuminate Malamud's treatment of history. First, however, let us understand the basis of Lukács's objection to this type of analysis.

The literary expression of existential resignation, his argument goes, leads the best of modern writers to relinquish the concreteness of social history for "the ghostly aspect of reality."[3] Escapist literature, like all forms of psychological and linguistic positivism, presumes, he concludes, an unchanging, dogmatic view of human nature. At stake is man's capacity to *make* history through political action.[4]

Lukács speculates that in writers like Kierkegaard, the denial of unity between the inner and outer world leads necessarily to the isolation of man's inwardness. Threatened by cosmic absurdity, human personality comes to be identified more and more with an abstract subjectivity: "According to Kierkegaard, the individual exists within an opaque, impenetrable 'incognito.' "[5] In this sort of religious romanticism Lukács finds the seeds of a dangerous religiosity that ripens with Heidegger's glorification of Hitler.

To understand the motivation of writers like Kierkegaard and Malamud demands a distinction — one that Lukács is apparently unwilling to grant — between religious faith and the romantic quest for permanence. Ironically, it is precisely Kierkegaard's rejection of objective certainty implicit in all forms of dogmatism that motivates his religious faith. "The faith to doubt" describes Kierkegaard's intention here, and, if I am correct, Malamud's as well.[6] Consequently, authenticity remains for both writers a thoroughly imperfect achievement. This assumption clarifies Malamud's treatment of God and of value in *The Fixer*. The refusal of Kierkegaard and Malamud to sanctify their experience of estrangement — in Lukács's idiom their refusal to establish dogma out of the *condition humaine* — illustrates the distinction I wish to emphasize between existential and romantic heroism.

The Jewish-American novelist offers rich ground on which to explore this distinction. While writers like Bellow and Malamud experience (as did Kierkegaard) the aesthetic rewards of romantic self-pity, of creating a world bounded by the limits of their own personal suffering, they resist the appeal of *Weltschmertz*. Their heroes — Herzog, Morris Bober, Yakov Bok — struggle against capitulation to inner as well as outer compulsions that diminish growth. An inherent sense of "incognitio" leads them not outside history but rather to a more Biblical sense of time and place.[7] We recall here the qualities that drew Faulkner to the Old Testament: the concrete faith of a people rooted in society and yet strangely committed to a significance underlying all literal manifestations of diety.

As I have suggested in discussing *Go Down, Moses*, the Judaic conception of God lives in nameless mystery. This notion of the divine beyond all human grasping yet "living" in law and covenant posits an unacceptable contradiction to many Marxists, unless mediated through some form of Hegelian dialectic. To Christian and Jew, however, contradiction is a necessary paradox that accompanies the effort to establish relationship between finite "I" and eternal "Thou," between existence and essence. Whether or not by authorial intention, both the secular and overtly religious heroes under discussion experience some aspect of this paradox. The values that motivate their will to resist inauthenticity may be derived, as Tillich has suggested, from religious sources;[8] any such value, however, "exists" through the hero's capacity to endure history.

Yakov Bok is victimized through his own efforts to escape the consequences of being a man, in Malamud's idiom, of being a Jew. Deserted by his wife, Raisl, he has left the shtetl for Kiev, determined to find better days. Living as a Christian in a district forbidden to Jews, he finds himself implicated in the alleged ritualistic muder of a Russian school boy. During his long imprisonment, waiting for the trial, the fixer comes to see his decision to leave the shtetl as a denial both of himself and of history.

Although Yakov seems aware that the surrounding power structure of Russian society has deprived him of a humane standard of living, his response at the outset shuns action for rhetoric. He has good arguments and he uses them when talking with his father-in-law. "What can anybody do without capital?" he asks Shmuel with sustaining self-pity. The answer is: not much! "Opportunity here is born dead" (p. 7). Why then, the fixer asks himself, had he ignored his wife's plea to move from the shtetl? Looking back on the static nature of his past experience, Yakov blames the incapacity of body and spirit on his Jewish fate.

Like Shmuel, who owning almost nothing must sell his services, Yakov earns the barest living by fixing the broken ware of his impoverished community. When he finds work it is usually for nothing. The notion that he is more sinned against than sinning sustains him; drinking his tea unsweetened, the fixer gains more than the price of sugar: "it tasted bitter and he blamed existence" (p. 5). A Jewish Byron, Yakov's fatality is to live. Rhetoric is not the only means he finds for distraction: "Generally he moved faster than he had to, considering how little there was to do, but he was always doing something. After all, he was a fixer and had to keep his hands busy" (p. 9). His decision to move in many regards extends this need. Like an unlucky card player, he feels compelled to do something — "Change your place change your luck, people say" (p. 12). Without a basis for action, at least none grounded in his own ability to affect the course of events, Yakov finds that in leaving the shtetl for Kiev he has merely exchanged one prison for another. His choice to leave reflects the same captivity of spirit that held him rooted to the shtetl. More driven than driving, he does not experience the anticipated relief once on his journey, but, rather, "a deeper sense that he had had no choice about going than he wanted to admit" (p. 19).

From the opening sentence of Malamud's novel we are introduced through the fixer to a world in which the motions of life reflect the absence of inner decision. Making a living, in Yakov's terms, involves a pursuit of capital which impugns his power to be moved inwardly. Not unaware of this, he confesses early to Shmuel: "I fix what's broken — except in the heart" (p. 7). His incapacity is symbolized on the road to Kiev through the infuriating quiescence of the horse Shmuel has sold him for the journey. His failure to force movement from the unwilling creature conveys the psychological inability to project movement from within himself.

When the horse stands motionless, Yakov's dreams "of good fortune, accomplishment, affluence" are diminished by thought: "becalmed on the nag he thought blackly of his father-in-law, beat the beast with his fist, and foresaw for himself a useless future. Yakov pleaded with the animal to make haste" (p. 24). Such a projected act of self-hatred reveals the fixer's unconscious dependence upon those who victimize him. After selling the horse — "He's only given me trouble" — for fare to get across the Dnieper, he looks back at the nag whinnying after them from the shore: "Like an old Jew he looks, thought the fixer" (pp. 26–27). His new self has not supplied an alternative that is any more than the capitulation of existential preference. Even before the gates of Kiev, it is the reality "that the ferry had stopped running [that] sharpened the fixer's desire to get across the river." And when the anti-Semitic boatman, finishing his violent diatribe against the Jews with the hope that they will all be annihilated, makes the sign of the cross, Yakov confesses that he had to fight "an impulse to do the same" (p. 28). Like Invisible Man, Malamud's hero is growing into the realization that, driven by others, his life has been without a meaningful center. And, as the opening of the second chapter suggests, "Where do you go if you had been nowhere?" (p. 29).

Malamud's uprooted protagonists continually seek forgetfulness through cultural metamorphosis. Fidelman in "The Last Mohican" comes to Rome in the hope of escaping his past failures: "He had read that here, under his feet, were the ruins of Ancient Rome. It was an inspiring business, he, Arthur Fidelman, after all, born a Bronx boy, walking around in all this history."[9] The art student's first sight of the Eternal City is interrupted by an itinerant Israeli immigrant named Susskind who greets him with — "shalom." "My first hello in Rome," mutters Fidelman, "and it has to be a schnorrer."[10] In the course of this hilarious tale, Fidelman finds that he cannot escape the schnorrer's demand for charity without diminishing his own humanity. Existence for the Jew, as for the

Christian, remains a communal relationship. When Susskind steals the first and only chapter of his Giotto manuscript because Fidelman will not give him an old suit, Fidelman finds his new life deprived of a starting point. "He had tried writing the second chapter from notes in his possession but it had come to nothing. Always Fidelman needed something solid behind him before he could advance."[11] It is, of course, the concreteness of his Judaic past that his flight to Rome has sought to obliterate.

For Malamud, to deny one's own history is to deny one's capacity for growth; it means to commit the self necessarily to an abstract system of value that is distinct from the existential dimension of human personality. Fidelman's desire to be a critic of Renaissance art does not spring from his passion to know Giotto and consequently to explore new sources of creative energy. He seeks rather an academic respectability that answers his need for distraction.

The appeal of other cultures, particularly the exoticism of the unexperienced, is often an invitation for romantic regression. This does not mean ideas cannot cross cultures but rather that new ideas seldom eliminate the environment they seek to affect. If Buddhism, for example, were to appear as a transforming force in American religious life, its authentic manifestation would have a distinctly American inflection. The effort to leap out of one's historical culture reveals for most existentialists a choice for self-destruction. The self, formed always by the particularity of its past, cannot escape the effects of its history. Being is rooted in time. To deny one's history is equivalent to denying one's self.

If Malamud's heroes often make the wrong choice, understood in terms of the preceding discussion, they initiate thereby a process that facilitates self-discovery. When Susskind steals Fidelman's manuscript, thereby disrupting his plans for an orderly year of scholarship, Fidelman is lost because he has nothing to do. He has not yet learned to make use of nothing. His culminating pursuit of Susskind reminds us of the comic flight of Invisible Man before the advance of Ras the exhorter. In both cases, insight occurs in the process of disruptive passion. In the case of Invisible Man it is fear; with Fidelman it is hatred. Although one is pursued and the other pursues, both discover themselves in relationship to the pursuer and the pursued. Their moment of self-realization is accompanied by a decision to stop running from others and from themselves.

Malamud's novel opens with the sight of people "running somewhere . . . everybody in the same direction." On the particular morning we hear "something bad has happened." The crowd's movement, we discover, is motivated by the news of ritual murder.

Hatred of the Jew throughout *The Fixer* appears in Sartrean terms. If anti-Semitism involves a choice, it is a choice without reflection. The picture of the Jew impressed upon the common man has been stamped there by church and state. Kogin, one of Yakov's more humane jailors, expresses the source of his mythology concerning Jewish "blood ritual" in the frankest terms: "I've heard about it ever since I was a small boy" (p. 233). In establishing the metaphysical principle that evil is localized in the Jew, leaders reap the political benefits of a scapegoat while encouraging an unreflective unity in the masses they seek to control. As I have suggested earlier, Sartre's *Anti-Semite and Jew* describes this inclination in every man as essentially anti-intellectual. In bias, the anti-Semite finds the instant certainty that reflection so easily dissipates. He chooses the sort of static existence Lukács condemns. Running away continually from any intimation of inwardness, his hatred of the Jew becomes his compensatory need "to confuse [passion] with personality." The motivating force in his bias is not hatred of the Jew but a basic fear "of himself, of his own consciousness, of his liberty, of his instincts, of his responsibilities, of solitariness, of change, of society, and of the world."[12] So understood, his desperate movement is a movement without intention.

While Sartre's words define the victimizers of Yakov, they apply equally to the victim. The fixer's passivity reflects society's more general disinclination to be free. Malamud emphasizes his protagonist's willingness to be led in his submission to the boatman and before his employer Nikolai Maximovitch, as well as through his brief relationship with the latter's crippled daughter. If his hesitation to yield to Zina's seduction results from understandable caution, it also represents Yakov's more general failure to make history: "For himself he was willing to experience what there was to experience. But let her lead" (p. 49). When she suggests that they retire to her bedroom, he replies: "Whatever you say," prompting Zina to demand: "What do *you* say, Yakov Ivanovitch?" (p. 51). We soon find that he hesitates because of the thought she may be a virgin. Zina takes his concern as a sign of old-fashioned morality. What Yakov wishes is to avoid an involvement. "Should I stay or should I go?" he speculates. His choice to live as a goy, to make a new history for himself, is suddenly suspect. For the time being he is neither goy nor Jew. Without intention, he is still nowhere.

If Yakov lacks the spirit to commit himself wholeheartedly to one course of action or the other, the fault is not solely his own. The fixer's neutrality arises from a greater skepticism about the nature of life, both its depth and its surface. As Kogin sums up his personal history — "You plan one thing and get another. Life plays no favorites and what's the use of hoping for it?" (p. 271). Kiev, that holiest of Russian cities, mirrors Yakov's soul as in a larger respect Malamud intends it to reflect the operative values of Western civilization. What is "holy" in Kiev, which is to say the ontological presuppositions of existence in Czarist Russia, are precisely those idols of the market place that have prompted philosophers as diverse as Bacon and Sartre to redefine human value. In this regard, we should recall the latter's assumption that existentialism is a humanism.

If freedom and movement do not mean the freedom to gain capital and security, what is left to hope for? Yakov's answer appears only too obvious. His life in prison, reduced by torture to the barest level of existence, is a living death. Understandably, the deepest wish throughout his ordeal is to be freed from this suffering. In the gentle and just Bibikov he finds a "potential savior" defending his "innocence" on the grounds of human law. Yakov at this time, relying on Russian justice, hopes he will be judged not guilty. But if free, what then? "He had pictured himself freed, hurrying back to the shtetl, or running off to America if he could raise the funds" (p. 182). Trusting in the very system of values that has led him to crisis, he continues, naively, to ignore Shmuel's historical insight that as Jews—"we live in the middle of our enemies." The urgency of Yakov's hope reaches a critical stage when he discovers the body of the prosecuting magistrate hanging dead in the adjoining cell. With Bibikov's murder, he has nowhere to turn: "Who would help him now, what could he hope for? Where Bibikov had lived in his mind was a hopeless hole . . . 'Mama-Papa,' he cried out, 'save me! Shmuel, Raisl—anybody—save me! Some-body save me!' " (p. 183).

Avoiding the existential act of self-affirmation, the fixer retreats once again to feverish activity. Walking in circles, he invents fantastic plans for escaping, indulging himself in the pain of their impossibility: "He walked all day and into the night, until his shoes fell apart, and then walked in his bare feet on the lacerating floor. He walked in almost liquid heat with nowhere to go but his circular entrapment, striking himself on his journey—his chest, face, head, tearing his flesh, lamenting his life." The scene recalls an incident on the empty road to Kiev, when an old woman, kneeling before a large crucifix, repeatedly hit her head on the cold ground. The sight had given the fixer a headache, Malamud's humorous comment on his hero's psychological captivity. With metaphor become truth, self-mortification discloses another form of self-denial. In suffering for his innocence (he has done nothing) Yakov discovers his guilt: capable of neither love nor hate he is neutral. To resist, one must start from something; Yakov believes in nothing.

Opposition, while no foundation upon which to build social struc-ture, is often the catalyst for existential growth. Lukács sets this principle in literary terms. Among the great heroes of fiction, he suggests, "it is just the opposition between a man and his environment that determines the the development of his personality."[13] Without resistance man becomes a static extension of the environment that claims him by birth. In this light we understand why William Styron's Nat Turner must shake his fellow slaves from docile complicity into a realization of the white Southerner's uncompromising depravity before he can hope to initiate significant change. Echoing Bruno Bettelheim's experience of the Nazi concentration camp, Styron comments on the internal obstacles to self-liberation: "A Negro's most cherished possession is the drab, neutral cloak of anonymity he can manage to gather around himself, allowing him to merge faceless and nameless with the common swarm: impudence and misbehavior are, for obvious reasons, unwise, but equally so is the display of an uncommon distinction."[14]

"Neutrality" is an important word in *The Confessions of Nat Turner* and *The Fixer*. The protagonist of each novel opposes his own inclination to take the course of least resistance; like Ralph before Jack Merridew's painted tribe, both withstand the temptation to merge with the enemy. The notion of rebellion, like that of revolution, had been anathema to the essentially apolitical Yakov. While he admits early to Shmuel that by predilection he ought to be a socialist, he confesses distaste for all forms of political activism: "the truth of it is I dislike politics, though don't ask me why. What good is it if you're not an activist? I guess it's my nature." The fixer's retreat into philosophical fatalism is another effort to avoid existential commitment. Dismissing God — "A meshummed gives up one God for another. I don't want either" — he allows an uncritical self-interest to define his concerns: "We live in a world where the clock ticks fast while he's on his timeless mountain staring in space. He doesn't see us and he doesn't care. Today I want my piece of bread, not in Paradise." Yakov's conception of the Judaic God, ironically abstract, reveals his preference for speculative resolutions: "I incline toward the philosophical" (p. 17). Once he has been arrested for murder, however, rationalization collapses. The picture that remains is one of crawling subservience with neither dignity nor meaning.

Following the death of the prisoner Fetyukov, "shot for disobeying orders and resisting a guard" (p. 184), the fixer is lectured on the consequence of insubordination. The instructions posted on the wall of his cell, like the demands upon Invisible Man, instruct him in the ways of his world: "Obey all rules and regulations without question" (p. 187). The alternative is to face death. Stunned by the loss of yet another individual who had shown him sympathy — Fetyukov, though a Christian, had urged him not to lose hope — Yakov submits. Unable to walk, he follows the warden's command and crawls "like a dog" to the infirmary. Through resistance, however, the uneducated peasant Fetyukov has preserved the idea of opposition. His act stands in meaningful contrast both to the fixer's temporary capitulation and to Gronfein, the informer whose betrayal of Yakov arises from a candid fear of death. Gronfein's submission to the existing power structure holds a certain pragmatic validity. Against such force all talk of heroism appears naively idealistic.

In the past, Yakov had been as casual about death as he had been about life: "Death," he tells Shmuel, "is the last of my worries" (p. 14). The deaths of Bibikov and Fetyukov and Gronfein's arguments for survival threaten his cultivated disinterest. Deprived of the means of doing anything — "His hands ached of emptiness" (p. 201) — and facing a charge that could result in his own execution, he tries to find distraction in thought. Spinoza, whom he has read most recently, comes readily to mind, but now it is not philosophical principles he recollects but the picture of a man like himself, denied by his own Jewish community, who "died young, poor and persecuted, yet one of the freest of men" (p. 207). The question of freedom recurs as the fixer's thoughts turn to fragments of Psalms once memorized. No longer safely abstract, the notion of God becomes an image of himself "pursuing his enemies with God at his side, but when he looked at God all he saw or heard was a loud Ha Ha. It was his own imprisoned laughter" (p. 209). Yakov cannot escape such implications.

When charged with revolutionary intentions, however, he reverts once more to his former neutrality: "I am not a revolutionist. I am an inexperienced man. Who knows about such things? I am a fixer" (p. 226). We know this is sham. Yakov is not a man without experience but, rather, one who has sought to deny his own experience. Back in his cell after the interview with Grubeshov, Yakov's personal crisis reaches a peak as he identifies with his own victimizers in one last orgy of self-effacement: "His fate nauseated him. Escaping from the Pale he had at once been entrapped in prison. From birth a black horse had followed him, a Jewish nightmare. What was being a Jew but an everlasting curse? He was sick of their history, destiny, blood guilt" (p. 227). As he protests too much, his conversion is imminent.

Malamud's secular hero rediscovers the liberating depth of Judaic life through two unlikely sources, Spinoza and Jesus. His imprisonment reveals the historicity of Jesus in much the same manner as it had found in the life of Spinoza new possibilities for human freedom: "the story of Jesus fascinated him . . . he was deeply moved when he read how they spat on him and beat him with sticks; and how he hung on the cross at night. Jesus cried out help to God but God gave no help. There was a man crying out in anguish in the dark, but God was on the other side of his mountain . . . Christ died and they took him down. The fixer wiped his eyes" (p. 232). As in Styron's *Nat Turner*, God's absence paradoxically sparks religious faith.

Each of Yakov's pictures of God reflects stages of the hero's inner development. When trapped within himself, the fixer's image mirrored the reality of self-chosen solipsism. The widening of his sense of experience to include the being of others and the reality of time, past and present, results in an historicized image of God.

For history to begin, Israel must accept God's offer of covenant. Pursuing this insight, Yakov's thoughts lead him, like Kierkegaard, to consider God's existence as dependent upon man's willingness to respond. For God to be (in history), man must believe. God has chosen the Hebrews to preserve him, Yakov reasons: "He covenants, therefore he is" (p. 239). The historical reality of God involves the "experience" of God, for the Christian through Christ, for the Jew through covenant. In each case, the religious experience posits I and Thou. Here, the fixer's thinking, through its secular disposition, takes an interesting turn. Stressing the personal quality of Thou, his conception of God loses the perfection of an abstracted deity. When God is bound up with *zoon politikon*, his attributes take on the quality of phenomena ("things for us") as distinct from noumena ("things in themselves").[15] Such a God does not answer man's need for escape. The resistance of bourgeois Christianity to the idea of Jesus as a man with human needs and functions suggests its desire to find in abstract ideality compensation for the imperfection of existence.[16] Similarly, the secular as well as the "religious" bourgeoisie have consistently sought relief from the complexities of an industrialized society through the worship of idealized heroes. The phenomenon of hero worship in nineteenth and twentieth century Western society, apparent at every level of the social scale, reveals impulses that shun history for romance.[17]

The fixer's iconoclastic conception of an imperfect God opposes all such idolatry. Yakov speculates that God is so human, He may even envy man his humanness: "Maybe he would like to be human, it's possible, nobody knows" (p. 240). His words recall Shmuel's earlier apologetic: "Remember, if He's not perfect, neither are we" (p. 18). Out of such imperfection, as I have suggested, arises the efficacy of relationship. The God unaffected by the human condition, appears, like Spinoza's abstract deity, on a timeless mountain, an "eternal, infinite idea" careless of that which cannot touch him. Experience cannot pull this conception of deity from the realm of noumena to phenomena.

The idea of an experiencing God leads to certain difficulties. As a Jew, Yakov cannot posit an intermediary in the form of Bibikov, Jesus, or Jaweh, and so he is confronted once again with the question: How can an eternal God "suffer" or "love"? With existential passion, Yakov reasons: "If God's not a man he has to be" (p. 274). The acknowledgment that God and The Law depend upon his response transforms the fixer's concept of experience. No longer the passive recipient of luck or patronage, he begins to look upon his life in terms of the history that has claimed him. His identity, no longer conceived as an abstract potentiality, moving through or standing aloof from historical events, takes on new immediacy: "the experience was his; it was worse than that, it was he. He was the experience." In realizing that his existence is bound up with his suffering ("I suffer therefore I am"), Yakov finds himself reunited with his past, personified through Shmuel and Raisl. Resignation leads him to a new maturity:[18] "I learned this but what good will it do me? Will it open the prison doors? Will it allow me to go out and take up my poor life again? Will it free me a little once I am free? Or have I only learned to know what my condition is—that the ocean is salty as you are drowning, and though you knew it you are drowned? Still, it was better than not knowing. A man had to learn, it was his nature" (p. 316).

Were *The Fixer* to end here, it would portray Lukács's conception of existential resolution. Malamud's intention, however, is far from realized. As Yakov's suffering increases following Shmuel's illegal visit, he experiences a heightened sense of social responsibility. Shmuel, for example, faces arrest as a consequence of his involvement just as Bibikov paid with his life to uphold the law through defending him. The fixer's new awareness has won him more suffering. But now it is suffering *for* something other than his own psychological liberation. " 'I'll live,' he shouts in his cell, 'I'll wait, I'll come to my trial' " (p. 275). No longer neutral, he sees that life involves reciprocity, that he can suffer for others as well as for himself. The insight has both tragic and political implications.

Kogin, we remember, despairs of meaning in the world. His own cynicism regarding love mirrors the fixer's, for both have seen the failure of all their plans. Our first sight of the jailer anticipates his future actions and hints of his role as Yakov's double. Outside the fixer's cell "he paced the corridor as if he were the prisoner" (p. 190), his gaunt face worn with the marks of worry. Listening to the Jew reading about the trial and suffering of Jesus, he sighs with sympathy; when his prisoner requests a small favor, a piece of paper and pencil, Kogin does not return to hear him reading the gospels. The reasons for his unwillingness to become involved recalls Gronfein. "Don't think I am not aware of your misfortunes," he confesses, "but to be frank with you I don't allow myself to dwell on it much." If he helps the fixer, Kogin adds prophetically: "I could get myself shot" (p. 271).

His frankness about his own motives parallels the fixer's growing honesty about himself. While the jailer's service to his prisoner remains for the moment advisory — quoting the scriptural promise he has heard from Yakov's lips that "he who endures to the end will be saved" (p. 272) — Kogin soon perceives that to live this faith means to sacrifice safety and take sides against those who would deny man hope and justice. Intervening to save the fixer, he gives his life for the same principle that has motivated Yakov's endurance: " 'Hold on a minute, your honor,' said Kogin to the Deputy Warden. His deep voice broke. 'I've listened to this man night after night, I know his sorrows. Enough is enough, and anyway it's time for his trial to begin' " (p. 326). His heroic resistance helps form the events that follow.

When Grubeshov first called Yakov an animal, the latter rebelled neither outwardly nor inwardly. Now, his decision to live, to come to his trial, accompanies the rage he experiences toward those who seek to dehumanize life. Facing Grubeshov's pharisaic judgment, he is no longer safely defensive: " 'And death is what you will get. It's on your head, Bok.' 'On yours,' said Yakov. 'And for what you did to Bibikov' " (p. 302).

Yakov's realization that the meaning of his life has expanded to include other people leads him to reconsider the reality of those external events that placed him in prison. Outside the shtetl, he has experienced the contradictions of living in a world where kindness is rewarded by suffering and reflection merely foresees complexity. "Who, for instance, *had* to go find Nikolai Maximovitch lying drunk in the snow and drag him home to start off an endless series of miserable events?" (p. 314). Stepping into history, however, *has* made a difference. An inner voice, in the image of Bibikov, professes Yakov's new sense of Being and time: "if you should ever manage to get out of prison, keep in mind that the purpose of freedom is to create it for others" (p. 319). In developing this insight, Malamud employs a metaphor that recurs with significant frequency in his fiction: "Once you leave you're out in the open; it rains and snows. It snows history, which means what happens to somebody starts in a web of events outside the personal. It starts of course before he gets there. We're all in history, that's sure, but some are more than others, Jews more than some. If it snows not everybody is out in it getting wet. He had been doused. He had to his painful surprise, stepped into history more deeply than others" (p. 314).

Snow, throughout Malamud's work, symbolizes the flux and possibility of history. Those who remain passive under the falling snow, like the evicted Kessler in "The Mourners," are doomed to a life without meaning. It is the great leveller of man's humanity. Under a common blanket of whiteness, Kessler's figure appears indistinguishable from the pieces of dispossessed goods that surround him. His failure to survive history represents his failure to love. Like Dante, who stands in the background of many of his works, Malamud characterizes the incapacity of mankind to love through figures of frozen immobility. Frank Alpine's name expresses the problem.

The discomfort of snow is not solved by moving to warmer climates. Malamud's characters continually face the temptation to flee the cold. Winter torments Helen in *The Assistant*: "She ran from it, hid in the house."[19] When she meets Frank Alpine in the pubic library (where she came often to escape the cold), the threat of intimacy frightens her. Walking home with him, under a cloudless sky, she hides her growing sense of vulnerability with a revealing non sequitur: "It feels like snow." What Helen dreads is the possibility that love will draw her into history. She shuns being out in the open where others (those who hate as well as those who love) may choose to involve themselves in her life and perhaps her death.

Snow, throughout *The Assistant*, points us toward an openness which includes life and death. Morris Bober dies as a result of clearing it from the sidewalk in front of his store, an act that paradoxically fulfills his need for a wideness he has not found in America:

> The spring snow moved Morris profoundly. He watched it falling, seeing in it scenes of his childhood, remembering things he thought he had forgotten. All morning he watched the shifting snow . . . he felt an irresistible thirst to be out in the open.
> "I think I will shovel snow," he told Ida at lunchtime.[20]

Frank Alpine, in choosing to make himself a Jew, preserves the old grocer's faith by taking up his burden. Again Malamud conveys the inspiration for this act through the metaphor of snow. The assistant has read a story about St. Francis in which the saint awakens one winter night with grave doubts about his religious life. Unable to sleep with the thought that he will never marry and have children like other people, he walks out into the snow. In an act of creative spontaneity the saint shapes a family out of snow, wife and children, then, kissing them, goes inside to sleep in peace. Frank, whose inner turmoil has continually led him to further acts of self-destruction, senses the significance of the tale.

Yakov's history begins when he sees Maximovitch half buried in the snow. At the close of the novel as he rides, through flurries of snow, toward his trial, he has learned to live in an imperfect world. Like Frank Alpine, his freedom is manifest in his choice to create order in a world of internal and external chaos. When an explosion wounds a cossack guard riding next to the carriage, the fixer is not immobilized by the apparent absurdity of this incident. The wounded man, his leg shattered by the bomb, looks through the window at him, "in horror and anguish . . . as though to say 'What has my foot got to do with it?' " (p. 331). No longer paralyzed by his own guilt, Yakov's thoughts direct him to the heart of the matter: The guard's suffering, like his own, is the consequence of living in "the poorest and most reactionary state in Europe" (p. 333). Conjuring a vision of Nicholas the Second, Yakov charges the Tsar of Russia with responsibility for the failure.

Malamud's final scene reveals the passive and self-pitying Tsar as a projection of the fixer's former self. Admitting that inequity exists in Russia, Nicholas defends his own failure to act on fate: "I never wanted the crown, it kept me from being my true self, but I was not permitted to refuse." Like Yakov in the shtetl, his weakness reflects an age that has lost faith in its own capacity to make history. The Tsar's continual plea— "What can a man do. . . ? One is born as he is born and that's all there is to it"—culminates with a final disavowal of responsibility: "I am the victim, the sufferer for my people. What will be will be" (pp. 333–334).

A concentration camp such as Treblinka existed, George Steiner suggests, "because some men have built it and almost all other men let it be."[21] Yakov sees that neutrality masks compliance, that in doing nothing Nicholas is equally guilty. Raising his pistol, he shoots the Tsar (Russia's "Little Father") dead. The act is a symbolic one. Like Invisible Man, he is determined to be his own father. When Nicholas asked him—"Are you a father?" the fixer replied—"With all my heart," for he has taken responsibility for Raisl's illegitimate child, as well as for his own deeper feelings. No longer a fatalist, Yakov's last words, "Long live Revolution! Long live liberty!" affirm his belief that there are ways to reverse history. It remains to be seen, for Malamud as well as for Golding and Ellison, if politics can ever be an expression of love.

Notes

1. Bernard Malamud, *The Fixer*, copyright 1966 by Bernard Malamud (New York, Farrar, Straus and Giroux, 1966), p. 335. Reprinted by permission of Farrar, Straus & Giroux, Inc. All page references are to this edition.

2. Paul Tillich, *Systematic Theology*, vol. II (Chicago, University of Chicago Press, 1967), p. 25. Tillich's response to the question of whether he regarded himself as an existentialist was often equivocal. At Stanford in 1965 he replied: "Fifty-fifty."

3. George Lukács, *The Meaning of Contemporary Realism* (London, Merlin Press, 1963), p. 25.

4. For a discussion of this idea see George Lichtheim, *George Lukács* (New York, Viking Press, 1970), pp. 52–53.

5. *Contemporary Realism*, p. 27. From a theological perspective, Rubem A. Alves in *A Theology of Human Hope* (Washington, D.C., Corpus Books, 1969), while acknowledging that "existentialism has a great affinity with political humanism" (p. 34), describes Kierkegaard as one whose "thought moves in the sphere of a radical asceticism regarding everything that means time or objective" (p. 36). Like Lukács, Alves considers Kierkegaard's thought essentially ahistorical.

6. The phrase is the title of M. Holmes Hartshorne's *The Faith to Doubt* (Englewood Cliffs, N.J., Prentice-Hall, 1963).

7. The distinction William Barrett makes between Hebraism and Hellenism is relevant here. *Irrational Man* (New York, Doubleday, 1958), chap. IV.

8. *Systematic Theology*, vol. II, pp. 25–26.

9. Bernard Malamud, *The Magic Barrel* (New York, Farrar, Straus & Cudahy, 1953), p. 162.

10. Ibid., p. 157.

11. Ibid., p. 172.

12. Jean-Paul Sartre, *Anti-Semite and Jew*, trans. G. J. Becker (New York, Schocken Books, 1968), pp. 52–53.

13. *Contemporary Realism*, p. 28.

14. William Styron, *The Confessions of Nat Turner* (New York, Random House, 1967), p. 65.

15. Lichtheim, pp. 58–59: Lichtheim suggests that all forms of positivism, from the realism of the scholastics to the presuppositions of social and natural science, tend to ignore this distinction.

16. The pursuit of such transcendence wherein all human contradiction is mediated and existence stripped of contingency often claims a transhistorical, "religious" intention. Deprived of history, the holy finds its only sanction in a world above the world. For a discussion of the Greek character of this assumption see Tom F. Driver, *The Sense of History in Greek and Shakespearean Drama* (New York, Columbia University Press, 1960). Thorleif Boman, *Hebrew Thought Compared with Greek* (New York, W. W. Norton, 1970) also develops some relevant distinctions here.

17. A recent example of the need for charismatic leadership is found in the attack of ten black writers on Styron's *Nat Turner*. Indicting Styron for creating a neurotic protagonist, replete with white America's "hang-ups," these critics largely refuse to see the historical Nat Turner in anything but idealistic terms. Eugene D. Genovese's review of *Ten Black Writers Respond*, *The New York Review of Books*, September 12, 1968, p. 34, makes the following point: "those who look to history to provide glorious moments and heroes invariably are betrayed into making catastrophic errors of political judgment. Specifically, revolutionaries

do not need Nat Turner as a saint; they do need the historical truth of the Nat Turner revolt, its strength and its weakness."

18. Eric Levy develops this idea of historical redemption in a 1971 Stanford Ph.D. thesis. Ihab Hassan suggests, on the other hand, that the widespread presence of revulsion in modern thought "is a confession that man finds no redemption in history." *Radical Innocence* (Princeton, N.J., Princeton University Press, 1961), p. 13.

19. Bernard Malamud, *The Assistant* (New York, Farrar, Straus and Cudahy, 1957), p. 88.

20. Ibid., p. 221.

21. George Steiner, *Language and Silence* (New York, Atheneum, 1967), p. 156.

The American Schlemiel Abroad: Malamud's Italian Stories and the End of American Innocence   Christof Wegelin*

"What is an American?" The question asked by the French immigrant Hector St. John de Crèvecoeur even before the Revolutionary War was at an end has haunted many Americans down to our own time. Our colonial beginnings left us with the task of defining our national identity, and from the same source came the habit of defining it in terms of our deviation from European patterns — social, political, moral, cultural patterns — a habit reinforced by later waves of immigration. All white Americans, after all, have European ancestors. This is why until recently most of our major novelists sooner or later felt they had to come to terms with the Old World and why many of them have explored their relationship to it by writing "international" stories and novels in which Americans are brought in contact and conflict with Europeans and European ways of life.

One element is universal in this literature throughout the nineteenth century, whether we think of travel essay or fiction and whether the focus be aesthetic or social or political: the contrast between a new Western world where, to paraphrase Henry James, the forms of human life are being forged in a deafening daily present, and on the other hand, a Europe where the past lingers over the present like a dream made visible. The American view of this contrast has tended to have a strong moral flavor derived from the seventeenth-century Edenic vision of the early settlers. In the late nineteenth century, when more and more Americans travelled in Europe and their social adventures were recorded in the burgeoning genre of the "international novel," ignorance of the world and artless manners on their part were therefore given great moral value. But

*Reprinted, with permission, from *Twentieth Century Literature* 19 (April 1973):77–88.

this view went under with other optimisms in 1914 in the cataclysm of what used to be called The Great War.

After 1918 the fiction in which Americans recorded their experience of Europe changed. The country-houses and genteel drawing-rooms of the pre-war decades, the realm of social conquest and of marriage between European nobility and American wealth—these were replaced by cafés, studios, fiestas, with their less eminent, more casual alignments. In the "century of the common man," private scenes gave way to public at the same time that relationships and roles lost their official and representative functions. The young American women of Howells and James, with their bright spiritual spontaneity, turned into the sophisticated, rootless, and sometimes deadly heroines of Edith Wharton and Scott Fitzgerald; tycoons and their wives were displayed by journalists and artists. The genteel society and the American innocence of former years still haunted a number of lesser novels often imitative of James, but the more pominent, the more original and more representative authors projected other scenes, other social elements and other themes.

Now, forty years later, we are even further along the road of historical change. Another world war, political and technological revolutions, and the cultural enrichment of the American scene have transformed the nature of transatlantic confrontation. In 1955 one of our leading quarterlies initiated a symposium to assess the state of American culture. The question of the American relation to Europe arose repeatedly, but the only thing that seemed certain was that transatlantic cultural relations were not what they used to be. Mid-twentieth-century America seemed less culturally deprived than the America of Hawthorne or James, Europe less compelling.

Fiction translates this general cultural view into dramatic and psychological terms. In the relations between Americans and Europeans contrast now is minimized. No longer is the American in Europe an innocent abroad. Having participated in wars and revolutions which have naturalized violence and cruelty, he has become an equal among the knowing, the corrupt. In this respect the difference between what followed the first world war and what followed the second is slight. The new relationship is documented by the fiction of Hemingway, Dos Passos, McAlmon in the twenties and thirties, by Hawkes, Styron, and others in the forties, fifties and sixties. The search of black Americans for their cultural roots poses a special problem, which may well help us to realize that the old transatlantic perspective is becoming less pertinent to the assessment of the American place in the world. But this loss of pertinence is implicit in much of the international fiction since World War I: generally speaking, the white American in this fiction is no longer in conflict with the European but at one with him in cruelty, anxiety, need.

In a moral sense, then, this late stage in the history of the American relation to Europe as recorded by the novelists may be described as a return from the western paradise to the world. If in the white man's version this history began in the seventeenth century with the escape of the Pilgrims from the bondage of the Old World into a new Canaan and later into the moral health of Jeffersonian society, the return movement too began very early — first to the mementos and monuments of the American past in Europe (for example, in Irving), then to the social complexities and the intellectual and artistic resources our ancestors had abandoned (in Cooper, James, and others). And now, finally, it has come to the darkening condition of the human community independent of national variants. This last is frequently the subject of our contemporaries, even when they write about Americans in Europe.

Bernard Malamud is an interesting case in point. He is a sophisticated artist aware of his literary antecedents. Titles like *A New Life*, "The Last Mohican," "Lady of the Lake" may suggest this. His Italian stories contain numerous Jamesian motifs, sometimes in strangely Kafkaesque distortion, as in "Behold the Key," where Rome remains as impenetrable to the American visitor as Kafka's castle is to K. "Lady of the Lake," another of his Italian stories, stays even closer to James though demonstrating clearly the change a century has brought in the American consciousness. Like Christopher Newman, a representative American from James's early work, Malamud's Henry R. Freeman is abroad in search of romance. But whereas James's Newman lives up to the large implications of his name, Freeman is not really Freeman but Henry Levin, a floorwalker at Macy's department store. And his hope for a romantic marriage to nobility collapses, not because the lady he courts turns out to be only the caretaker's daughter, not because she is less than he imagined, but because she treasures what she has suffered for in Buchenwald, treasures, that is, the very Jewish solidarity which he has denied by changing his name. "Lady of the Lake" plays a variation on the traditional contest between natural and artificial aristocracy which James's Newman, one of Nature's noblemen, wins hands down. In Malamud, the lady's title may be spurious, but her innate nobility has been certified in experience; it is Freeman who turns out to be sham. The basic pattern of the story — the American's quest for romance and his discovery of reality — is traditional, but innocence has ceased to be the American's distinguishing mark.

Malamud's most extended and most interesting treatment of the American in Europe is contained in *Pictures of Fidelman* (1969), which unites three earlier stories of Arthur Fidelman, an American in Italy, with three recent additions to round out his career in what may be called an episodic novel. Some of the chapters again invite comparison with James's treatment of similar themes and in fact become more meaningful when the reader is aware of the parallels. But the moral ambience of the older writer is changed almost beyond recognition, indeed is changed so much that at first glance it may seem frivolous to try and fit Malamud's schlemiel into the traditional pattern. But when the attempt is made, the parallels and incongruities between Malamud and James reveal that the Fidelman cycle traces the very curve of the American's emancipation from his earlier roles on the international scene.

The search for romance, in life and in the stores of European art, and the discovery of reality, particularly the reality of the quester's own true nature and condition, are again at the thematic core. But Fidelman is an artist manqué and the particular form his search takes is determined by his bungling efforts to find his true vocation, his proper relation to the artistic life. As the epigraph from Yeats says,

> The intellect of man is forced to choose
> Perfection of the life, or of the work. . . .

But Fidelman wants both. And his story consists of a series of picaresque adventures in Rome, Milan, Florence and Venice, in which he tries to find his way between the demands of his intellectual and physical needs at the same time that a series of confrontations with various Old-World characters leads him to self-realization — as Jew, as lover, as artist. Italy supplies the traditional locale of the artistic quest. But the divergences between Fidelman's experiences and those of his predecessors become increasingly emphatic from story to story, the tone increasingly ribald, Fidelman's adventures more and more indecorous, extravagant. His career is a burlesque of the earlier patterns of transatlantic discovery and can in fact be summed up as the transformation of a nineteenth-century American cultural pilgrim into a twentieth-century man stripped of genteel pretensions and *thereby* achieving the harmony of life and work.

We first meet him in "Last Mohican" in front of the railway station of Rome "absorbed in his first sight of the Eternal City." Although he is equipped in the best twentieth-century fashion with tweed suit and Dacron shirt his stance is old-fashioned, that of the innocent from the New World (perhaps the western barbarian or noble savage ironically suggested by the title) before the wonders of an old civilization. The concluding lines of the first paragraph make this clear: Fidelman "was conscious of a certain exaltation that devolved on him after he had discovered directly across the many-vehicled piazza stood the remains of the Baths of Diocletian. Fidelman remembered having read that Michelangelo had helped in converting the baths into a church and convent, the latter ultimately changed into the museum that presently was there. 'Imagine,' he muttered. 'Imagine all that history.' " The opening passage represents an American archetype and may remind us, for instance, of Hawthorne's sense a century earlier that in Rome all ages are simultaneously present. Fidelman is conscious of an exaltation and a role inherited from earlier Americans; the role has devolved on him. Malamud's choice of the verb is precise though quiet. That role of representing the New World, the role of the Mohican, is played by the Jew, gazing in innocent wonder at a civilization after all younger than his own, gives the portrait added ironic point and helps to set the comic tone which is to dominate the book.

Fidelman's representative quality is underlined by his mission. Feeling that he has failed as a painter, he has turned to art history and come to Italy to write a critical study of Giotto. But the present will not let him indulge his essentially sentimental vision of the past. Almost at once he is pursued by Susskind, a mysterious refugee from Germany, Hungary, Poland, even from Israel, a Wandering Jew and incarnation of the reality of poverty and want. Susskind keeps demanding that Fidelman give him one of his two suits, a demand Fidelman refuses: "All I have is a change from the one you now see me wearing. Don't get the wrong idea about me, Mr. Susskind. I'm not rich," he says reasonably and truthfully. But Susskind keeps up the pressure and ultimately, in a dream revealing himself as the Virgil to Fidelman's Dante, teaches him that his study of the past has been an escape from responsibility, that the knowledge of the past must prove itself in the present. Fidelman has failed as art critic; his indifference to the refugee's need shows that he has not understood the lesson in charity taught by Giotto's Saint Francis, who gives his golden robe to a poor old knight.

This lesson is the first of many suggesting the interdependence of the two perfections, of the life and the work. It causes Fidelman to shed the inherited pilgrim's role. Other lessons follow until in the end he finds his own proper mode of existence and returns home.

In "Still Life," the second story, he has gone back to painting; the investigation of history has given way to the creative exploration of his own experience. Still in Rome, he rents a corner in the studio of a young woman painter, and the story traces his progress as painter and lover. Landlady and canvas are equally resistant until one day, when Fidelman gazes down on the rooftops and monuments of Rome, still feeling a stranger to its elusive spirit, a thought strikes him: "if you could paint this sight, give it its quality in yours, the spirit belonged to you. History become aesthetic!" And if history, why not Annamaria, his landlady? "What more intimate possession of a woman!" But only when he remembers the lesson of the great masters and paints her as "Virgin with Child" does he succeed. Then he catches an immediate likeness, then he penetrates to the mystery of her soul: for she too has had a child, incestuously conceived and murdered in a moment of terror. With the aid of the traditional archetype, the Madonna and Child, the artist's imagination has discovered not only her beauty but also the guilt which she has never dared tell the priest. In a sense Fidelman has become her confessor. In a final tableau the physical and moral mingle grotesquely. He has dressed up to paint himself as priest, and seeing him thus, the woman is moved to pour out her guilt and demand that he impose penance; much, much more than prayers, she demands. "In that case," says Fidelman, "better undress." "Only . . . if you keep your vestments on," she insists. The cassock is too clumsy, but he agrees to the biretta, which must do for the Jewish skull cap. In the final act it is the Jew who possesses her, the Jew represented from the start by the emblematic Star of David concealed in his pictures possessing the Catholic Annamaria represented by an emblematic black cross always concealed in hers. "Annamaria undressed in a swoop," the story concludes. "Her body was extraordinarily lovely, the flesh glowing. In her bed they tightly embraced. She clasped his buttocks, he cupped hers. Pumping slowly he nailed her to her cross." The image, boldly merging crucifixion and fornication, represents his discovery of the Roman sense of guilt and of his own different nature. The story, it must be added, is, like the whole book, a masterpiece of tonal variations and atonal combinations — solemn, crass, ironic and mocking and always intriguing — which may puzzle us at times but which underline the change a century has brought about in the American exploration of Europe — in the nature of the quester and of his quest.

In the rest of the "pictures" of Fidelman the development begun in "Still Life" continues. Generally he grows in self-knowledge and courage as he declines in respectability. In "Naked Nude" he is held captive in a hotel run for the convenience of prostitutes by a brace of strongmen, lovers, since in this modern and democratic seraglio the safety of the eunuch of old has been replaced by that of the homosexual. The price of his freedom is that he help them steal Titian's great picture of the Venus of Urbino from a nearby museum by painting a copy which they will substitute for the original. Fidelman does not like to steal from another painter, but his captors assure him that it is the way of art as it is the way of the world: "Tiziano will forgive you. Didn't he steal the figure of the Urbino from Giorgione? Didn't Rubens steal the Andrian Nude from Tiziano? Art steals and so does everybody." But Fidelman wants to be honest, at least to himself, and what follows is a variation on the theme of the vital relation between life and art. He tries innumerable schemes for producing the copy — painting over photographic reproductions, studying models of every kind — all without success until one day he accidentally sees one of the ladies of the house naked. The sight fires his memory and imagination and he paints every nude he has ever seen into his picture, every woman he has ever dreamed of or lusted after. Ultimately it is the life urge, including the knowledge that if he does not produce the gangsters will do away with him, which brings success in the artistic task. The nude he paints is "naked," as the title of the story proclaims, because it represents his own life, himself: "The Venus of Urbino, c'est moi!"

The liberation of the creative flow initiates the liberation of the man. First the gangsters give him his passport back, the official token of his identity. When the theft of the Titian is accomplished he is to receive his stipulated pay, the return fare to America. But the master stroke of the author and his creature is yet to come. At the last moment, in the dark museum, when the original has been taken off the wall and is standing next to the copy on the floor, Fidelman rehangs the Titian and steals his own copy. At this moment, he becomes superior to the accompanying gangster, knocks him unconscious and, sacrificing the promised reward, achieves his freedom — from more than his jailers. For by choosing his own creation he has chosen himself. The story ends, as many of Malamud's stories do, in a suggestive tableau: after the escape Fidelman unwraps the Venus in the pitch black night and "by the light of numerous matches adores his handiwork." This proud obeisance distinguishes him radically from his earlier self, the cultural pilgrim and art historian of his first entry on the European stage.

For five years "Naked Nude" (1963) seemed to record the triumphal end of the saga of Fidelman. Then Malamud took his burlesque odyssey up again, ultimately to bring him home, from Europe as well as from the existential solitude. "A Pimp's Revenge" finds Fidelman in Florence in need of further liberation, this time from apron strings, another tie to the past. If his struggle with Titian led him to an almost Emersonian declaration of independence from the courtly muses of Europe, his struggle with a childhood photograph of himself with his mother teaches him a lesser dimension of his nature. He is engaged in a dual struggle: trying to paint his masterpiece, a "Mother and Son," and finding the right relation with Esmeralda, a young prostitute he has taken from the street and set up housekeeping with. He takes a rather high tone with Esmeralda's former pimp. But as he finds it more and more difficult to live by his art, he himself assumes the pimp's role, condoning in himself what earlier he had condemned in the other. In all other respects, he settles into a comfortable bourgeois existence, summed up in a telling image: a checking account with the Banco di Santo Spirito, where Esmeralda's earnings are deposited. But while Fidelman the man may take his ease, the artist struggles. His attempt at the "Mother and Son" remains frustrated. Only when Esmeralda burns the fatal photograph and thus stops him from trying to paint himself back into his mother's arms, as she puts it, only then is the artist in him liberated. Then he paints with confidence, amusement, a sense of discovery. For almost imperceptibly his subject changes: "Mother and Son" turns into "Sister and Brother" and finally into "Prostitute and Procurer." In the course of these transmutations the face of the female figure changes too: first it was his mother's taken from the snapshot, then his sister's from memory, finally Esmeralda's from life. But the face of the male figure remains his own. And though he considers substituting that of the pimp, "the magnificent thing," Malamud tells us, "was that in the end he kept himself in." If the artist has again grown in self-realization, however, the man cannot live with his discovery, and the story ends in a macabre catastrophe. Goaded by the subtle poison of the pimp's faint praise, Fidelman ruins the painting by trying to improve it. The rest is one quick rush of destruction. When he discovers what he has done he smears a tube of black all over the canvas:

Esmeralda, shouting "murderer," dashes at him with the bread knife; he twists it out of her grasp and in despair lifts the blade "into his gut." Esmeralda's *former* pimp reaps satisfaction from this revenge, but it is the act of Fidelman's own self-abused spirit.

Rehabilitation comes in the concluding story, "Glass Blower of Venice," in which we find him recovered or resurrected but at any rate reduced to humble service as a kind of St. Christopher, carrying passengers piggy-back through the flooded squares of Venice. This useful function initiates his incorporation into the human community. He establishes "the first long liaison of his life" with one of his passengers, the wife of Beppo the glass blower. It is a relation of sexual convenience but in time accompanied by a friendship with the husband, which grows and grows until, in a scene of wild grotesquery, Beppo slips into his wife's place and he and Fidelman become *real* lovers. Never before has Fidelman loved anyone without reservation; now he loves Beppo. Beppo leads him to his real self, the place where perfection of life and work is one. He strips him of past artistic pretension, then proceeds to teach him the rites of love and the art of blowing glass. The two merge on the level of broad pun and of theme. In a page or two of descriptive legerdemain devoted to their work with the hot molten glass, every move they make is in essence sexual, "a marvelous interaction," Malamud tells us. For the first time in his life Fidelman works instructed by love in a medium which is his very own. The cant of theory and the false starts derived from imitation are left behind. Now he creates beauty not out of despair or desperation but out of joy. His education finally completed and partly in deference to the duty which Beppo owes his family, the American sails home, where, his story concludes, "He worked as a craftsman in glass and loved men and women."

In large outline the story of Fidelman conforms to the basic plot of international fiction in which the American goes to Europe, where he is tried and where is identity is defined. Not surprisingly, as a number of critics have noted, Malamud intones some Jamesian motifs. Doubtless he knows his James well. But *Pictures of Fidelman* is a portrait of the American specifically as artist, and the treatment of a similar theme in "The Madonna of the Future," one of James's very early stories, seems to have haunted Malamud. A comparison, therefore, may point up how the intervening century has modified the American relation to Europe.

James's concern with the nature of art is dramatized in the contrast between two artists in Florence, an American and an Italian. The American, an unworldly idealist who has Raphael's brain but not his hand, aspires to paint a "résumé" of all the Italian Madonnas, but dreams away his life in front of an empty canvas; the Italian meanwhile employs his manual aptitude in turning out unbreakable but suggestive and therefore marketable figurines of cats and monkeys illustrating the various combinations of "the amorous advance and the amorous alarm." Both artists get their inspiration from the same woman — the American in pure contemplation of an idealized image unchanged by time, the Italian in domestic intercourse with a mistress visibly coarsened by life. A similar triangle is at the center of Malamud's "Still Life." In each story, moreover, the woman, a "maiden mother" who has lost her child, represents a mundane version of the painter's holy subject. And the contrast between sacred and profane in each story bears on the central problem of artistic creation. James's American is incapable of realizing his idea in shape and color on canvas because in ecstasy before the magic of the old masters he has lost his eye for life; the Fidelman of "Still Life" from a similar preoccupation with the great images of art escapes into abstraction — until he realizes with what seems a side-glance at James's story that the "furthest abstraction . . . is the blank canvas," a dead end: "If painting shows who you are why should not painting?" It is only when the imagination and life interbreed, as in the portrait of Annamaria as an archetypal "Mother and Child," that waiting succeeds, that is, that it moves by revealing truth.

If all this suggests that James and Malamud both see art as closely related to life, a theme we shall return to presently, their portrayals of the international scene differ profoundly: the moral distance between American and Italian has shrunk. And "A Pimp's Revenge," in which the same triangle of characters recurs, demonstrates the loss of the dear old American innocence even more explicitly. Now Fidelman, like James's visionary, is in Florence, set on painting a Madonna but somehow incapable. The psychological action of the story traces his and our discovery of his true nature and condition in the evolution of his painting. And the macabre end of the process expresses his despair at finding that he has become morally indistinguishable from the Italian pimp, in fact his double. Even as artist he now combines the roles James assigned to his American and Italian separately. While he wrestles with his lofty subject, the natural demands of the body cause him to produce small carved Madonnas for the tourist trade. Unlike James's Italian, he keeps his commercial art respectable. But when machine-made products drive his from the market and to make a living he turns pimp, he more than matches James's Italian pornographer. Prurience now enters his artistic activities and the parallel with James's story becomes so specific that it is difficult to imagine Malamud unconscious of it. While Esmeralda is on her job Fidelman sits nearby, ready to protect her from unruly customers, meantime appropriately occupied with a sketching pad in which, Malamud tells us, "he sometimes finds himself drawing dirty pictures: men and women, women and women, men and men." James's practical Italian described his "dirty" figurines in an impertinent murmur, repeated as the final phrase of the story: "Cats and monkeys, monkeys and cats; all human life is there!" The reappearance of the cadence in Malamud's description of Fidelman's sketches underlines how far the American artist has travelled from his splendid vision. There are other moments when something close to a verbal echo accentuates the divergence. James said of his exemplary American idealist:

> A creature more unsullied by the world it is impossible to conceive, and I often thought it a flaw in his artistic character that he hadn't a harmless vice or two. It amused me vastly at times to think that he was of our shrewd Yankee race; but, after all, there could be no better token of his American origin than his high aesthetic fever. The very heat of his devotion was a sign of conversion; those born to European opportunity manage better to reconcile enthusiasm with comfort.

A century later esthetic and other fevers, allied in Fidelman, seem to have abated. Frustrated in artistic ambition Fidelman feels he "could stand a little sexual comfort"; and once he has settled down with Esmeralda, his whole existence is a picture of middle-class ease recalling the tableaux of James's Italian artist and model united suggestively at dinner or a late breakfast. "Shopping for food's a blessing," Fidelman thinks: "you get down to brass tacks. It makes a lot of life seem less important, for instance painting a masterwork." Though not born to the manner, he has learnt "to reconcile enthusiasm with comfort" like any European.

The contrast with James's story of almost a century before draws our attention not only to the changed moral ambience and the shrinking of transatlantic differences but also to Malamud's concern with the relation of art and life, to Fidelman's refusal to choose between the two perfections. As we have seen, the question of their relationship concerns him in all his adventures; but only in the last one in Venice does he achieve their reconciliation when both are energized by love, and ambition and talent are one. Between the Florentine quest and the Venetian fulfillment, however, Malamud has interposed a fifth chapter, fittingly entitled "Pictures of the Artist." Unlike the other chapters, it is a surrealistic dream sequence, filled with allusions to historical painters, candid snapshots or jaundiced sketches of the artists ("I paint with my prick. Renoir. I paint with my ulcer. Soutine. I paint with my paint. Fidelman . . . Painting is nothing more than the art of expressing the invisible through the visible. Fromentin . . .") There are allusions also to a multitude of paintings—a whole catalogue of saints, for instance—and to literary works, above all the *Chants de Maldoror* by that forerunner of the surrealists, Ducasse alias Lautréamont, with which this chapter shares the abandonment to the inner vision, to memory and fantasy. And finally, there are allusions to the other chapters in the book, more probably than he who reads and runs is likely to realize. One hesitates to speak with much assurance of the meaning of a piece as dense and in part obscure as this tour de force, but so much is clear: in all its variety of tones and modes it elaborates the central theme of the Fidelman story—the question of the relation of art to life. Let a single illustration suffice.

In a moment of frustration in an earlier chapter, Fidelman exclaims:

"That's my trouble, everything's been done or is otherwise out of style—cubism, surrealism, action painting. If I could only guess what's next." Now, in Chapter Five, he has invented what's next. In his frantic search for originality he has taken to digging "spontaneously placed holes" in the ground which, when seen together, constitute "a sculpture." He exhibits them for a fee and proudly advertises them as "new in the history of Art." But when called on to explain himself, all he has is theoretical claptrap:

> Primus, although the sculpture is more or less invisible it is a sculpture nevertheless. Because you can't see it doesn't mean it isn't there. . . . Secundus, you must keep in mind that any sculpture is a form existing at a point radiating in all directions, therefore since it is dug into the Italian earth the sculpture vibrates overtones of Italy's Art, history, politics, religion; even nature as one experiences it in this country. There is also a metaphysic in relation of down to up, and vice versa . . .

Fidelman's listener, a poor young man who has spent his last ten lire to buy an admission instead of bread for his hungry babes, disagrees but is sent packing—only to return not long afterwards, transformed into a mysterious and threatening stranger. Now *he* initiates a metaphysical discussion of Fidelman's holes but without Fidelman's ostentation: "To me if you'll pardon me, is a hole nothing"; and he proceeds to prove his point by throwing an apple core. "If not for this could be empty the hole. If empty would be there nothing." The Yiddish plainness underlines the contrast with Fidelman's vacuity. But Fidelman persists: "Form may be and often is the content of Art." Malamud himself begs to differ. Like James, he thinks of fiction as closely related to life and history. After Dachau and the Moscow trials, after Pearl Harbor, Hiroshima, Korea, Dallas, and Vietnam, "who runs from content?" he asked when he accepted the National Book Award for *The Fixer* in 1967. The rejection of "signification" in the novel, he suggested, would lead to its death: "To preserve itself [art] must, in a variety of subtle ways, conserve the artist through sanctifying human life." And while as a writer he welcomed "the invention of new forms that may bring the novel to greater power," he repudiated a theory which "ultimately diminishes the value of a writer's experience, historical and personal, by limiting its use in fiction." Content, in a word, "cannot be disinvented." Fidelman's mysterious stranger argues more palpably: "You have not yet learned what is the difference between something and nothing," he says. Then, administering to the horrified Fidelman a resounding blow with the shovel, he topples him into the larger of the two holes and fills it up with earth, thus extinguishing both sculptor and sculpture. "So it's a grave. . . . So now we got form but we also got content." And so, we may add, life and art are inextricably fused. It is the lesson Fidelman has to learn. And after the grotesque flashes of merriment and the methodical madness of Chapter Five, Beppo the Glass

Blower teaches it in the positive way of love to a once more resurrected Fidelman in the last chapter.

His final adventure in Venice, as we have seen, leads this schlemiel abroad to the recognition of who he is: not the critic of Giotto, not the painter of traditional subjects or abstractions, nor the extravagant inventor of a totally new form, but the craftsman whose art is the product of the spontaneous response to life, and who is thereby enabled to bridge Yeats's division and achieve "perfection" in life and work. The quotation marks have become necessary, however, for the meaning of "perfection," along with much else, has changed since James, the imperative of self-fulfillment having at least in part replaced that of principle. In a general sense, Italy has served Fidelman as Europe has served Americans before him. But Fidelman's self-discovery is distinguished from those earlier ones in two important ways. For one thing, it is private instead of generic; it has nothing to do with the difference between American and European systems of government or society; it involves no international contrast. Fidelman has discovered himself as individual, not as American or democrat or natural nobleman. Nor is he distinguished by moral superiority, as the American heroes and heroines in James and Howells, for instance, frequently are. Far from staying aloof in critical detachment or native innocence, he meets his European counterparts on their own level. He picks pockets, makes love to bony chambermaids, pimps for his young whore, cuckolds Beppo and then becomes his lover. And he takes to the ways of this world he has entered like a fish to water, for it reveals to him what has been in him from childhood. "I am what I became from a young age," he says when he contemplates his self-portrait of the artist as pimp. Not that he judges himself, however. The very idea of moral judgment is foreign to this American in Europe. And this — that moral judgment is simply not in it — more than anything else characterizes the change from the earlier treatments of transatlantic confrontation. Fidelman's self-portrait is both example and symbol of this change. In the hands of James's American visionary the image of purity, the Madonna, had turned into the ultimate abstraction of the blank canvas; now it turns into the all too earthly-concrete "Prostitute and Procurer." To Fidelman the modern pair is no less sacred than the "Mother and Son" out of which they evolve:

> This woman and man together, prostitute and procurer. She was a girl with fear in both black eyes, a vulnerable if stately neck, and a steely small mouth; he was a boy with tight insides, on the verge of crying. The presence of each protected the other. A Holy Sacrament.

The change which has come over the treatment of the American experience of Europe expresses itself finally in a tone which frequently jolts the reader by the deadpan treatment of melodramatic or grotesque situations, the matter-of-fact coarseness which may sometimes tempt him to question the author's taste. At times one feels that Malamud is playing rather frivolously, not to say contemptuously, with his antecedents and with his audience. The defense that comes to mind immediately is that this dancing on graves, this affront of the reader's sensibilities, underlines the studied rejection of the idealism which characterized former American champions in the international contest and seals the loss of innocence.

"Ecco la chiave!": Malamud's Italy as the Land of Copies

Guido Fink*

When admitted by the *soi-disante* Isabella Del Dongo to a private tour of the galleries in her Palazzo, the protagonist of Bernard Malamud's story "The Lady of the Lake" — a vacationing New York Jew called Henry Levin, who for some reason has recently assumed the name "Henry C. Freeman" — is extremely disappointed by the girl's confession that most of the art treasures in display are, indeed, copies. First of all, there is no evidence that Napoleon had actually slept in the so-called Napoleon's Chamber; maybe it was his brother, or his sister Pauline; also, the Titians, Tintorettos, Bellinis, and the other paintings which make him hold his breath are not originals at all. "We often pretend," Isabella says. "This is a poor country."[1] The idea of fake, and the opposition between original and reproduction, are recurring preoccupations with American writers who choose Italy as a setting for their works. The most obvious reference, and a brazenly heterodox approach, may be found in Mark Twain's playful attitude, as expressed in the Milanese chapters of *Innocents Abroad* (1869):

> As usual, I could not help noticing how superior the copies were to the original, that is, to my inexperienced eye. Wherever you find a Raphael, a Rubens, a Michelangelo, a Carracci, or a da Vinci (and we see them every day), you find artists copying them, and the copies are always the handsomest. Maybe the originals were handsome when they were new, but they are not now.[2]

Normally, however, discrimination occurs in favor of the "real things." Henry James's aesthetic pilgrims, for instance, would never hesitate in these matters of taste: should they commit similar blunders, this could only mean that they still have a long way to go in their difficult path toward refinement and moral perfection, as is the case with Christopher Newman, who in the opening scene of *The American* (1876) pays an extravagant sum for Mlle. Nioche's copy of a Madonna in the Salon Carré of the Louvre museum.[3] But the issue is not that simple. Copies may be

*This essay was written specifically for this volume and is published here for the first time by permission of the author.

more advisable or less dangerous than originals because of morbid, vaguely Puritanical obsessions: in Hawthorne's *The Marble Faun* (1860), Miriam's chiaroscuro art, with its disturbing overtones, seems responsible for the evocation of threatening shadows out of the Roman catacombs, while Miriam's friend Hilda, another American artist in Rome, seems much wiser in her humble decision of just imitating Guido Reni and other masters instead of creating new pictures of her own. Again, the very existence of copies may be seen as the best evidence of authenticity and uniqueness for a work of art: a sort of seal of approval. This point, among many others, is debated by Walter Benjamin, in his seminal work of 1936 on the way modern art has been affected by the phenomenon of technical reproduction.[4]

At first sight, the problem seems quite peripheral in Malamud's story. Levin, or Freeman, is only annoyed because he cannot tell "the fake from the real": even when told by Isabella that the copies are "exceedingly beautiful" and that it takes an expert to recognize them as such, he is bound to realize that, not unlike James's Christopher Newman, he still has "a lot to learn." Yet, the tricks and the deceits of the Palazzo del Dongo are particularly relevant to his own predicament, and a Dantesque detail in the allegorical tapestry that Isabella points out to him—a leper suffering horrible pains, after falsely affirming he could fly—somehow anticipates the final twist of the story, when another false statement, his often repeated denial of being Jewish, brings all his hopes of romance with Isabella to an abrupt end. The girl, on the other hand, is no less deceitful than he is—she belongs to a "poor country"—and therefore has more justification if she "often pretends." As the land of trickery and delusion, Italy ought to be a convenient haven for such a Protean antihero as Malamud's "schlemiel abroad"; but in this case the comedy of errors is pushed too far, and Levin / Freeman is finally left with a cold marble statue—a copy?—instead of the soft, warm, real thing (i.e., Isabella's breast) he desperately tries to clutch. It is the appropriate ending—complete with mist, moonlight, and Gothic atmosphere—for a story the title of which is "copied" from or at least hints at another text, as is the case with at least another "Italian" story, "The Last Mohican" (1958).

The unavoidable *décalage* between mythic (i.e., ancient, Classic, or Renaissance) and real (modern) Italy is a recurring motif in many American works of fiction set in this country. Henry James's Theobald—the protagonist of *The Madonna of the Future* (1873), a novella that could easily be the "original" for one of Malamud's exercises in rewriting, "A Pimp's Revenge" (1968)[5]—is a would-be painter and a staunch admirer of Renaissance art who, living in late 19th-century Florence, prefers to haunt its empty streets at night, when "the present is sleeping" and "the past hovers about us like a dream made visible."[6] Without going that far, the protagonists of Malamud's Italian stories do realize—often at the very beginning of their Italian experiences—that there must be a difference between their fantasies or expectations and the actual impact of the country as it is or as it was in the fifties. Particularly naive, Levin / Freeman raves about the names of the islands he sees from the Stresa shore ("Ah, what names of beauty: Isola Bella, dei Poscatori, Madre, and Del Dongo. Travel is truly broadening, he thought; whoever got emotional over Welfare Island?")[7] until he almost becomes a comic version of Proust's young Marcel, ecstatic about the names of Venice and Florence (and Parma, and Pisa) in the last section of *Du coté du chez Swann*. But as we have already seen there will be no beauty for him in Italy — only the parody of a Gothic romance, where the tragic echoes of Buchenwald, the (reproductions of) classic art treasures, and the romantic scenery itself are somehow dissolved in a low-comedy context of *pensioni*, tourists, and garlic-smelling *barcaioli*. Similarly, Carl Schneider, the graduate student in Italian who vainly looks for an apartment in Rome ("Behold the Key," 1958), is soon disappointed by the "city of his dreams: Rome, a city of perpetual surprise, had surprised unhappily."[8] And the artist / art student Arthur Fidelman, upon his arrival at the Stazione Termini, in the opening paragraph of another story, "The Last Mohican" — which will prove just the first of his Italian unfortunate adventures or "exhibitions" — is overwhelmed by the ruins of the Baths of Diocletian, well remembering that in Michelangelo's times the building had been converted into a church, later again into a museum: " 'Imagine,' he muttered. 'Imagine all that history.' "[9] Like those often altered remains, Fidelman's Rome has several faces, some belonging to its traditional, well-established iconography (Saint Peter's Cathedral, for instance), others less familiar to the average tourist, such as the open markets in Porta Portese, Piazza Fontannella Borghese, Piazza Dante; some imbued with an eerie, dreamlike atmosphere (the decrepit Ghetto, where among crumbling tenements and narrow cobblestone streets one can have a passing glimpse of hidden Oriental treasures, "dark holes ending in jeweled interiors, silks and silver of all colors"); others again quite nightmarish, such as the empty graves of Nazi victims in the Jewish section of the Verano cemetery, or the "blank wall" in front of which, following a ghost "through a thick stone passage," Fidelman only finds a disturbing smell and a painted inscription weakly lit by an electric bulb: "*Vietato urinare.*"[10] (Ruins, caves, evil smells, "Roman fever," and other mysterious infections are part, of course, of the poisonous charms of the "Eternal City" as seen by American authors, since the times of *The Marble Faun* and of James's *Daisy Miller* [1878]. In more recent times such miasmatic effluvia have been openly assuming sexual or excremental connotations, as shown by Tennessee Williams's *The Roman Spring of Mrs. Stone* [1950], or by Leslie Fiedler's novel, *The Second Stone* [1963].)

"Behold the Key," a story which has been seldom discussed or appreciated by Malamud devotees,[11] is perhaps the most emblematical of the "Italian" stories, or, at the very least, a significant introduction to

Levin Freeman's and Fidelman's experiences. The first story with a Roman setting to be encountered by the reader of *The Magic Barrel*, it deals with a quest, or the parody of a quest, that may seem irrelevant or trivial — the desperate search for an apartment. But for Carl Schneider, whom we may consider Malamud's first version of the "schlemiel abroad," finding an inexpensive flat for himself and his family, after many depressing experiences in *pensioni* or cheap hotels, is not only an economic necessity but also a personal need. Carl Schneider dreams to live *in* the city, as a member of its community, apart from other tourists or visitors, at least for one year. The one apartment he would desperately like to move into — after being dragged by a pathetic, unlikely Virgil named Bevilacqua through a maze of Roman rain-drenched streets or endless streetcar rides to a series of impossible or unavailable or fatally flawed places — is a Contessa's home in the Monte Sacro district, which among other beauties contains one of the few clearly Edenic gardens in Malamud's strictly postlapsarian world. In a predictable anticlimax, however, neither Carl Schneider nor his awkward famulus are allowed to enter that dreamlike place, the key to the apartment having been stolen by villainous De Vecchis, the Contessa's former tenant and rejected lover, who after failing to blackmail the protagonist, out of sheer spite destroys all the valuable pieces of furniture, smashing sofas, books, and window panes, and desecrating the immaculate walls with wine and obscene graffiti: "*Ecco la chiave!*" he shouts, finally throwing the key to Carl and Bevilacqua when it has become plainly useless.

Never has the opposition between myth and reality of modern Italy been drawn in sharper contrast. On the one hand, Carl's dream of Paradise — "they had moved out of the hotel into the Contessa's apartment. The children were in the garden, playing among the roses" — contrasts with a real Inferno, expressed by the explosion of hatred and violence between the two fellow citizens, Bevilacqua and De Vecchis, among the shattered remains of what had been an ideal home. "He lives for my death," says Bevilacqua of his enemy, "I for his. This is our condition."[12] Better not to inquire which of these two versions of Italian life is, in Malamud's view, the more authentic — they are probably overlapping and closely related to each other, like an original and its copy.

Bernard Malamud first came to Italy in 1956, on a Rockefeller grant.[13] Previously, he had several contacts with Italian immigrants in New York, during and since the Depression.[14] Apart from Frank Alpine, the hero of his second and possibly most celebrated novel, *The Assistant* (1957), many Italian-Americans appear in the background of his New York Ghetto stories.[15] The time of Malamud's first sojourn was not an easy one for Italy. Even in the late fifties, the aftermath of World War II was still visible, especially as far as housing was concerned, since the reconstruction of the many destroyed or damaged buildings and the practically unplanned, chaotic growth of the major cities had failed to keep pace with the heavy demand for housing created by the rapid change in the economy and to the steady influx to the cities of peasants who had abandoned the impoverished land. At that time also, political change, evidenced by the heavy loss of votes for the center coalition in the 1953 elections, when the dominating parties had vainly tried to strengthen their position with the so-called "Fraudulent Law," had brought to an end whatever stability, or stagnation, the Catholic leader De Gasperi had given to the country. A long period of unrest and uncertainty had begun, which was eventually solved with the "opening to the left" and the agreement between Socialist and Catholics in 1962.[16] Actually 1958, the year when the first "Italian" stories were published, was to be the beginning both of a detente (with the advent of the new Pope, John XXIII) and of a period of development and increase in living standards, later to be called "economic miracle."[17] Rome, in particular, was emerging as not only the casual, easygoing haven for artists, drifters, and the motley crowd involved or hoping to be involved in the film industry — largely Americanized thanks to the so called "runaway productions" — but also as a sort of European capital of entertainment, endowed with all the glitter and the scandal later reinvented by Fellini's imagination in *La dolce vita* (1959). Fidelman's second adventure, "Still Life" (1962), could be a timid, peripheral step in that direction. But Malamud is mainly in touch, and in tune, with the milieu of losers and pathetic failures that an Italian journalist, Giovanni Russo, called in those very years *L'Italia dei Poveri*.[18]

Even if both Schneider and Levin / Freeman, in different moments of their Italian experience, are either embarrassingly admired or venomously attacked because of their mythical American affluence, they are far from being rich, and their being part of a minority somehow prepares them to be sympathetic to their new acquaintances. Of course, to Italian eyes (Isabella's being an understandable exception) they are not identifiable as Jews: they are one hundred percent Americans, without the hyphen they may be conscious of in their own country. But even Arthur Fidelman, who appears on the Roman scene with a new pigskin leather case, new shoes, and a new tweed suit, cannot resist the subtle fascination of the past centuries, which are still perceivable in the city, and, so to speak, rapidly deconstruct the protective shell of novelty and efficiency hiding his real self. Just outside the railroad station in Rome, Fidelman experiences "the sensation of suddenly seeing himself as he was"; he finds himself locked and mirrored in another man's gaze; and this other man is a Jew. ("Shalom!" is the first word which is addressed to him in Rome.)[19] This means, among other things, that Italy is not really as unfamiliar as a landscape; in other words, these "schlemiels abroad" are liable to become part of that landscape. That compulsive liar, "Freeman," pretends not to understand when Isabella points out that the profile of the Alpine peaks from Mount Rosa to Jungfrau "looks like a Menorah" ("Like a what?" he asks, and the girl must explain, "Like a seven-branched candelabrum holding white candles in the sky.")[20] But to Fidelman, as long as he proceeds in the frantic search for the schnorrer who may have stolen his precious manuscript, Rome undergoes a double change. First the city becomes a maze of open-street markets, second-hand goods, junk peddlers, beggars, prostitutes, or petty thieves (there may be a reminiscence here of De Sica's celebrated 1947 film *The Bicycle Thief*). Then, after a particular Friday night, when Fidelman mingles with a group of Sephardic Jews in a Left Bank synagogue, Rome is transformed, both in the protagonist's dreams and in actuality, into an eerie succession of nocturnal visions—the Ghetto, the Jewish section of the cemetery, the Hebrew catacombs under the ancient Appian way—that again once remind the reader of *The Marble Faun*, or perhaps a Jewish travesty of Hawthorne's novel. To Sidney Richman, Italy is "a setting which Malamud seems to delight in almost as much as in New York's East Side, and for similar reasons"; but both "Behold the Key" and "The Lady of the Lake" demonstrate the author's "weakness" whenever he attempts "to extend his themes into non-Jewish areas."[21] Yet, whatever the critic may feel about these specific stories, this does not seem to be the case. It takes just a few pages, a few subtle hints, before a sort of contagion takes place—those "areas" becoming no longer "non-Jewish" at all.

In the much-discussed ending of *The Assistant*, Frank Alpine, the young American of Italian extraction, literally and symbolically crowns his excruciating period of "apprenticeship" by having himself circumcised and becoming a Jew.[22] Perhaps it could be argued that the ironically useless key to the Italian Paradise in "Behold the Key" thrown by perfidious De Vecchis at Carl Schneider—actually aimed at De Vecchis's enemy Bevilacqua, but hitting the American instead, and leaving "a mark he could not rub out"[23] on his forehead—is after all a clue, or a symbolic passport toward honorary citizenship in the land of suffering, litigation, misery, and endless maneuvering. The very words, sarcastic yet solemn, with which De Vecchis accompanies his gesture—words that are translated even more solemnly in the title of the story, while the standard English equivalent would be something like "here's the key"—evoke the ritualistic public ceremonies in which illustrious visitors are symbolically given the keys to the city by local authorities. Becoming a member of that particular community may seem a dubious honor, especially to patriotic American readers; but exactly like Frank Alpine's, this rite de passage is not important in itself. What is really at stake here, as well as in much of Malamud's work, is the individual ability to transcend one's own prejudices and limitations, to emphathize and project one's personality, to become so to speak, one's own image of the Other.

The issue is particularly complicated in these Italian stories by the double track they follow. The path toward Italian-ness overlaps with the road leading back to the protagonists' Jewish roots, and vice versa. By denying his Jewishness, Levin / Freeman misses his chance of marrying into a (supposedly) aristocratic Italian family. In "The Last Mohican," Fidelman, by contrast, seems to avail himself both of his American-ness and his easy adaptability to Roman habits as of a double armor against recognizing his own responsibilities toward his cumbersome, exasperating Jewish alter ego, the schnorrer named Susskind. But the very fact of loosening his tight, efficient program of library hours and visits to the museums, by adopting the lax Roman custom of late dinners, too much wine and spaghetti, naps and *passeggiate*, somehow paves the way to another transformation, more or less like the Baths of Diocletian have been doubly converted, and the city itself twice changes under his and our eyes. At the end of the story, Fidelman, in a dream, is led by "Virgilio Susskind" into a synagogue, where he sees the unlikely painting on the vaults of the building of Saint Francis of Assisi giving his clothes to a "Cavaliere Povere," a fresco by Giotto whose unusual relocation is in itself a revealing case of osmosis and overlapping. Only then does Fidelman realize—he, incidentally, has been pestered by the schnorrer with the repeated request of a new suit, and strongly suspects him to be responsible for the theft of his valuable manuscript on Giotto—that Susskind is, in fact, inextricably linked to his own destiny and that he cannot possibly deny or postpone his help any longer. It is, of course, too late: Susskind, not listening to him, continues his eternal running (he has been introduced as a "Jewish refugee from Israel," and from everywhere else as well); Fidelman is frozen in the ritual tableau that usually concludes Malamud's novels and stories. But the additional stories will provide him with an abundant share of running of his own.

Mobility is not the most striking characteristic of Malamud's heroes. They may travel, migrate, cross symbolic boundaries, like S. Levin (in *A New Life*, 1961) or Yakov Bok in *The Fixer* (1966); they may have gone a long way *before* the beginning of the story, like both Morris Bober and Frank Alpine in *The Assistant*. But they are usually remembered as being trapped, symbolically or not so symbolically entombed in their own depressing environment.[24] In the New York's East Side stories, at least, they seem motionless and paralyzed even when taking an occasional subway ride to Harlem or the Village. Italy, a more chaotic and less rigidly structured milieu, seems to inspire much more dynamism, once again beginning with the endless and fruitless apartment hunting poor Carl Schneider is condemned to undertake. In his successive "exhibitions" after "The Last Mohican," Fidelman may be trapped (once he is the prisoner of two brothel-keepers in Milan, who also confiscate his American passport; another time he is buried alive in a dream), but apparently he may escape from one prison to the next, assuming the Protean identities of a perennial wanderer that almost transforms him into a replica of his lost Jewish alter ego, Susskind the eternal refugee. Indeed, he possesses the "fluidity" and "formlessness" that Tony Tanner detects, both as a threat and a secret aspiration, in the heroes of many American novels of the fifties and the sixties.[25]

There is never, or almost never, a question of being Jewish with this Italianate Wandering Jew, who reappears as "ravaged Florentine" or "assistant glass blower in Venice," and even obtains one of his painfully few sexual triumphs disguising himself as a priest. But in a way he goes even farther. In addition to recovering his Jewish identity, and acquiring a temporary Italian one in different cities, he becomes a citizen of the Land of Copies, not only as an artist, in various occasions involved in operations of forgery or imitation ("I reject originality," he says), but also as a person. In "A Pimp's Revenge," for instance, he confronts himself with a smooth, soft-spoken con man in yellow gloves, Ludovico, who in more than one way is the final embodiment of all that looks vulgar, repulsive, or sinister in the Italian as Rival or Other Man (Augusto in "Still Life," Angelo and Scarpio in "Naked Nude," as well as Carl Schneider's and Bevilacqua's arch-enemy, De Vecchis). Yet he practically merges with Ludovico's image, becoming his double. His next encounter with an Italian as Rival (Beppo the Venetian glass blower, who is the husband of his mistress Margherita), however, will be frankly romantic, a particularly rewarding version of the master-apprentice relationship which is obviously so important in Malamud's world. There is a compensation after all, for the loss of a passport, and of a nationality.

Shifting, restless, unreliable as it is, the Land of Copies is at the very least a complete break with the well-established tradition of dreamy visions and painted backdrops to which American Romantics — one may think of Venice as seen by Poe, Cooper, or Irving — have given a remarkable contribution, long before the culmination of the trend with Mann's *Der Tod im Venedig* (1911).[26] Even in a recent American novel, the already quoted *The Second Stone*, the protagonist seems surprised by the fact that real and loud human beings do, after all, inhabit a Roman square: "*Eppur si muove!*" he mutters, echoing Galilei's famous statement.[27]

The bustling, dynamic pace of Italian life as seen by Malamud may, at times, exclude the outsider from its dubious privileges; and Fidelman, as well as Schneider and Levin / Freeman, often experiences the loneliness of exile. Yet, Italy may be motherly, or harsh and motherly at the same time, like the bronze statue of the Etruscan she-wolf suckling the infants Romulus and Remus which strikes Fidelman's eyes upon his first meeting with his spiritual twin brother, Susskind. Erotic and Oedipal overtones are nothing new, however, in the American experience of Italy. "It's the fashion to talk of all cities as feminine," says Theobald in James's *The Madonna of the Future*. "But, as a rule, it's a monstrous mistake. Is Florence of the same sex as New York, as Chicago? She's the sole true woman of them all; one feels towards her as a lad in his teens feels to some beautiful older woman with a 'history.' It's a sort of aspiring gallantry she creates."[28] Accordingly, Malamud's "schlemiel abroad" seems much more dominated by or dependent upon the Eternal Feminine than his American counterpart, usually belonging to a safely patriarchal family where the woman's role is minimal or instrumental. Once again, Carl Schneider leads the way. First of all, he is not alone, as his followers will be: he has a wife, two years older than he is, as well as two kids. Even if we mostly assist at his ordeals and showdowns with male helpers or opponents, he obviously depends on a sort of female trinity: his wife Norma, whose savings pay for his studies; Norma's unseen mother, who has paid for their transportation to Italy; and, we hope, the Contessa — a plain woman past fifty, with wrinkled skin and dyed hair, but also a big maternal bosom, smelling like a rose garden — who might accommodate the Schneiders in the heavenly apartment she owns, were she not so busy with her imminent wedding, and so nonchalant. More traditionally, Levin / Freeman (albeit unsuccessfully) and Fidelman (with limited success) are given the chance of regular love affairs with Italian girls, but these affairs are usually beset with almost insurmountable problems. Annamaria Oliovino, the hysterical and frigid *pittrice* whom Fidelman humbly worships in "Still Life" somehow represents a violent denial of motherhood (she has thrown her baby, born of a semi-incestuous relationship, into the Tiber). For Esmerelda, the young prostitute who shares Fidelman's Florentine room in Via Sant' Agostino, the image of the artist's dead mother proves to be a dangerous rival to the Fidelman-Esmerelda relationship — Fidelman is obsessed with painting his mother as a modern madonna or a visualized Kaddish, drawing inspiration from an old, faded photograph. "To me," says the girl, rather perceptively, "it's as though you were trying to paint yourself into your mother's arms."[29] Her observation suggests the rather complex Oedipal knot upon which the story is based. An even more significant Oedipal connection involves Margherita (in "Glass Blower of Venice"), an overt mother figure, whom he appreciates not only for her generous offer of herself but especially for her generous offering of ravioli. It is Margherita who sends Fidelman back home to America: his apprenticeship is concluded. In the last of the stories, he has learned to give up any pretense as a man or an artist, he has become an assistant artisan, and he has finally found true love (with Margherita's husband). The good substitute mother, the one he has met in this land of substitutions, knows well that it is high time for the reborn Fidelman to cross the ocean and begin a new life, just as the real mother has felt in her time.

What is the culmination of the Italian experience for Malamud's heroes? Should we dismiss it as a repetition in a minor key of the tragicomedy of escape, loneliness, failed integration, and possible spiritual reward, as performed by similar characters in the familiar milieu of New York's East Side, as well as in prerevolutionary Russia or the Western state of "Cascadia"? Is it just a parodic version of this individual rite de passage, in a teeming, colorful, but finally irrelevant context of duplicates and stereotypes? Actually, the many possible combinations among these doubles and mirror images do produce oddities and freakish monstrosities of their own, as revealed by the linguistic *mésaillances* to which Malamud, the post-Babelic writer, already an expert in the subtle blending of English and Yiddish, abandons himself. Somehow he has learned to cope with the standard, almost unspoken national language and with the fanciful jargon which is deemed necessary in order to communicate with rich tourists. First, Italian expressions infiltrate the text by the dozen, not only as quoted "reports," but also as fragments of the protagonists' consciousness or free indirect speech — "*Ecco la chiave!*" says Da Vecchis, but "*ecco, Susskind!*" thinks Fidelman, when he finds the schnorrer selling beads in the porch of Saint Peter's. Also, the hybridization process — the same one that deeply irritated Mark Twain in *Innocents Abroad*[30] — is pursued on various levels. When trying to speak English, Malamud's Italians fall into all the traps of the most pathetic pidgin ("Weesh you an apotament?"; "Are you in biziness?"), thus transforming, by way of contrast, the "schlemiels abroad" they are conversing with into impeccable models of nonethnic Americanism. But when they presumably speak their own native Italian, the narrator automatically translates their words into something resembling Malamud's Anglicized, oracular Yiddish, having no possible equivalent in Italian language or dialects: "Assassin! Turd! May your bones grow hair and rot!"; "A prayer is a prayer; I suffer for mine"; "Look at what I'm wearing . . . Look at this junk pile, can you call it a house? I live here with my son and his bitch of a wife, who counts every spoonful of soup in my mouth. They treat me like dirt, and dirt is all I have to my name."[31] Of course the treacherous, all-pervading interplay of copies and doubles is not only grounded in the linguistic texture of the stories but is also present as structural principle or plot device. In "Naked Nude" (1963), Fidelman the artist, who often draws inspiration from his memories or the reproduction of some already existing work of art, is forced by his evil padrone, Angelo the brothel keeper, to imitate a Venus by Titian which he plans to steal from a gallery on Lake Stresa's Isola Bella, substituting Fidelman's copy for the real thing. Fidelman has obvious misgivings, ethical as well as professional, about "stealing another painter's ideas and work," but Angelo provides him with a ready-made theory that justifies this and other thefts:

> "Tiziano will forgive you. Didn't he steal the figure of Urbino from Giorgione? Didn't Rubens steal the Adrian nude from Tiziano? Art steals, and so does everybody. You stole a wallet and tried to steal my lire. What's the difference? We're only human."[32]

Fidelman complies, only to steal his own copy instead of the original, falling in love with his own imitation. In "A Pimp's Revenge," having realized that all has been *done* already, he copies an old photograph of himself and his mother, chalks a Raphaelesque Madonna on a pavement near Santa Maria Novella, refuses to carve a nude Marilyn Monroe and a Baptist in leopard skin, but does carve wooden Madonnas which he either sells to a Ponte Vecchio souvenir vendor or peddles to shops in via della Vigna Nuovo. At the same time, his author and sole inventor, Bernard Malamud, is consciously rewriting and updating a Henry James novella dealing with the impossibility of creating modern Madonnas and with the hideous vulgarity of mass-produced and mass-distributed artifacts.[33] *Pictures of Fidelman*, as it has been often remarked, abounds in direct or indirect references to various painters, paintings, and techniques,[34] but all of Malamud's "Italian" stories contain oblique echoes of, and allusions to, other texts and authors: Byron, Scott, Cooper, Thomas Mann, and above all James. (Another, less successful exercise in rewriting, this time inspired by "The Altar of the Dead," is the Roman story of "Life Is Better Than Death" [1963].)[35] While it would be absurd to forget that the game of literary references does occur throughout the whole body of Malamud's work, it seems only fair to recognize that Malamud's Italy is an extremely favorable territory for such exercises in playful and not so playful intertextuality. Like the "hot molten glass" which, after abandoning creative art, Fidelman takes delight in for both sexual and professional reasons ("with pipe, tongs, shears, you can make a form or change it into its opposite," says his lover, master, and mentor; "for instance, with a snip or two of the scissors, if it suits you, you can change the male organ into the female"[36]), Malamud's writing becomes a flexible medium that can produce almost anything—as well as its double, contrary, or parody. Fidelman's period of "assistantship" as well as his Italian experience reaches its culmination in the "huge glass bubble" out of which he makes a bowl, "severe and graceful," reminding his friend of "something the old Greeks had done" and his readers of something else—a beautiful but fatally cracked "golden bowl" having nothing to do with the Old Greeks. This glass bowl, a farewell gift to his friend Beppo, will last only one day: the following morning it is nowhere to be found, the "assistant manager" (another assistant!) being suspected of having stolen or smashed it. But resembling as it does the "spheric body without orifices" that Leo Bersani in a later book would propose as the modern, sterile equivalent of the traditional images of motherhood or generation,[37] it is an appropriate correlative—and a climax—for this complex comedy of mirrors, copies, uncreative creation, and artificial family plots.

It may seem disappointing, or predictable, or déjà vu. Anything can turn into anything else; Proteus is our modern, transethnic, transpersonal, transsexual hero; Levin / Freeman, after all, was right in assuming a new identity, only less so in disclaiming his former one. Did not Malamud himself, in another context, warn us that all men are Jews? Did not Nietzsche affirm that even anti-Semites are only frustrated by their secret desire to be Jewish?

Probably we should not push the matter so far. Yes, all men are Jews; but some, at least in Malamudland, are more Jewish than others. One has only to think of the lonely, famished crowd — widows, apprentices, idiots, refugees, old black jewbirds losing their plumage — peeping through the windowpanes, waiting, humbly begging or unreasonably claiming a share of the often miserable meal which is being served indoors. And Italians may legitimately be considered as strongly recommended candidates for promotion to that dubious grace, Jewishness as suffering, which has been granted, but not without difficulties, to members of other ethnic groups (*The Tenants*, 1971), and even to nonhumans (*God's Grace*, 1982).[38]

Oddly enough, however, the only character both Italian and Jewish ever conceived by Malamud — Isabella Della Seta, *not* Del Dongo — hides forever among "her" statues and in the thick of the wood at the very moment when we discover her religious affiliation. Her elusive figure in "The Lady of the Lake" is a premonition of other female appearances, equally mysterious, that Malamud will later evoke among the masks and gondolas of his Venice: the woman that giggles while Fidelman carries her on her back during the *acqua alta* (but she will be back, as the not-so-enchanting Margherita) and the red-haired girl that Dubin vainly pursues through *calli* and canals, thinking she might be his daughter Maud, while he vacations in Venice with the young girl he plans to take as his mistress. The whole Venetian episode in the latter novel, *Dubin's Lives* (1980), is of course déjà vu — Italy and Italians being no longer necessary elements of Malamud's imagination at this stage.[39] But somehow the running and the excitement continue, and so does the carnival of masks and doubles. Is the girl really Maud Dubin? Is she a girl at all? The manager of the *pensione* is not so sure:

> "She's red-haired," Dubin explained, and the padrone laughed and said, "We've got two different redheads this week. Eh, signore, they're a deceptive lot. You can't tell what they really are until you've looked up their legs."[40]

"Believe me, there are Jews everywhere," said old Manischevitz, the tailor, after seeing his Angel in Harlem. One might add that there certainly are double, copies and mirror images everywhere. Italy, however, seems to have proved good territory for the test and the confirmation of Malamud's views about today's world — or perhaps tomorrow's.

Notes

1. Bernard Malamud, *The Magic Barrel* (New York: Random House, 1958), 122–23. This particular story, "The Lady of the Lake," is not included in Rita Nathalie Kosofsky's checklist, so no original date of appearance can be given.

2. Mark Twain, *Innocents Abroad* (New York: Signet Classics, 1966), 137.

3. On this aspect of *The American*, and of James's dislike of copies and reproductions, see Barbara and Giorgio Melchiori, *Il gusto di Henry James* (Turin: Einaudi, 1974), 11–12 ff.

4. According to Walter Benjamin (*Das Kunstwerk im Zeitaler seiner technischen Reproduzierbarkeit*), *medieval Madonna* was not really authentic: it only became such in later centuries, especially in the last one. I am quoting from the Italian edition, *L'opera d'arte nell'epoca della sua riproducibilità tecnica* (Turin: Einaudi, 1966), 49.

5. The relationship between these two texts has been explored by Christof Wegelin, "The American Schlemiel Abroad: Malamud's Italian Stories and the End of American Innocence," *Twentieth-Century Literature* 19, no. 2 (April 1973):84–85, and by myself in "Il colore sul vuoto: James e Malamud a Firenze," in Tiziano Bonazzi, ed, *America-Europa, la circolazione delle idee* (Bologna: Il Mulion, 1976), 11–34. I am indebted to Mr. Wegelin for the expression "schlemiel abroad," which I am freely using in this essay, as well as for many more suggestions.

6. Henry James, *The Complete Tales*, ed. Leon Edel (London: Rupert Hart-Davis, 1962)3:13.

7. Malamud, *Barrel*, 106.

8. Ibid., 57. The story, according to Kosofsky, first appeared in *Commentary* in May 1958, while "The Last Mohican" is listed as the preceding item, having appeared in the Spring 1958 issue of *Partisan Review*. Since "Behold the Key" is the first of the "Italian" stories to appear in *The Magic Barrel*, I am considering it a beginning of, or introduction to, the whole Italian experience, for reasons that I hope will be clear in the essay.

9. Bernard Malamud, *Pictures of Fidelman: An Exhibition* (New York: Dell, 1970), 11–12.

10. Ibid., 33.

11. Earl H. Rovit, *Critique* 5, no. 2 (1960), includes both "Behold the Key" and "The Lady of the Lake" among "the less successful" of Malamud's stories; Sidney Richman, *Bernard Malamud* (New York: Twayne, 1966), calls the former "deceptive" and "far from his best work." Both are included in Leslie A. Field, Joyce W. Field, eds., *Bernard Malamud and the Critics* (New York: New York University Press, 1970), 7, 321, 323.

12. Malamud, *Barrel*, 82.

13. Malamud briefly recollects the episode in his introduction to *The Stories of Bernard Malamud* (New York: Farrar, Straus, Giroux, 1983), ix.

14. In his September 1985 brief stay in Italy, where he had been awarded the Mondello Prize for both his first and last novel — *The Natural* having been belatedly published in Italian the year before — Malamud gave various interviews, expressing his particular affection for the country he was unfortunately visiting for the last time. Particularly interesting, his conversation with Antonio d'Orrico, "Io, Malamud, vissute al 50 %," appeared in the Communist daily paper, *L'Unità*, 14 September 1985. In this interview, according to d'Orrico, Malamud related his admiration for the high spirits with which his family's Italian neighbors faced the Depression.

15. Italians appear, in addition to *The Assistant*, in the following stories: "The Prison," "A Summer's Reading," "The Bill," "The Death of Me," and "The Cost of Living." On Italian-Americans and transethnicity in Malamud's work, see Elèna Mortara di Veroli, "Italian-Americans and Jews in Malamud's Fiction," *Rivista di Studi Angloamericani* 3, nos. 4 and 5 (1985):195–211.

16. On the social and political situation in Italy during the fifties, see Giuseppe Mammarella, *Italy after Facism: A Political History* (Notre Dame, Indiana: University of Notre Dame Press, 1966), 121–23, 249 ff., 309–11, 316. On housing conditions in Rome, see Robert C. Fried, *Planning the Eternal City: Roman Politics and Planning Since World War II* (New Haven/London: Yale University Press, 1975), 229 ff.

17. ". . . In the two decades of the '50s and the '60s, taken together, the Italian rate of expansion of gross national product was exceeded in Wesern Europe only by that of the German Federal Republic. Yet, contrary to the view generally held, the Italian "economic

miracle" was really concentrated in the brief period from 1959 to 1963. . . ." (Gisèle Podbielski, *Italy: Development and Crisis in the Postwar Economy* (Oxford: Clarendon Press, 1974), 15.

18. Giovanni Russo, *L'Italia dei poveri* (Milan: Longanesi, 1958), is particularly interesting as a background to Malamud's Italian stories of that period. The chapter "Rome By Night" (127–40) first appeared in 1954.

19. Malamud, *Fidelman*, 13.

20. Malamud, *Barrel*, 128.

21. Fields, *Malamud and the Critics*, 323.

22. For contrasting readings of the ending in *The Assistant*, see, as a few of the possible examples, the Hassan, Shear, Hays entries in Fields, *Malamud and the Critics*, 199 ff.

23. Malamud, *Barrel*, 83.

24. The prison motif, and the idea of Jewishness as imprisonment, were developed by Robert Alter in *After the Tradition* (1966). See Fields, *Malamud and the Critics*, 33–34.

25. In the introduction to his own *City of Words: American Fiction 1950–1970* (London: Jonathan Cape, 1971), Tony Tanner finds a central concern for the heroes of many American novels of the period in the search for a freedom that is not entirely formless (a "jelly") and for "an identity which is not a prison" — a search also extended, on a stylistic level, to authors of those novels (p. 19). Following this approach, Tanner later in the same book analyzes several Malamud characters, including Fidelman, 339–43.

26. On the theme of Venice in literature, see the fine essay by Giorgio Bassani, *Le parole preparate* (Turin: Einaudi, 1966), 17–36.

27. I am quoting from the Italian edition, *Il congresso dell'amore* (Milan: Longanesi, 1964), 133.

28. James, *Complete Tales*, 23–24.

29. Malamud, *Fidelman*, 115.

30. In the French and Italian sections of *Innocents Abroad*, Mark Twain obviously delights in quoting verbatim certain examples of *franglais* (such as Blucher's "*Monsieur le* Landlord. Sir: *Pourquoi* don't you *mettez* some *savon* in your bedchambers?"). His future, contradictory relationship with "English as She Is Spoke" seems to suggest that he was not entirely joking when preaching against such hybrids — "a thing that is neither male nor female, neither fish, nor fowl — a poor miserable, hermaphrodite Frenchman!" (*Innocents Abroad*, 133, 168).

31. The above quoted lines are respectively uttered by Bevilacqua (Malamud, *Barrel*, 82), Etta in "Life Is Better Than Death" (Malamud, *Stories*, 295), and Rosa in "The Maid's Shoes" (Malamud, *Stories*, 110).

32. Malamud, *Fidelman*, 75.

33. See Note 5. It may be significant that, while Fidelman is trying to do both his Madonna-like masterpiece and the vulgar statuettes that help him to survive, at least until he resorts to pimping, Henry James's Theobald is only dedicated to his Madonna (never, alas, to be painted) while the producer of hideous, plastic statuettes of "cats and monkeys" is Serafina's lover (the usual, vulgar, Italian Other Man).

34. See, on this and other aspects, Tanner, *City of Words*, 340.

35. Obviously Byronic are such names as Beppo and Margherita ("Glass Blower in Venice"); Cooper and Scott are echoed, as previously hinted, in the titles of two among the first "Italian" stories, "The Last Mohican" and "The Lady of the Lake"; in "A Pimp's Revenge," the prostitute's name (Esmerelda), as well as some fiendish connotations of Ludovico's, may be an oblique allusion to Thomas Mann's *Doktor Faustus* (1947).

36. Malamud, *Fidelman*, 183.

37. Leo Bersani, *A Future for Astyanax: Character and Desire in Literature* (Boston/

Toronto: Little, Brown & Co., 1976) detects this "spheric" motif both in the so-called "gay" culture and in such authors as Samuel Beckett (265 ff.).

38. Discussing *The Tenants*, Robert Alter significantly writes: "The Negro is a far more obstreperous and hostile disciple than the Italian Frank Alpine . . . but, like Alpine, he finally becomes a "Jew" in Malamud's special sense. . . ." See "Updike, Malamud, and the Fire This Time," *Commentary* 54, no. 4 (October 1962):69.

39. After *Fidelman*, and prior to *Dubin's Lives*, the only reference to anything Italian in Malamud, if I am correct, is the "abandoned Italian cellar restaurant" in the condemned neighborhood of *The Tenants* (Harmondsworth, Middlesex: Penguin, 1972), 12.

40. Bernard Malamud, *Dubin's Lives* (New York: Avon, 1980), 86.

The Tenants in the House of Fiction

Steven G. Kellman*

With *The Tenants* (1971), Bernard Malamud ostensibly addresses himself to the most urgent problems besetting contemporary American society. Although based on authentic details of the Mendel Beiliss blood libel case in Czarist Russia, *The Fixer* (1966) was still concerned with other times and other places. The years during which *The Tenants* was gestating were a period of unrelieved and perhaps unparalleled crisis in the United States. Two of its most distressing symptoms were accelerating urban decay and the substitution of racial warfare for race relations. *The Tenants* is set in the very heart of the heart of our troubles; its major protagonist, Harry Lesser, lives in midtown Manhattan, the solitary resident of a crumbling, condemned tenement house on Thirty-first Street and Third Avenue. "In New York who needs an atom bomb? If you walked away from a place they tore it down."[1]

Nothing can be sole or whole that has not been rent, and, in its account of Lesser's stubborn refusal to be evicted from a home which is barely a house, *The Tenants* points apocalyptically toward a resolution of current woes. The insurgent pose of Willie Spearmint must be seen against the background of virtual civil war in Watts, Newark, Detroit, and Cleveland and of the birth of the Black Power movements. For any contemporary American who reads newspapers as well as books, who walks streets as well as bookstore aisles, the violent confrontation between the Jewish Lesser and the black Spearmint echoes against the canyon carved between liberal and radical. In the autumn of 1968, for example, the New York City school strike produced an ugly showdown between Jewish teachers and black community groups. The particularly painful antagonism between America's two most articulate minorities is reflected in the novel's concluding scene, in which Jew and black have at each other

*Reprinted, with permission, from *Studies in the Novel* 8, no. 4 (winter 1976):458–67.

with ax and saber. Perhaps this is what the age demanded—the artist a social prophet and his art above all "relevant."

Nevertheless, as a product of and a mirror held up to this burning roadway, *The Tenants* commits a startling omission of sin. The single most disruptive trauma in American life during the late sixties is referred to only once and in such an oblique manner as to suggest deliberately extreme understatement. Harry Lesser's older brother died "in the war before this war" (p. 182). That "war before this war" is apparently the Korean War, and "this war" becomes a very curious euphemism for the Vietnam War. Whereas another Jewish novelist and one-time mayoral candidate had in fact directly entitled his 1967 novel *Why Are We in Viet Nam?*, Malamud contents himself with one passing, furtive allusion to an involvement which threatened as much destruction to American society as it entailed on the Asian mainland. This fact alone should raise doubts about locating Malamud in the company of such social realists as Dos Passos, Farrell, and Steinbeck.

Writing of *The Magic Barrel* and *The Assistant* in 1961, Philip Roth noted Malamud's "spurning of our world."[2]

> Malamud, as a writer of fiction, has not shown specific interest in the anxieties and dilemmas and corruptions of the modern American Jew, the Jew we think of as characteristic of our times; rather, his people live in a timeless depression and a placeless Lower East Side; their society is not affluent, their predicament not cultural.[3]

Alfred Kazin, as well, early called attention to Malamud's antirealism. Relating him to a Jewish tradition of otherworldliness, Kazin asserts: "Unlike those who are abstract because they have only their cleverness to write from, Malamud is abstract out of despair: despair of the world itself, which can no longer be represented."[4] And Robert Alter finds it instructive to juxtapose *The Tenants* to John Updike's *Rabbit Redux*.[5] Both works were published in the same year, and both are located in a recognizably contemporary America. Yet, by comparing the styles of similar passages in the two novels, Alter convincingly argues for a peculiarly solipsistic quality to the world of *The Tenants*. We rarely get outside Harry Lesser's imprisoning consciousness.

Malamud's fiction has consistently demonstrated a strategy of escape—whether from the banality of popular culture into the timeless significance of myth in *The Natural*, or from the deadening particulars of a prison cell into rejuvenating dreams in *The Fixer*. While his work begins in attentive obedience to the messy details of our world, it soon takes on a life of its own. Its central protagonist himself a novelist, *The Tenants* is Malamud's most self-conscious work. In an obvious echo of Proust, Harry Lesser reminds himself: "Time past is time earned unless the book was badly conceived, constructed, an unknown lemon; then it's dead time"

(p. 11). This is only one of hundreds of literary allusions scattered throughout a novel which is best understood within the tradition of *A la recherche du temps perdu*. It is one of that sizeable family of reflexive novels, including *Les Faux-Monnayeurs*, *La Nausée*, *La Modification*, *At Swim-Two-Birds*, *Under the Net*, and the Beckett trilogy which through a variety of devices refuse to allow the reader to forget they are fiction. When Shakespeare devises his numerous plays-within-a-play (*Pyramus and Thisbe*, *The Murder of Gonzago*, Prospero's Masque), when Alfred Hitchcock manages ingenious cameo appearances within his own films, and when William Butler Yeats parades his circus animals before our eyes, the effect is an intense awareness and questioning of artifice by artifice. As Künstlerroman, *The Tenants* features not one but two leading novelist figures. In addition, Irene is an actress performing Ibsen, and the deceased but important Lazar Kohn was a painter. In Gide's *Les Faux-Monnayeurs*, two different novelists, Edouard and Passavant, are competitors for authorial sovereignty within the fictive universe, as are the historian Desprez and the novelist Carnéjoux in Claude Mauriac's *La Marquise sortit à cinq heures*. In *The Tenants*, Harry Lesser and Willie Spearmint are literary rivals. Each desperately seeks to encompass the other within his art. The result is a novel which relentlessly probes the nature of literature — especially this particular work of literature — and of the social conditions from which it arises.

The very first sentence of *The Tenants* aptly depicts Harry Lesser glancing at himself in the mirror as he awakens to work on his book. The mirror motif recurs later, most notably when Lesser is leaving the Museum of Modern Art. In the Museum lobby, a black woman drops a mirror from her purse, shattering it. As Lesser stoops to pick up the pieces, he sees Irene and, somewhat portentously, thus begins a romantic involvement with someone other than himself. The mirror obviously points to both the narcissism of Lesser and to the introspective brooding on itself which characterizes *The Tenants*.

Even before its first sentence, *The Tenants* is framed by not one, but two epigraphs. One of the most traditional devices of editorial intrusion, the epigraph subverts in advance a narrative's illusion of being a slice of life. The effect here, at the very outset of Malamud's novel, is to caution us that we are about to encounter yet another exhibit in a museum without walls. It is Malamud the author telling dear reader that *The Tenants* finds its parallel as much in two other works of art as in the city streets. The first epigraph, "Alive and with his eyes open he calls us his murderers," anticipates Willie Spearmint's rage against a racist social order. At the same time, its source, the classical rhetorician Antiphon's *Tetralogies*, suggests Harry Lesser's identification with the mainstream of serious Western literature. With the second epigraph, the roles are reversed. "I got to make it, I got to find the end" clearly points to Lesser's obsession with providing an ending for his novel. However, the source of the quotation, the black jazz singer Bessie Smith, certainly belongs more to the world of Willie Spearmint.

The New York which Willie and Harry inhabit, like the art on which they toil, is easy prey to the demolitionist. Realistic illusion is shattered by literary allusion, and *The Tenants* deliberately and on almost every page reminds the reader of the existence of other works of literature. Brief reference to "Lesser's pleasure dome" (p. 4), for example, emphasizes the wretchedness of Harry's existence by contrasting it with the magnificence of Kubla Khan, at the same time as it reminds us that the words we are reading occupy the same ontological status as Coleridge's poem. Lesser's meditations on his situation assume unmistakeably Shakespearean cadences: "Ah, this live earth, this sceptered isle on a silver sea, this Thirty-first Street and Third Avenue. This forsaken house. This happy unhappy Lesser having to write" (p. 3). This allusion, by referring us back to *Richard II*, to the noble John of Gaunt and the glory that was England, once again mocks and defines a contemporary schlemiel, while it suggests Malamud as a colleague of Shakespeare, not Holinshed. Willie Spearmint's name is an overt salute to Shakespeare's, and Harry Lesser's projected novel will borrow both title and epigraph from *King Lear*. Its name, *The Promised End*, echoes Kent when, touched by the sight of the King carrying the dead Cordelia onto the stage, he asks: "Is this the promised end?" (V. iii. 264). And the epigraph, "Who is it who can tell me who I am?" recalls Lear's disappointment at the discourteous way Goneril has received him early in the play (I. iv. 220). Both serve to set a lesser figure against the background of high tragedy while reminding us that Lesser and Malamud ply the same trade as did Shakespeare.

Harry considers the possibility that Mark Twain once lived in the house next to his (p. 5), and a work of literature winks at us again when one of Willie's friends turn up named Sam Clemence. Lesser's hashish dream of drifting with Willie on a floating island (pp. 43–44) echoes Leslie Fiedler on Twain: the recurrent literary conceit of a white man and a black man together gliding free of civilization. The hero of Willie's novel reads an extensive list of authors while in prison, and, when his manuscript is destroyed, Harry consoles himself with the thought that both Thomas Carlyle and T. E. Lawrence rewrote entire works after losing the originals (pp. 164–65).[6] These and many, many other literary references with *The Tenants* lead us to a conclusion similar to that of Alice at the end of her curious adventures; we have had to do with "nothing but a pack of cards." Jan Mukařovský and the Prague School in general have popularized the concept of foregrounding as a distinctive feature of poetic language,[7] and Tony Tanner sees foregrounding as characteristic of American fiction between 1950 and 1970.[8] Persistent reminders within *The Tenants* of the world of literature foregrounds the novel, calls attention to the truth that this is a novel, one whose central concern is the relationship between novels and the experiences they transcend.

Willie solicits Harry's judgment of his writing, and, in the counterpoint of blocks of Willie's narrative with Harry's comments on them, a kind of metaliterature, literature which is simultaneously its own criticism, emerges. The figures of a Jewish writer and a black writer enabled Malamud to juxtapose the two most publicized "movements" in American fiction during the sixties. Such authors as Wright, Ellison, Baldwin, and Jones form even less of a coherent "school" in the Continental sense than do Bellow, Mailer, Roth, and Malamud himself. And Malamud's black and Jew seem at times caricature of charcoal face and carrot nose. A more sympathetic, and accurate, description is that they are metaphors, tools for exploring two poles of the creative mind. In Malamud's idiosyncratic universe in which to be a self-denying sufferer is to be a Jew, a belated circumcision only confirms that the Gentile Frank Alpine of *The Assistant* is in essence a Jew. Philip Roth, again, observes that Malamud's are not real Jews but rather "a kind of invention, a metaphor to stand for certain human possibilities and certain human promises. . . ."[9] In *The Tenants*, Malamud at his best is neither sociologist nor literary historian. His Jewish and black writers serve to probe two distinct possibilities of literary expression.

Willie Spearmint's writings are confessional, picaresque, naturalistic, and *engagé*. First person narratives, they appropriate elements from the autobiographies of Malcolm X, Eldridge Cleaver, and George Jackson. The main character traces his progress from a broken home, through a sentimental education in the underworld and in prison, to the growth of a transforming self-awareness. A hostile environment is the villain, and the narrator portrays himself as both victim and rebel. Throughout the various versions and stories Willie attempts, details change, and it is impossible for Harry or Irene to determine which are more biographically authentic. But, though the narrator is born now in Mississippi, now in Harlem, now in Georgia, the fundamental pattern and style remain. Furthermore, to be able to compose a powerful story is not enough for Willie; it must have some effect on the society from which it arose. Lesser imagines Willie scrawling in charcoal the defiant assertion: "REVOLUTION IS THE REAL ART" (p. 163).

While admiring the energy in Willie's prose, Lesser regrets that his ideas "fall short of effective form" and "that his writing shows impatience with the craft of writing" (p. 61). Some of Henry James's most articulate champions have been American Jews, and, in contrast to Willie's compulsion to say *something*, Harry Lesser devotes himself to the imperious demands of form. He has spent nine and a half years toiling on just one novel, and it is only a scrupulous concern for the organic relationship which must exist between an ending and what has gone before that has kept him in monastic confinement in his tenement searching for *la fin juste*. To the hard-boiled premise that truth is crude and only distorted by the niceties of style, Malamud's black writer brings a stubborn Will and a potent Spear. His harried Jew is a servant of beauty, a Lesser god in the primitive pantheon. And Willie's physical presence and his sensual distractions identify him with the body, while Harry's wide reading and his ascetic existence mark him as mind. Furthermore, in the clash between the two writers, Harry is a universalist; in the name of tireless principles, he challenges Willie's assertion that you must share an author's experience in order to understand his book.

> "Black ain't white and never can be. It is once and for only black. It ain't universal if that's what you are hintin up to. What I feel you feel different. You can't write about black because you don't have the least idea what we are or how we feel. Our feelin chemistry is different than yours. Dig that? It *has* to be so. I'm writin the soul writin of black people cryin out we are still slaves in this fuckn country and we ain't gonna stay slaves any longer. How can you understand it, Lesser, if your brain is white?"
>
> "So is your brain white. But if the experience is about being human and moves me then you've made it my experience. You created it for me. You can deny universality, Willie, but you can't abolish it" (p. 68).

This feud between content and form, truth and beauty, mind and body, the One and the many is of course even tautologically unwholesome. The complete work of art, whether *The Tenants* or *The Promised End*, must succeed in harmonizing such contraries. The novel's final fantasy is of an apocalyptic combat and fusion between Jew and black. "Each, thought the writer, feels the anguish of the other" (p. 211). However, even before that moment, each initiates a conversion in the other. After moving into the tenement house, Willie becomes more and more slave to a Flaubertian art. He spends an expanding number of hours each day laboring on his manuscript, until he eventually has no time left for Irene. Harry, in turn, is drawn increasingly into a sensual life, inheriting Irene and abandoning, at least temporarily, the word for the world. The reversal of Jew and black is underscored when Willie, physically emaciated by long bouts with his writing, complains to Harry: "You young bloods have got it all over us alter cockers" (p. 143).

Eventually, Harry, like Willie, abandons Irene to return to the demands of his craft. Despite dramatic differences, both Harry and Willie are writers, and both assume the austere, isolated role of *le poéte maudit*. Willie's writing is an outraged expression of social concern, yet to be a writer he withdraws from society to the vacuum of an abandoned tenement. And Harry, who informs Irene he is writing a book about love, must lead a singularly loveless life to do so. In Willie's first manuscript, the narrator, serving time for burglary, discovers he is able to escape prison walls, at least in his imagination, as soon as he begins to write. "From then on I am not afraid of the fucking prison because I am out of it as much as I am in" (pp. 57–58). Both Harry and Willie withdraw from the world in order to embrace it. By doing so, they recall the line, not alluded to by Malamud, in which Lear welcomes captivity: "We two alone will sing like birds i' th' cage" (V. iii. 9).

In contrast to both caged writers, the landlord Irving Levenspiel is a sort of reality principle. Recurrent visits to his tenement house in order to plead with Lesser to vacate represent an intrusion of the outside world into an aesthetic retreat. He is analagous to the wet mutt with bleeding eye which makes its way up six flights of stairs, only to be evicted by Lesser (p. 21). Thus does the writer defend himself against the surrounding chaos which threatens to overwhelm him. As the Hebrew and German etymology of his name suggests, Levenspiel exists to play on the heart — "Art my ass, in this world it's heart that counts" (p. 19) — and to remind his stubborn tenant of the dangers of insulating himself from human emotions — "What's a make-believe novel, Lesser, against all my woes and miseries that I have explained to you?" (p. 18). Nevertheless, Levenspiel's appearances provide comic relief, and he is an object of fun. With each inflated bribe offer to get Harry to leave, Levenspiel provides a catalogue of his sorrows: his mother's insanity, his daughter's abortion, the economic pressures forcing him to demolish the building. Levenspiel is a grotesque, and his version of reality emerges as even more incredible than the artist's facsimile.

If Harry Lesser, unmarried and absolutely alone, is to come to life, he must beget himself. His mother died when he was still young, and his aged father, whom he has not seen in years, is in distant Chicago. Like the Gideon bastards who exult in the challenge of molding their own identities, Harry in effect must be his own parent. He is thirty-six, and, like Dante midway in his life's journey or like Huysmans's Des Esseintes, Sartre's Roquentin, or Murdoch's Jake Donaghue, all in their thirties, Harry looks forward to a rebirth. Like most Malamud protagonists, he awaits A New Life.

In Harry's case, the new life will be through and in the novel on which he is laboring. Totally absorbed by his work, he *is* his novel — "Thus Lesser writes his book and his book writes Lesser" (p. 177). Who touches his book touches the new man Lesser creates. In *Pictures of Fidelman* (1968), Arthur Fidelman must begin all over after Susskind burns his Giotto manuscript in Rome and after Beppo destroys his paintings in Venice. When Willie Spearmint burns the only copy of the novel Harry Lesser has been struggling with for over nine years, it is as if he has murdered Harry; staring at the charred remains of his manuscript, Lesser "saw himself buried in ashes" (p. 164). In order to arise Phoenix-like, Harry must forge a fresh identity from the beginning. Willie Spearmint, who is born again as the novelist Bill Spear, demonstrates this identification of self and creation. Classical mythology exalts the power of the artist when it depicts Pygmalion bringing the statue Galatea to life. Yet the figure of Willie suggests the autogenesis of a Pygmalion who is simultaneously his own Galatea—"nobody, his presence stated, was his Pygmalion. He had sculpted himself" (p. 64). Both of Malamud's writer figures enter their house of fiction as into a maternity ward, and Harry is in fact called "to midwife" (p. 77) Willie's work.

One of the quotations Arthur Fidelman stencils on his wall in Florence is Whistler's "A masterpiece is finished from the beginning."[10] In an organic work of art, the end is of course promised and contained in its seed. But Harry Lesser's promised end never comes, and *The Tenants* is riddled with false conclusions, passages representing Harry's attempt to put a stop to nine and a half years of labor. Each is followed by the formulaic "The End," yet each is also followed by other alternatives. Harry puzzles over the achievement of his dead friend, the painter Lazar Kohn. Kohn was able to complete a portrait of a woman simply by deciding to hang it on a wall.

> In painting, Lesser thought, you could finish off, total up, whether done or undone, because in the end (the end?) you hung a canvas object on the wall and there was no sign saying, "Abandoned, come back tomorrow for more." If it hung it was done, no matter what the painter thought (pp. 102–3).

In a work of fiction, on the other hand, the end must be not only terminal, but teleological as well. While painting deals with immediate sense impressions, literature organizes thoughts. It attempts to impose a complete pattern, a meaning, on experience, even if that experience, like the sick stray dog or like Irving Levenspiel and his troubles, is inherently disruptive of all order.

Moreover, if in fact the artist succeeds in re-creating himself through his writing and can achieve an identification of self and book, the book cannot have an end as long as the life does not. Both are works in progress. As long as Harry Lesser, unlike the late Lazar Kohn, continues breathing and struggling, his life goes on, deprived of the significance of definitive retrospection. Kohn is able to arise, Lazarus-like, from the grave, reborn as a work of art, but Lesser, who tells Irene that the name of his novel's main character is Lazar Kohn, as yet cannot. The living novelist—whether Harry Lesser or Bernard Malamud—who attempts to compose against the background of contemporary American society is destined to do so without end. Harry's new life, whether as completed novel or as marriage to Irene in San Francisco, can never come. In front of Harry's tenement "stood a single dented ash can containing mostly his crap, thousands of torn-up screaming words and rotting apple cores, coffee grinds, and broken eggshells, a literary rubbish can, the garbage of language become the language of garbage" (p. 4). The failure of a realism committed to cataloguing the trash of our lives is that the language of garbage is an endless flow.

But *The Tenants* does have a back cover. After a fantasy of violent confrontation between Jew and black, Levenspiel enters the scene with a plea for mercy. After ninety-eight repetitions of the word "mercy," the novel halts, without a period. Typographically, this long chain of identical words resembles an ellipsis, and it emphasizes the fact that *The Tenants*, like Harry Lesser's novel, remains open-ended. In Shakespeare's use of the Jew as metaphor, an emotionally constricted character is reminded that the quality of mercy is not strained but flows freely, as does the word itself on the last page of *The Tenants*. Mercy entails concern for someone else, an absolute denial of solipsism. Trailing off into a potentially endless series of *mercys*, the novel halts with a recognition of the insufficiency of the self. In Huysmans's *A rebours*, Des Esseintes, like Harry Lesser, retires from the world in order to be reborn in a life which is as deliberate as a work of art. Yet the conclusion to *A rebours*, like that of *The Tenants*, suggests failure for the project of individual autonomy; Des Esseintes is left invoking God's pity. Malamud's Jewish novelist is incomplete as human being and as artist. And *The Tenants*, faced with composing the unresolved tensions of contemporary society and with fixing the novel's relationship to life, does neither, memorably.

Notes

1. Bernard Malamud, *The Tenants* (New York: Pocket Books, 1972), p. 5. Numbers within the essay refer to pages in this edition.

2. Philip Roth, "Writing American Fiction," *Commentary*, 31 (March 1961); rpt. in *The American Novel since World War II*, ed. Marcus Klein (Greenwich, Conn.: Fawcett, 1969), p. 150.

3. Ibid., p. 151.

4. "The Magic and the Dread," *Contemporary Literature*, ed. Richard Kostelanetz (New York: Avon, 1969), p. 441.

5. "Updike, Malamud, and the Fire This Time," *Commentary*, 54 (Oct. 1972), 68–74.

6. Coincidentally or not, in *Mr. Sammler's Planet*, published one year earlier, Saul Bellow makes use of the same anecdote (New York: Viking, 1970), p. 113.

7. See especially Mukařovský's "Standard Language and Poetic Language," in *A Prague School Reader on Esthetics, Literary Structure, and Style*, ed. Paul L. Garvin (Washington, D.C.: Georgetown Univ. Press, 1964), pp. 17–30.

8. *City of Words: American Fiction 1950–1970* (New York: Harper and Row, 1971), p. 20 ff.

9. Roth, p. 151.

10. Malamud, *Pictures of Fidelman* (Middlesex, England: Penguin, 1972), p. 71.

Mirrors, Windows and Peeping Toms: Women as the Object of Voyeuristic Scrutiny in Bernard Malamud's *A New Life* and *Dubin's Lives*

Chiara Briganti*

It is generally acknowledged that it is through the abandonment of egocentrism that the protagonists of Malamud's novels arrive at self-definition.[1] Any attempt to escape reality is doomed to failure and solipsism, and the individual who conjures up his own interior world condemns himself to impotence because he does not have a world to act in any more. Malamud's characters are presented in the act of self-creation which involves reconciliation with their own past and giving up false notions of freedom; they become accomplished individuals, with a commitment to a profound relationship, defined values, and a space in society. The quest for identity engages them in a sentimental education, and those who succeed in the struggle against their own egocentrism not only conquer a new life, but learn how to respond to the other with that charity and sympathy without which for Malamud there is no possibility for regeneration. It is through commitment that the protagonists realize their freedom.

In this quest, women serve primarily as antagonists and as a means to precipitate the crisis in the male protagonist. In *The Natural*, Memo Paris and Iris Lemon, far from being complex characters, are there to confront the protagonist with temptation and ruin on one side and possibility of redemption on the other. So Memo Paris, a new version of the "dark lady" of much British and American literature, is the vindictive temptress whose "sick breast" seems to exemplify an inability to love, while Iris Lemon (and the name itself is only too openly symbolic) is presented like a somewhat simplistic Great Mother of fertility. This same duality reappears attenuated in *A New Life*, where S. Levin finds out that Avis Fliss (like Memo suffering from breast fibroma) has been spying on his adulterous relationship with Pauline Gilley and has been collecting evidence with the intention of reporting it to Pauline's husband. But Avis is more a pathetic lonely woman than a vindictive temptress, and Pauline, although pregnant by the end of the novel, is hardly a goddess of fertility. In *The Fixer*, Raisl's function is to offer her husband the possibility of redemption through sacrifice. Like all the other female figures, she too is relegated to her sexual role, and Yakov Bok curses her "miscarrying womb and dry breasts." In *The Tenants*, Irene, initially Willie's "white bitch," and for some obscure reason suffering from cystitis, is the cause of the two male

*Reprinted from *Studies in American Jewish Literature*, no. 3 (1983):151–65, by permission of the State University of New York Press. © 1983, State University of New York.

characters' rivalry, and therefore, indirectly, of their literary crisis. We ignore everything about her, except that she used to be, as she confesses to Harry Lesser, "a fucked-up kid," who "drew men like flies until [she] began to wake up frightened" (*TT*, 108). She seems to be the prototype of the Fanny Bick of *Dubin's Lives* and, like her successor, her only function in the novel is to precipitate a crisis and to offer a potential for redemption which is rejected by the male protagonist.

It will be argued in the present paper that two tendencies can be distinguished in Malamud's fiction: in one group of novels (*The Natural*, *The Tenants, Dubin's Lives*), the protagonist is unable to free himself from his subjectivity because of an intrinsic passivity, while in the other (*The Assistant, A New Life, The Fixer, Pictures of Fidelman*), the protagonist succeeds in overcoming his earlier traits and assumes an active role, and, consequently, achieves a positive identity. I will illustrate this argument in terms of the voyeuristic impulse in the characters of S. Levin in *A New Life* and William Dubin in *Dubin's Lives*, showing how women, being the object of a voyeuristic scrutiny, never rise above the sexual roles which strictly determine their function in the narrative.

Theodore Solotaroff observed that "As in the romances of another moralist, Nathaniel Hawthorne, there are a good many mirror images in Malamud's tales, and they signify much the same preoccupation with those moments when the distinction between the objective and the imaginary is suspended and the spirit sees either itself or, in Hawthorne's term, its 'emblems.' "[2] To lights and mirrors we can add the images that refer to eyes and windows and the verbs that abdicate the visual function. These images, although always present in Malamud's works, recur more frequently in *A New Life* and in *Dubin's Lives*, where they serve well the purpose of characterizing these two novels and of defining their positions at the two extremes of Malamud's production.

In *A New Life* all characters seem to be affected with what Freud refers to as "scopophilia," the obsessive tendency to watch others and themselves; and in this act they reveal their own impotence: they look without seeing, compelled to indulge in their visual faculty through a medium which itself becomes an obstacle. The landscape, which Levin looks at from his office window, becomes ominous: "Staring out of the window, Levin noticed that the cracked glass resembled a forked lightning" (*ANL*, 227). Levin watches Pauline, the woman who has become his lover, through fogged windowpanes, half-closed windows or curtains, which become symbols of his impotence to overcome a sense of estrangement and to establish a relationship with the woman. Gerald Gilley, Pauline's husband, shows the same kind of impotence, that is, of inability to see: "Gilley . . . stood there for a wavering minute, a redheaded owl *peering* into the dark . . . blinked *without seeing* them although *staring* in their direction" (*ANL*, 188) (emphasis added).

On his first night in Cascadia as a guest of Gerald and Pauline,

"[Levin] caught a glimpse of the Gilleys, man and wife, embracing in their nightshirts" (*ANL*, 24). This scene foreshadows the anomalous position of Levin, outsider and spectator, which will reach its climax when, having become the lover of Pauline, he seems to abdicate in favor of Gilley, and choose the role of a voyeur:

> He watched for a touch of Pauline, a glimpse of her dress as she passed the half-shaded window, or whatever morsel luck would let fall into his empty hands. . . . Levin was startled by a touch on the arm. A cop, staring at his beard, said a taxpayer had called and complained of a Peeping Tom. . . . He crossed the street and stood . . . a few feet from her partly-open, dark bedroom window. . . . In the stillness he heard the rhythmic creaking of a bed, and then on the night — a bird, catch it, hold it — the soft cry of a woman at the height of her pleasure.
>   Gilley had, in an inspired moment, satisfied her for him. (*ANL*, 243–44)

However, Levin, newcomer in Cascadia, and haunted by old terrors and by the fear of another failure — "A white-eyed hound bayed at him from the window — his classic failure after grimy years to master himself" (*ANL*, 164) — not only watches, but is watched by all the characters that move around him, and these two elements, watching and being watched, interplay throughout the novel in a complex way: "He . . . found himself staring into a pair of brown eyes. . . . then he saw Pauline Gilley watching him through the glass top of the back door, something like pity in her eyes" (*ANL*, 164). What seems significant is that through the novel Levin moves from the voyeuristic attitude that characterizes his lack of commitment to reality, his role of impotent spectator, to becoming a victim of the voyeurism of the other characters. From being a watcher, he gradually becomes the object of scrutiny, as through errors, *faux pas*, uncertainties, he takes in his hands the reins of his own life and accepts the need to act in reality, even though this ultimately means giving up his aspirations.

Although at first he "thought in terms of experience with [Pauline], not necessarily commitment," he finally accepts the responsibility that she represents. However, Pauline, like Laverne, Nadalee and Avis has still little human significance for Levin. She is only the pretext for his crisis; by becoming his mistress she precipitates the events and forces him to dive deep into his own nature and past existence; but as a character, she is another example of Malamud's inability to create believable three-dimensional female figures. Throughout the novel she never acquires a real substance and her image remains somewhat blurred. Gilley sees her as a neurotic wife, Levin as a potential lover, and even the image she has of herself is only that of "a mother of two." At first put off by her barren chest, Levin finally falls in love with her "because she had one unforgettable day given herself to a city boy in a forest. And for the continuance of her generosity in bed. . . . Or was he moved to love because her eyes mirrored Levin when he looked" (*ANL*, 217).

If to Levin she is the "masked lady" just long enough to stir his excitement and confront him with the thrill of mystery, the reader is never allowed to remove the veil and gain a deeper insight into her character. By showing her behind half-drawn curtains and misty windowpanes, Malamud makes her the object of Levin's voyeuristic scrutiny and denies her a complex personality. She doesn't exist. When debating between his desire to continue the relationship and his feeling of remorse, Levin never takes Pauline into consideration but "he feared the husband of the wife, ashamed of eating his apple" (*ANL*, 222). Even when Levin somehow overcomes his voyeuristic impulse and assumes an active role, Pauline's function remains simply that of the instrument through which Levin can prove that his old self has changed and is now ready for a new life. His "falling in love with her breaks his tie with his old self: he is not any longer on the periphery of things, watching and observing the local flora and fauna with his binoculars and nature book."[3]

A *New Life* ends positively not because Levin succeeds in fulfilling his dream of a brilliant academic career; on the contrary, he is forced to give it up, but because for the first time in his life he accepts the burden of his responsibilities and chooses an active role. When Gilley asks him, " 'An older woman than yourself and not dependable, plus two adopted kids, no choice of yours, no jobs or promise of one, and other assorted headaches. Why take that load on yourself,' " Levin can answer: " 'Because I can, you son of a bitch' " (*ANL*, 360).

Levin symbolically breaks the circle of his stifling subjectivity when in a fit of anger he punches the cracked windowpane that he inherited from Duffy, his unfortunate predecessor, whose footmarks, for a series of coincidences, he has been following so far. It is his first act of rebellion, symbolic of his decision to act and to shake off his shoulders the shadow of his predecessor who ended up committing suicide.

Once he has acquired the courage to expose himself and to face his own eyes as well as those of the people around him, he shaves the beard that he had grown "in a time of doubt . . . when [he] couldn't look [him]self in the face." The mirror where he confronts himself does not reflect a flattering image, but what matters is that Levin survives the ordeal:

> He had searched long in the mirror, felt ill but lived. Too much face, the eyes still sad candles, blunt bent nose, lips without speech telling all, but the jaw looked stronger, possibly illusion. (*ANL*, 246)

The role of voyeur is now taken by Gilley, Pauline's sterile husband, amateur photographer, "very talented at candid shots" (*ANL*, 15), what Barthes would call "un agent de la Mort."[4] The analogy between the lens of the camera and the keyhold, privileged stimulus of voyeuristic imagination, comes naturally to mind. Photography, which in Sundquist's words, "perfects the fantasy of the voyeur who sees all without being implicated in the scene,"[5] provides Gilley with a gratifying and, as he himself will admit, useful hobby. Thanks to this hobby, he finds out the relationship between his wife and Duffy. For Duffy, in turn, photography turns out to be fatal, since it makes him lose the support of Fabrikant, the only person who was willing to defend him, and consequently provokes the loss of his job and his suicide. The camera, the means that Gilley uses to act out his voyeuristic aggression, becomes an actual deadly weapon. The last action of Gilley, consistent with his role, consists in taking a picture of Pauline and Levin as they are leaving Cascadia:

> Gilley was aiming a camera at the operation. When he saw Levin's Hudson approach he swung the camera around and snapped. As they drove by he tore a rectangle of paper from the back of the camera and waved it aloft.
> "Got your picture!" (*ANL*, 367)

In this act, Gilley's voyeuristic aggression explodes. Taking a picture amounts to reducing the subject to "Tout-Image" that is the death in person; it means to expropriate him of himself and make him an object; to put him in a file, ready for any kind of subtle manipulation.[6]

Dubin's Lives, Malamud's most recent novel, ends in ambiguity, but still in such a way as to be grouped with *The Natural* and *The Tenants*, where the protagonists are hopelessly sealed in their egos and whose quests for a new life always lead to failure. The failure of Roy Hobbs and Harry Lesser is partly due to their incapacity to commit themselves and to accept a relationship with another human being. They both remain isolated and, therefore, sterile, frustrated in that quest for an identity to love and to lose themselves in the "other" in a constructive relationship.

The most common means of acquiring a personal identity in Malamud's novels is provided by work; but Malamud constantly suggests that devotion to work should not be obsessive; instead, it should be tempered with respect for the reality of life. Roy Hobbs is so carried away by baseball that anything he says, does or thinks, is related to that sport. The same bias shows in the total devotion of Harry Lesser to his art: since he sees himself only as a writer, all other human, social and emotional activities are secondary to him. In *The Tenants*, Malamud, besides elaborating on his fundamental literary preoccupation — the development of a personal identity, focuses on a recent interest of his, the relationship between the artist and art, on one hand, and art and reality on the other, the issues of which are made even more explicit in *Dubin's Lives* where the protagonist is a biographer.

Dubin started to write biographies because "He felt that the pieces of his own life could be annealed into a unity. He would understand better, be forewarned. He felt he had deepened, extended his life; had become

Dubin the biographer (*DL*, 98). But gradually his profession becomes an alibi not to live his own life, while at the same time providing him with a way, although an illusory one, to break the boundaries of his existence: "Everybody's life is mine unlived. One writes lives he can't live. To live forever is a human hunger. . . . Prufrock had measured out his life with measuring spoons; Dubin, in books resurrecting the lives of others" (*DL*, 11–12). This is one of the most effective passages focusing Dubin's personality, which immediately reveals itself as strongly narcissistic.[7]

The biographer struggles to extract art from experience, watching himself live, write and cope with the complex interplay of life and literature, individual and society. Art becomes for him the only means of controlling life and exorcising the terror of death. To create with words and images becomes a mode of transforming writing into some ascetic but self-fulfilling practice of the soul, into a value substitutive of any other truth. But at this point, Dubin approaches a crisis: D. H. Lawrence, the character he has chosen for his next biography, after his initial choice of Virginia Woolf, "whose intelligent imagination and fragile self had drawn him to her," seems to be elusive and recalcitrant; his personality, extremely different from the biographer's, does not provide Dubin with any clue to effect that process of identification that is necessary for him in order to deal with it in its complexity. Confronted with a character such as Lawrence, who " 'lived a vast consciousness of life. At his best he wants man to risk himself for a plenitude of life through love' " (*DL*, 303), Dubin goes through a crisis, as a biographer and as a man. And because of this interplay, if not confusion between art and life, which characterizes Dubin, it is not clear whether his sudden passion for Fanny, the attractive dropout whom his wife has hired as house helper, is, at least to some extent, stimulated by the biography of Lawrence. It seems evident, however, that the voyeuristic relationship of the biographer with the lives he writes about, from the very beginning marks his relationship with Fanny:

> He enjoyed coming on Fanny in motion: forcefully stroking the rugs with the vacuum cleaner; the choreography with a mop over the kitchen floor . . . she was gifted in femininity, Dubin had decided. Fanny wore miniskirts; on hot days she appeared in shorts and gauzy blouses . . . her white or black bra visible through the garment". (*DL*, 26)

Here too, as in *A New Life*, the recurrence of images related to mirrors, eyes, windows, defines a relationship voyeuristic as well as narcissistic with reality. Dubin, immoderate Narcissus, confronts daily his image in the mirror: "He beheld in the mirror . . . a flash of himself in his grave, and with a grimace clutched his gut where he had been stabbed" (*DL*, 15). The spell thrown on Dubin by the reflecting surface might indicate a fragmentary identity in need of constant verification, as it seems to be proved by the tendency to catch glimpses of himself that hit him as violently as traumas: "The biographer caught a glimpse of himself in the mirror. Shock of recognition. . . ." and by his need to define himself over and over according to the role played at that particular moment: "Old Billy Goat," "Dubin Prometheus, bringer of heat in a cold house," "Dubin frozen stiff, snowman. Death's scarecrow," "Dubin, man of the world," "Dubin the single."

The way Dubin indulges in watching and defining himself reveals also a tendency to narcissistic self-contemplation and a voyeuristic rela- tionship also with himself—Dubin will stop to watch himself, he will come out of himself to be a spectator of his own actions—which reflect in turn detachment and lack of commitment in his life. In Hawthorne, from whom, as mentioned above, Malamud may have derived this type of imagery, the insistence on mirrors and reflected images symbolizes a tendency to voyeurism. According to Eric Sundquist, in Hawthorne this tendency "often takes the form of his fear of being subjected to the gaze of the other and his obsession with voyeurism and detective-like surveil- lance."[8] This is certainly true also for Malamud, whose characters, when not spying, are haunted by the idea of being spied upon, and often are at the same time voyeurs and victims of voyeurism.

For a curious coincidence, to support his thesis, Sundquist quotes D. H. Lawrence who, in his essay on *The Scarlet Letter*, noting the relation between voyeurism and transgression, points out that during their sexual intercourse after the Fall from Eden, Adam and Eve "kept an eye on what they were doing, they watched what was happening to them . . . before the apple, they had shut their eyes and their minds had gone dark. Now, they peeped and pried and imagined. They watched themselves." Dubin's voyeurism is being linked to transgression and showing itself explicitly when the biographer finds himself spying on Fanny, and watching himself while spying on her; but it also shows a refusal to live and to be involved in human relationships, to come out of his subjectivity. This tendency marks all of Dubin's relationships, starting with the one with nature, that he seems to derive from Thoreau, of whom he wrote a biography: "In sum, William Dubin, visitor to nature, had introduced himself along the way but did not intrude. He gazed from the road, kept his distance even when nature hallooed . . . on the whole, in varying moods Dubin looked at the scenery, and the scenery, in varying moods, looked at him. . . . If you dared to look you earned seeing" (*DL*, 9–10). The analogy with Thoreau's clandestine gaze seems clear: "Man cannot afford to be a naturalist, to look at nature directly, but only with the side of his eye. . . . To look at her is [as] fatal as to look at the head of Medusa."[9]

This same voyeurism characterizes Dubin's relationship with his wife. In a scene at the beginning of the novel, that seems particularly signifi- cant, Dubin, looking at Kitty from the window, believes he is watching some ritual dance; he thinks he may have discovered a new side of his wife's personality, and the banality of what is actually taking place escapes him completely:

> Kitty, as he dried his razor by the sunlit window, seemed to be dancing on the lawn. . . . It was a running dance, very expressive — fertility rite? . . . He tried to figure out what the ceremonial meant: wounded bird, dying swan? . . . He felt how strange life was, then began thinking of Passions of D. H. Lawrence, before he realized Kitty was in the house, screaming to him, her face red, eyes angered, frightened.
> "Why the hell didn't you come and help me?"
> "What for?"
> "A *bee*, William," she cried. (*DL*, 17–18)

Kitty is a perceptive and attractive middle-aged woman. As most of Malamud's female characters, she doesn't have a profession nor any special vocation. In fact, except as mother and wife she hasn't accomplished much in her life — she is rather what one would define an accomplished woman, with a conspicuous interest in psychoanalysis developed after her first marriage with a doctor. Full of idiosyncrasies and neuroses, she suffers from insomnia and worries about cancer and leaking stove-gas. After having been married twenty-five years to Dubin, she starts ruminating on her first husband, who died of leukemia at forty. She is so constantly intent on brooding on the past, analyzing the years of her marriage, that finally to Dubin she comes to represent the past with all its disillusions and failed expectations. Malamud, however, is not interested enough in his female characters as to tell us more about the way Kitty deals with her ghosts and with the progressive estrangement of her husband; we see her only from Dubin's point of view as a neurotic and dependent woman groping about to keep her balance. On the other hand, we know that if change for Kitty depends on her husband, for Dubin the only possible way to bring a change into his life would be to come out of his own ego and commit himself to a responsible relationship with another human being; but he is distracted and lacking in generosity. His marriage, which at first he thought would provide him with a way to give a purpose to his life and to give up loneliness, has proved unable to fulfil his expectations: Dubin at fifty-seven is not very different from the twenty-year old "self-reclusive too subjective romantic youth." He doesn't sympathize with his neurotic wife — "He left her standing sadly naked before the glass" — and is relieved when she decides to see a psychoanalyst. After twenty years spent together, the two only share their weaknesses and loneliness: "You're out on your private little black sailboat in the rough green sea and here I'm alone on a dreary lava-like shore," says Kitty bitterly.

The past, although Dubin seems to be continuously analyzing it, is not reconciled with the present and accepted; it does not become a useful experience; instead, it is only a burden. Of his childhood, Dubin only remembers his mother's insanity (Dubin's mother belongs to a long series of suicidal and insane women in Malamud's fiction). Of his father, he recalls the indolence and resignation, and is unable to grasp the meaning of a life redeemed by the struggle for a dignity achieved through the sorrow experienced together with and for another human being.

It is known that the dialectic counterpart of voyeurism is narcissism, and Dubin not only relishes his daily confrontations in the mirror, "In the lusterless mirror his left eye was fixed, distant, cold; contemplating his frightened right eye," but goes so far as to use other people as reflecting surfaces: "The unconscious is mirrored in a man's acts and words. If he watches and listens to himself, sooner or later, he begins to see the contours of the unconscious self . . . You see in others what you are" (DL, 130).

In such novels as The Assistant, A New Life, and The Fixer, the protagonist seems to have gone through a positive change by assuming a fatherly role. In The Natural and The Tenants, where the protagonists fail in their quest for identity, their failures come together with the refusal or the absence of the fatherly role.[10] In Dubin's Lives, although the protagonist is a father of two children, of whom one is adopted, his relationship with them turns out to be fragile and unresolved. When he goes to visit his adopted son in Sweden, more to appease his guilty conscience for having betrayed his wife than for a genuine interest in the boy, Dubin discovers that Gerald has taken back the name of his real father, Kitty's first husband. Their encounter is made pathetic by the absolute lack of communication: "Dubin talked to the youth's back and Gerald talked to the night. . . . The biographer limped behind him" (DL, 110-11). The reason for this incapability to communicate has already been provided by Dubin, in a rare attempt to analyze his relationship with his adopted child:

Q. "Tell me, Dubin, what did the boy really mean to you?"
A. "I saw myself in his eyes—a fatherly type."[11] (DL, 270)

With Maud, the daughter born from his marriage with Kitty, Dubin is not more successful. Sealed in his own egocentrism, careless and distracted, he cannot even remember his daughter's age. The only ties he has are sentimental ties with the past: "He had wanted one of Maud's affectionate notes as a child to keep in his pocket. The uses of the dwindling past" (DL, 120). And when Maud asks for help, he is unable to respond. Needless to say, in spite of Zen meditation and heightened sensibility, Maud has to succumb to the destiny of Malamud's female characters, and her crisis of identity is closely related, in fact it has its origin in her sexuality: she is made pregnant by a man thirty years her senior, married, black.

The numerous parallels between Maud and Fanny—they are the same age, they both drop out of school to live in a Buddhist commune, and they both become involved with men old enough to be their fathers—seem to point out the motive of the unconscious incest desire which runs in much of Malamud's fiction. But they are not convincing and do not add substance to the personalities of the two women; Maud, in particular, never becomes more than the stereotype of the Berkeley vegetarian, health-nut, and faddist.

The "Promised End," the novel that Harry Lesser, the protagonist of *The Tenants* is writing, is not only a mirror of his own life, but can be considered also the paradigm of *Dublin's Lives:*

> It was about a writer, a . . . man who is often afflicted by the thought that he has wasted more of his life than he was entitled to . . . he finds it hard to give love . . . It's the old giving business, he can and he can't, not good enough, too many unknown reservations, the self occluded. Love up to a point is not love at all. His life betrays his imagination.[12]

The incapacity to give, exemplified by the voyeuristic attitude, also mark Dubin's relationship with Fanny. As in *The Natural* Roy does not realize what Iris Lemon is offering him, and refuses both her and what she stands for — love, fertility — when she reveals her past to him, so Dubin cannot overcome the "girl-of-my-dreams" syndrome. Although Fanny gradually turns out to be a positive character, with clear implications of fertility, because of her past, "Dubin saw clearly what she had and what she lacked: was unmoved by her. She lacked, he thought, experience of a necessary sort; certain mistakes are wrong to make" (*DL*, 193). The mistakes he cannot forgive her for can be identified with that fullness of life which Lawrence preaches and which Dubin is impotent to pursue, because even in the most ecstatic moments, rather than merge himself into the experience, he watches himself live: "Here is William the Bold, with upraised sword on a black charger, galloping onward under the bright blue sky (*DL*, 62).

In literature, one of the most recurrent symbolical structures is represented by the tendency to identify sexuality with sin. Therefore eroticism is placed in the equivocal position of being at the same time the most powerful expression of life instinct and the most essential experience of ego dissociation. Only love can resolve this dichotomy: the impulse to love becomes a motivation to find human order in chaos. Dubin cannot resolve this dichotomy, and his passion for Fanny proves to be another symptom of immaturity; his physical desire, another form of narcissism. Not even when he finds her again after a winter spent under a sterile and exhausting discipline of strict diet and jogging, and finally makes love to her, is he able to abandon himself to the experience. Twice he loses her and twice he finds her, and in both cases the magic of the moment is reduced to a sterile accounting transaction: "This evens it, Dubin thought, for the cruel winter. Was it this, he wondered, he had earned tonight?"

Like Lesser, who falls in love with Irene because he finds that she fits well in his life and in the novel he is writing. Dubin also falls in love with

Fanny because she represents that richness of life Lawrence writes about and from which he has always felt excluded: "Dubin felt heartened to have recovered her. He felt himself a gifted man, an excellent biographer" (*DL*, 211). Both Dubin and Lesser fail to understand that the delicate equilibrium between art and life is compromised when one of the two is pursued at the other's expense. When Fanny fails him, Dubin gets stuck in his writing, unable to use his imagination to free himself of the tyranny of that same imagination. "What also ran through his mind was whether he had responded to her as his usual self, or as one presently steeped in Lawrence's sexual theories, odd as they were" (*DL*, 23). Incapable of disentangling his life from the lives he writes about, he struggles in the prison that he has built for himself.

His view of the lover is as distorted as that of Kitty and of his children. The first impression the reader gets of Fanny, being filtered through Dubin's eyes, is that of a promiscuous ex-hippy; and only when the point of view shifts from Dubin to the narrator does the character of Fanny acquire some positive traits: late in the novel we learn that in Venice she had acted not out of a nymphomaniac impulse, but out of resentment at the role of Dubin had forced upon her, that of a young mistress to whom he refused to get emotionally close. While Dubin goes through an extenuating regime of diet and exercise in a pathetic attempt to fight against the undoing of time, she grows into a maturing young woman with a sense of direction and self-discipline. Dubin, as mentioned above, approaches nature with the ambivalent attitude of a voyeur; Kitty has a purely aesthetic view of it: she collects sunsets and endlessly rearranges the hedges in her garden to create pleasant color combinations, in a constantly frustrated attempt to grow something. Fanny, instead, buys a farm, because she says, "I've often felt I wanted to dig my hands into the soil and make something grow," and plans to get a degree in environmental sciences. Dubin is conscious only that "Her abundant body, though not voluptuous, had a life of its own" (*DL*, 21), and his view of her hardly changes with the progress of their relationship. In fact, just after one encounter with Fanny, Kitty shows more insight into her personality than Dubin after two years: "She's intelligent, has a mind of her own and the usual dissatisfactions of someone her age" (*DL*, 24).

Fanny appears gradually under a more favorable light, different from the provoking twenty-three-year old woman who transpires sex and expresses herself only through clichés. But the way the biographer perceives her remains unchanged; two years after the beginning of their relationship, Dubin is surprised when he realizes that she is able to think: "Fanny's term paper revealed qualities he had not often observed in her: of knowing more than she seemed to; of being organized as she thought things through" (*DL*, 231). Fanny is generous and giving. She represents the future and the possibility of a "new life" for Dubin; but Dubin is incapable of giving; he takes from her what he can transforming her into a new version of the inspiring Muse: "These visits of Fanny sparked his work. Ideas swarmed in Dubin's mind" (*DL*, 103). And while debating on whether Kitty or Fanny should have the privilege to typewrite his manuscript, he ends up alienating his wife's love and seeing Fanny only as a temporary palliative to his fear of aging.

Unable to make the leap, trapped in his subjectivity, but still desperately attracted to Fanny and to what she represents, Dubin confines himself voluntarily to the role of the voyeur, which seals his impotence and passivity:

> What a base thing to be doing, Dubin — at your age a Peeping Tom. He observed himself staring at them through the avocado leaves, a gray-haired old man with thick salt-and-pepper sideburns and jealous eyes. (*DL*, 330).

All the female characters in Malamud's fiction share a common shallowness and common values: they all respect marriage and family life, and, whatever their past, they all seek fulfillment through a permanent relationship with a man. They are unidimensional characters who are never confronted with the responsibility of a choice. While they never face a crisis, because their roles — of wives, mothers, mistresses — prove to be immutable once they are set at the beginning of the narrative, men appear to be problematic figures of writers, biographers, teachers, baseball players, striving to achieve an identity and to reconcile themselves to the demands of love and commitment. In *A New Life*, the protagonist succeeds in his struggle to free himself of his obsessive subjectivity. Determined not to repeat his past mistakes of escape from reality and detachment, he agrees to marry Pauline, to accept responsibility, and to reject the role of voyeur. In *Dubin's Lives*, although the conclusion remains somehow ambiguous, it seems legitimate to suppose that William Dubin will remain trapped in the prison of his own subjectivity, unable to adopt new models and to create a new life for himself. Haunted by his past, but unable to learn from it, he accumulates sterile suffering. Refusing to accept responsibility and to make a commitment, he condemns himself to failure and frustration.

Notes

1. Bernard Malamud, *A New Life* (New York: Farrar, Straus and Giroux, 1952, 1966), and Bernard Malamud, *Dubin's Lives* (New York: Farrar, Straus and Giroux, 1979), hereafter referred to as *ANL* and *DL* within the text.

2. Theodore Solotaroff, "Bernard Malamud's Fiction: The Old Life and the New," *Commentary*, 33 (March 1962), p. 199.

3. Neal D. Kreitzer, "The Quest for Identity in the Novels of Bernard Malamud," Ph.D. dissertation, University of California, Davis, 1974, p. 172.

4. Roland Barthes, *La chambre claire* (LeSeuil: Editions de l'Etoile, 1980), p. 144.

5. Eric Sundquist, *Home As Found* (Baltimore: John Hopkins University Press, 1977), p. 141.

6. Barthes, p. 31.

7. Béla Grunberger observes that "the idea of, and desire for immortality is linked to moral narcissism." From *Narcissism, Psychoanalytic Essay*, trans. Joyce S. Diamanti (New York: International Universities Press, 1979), p. 17.

8. Sundquist, p. 105.

9. *The Writings of Henry David Thoreau* (1906; rpt. New York: AMS Press, 1968), 11:45.

10. Kreitzer, p. 172.

11. Jean Starobinsky observes that "Au narcissisme indivis de l'adhésion à soi succéde et s'oppose une seconde forme de narcissisme: la projection de soi. Plutôt que de narcissisme, il faudrait parler ici de pygmalionisme, car c'est Pygmalion qui nous offre l'exemple mythique de cette attitude. Au lieu de se replier immédiatement su lui-même, l'amour s'aliène, devient *oeuvre*; mais, par le détour de l'oeuvre, il cherche encore à s'unir à soi: l'amour n'est ainsi sorti du moi que pour se préparer le bonheur d'un retour. . . . Narcissisme hyerbolique, plus exigeant, plus créateur, voué à l'imaginaire et à l'insatisfaction qui le tiendra indéfiniment — mais délicieusement en haleine." From *L'Oeil Vivant* (Paris: Gallimard, 1961), p. 180.

12. Bernard Malamud, *The Tenants* (New York: Farrar, Straus and Giroux, 1971), 6.

The "Perverse Economy" of Malamud's Art: A Lacanian Reading of *Dubin's Lives*

James M. Mellard*

Although working in the sophisticated realm of modernist fiction, Bernard Malamud has been a deceptively innocent craftsman throughout his career. More often than not, his characters and Malamud's own authorial personae assume the guise of the *eiron*, the apparent naif who speaks wisdom ostensibly beyond his or her capabilities. It is not surprising then that *Dubin's Lives* (1979) has appeared to some "merely" as a throwback to the more innocent age of realism,[1] and might therefore seem the least likely of novels to yield to a psychoanalytic poetics. But in the quests for identity of William and Kitty Dubin and Fanny Bick — in, that is, their searches for the sources of their being — the novel lends itself to a psychoanalytic reading — a reading, moreover, not from just any Freudian or post-Freudian perspective, but one from the controversial theory of Jacques Lacan (1901–81).[2] A brief summary of some of the key points of Lacan's theory will prove useful for an understanding of the psychoanalytic structure of Malamud's narrative, as well as emphasize not how naive but just how sophisticated Malamud's art has always been.

Lacan claims not to have replaced Freud, but to have rediscovered the

*This essay was specifically written for this volume and is published here for the first time by permission of the author.

essential Freud, especially the early writings in *The Interpretation of Dreams* (1900), *The Psychopathology of Everyday Life* (1901), and *Jokes and their Relation to the Unconscious* (1905). The core of Lacan's revision of Freudian theory is its insistence on the primacy of language, both within the subject and as the medium of exchange between the subject and the analyst. While Freud searches for evidence of primal events forming the principal contents of the unconscious, Lacan even more than Freud looks to the language in which the subject speaks, for his fundamental principle is that the unconscious is like a language and functions only in the ways language itself functions. Lacan takes his view of language from Ferdinand de Saussure, Roman Jakobson, and the Structuralists; for them, a universalized language (*la langue*) always exists prior to and determines individual utterance (*la parole*). Similarly, Lacan postulates an "I" (an individual subject) determined by a prior agency he calls the Symbolic, a concept similar to Ernst Cassirer's "symbolic forms." Consequently, where Freud assumes that the individual's identity and unconscious (and with them the notion of an autonomous ego or self) exist a priori and are projected outward toward his or her personal experiences, Lacan argues that the conscious "I" and the unconscious Being, which Lacan calls the *moi* and Freud calls the ego, are imposed from outside. As the Structuralists posit *la langue* as a domain that always comprehends more of the potentialities of individual language use than *la parole*, so Lacan posits a *moi* Being that always comprehends the individual "I" and is beyond its knowledge. The Lacanian *moi* or self, Lacan argues, is detached from the "I," by a kind of dehiscence, in two stages: first (and primally), through an other (beginning with the mother) in the conscious register of illusions and desires Lacan calls the Imaginary, by identifications that serve to create a place of unconsciousness; and, second, by the impositions, represented by the father, of the unconscious cultural Other in the Symbolic. For Lacan, the Symbolic Other (like *la langue*) is, finally, the cultural "object" that dominates knowledge and is mediated through a subject's actual language, but is imposed from the outside on the subject, who is split between the conscious "I" and the unconscious *moi*.

The mediations within language (*la parole*, not *la langue*) of "I" and Other through the "other" and through *moi*, Lacan claims, begin to illuminate the "hidden, but palpable, discourse which resides in unconscious networks of meaning."[3] The dominant feature of speech or speechacts that permits subjects to approach — if not actually grasp — the *moi* or "essential" Being that is the focus of conventional ego-psychology is repetition. Appearing mainly in the figures of speech known as metaphor and metonymy, the repetition occurs in the utterances of the "I" (the speaking subject) forming the verbal text. Lacan views verbal repetition as the means by which the individual both achieves and reveals identity within the dialectic of Desire and Law. This dialectic develops very early in the subject's life as a result of what Lacan calls "the mirror stage."[4]

Desire is created in that stage when the six-to-eighteen-month-old subject loses the unity Lacan postulates in the infant psychically still undifferentiated from the body of the mother. Simultaneously, Law is created there when separation occurs, the authority (the "no") of the father is perceived, and the threat of castration is accepted as the punishment for the illicit incestuous Desire to be all to or for the mother. The kernel of an individual's identity, from a very early age, then, is derived from the persistent reification of the complex of relations formed in the mirror stage. The form of repetition that Lacan calls *remémoration* (as opposed to mere reminiscence) "belongs to the *moi* [the essential self or Being] and drives human beings to relive unconsciously each instant of their history in the present,"[5] thus accounting for what the Lacanian critic Julia Kristeva calls the "perverse economy" found in thought, language, and the artistic text.[6]

I

Despite the brevity of this outline of Lacan's major ideas, perhaps one will be able to see how they illuminate a particular literary text such as Malamud's *Dubin's Lives*. In a Lacanian poetics, the place to start is with the *moi*, the essential self so difficult to get at. A poetics based on Lacan, as Ragland-Sullivan argues, will "reveal the *moi* as the true subject of being, and at the same time a compilation of myths, fantasies and desires taken on from others (become a repressed Other)."[7] In this endeavor, a Lacanian poetics, in focusing on the "*moi*'s identity quest," will reveal that a text's significant repetitions will occur in mirror-phase patterns of doubling and opposition that display the *moi*'s disparate voices in "their dialectical disharmony in relation to an Other's Desire."[8] The possibility of significant repetition of "*moi* voices" in *Dublin's Lives* can be inferred from the novel's title. It refers, obviously enough, to the biographies written by William B. Dubin, Malamud's "subject" and a biographer of Abraham Lincoln, Mark Twain, and H. D. Thoreau, as well as author of a life (in progress) of D. H. Lawrence, of a book called *Short Lives*, and, one learns at the end, of a life of Sigmund Freud's daughter, which Dubin co-authored with his own daughter, Maud. But the title also refers to the lives Dubin experiences within the discourse of family history, including not only that of his own family, but also histories of families drawn into contact with his. Observed through the novel's patterns of repetition, Dubin's "life" (like everyone's) is a network of intertwined "lives," all manifesting essentially the same familiar structures elucidated by Lacan.

All these lives or life-stories illustrate the dialectical workings of the force of Desire and the authority of the Law, both created in the subject's passage through the mirror phase, within which he or she also begins to assume language and a role within the Oedipal structure. In this largely

Oedipal premise, Lacan is most Freudian in his theory. But the specific manifestations or the Oedipal structure in *Dubin's Lives* have less to do with a Freudian primal scene than with the Desire of the mother and the subject's encounters with the authority of the Law. In Dubin's life, for example, while one can see the Oedipal problem rather clearly, it does not take on the usual configuration in which the parents provide strong identificatory (however illusory) imagos in the Imaginary to match the roles defined by the culture within the authority of the Symbolic. The Symbolic father in the Oedipal structure represents the Law of the Other, but in the case of William Dubin, the real father is a feckless, self-satisfied failure as seen from the point of view of the cultural Other. For her part, Dubin's mother offers no strong identificatory figure to match the maternal Symbolic value either. If anything, the real Hannah Dubin is a less attractive imago than Charlie Dubin, for, after the drowning of Dubin's nine-year-old brother, she becomes a paranoid schizophrenic: "She was afraid of the white window shades and of the long dark hallway of the railroad flat," Dubin reports; "She was afraid of footsteps on the stairs in the hall. She hid in the back bedroom, coming out to clean; or cook a chicken, then hid in the bedroom."[9] Worse, she becomes suicidal, and once, having tried to kill herself by swallowing disinfectant, she is rescued, quite fortuitously, by William, to whom she then promises never to try again if only he will not tell his father. Thereafter, "Hannah sat in the darkened bedroom, shades drawn, whispering to herself. She was meek in the house but when she ventured into the street to buy something to eat she shouted at those she said were following her" (69). Like her dead son, Hannah has one of those short lives William will someday try to resurrect: "She was dead at forty, of pleurisy and anguish. She did not thank her husband for waiting for her to get better; she did not thank her son for having kept her from taking her life" (69). As for Dubin, while "He hid from his memories of her" (69), he will nonetheless construct much of his own life around her and the image of Desire she will represent.

It is impossible for the *moi* to hide from its images of the mother and father. In Dubin's life, their presence is inferred readily from the "I" subject's representation of patterns of repetition observed in overt doublings or in oppositions arising from the Other. Consequently, whereas Dubin seems to seek a wife totally unlike his mother, his choice actually reinscribes her presence in his unconscious life. Dubin marries late, at the age of thirty-one, drawn (in a nice Lacanian irony) by a letter, one accidentally put on his desk at the journal office where he worked as an assistant editor.[10] He had read the letter, from a widow, but would have done nothing about it had she not written again, asking that her message for the personals section not be printed after all. Dubin is oddly attracted to the widow, whose first message seems to suggest a woman precisely the opposite of Hannah Dubin:

> Young woman, widowed, fairly attractive, seeks honest, responsible
> man as friend, one who, given mutuality of interests and regard, would
> tend to think of marriage. I have a child of three. (46)

But every detail as one learns more, insists upon an unconscious repetition
shaped by the force of Desire, for Kitty clearly becomes a displaced
representation of Hannah Dubin. Kitty, like Hannah, has emotional
problems, trouble sleeping, and a life she calls "such a chronicle of woe
I'm almost ashamed to write it" (47). Like Hannah, Kitty is aggrieved by
the short life of a loved one, though it is not a son, but Kitty's husband
who dies prematurely, dead at forty as Hannah herself had been. Furthermore, like Hannah, Kitty gives the sense that she is barely in control of her
life. "I can't say my emotional season is spring," she concedes; "Fortu-
nately, I have a strong reality element that keeps me balanced against
some of my more neurotic inclinations" (47). Ironically, even at a distance,
Kitty understands the nature of her magnetic pull on Dubin, for, better
than he, she has understood what it is about her that attracts him: "I don't
want to ensnare you with my unhappy history, Mr. Dubin," she writes; "I
sense you lean to that tilt" (47).

Inevitably, Kitty represents someone with whom Dubin can play out
his dialectical fantasy of Desire and the Law — of life and death. Indeed,
Dubin's *remémoration* of the way in which he met and "courted" Kitty
occurs in a powerful context of negation and death that actually provides
the first crux of the novel — Dubin's unconscious decision to pursue Fanny
Bick. Dubin's crisis begins with thoughts about his grown children — the
stepson, Gerald, and the daughter, Maud. Both Gerald and Maud have
left the family nest, Gerald AWOL from the Army and in Sweden and
Maud in school at Berkeley, across the country from the Dubins' home in
Center Campobello, in up-state New York, near the Vermont border. Kitty
is also away, presumably to visit the graves of her parents in Montreal.
Most significantly, that Malamudian intruder, Fanny Bick, is gone, having
just quit her job as housekeeper for the Dubins. Accounting for Kitty and
Dubin's pervading thoughts of self and other, sex and death, Fanny has
returned the repressed, the Oedipal drama, to the Dubin household.
Almost the same age as Maud, Fanny reminds Kitty of her advancing years
and diminishing sex appeal. She no doubt senses the truth, moreover, that
Fanny has become a figure of forbidden Oedipal Desire for Dubin:

> She was only a couple of years older than Maud and he sensed in himself
> something resembling incest taboo once removed — you don't bed down
> a girl your daughter's age. (31–32)

Consequently, when Fanny quits her job, she leaves Dubin in virtual panic
of death and negation of identity. He feels "a surge of loneliness . . . like
acid invading the bone" (39–40), thinks more on his children, prowls a
house left empty of children and wife, and feels "death's insistence of its

presence in life, history, being" (40). Puzzling over his own identity, once observed in the mirror of his children, Dubin wonders if his "almost soiled awareness . . . of one's essential aloneness" has been caused by

> The absence of his children. . . . You tried to stay close, in touch, but they were other selves in other places. You could never recover the clear sight of yourself in their eyes. (40)

Dubin, as must we all, inevitably takes part in a "discourse of the family."[11] That discourse is always multisided and provides that he will play a role in the fantasy lives of others around him, just as others play roles in his fantasies. Kitty, for example, repeats her search for parental love and recognition because they were never given unreservedly by her parents, whose story is tangled in images of death, betrayal, and rejection. Her "father had killed himself when she was a child" because her mother "had betrayed him," and her mother, she says, "deserted me for a lover she went to Europe with" (95). In Kitty's unconscious structuring of relationships, however, Dubin is forced to substitute not for the real father, but for the father surrogate her first husband, Nathanael, had been. Dubin is aware of his role, and he charges in one argument that he feels like Kitty's "step-husband" (254). Kitty had said from the very start, "In a way you remind me of my husband" (48). Moreover, she tells him late in their marriage that, had Nathanael not died, she might have "done better with" him than with Dubin (336). Nathanael had loved her, Kitty feels, "more than anyone else ever has" (95). But Dubin does recognize that she had "mythologized" Nathanael, not because of a lack in himself, but because of a "gap" (95) in her that might never be filled.

Nathanael had replaced the dead father in Kitty's real and fantasy life, and with her he was going to provide the healthy family she had not really had with either her parents or the loving grandmother who reared her after the mother had departed. Kitty's aim, it would appear, is that which Stuart Schneiderman has attributed to psychoanalysis: "the repairing of the relationships people have, not with other people, but with the dead."[12] Although in fact Nathanael could never have satisfied the hunger in Kitty's desiring self, his premature death not only reinforced Kitty's feeling that loss was to be her destiny, but also caused her to etch that feeling on the consciousness of both son and "step-husband":

> Kitty came to him with . . . the clinging remnants of trauma: modified mourning for the young dead, her ongoing burden, derived from a father a suicide at thirty-four, and a husband in his fortieth year destroyed by leukemia. . . . Kitty, telling herself it needn't be, feared more of the same. She feared her son's imagined fate; soon the child held it against her. Against her will she taught him how to miss a dead father. (89)

Thus, for Dubin, Kitty had never recovered from her mourning of Nathanael — nor of father or mother or, later, a dead fetus (95). In her "there's a presence besides the self, the self that opposes the self" (89), that causes her to feel the law that "Everyone's loss of someone's presence, significant or small, wakens a sense of prior loss" (90). But in Lacanian terms, those sought-after figures are really figures of Kitty's self. All those "absent presences," finally, are only signifiers of the *moi*, the self, she seeks. But the *moi* will always remain a mystery, and thus Kitty cannot ever achieve what she seeks. As Lacan's mirror phase determines, the *moi* is always a function of the recognition of an other or others, and so that which makes for "the uniqueness of personality" also "becomes one more proof of an unconscious (absent) space in being."[13] Thus if Kitty is neurotic — and her constant sniffing at the stove to detect escaping gas seems a symptom of neurosis — it is not because she seeks the *moi* or Phallic plenitude, but because she believes she can possess them immediately and consciously. Such possession, Lacan insists, is never possible, though seeking it in full awareness of its impossibility is not unhealthy: such is the pursuit of human ideals.

In the unconscious discourse mediated by the child's place in the family structure, Kitty and Dubin now "speak" to each other through Fanny Bick, who replaces Maud and Gerald in the chain of communication. Thus when Dubin learns that Kitty has returned to her husband's grave, rather than to that of her parents as she had originally meant to do, Dubin begins to speak totally from within an undisguised Oedipal structure. Consequently, Malamud suggests, Dubin's next meeting with Fanny becomes an Oedipal fantasy realized. The meeting displays the lineaments of dream, featuring a night, "dark deep and starlit" (41), a movie theater, and Fanny herself, "still into the film, conscious of herself" (42). Dubin had not consciously sought out Fanny, but, as he is mirrored in the theater's poster window outside at the moment a show ended, "Dubin sensed her before he saw her" (41). Following her at a distance, Dubin does not even then plan consciously to contact her, but that sense of absence, death, and "essential aloneness" that had assaulted him before Kitty's phone call from the site of Nathanael's grave returns again and replicates unpleasant sensations from his youth:

> He doubted he would talk to her; then he thought he *must* talk to her. His odd loneliness still rode him — a discomfort he wanted to be rid of, something from youth that no longer suited him. He felt hunger to know the girl, could not bear to have her remain a stranger. The lonely feeling would ease, he imagined, if he knew more about her. Crazy thing to feel it so strongly, as though he'd earned the right to know. Here I am hurrying after her as if we are occupying the same dream. (42)

But, of course, Dubin *is* occupying the same dream as Fanny, and it is equally Oedipal from Fanny's point of view. For Fanny, Dubin is the figure of the serious, scholarly, loving father who might replace a father who, she tells Dubin, "is about your age," but "screwed around a lot" (37). Just as entangled in an Oedipal fantasy as either Dubin or Kitty, Fanny has had many lovers in her short life, but the ones who seem to mean most to her are less identificatory projections in the Imaginary than links to Symbolic Others — or Fathers. Her initiation into sex was conducted by an orthodontist named Mitch, who "said he loved me," she tells Dubin, and who "even filled my cavities and straightened my front teeth" (204). Another of her lovers before Dubin was Mitch's father, Harvey, who had forced his son to break off with Fanny. Fanny's later relationship with Harvey, sparked by his reading Fanny's letters to Mitch, was marked by love, friendship, and concern — but not sex, though, for her part, Fanny was willing. Ironically, it had been Harvey who gave her a copy of the book — Dubin's biography of Mark Twain — that had prompted her to seek out Dubin. Harvey is almost precisely Dubin's age, and her relationship with him had helped create her desire to know the man who wrote the Twain book. "I hoped we could really talk," she tells Dubin; "I wanted somebody other than a shrink to advise me about my life, how to get it together better than I did. I had the feeling you could tell me useful things about myself" (206). Trying to find a father to replace the one who screws around a lot, Fanny is shocked to discover that she may have found one no better than the original. It was Dubin's book that had met Fanny's "needs," she confesses, and she has to adjust to the sexual need Dubin expresses to her. "I never thought we would end up going to Venice," she says; "When you asked me I felt let down" (206).

One sees the inscription of the Oedipal all through both sides of the "dream" Dubin inhabits with Fanny. Fanny's unconscious concerns are directed to the betrayal of maternal relations, whereas Dubin's are directed primarily to the interdiction of child-parent incest. From the first, Dubin projects Fanny into his own "incestuous" Oedipal history. Dubin's suggestion that Fanny read *Sons and Lovers*, by association, repeats Dubin's sexual initiation with an older woman, a teacher who was reading the Lawrence with him. Other, perhaps less overt, Oedipal associations occur as well. For example, Dubin's proposal that Fanny wait for him in New York at the Hotel Gansevoort apparently ignores the fact that he had first met his wife, Kitty, in person at the bar there. For Fanny, the maternal associations had been reinforced at the moment of Dubin's proposing the Gansevoort: "That's Melville's *mother's* maiden name" (45; my emphasis). In this changed context, one must surmise that it is the Oedipal conflict that prevents Fanny's waiting for Dubin at the right place in New York the first time. Fanny must have forgotten the Gansevoort's name in order, therefore, to suppress the Oedipal interdictions. As she explains to Dubin, she had waited at the *Brevoort* and even the Plaza (55), but could not recall Gansevoort. Whereas the effective interdiction in New York had been Fanny's sense of the Oedipal, in Venice the oppressive interdiction resides in Dubin. It surfaces once more, not in his overt concern for his wife, but in his incestuous guilt — overcome again — that Fanny could be his daughter.

> On the plane he had asked himself, "What am I doing here, a man my age with a young woman hers?" The answer came easily and happily: "Enjoying myself. I have it coming to me." (55)

Dubin's unconscious knows otherwise (the Other *is* wise). Dubin has no sooner arrived in Venice than, dimmed by fog and mist in a narrow defile, the figure representing the interdiction against incest arises in his vision:

> There, as the mist thinned and they could see others approaching, it seemed to the biographer that a red-haired girl clinging to the arm of a gray-haired man . . . was his daughter Maud. (53)

The man and the woman quickly disappear in the mist, before Dubin can be sure of the girl's identity. But the figures will return to haunt Dubin's pleasure trip. Dubin and Fanny fail to make love in Venice because Fanny comes down with diarrhea and because he worries about Maud. His thoughts of Maud only insist upon the child-parent relation in the Oedipal: "As he was falling asleep Maud appeared in his mind; Dubin awoke. Was it she he had seen in the fog with a man old enough, ironically, to be older than her father?" (64). Later on, as Dubin encounters an old waiter who reminds him of his father, his thought only reinforces the interdiction by an ambiguous command: "Go look for your daughter," Dubin thinks the old waiter tells him (69). Dubin looks, and seems to find daughters everywhere in Venice, but they are always in the presence of, Lacan would say, Fathers emanating from the site of the Other. At the Piazza San Marco, for example, the putative daughter is Fanny herself, blessed ("my child") by a priest (Father) who (like Dubin) is from Newark, New Jersey (73). Leaving the Accademia Gallery, Dubin thinks that he sees Maud again — "an auburn-haired girl with a gray-haired man, his arm draped around her shoulders. They were sitting with their backs to him, the girl resting her bronze head against the old man's breast" (80). Dubin's dream-assignation with Fanny has become a nightmare, for he frantically chases after the couple and succeeds only in wasting hours while Fanny, over her illness, is expectantly awaiting him back at the hotel. When Dubin finally returns to her, he suffers the most explicit reminder of all of his relation (as father) to Fanny (the daughter) in the Oedipal structure. The reminder, ironically, can only be called the primal scene of the Father: "On the rug, crouched on hands and knees," was a young gondolier encountered earlier, "his fiery hairy ass not so handsome as it had seemed in tight Levi's; and under him, alas, lay Fanny" (82). Later, thinking as father, not lover, Dubin can only detest "himself for falling into the hands of a child" (82).

II

The problem for Malamud as a writer — disregarding any relation of Dubin's fantasies to the author's — is how to transform the forbidden object of Desire in order to evade or disarm the authority of the Law. It is a virtue of Lacan's theory that it can join both the Imaginary objects of the text and *moi* or self through the repetition of the devices by which each makes meanings and makes meanings known. "Like the rhetorical tropes that operate language by laws of metaphor and metonymy," says Ragland-Sullivan, "psychic energy also functions by substitutions, displacements and referentiality. Not only is the *moi* originally 'put together' by these processes, it also continues to use the same 'laws' by which to function within the Imaginary order."[14] These same laws, moreover, operate through the functions of Desire, which aim always "at the objects (persons, things, or the use of language per se) that hold out the promise of satisfaction (and the [impossible] hope of final unity)."[15] Thus, Desire becomes the pivotal term here for *moi* and text, for it "infuses both language and the *moi* with a Real dynamism whose source is a lack of unity in the elemental structure of being."[16] As in most literary texts, the dynamism of Desire drives the metaphorical substitutions and metonymical displacements of *Dublin's Lives.*

Since Dubin is the central subject consciousness in *Dubin's Lives,* all the other characters somehow have to be reduced to functions of him if a *unity* is to be made of the book, to say nothing of one's sense of his *moi* being. Thus it must be said that all the elements observed so far are related to drives or needs manifested in Dubin himself. One may start with the interdiction against incest violated by Dubin's drive toward union with his daughter. Plainly enough, the burden of the Law against incest falls on Dubin when he tries to justify to himself his pursuit of a relationship with Fanny. In the text, one sees the weight of that Law in Dubin's conviction that he sees Maud and the gray-haired gentleman in Venice, there for the same illicit reason, no doubt, as Dubin and Fanny. But the fact is, these projections occur in Dubin's theater of the Imaginary; they represent a doubling of the image of the same forbidden Desire he pursues. In the register of the Imaginary, the image of Maud and the old man (whether or not they ever exist in the Real) helps Dubin to disarm the Law he means to violate with Fanny. Dubin's identification of Maud and Fanny in the Imaginary suggests to him that what he is doing can be permitted — at least it is "not forbidden." For Fanny not only is not actually his daughter, his actual daughter is herself similarly involved with an old man. The perception, no doubt, permits a sort of transference here for Dubin, for he can project any guilt he feels about Fanny toward the other, the "old man" with whom Maud "betrays" the father and the "Father" at the same time. Moreover, late in the novel, when Maud confirms that she has taken an elderly professor of Spanish for a lover and will permit him to be the father of her child, Dubin is more radically vindicated: for the "old man" is not just "other" as his duplicate; he is, as a black man, radically "Other." In Freudian terms, these moves in the text amply defend Dubin (but readers, as well) against Oedipal guilt.

A similar pattern operates in Dubin's relationship with his wife Kitty. Again, the fact that Kitty has an involvement with Roger Foster, young enough to be her foster son, indicates in the register of the Imaginary that she, like Dubin, feels an Oedipal desire, for her child. Quite literally, Dubin trades off this relationship for his involvement with Fanny, for in the scene where Kitty confesses her relationship to Roger, Dubin reveals his involvement with Fanny (without, it is important to note, naming her). Thus the psychic value of Kitty's transgression in the register of the Imaginary is transparent to Dubin and to readers: it represents a metaphorical substitution that signifies, at the same time it hides, the transgression Dubin desires to commit: Incest. Moreover, Kitty's transgression signifies a further betrayal of Dubin, for the name of the actual father (that is, Gerald's father) whom she would properly obey as what Lacan calls the phallic Signifier, the Other, is not Dubin, but her first husband, Nathanael. *That*, of course, is one of the major psychic problems persisting within Kitty's mind, as well as in the relationship between Dubin and his wife. Dubin always feels himself a "step-husband," and Kitty's dreams and conscious behavior, frequently reifying Dubin's sense of belatedness, efface him not only behind the signifier represented in her biological father, but also behind the sign of her first husband, the father of Dubin's stepson.

In the perverse economy of *Dubin's Lives*, since its subject is William Dubin, neither can the brief affair (really a one-night stand) of Dubin and Flora Greenfeld remain as a moral advantage for Kitty. As there had been an involvement for her with a younger lover to balance the one Dubin has with Fanny, so there is an affair for Kitty with a mature lover to redress Dubin's with Flora. Kitty, like Dubin, becomes involved with a friend of the family: Evan Ondyk, a psychotherapist. Kitty had been seeing him for therapy for quite some time. One of her problems, of course, is the guilt she assumes for her unconsummated involvement with Roger Foster, but another — probably more serious — one is her relation to the impotence that afflicts Dubin. The impotence had begun after Fanny's return to Center Campobello long after the Venetian fiasco; on this second incursion, as Dubin, unknown to Kitty, became deeply involved with Fanny, the marital impotence began, and it would recur as Dubin, again unknown to his wife, resumed his involvement with Fanny on her third incursion into the Dubins' lives. Dubin himself recognizes the source of the impotence in a reflection in a mirror. In its combination of Imaginary identification and the threat (signified by castration) of death, it is a repetition in adult life of what Lacan calls the subject's mirror phase. Fanny's displacing Kitty from her proper place in the Oedipal triangle eventually causes Dubin to imagine his negation:

> Dubin has two wives? Here's Kitty gazing out of a window reflecting herself, and beholds, in the wood in the distance, the shadow of a presence; aware of something not fearsome but a source of fear? Dubin, staring through the same glass, sees himself in view. Fanny, in white, standing dimly by his side, all but invisible. He searches the glass, amidst images of leafy trees and darkening shallow clouds, for Kitty, expecting her to be reflected nearby; but she stands alone, amid tall trees, in the deeper distance . . . He dreamed of Kitty pacing the black-railed widow's walk on the roof. (242)

The affair between Kitty and Evan Ondyk is more complicated still, for it also represents Dubin's desire for castration, punishment for real and imagined transgressions against fatherhood or the Father. Thus the affair is good news and bad news for Dubin. The good news is that, perversely, Dubin can see himself as Kitty's benefactor. Although Kitty does not know about Fanny specifically, she does understand that something ("the shadow of a presence") is intruding in her relationship with her husband. When she turns to Ondyk for therapy, Dubin admits that it works. She sleeps better, worries less, and seems more in control of her anxieties. Moreover, she solves the sexual lack with Dubin by taking on a more directly sexual form of therapy with Evan. "Do you think I might be deceiving you?" Kitty once had asked Dubin. "I wish you were" (240), he thinks but does not say. But when Kitty confesses to Dubin about the Ondyk affair, she recognizes Dubin's complicity in it: "If it weren't for you," she says, "I don't think I would have done it" (352). And that is no doubt precisely the point, for her affair with Ondyk fulfills an explicit wish of Dubin's. What is the bad news then? The affair, once again, represents Dubin's failure to supplant Nathanael Willis in Kitty's fantasy life, for Evan — the therapist who mirrors Nathanael's interest in Freud and psychoanalysis — can stand in the place of the Father for Kitty in ways that Dubin realizes he never has and probably never will. Her affair with Ondyk raises a question, then, about Kitty's watch on the widow's walk in Dubin's earlier dreams; does she watch for the absent Dubin or the return of her beloved Nathanael? Thus, ironically, just to maintain a moral equivalency in his unconscious discourse with Kitty, Dubin is forced to pay the price, in the Imaginary, of both castration and death, impotence and negation.

But in Dubin there is another desire that these displacements represent, for in fact he courts the relationship appearing to render him superfluous. The desire his behavior reflects, again, lies in the Oedipal structure. As a son himself, Dubin inevitably suffers from belatedness, for he will of necessity follow in the path of the father in his relations with the mother. Consequently, Dubin suffers more in his relationship to Kitty than otherwise he might if he had been at least the first husband and, perhaps equally important, the father to the son. That Gerald until the novel's end, indeed, goes by his father's last name — Willis — is just one further reminder that Dubin, vis à vis Kitty, does not represent the name of the father. These significant reminders of Dubin's displacement as the father are linked to his consequent desire to punish himself for assuming he can appropriate that place. Thus the most powerful reminder of his guilt lies in his relationship to his mother, Hannah. Dubin carries a burden of guilt because, though in the Imaginary he has possessed his mother, he has never been subject to the punitive castration such an act demands. That possession, of course, is entirely figurative, though its effects are real enough. It came about because of that deadly secret — "Willie, don't tell Papa I'm going crazy" (68) — Hannah had asked him to keep from his father the time she tried to kill herself. Thus his possession is the secret, but a guiltier possession is the sexual secret — the desire the son feels for the mother, a desire seen in the language of his memory of the scene: "Yes, she whispered, yes, yes." (68).

Although Dubin admits that he "hid from his memories" (69) of his mother, his need to eliminate his guilt for having possessed her in the place of his father surfaces in a rather explicit, but still Imaginary, way in the novel. Charlie Dubin never represents a powerful figure of negation or castration, so he can never represent a very adequate figure of forgiveness either. Thus, in the climax of the novel, having again committed a transgression of the Oedipal law and this time suffered the Father's denial, Dubin eventually gains an explicit, and powerful Symbolic forgiveness. Dubin encounters his father through the displacement of a double. His surrogate father is the figure of Greenfeld, the flutist; Dubin betrays his symbolic Father through possession of Greenfeld's wife, Flora. Greenfeld, appearing on the novel's first page, is obviously a multivalent character. Dubin often encounters him on the road as the two jog in their opposite directions, and as an image in the mirror Greenfeld could as well be brother to Dubin as Father. But Greenfeld more apparently signifies the Father in the Symbolic than the identificatory brother in the Imaginary. First, Greenfeld is associated with Dubin's religion — always an Other. Both are Jewish, and Greenfeld, in one brief, typifying encounter on the road, tells a rabbi joke in passing. Furthermore, Dubin's father and Greenfeld are linked by a letter. Dubin thrusts upon Greenfeld an occasional note, reminding of the way he had once left a letter with his father. That letter linked his manhood to his religion and subordinated the Law of the father to personal Desire. Associated with the death of the father, moreover, the letter is still in Charlie Dubin's pants pocket when he dies:

> Dear Papa, How can a man be a Jew if he isn't a man? How can he be a man if he gives up the woman he wants to marry? (69)

Finally, Greenfeld is Symbolic Other to Dubin in another way. Greenfeld is associated with the place of origins, the crux of the world; for of the crossroads where they meet, Greenfeld says, "This has to be the center of the universe, my friend" (3). Thus, it seems only appropriate that Dubin direct his "thoughts" to Greenfeld rather than to "the gods" themselves. Greenfeld, as Other, represents the Father *and* the Law of the Father. Thus when Dubin makes love to Flora Greenfeld, he is betraying not just a friend, but also the father, and not just any father, but the Father in the Symbolic. And when Dubin, in the hospital recovering from his brush with death near the novel's end, is forgiven by Greenfeld, the forgiveness functions as that of the Father bestowed on the son and signifies that which Dubin had sought from his real father.

III

The roles that figures such as Roger and Maud, Flora and Greenfeld, or even Kitty and Dubin play in the transformations engendered by the plot do not change, though they do reveal, their *moi* essences as characters (or, in the Real, as persons). The one character who does seem to change in some essential way is Fanny Bick. At first glance, she functions in the plot as a catalytic agent that acts, without change, to change the other reagents. True enough, when Fanny is introduced into the nuclear family structure represented by Dubin and Kitty, she seems to cause chemical reactions, but is herself left the same. Her conscious aim is to introduce herself into the Dubin household in order to get advice about her life from Dubin; unconsciously, her desire is to find a father who can substitute adequately for the one she could never respect, and there is an unconscious sexual agenda, too, otherwise the role she thinks she seeks for Dubin could have been filled by old Harvey, who can dispense wisdom, but because of drugs and poor health is sexually impotent. Given Fanny's conscious and unconscious desires, she must inevitably be a catalytic agent in the structure of the Dubin family. But it happens, ultimately, that the apparent catalyst is also changed, bonded into a stable unit of the family, thereby merely showing just how powerful is the structure she had unwittingly challenged.

In *Dubin's Lives* the fact that Fanny changes will have little to do with her, however, for she remains an object in the fantasy life of the novel's true subject: Dubin himself. Consequently, the *moi* transformations that appear to occur in Fanny are part of the process by which Malamud transforms the forbidden element in Dubin's desires. Moreover, the process by which this transformation of the forbidden takes place marks off the plot of the novel. The novel's plot is punctuated by Fanny's rhythmical appearances and disappearances (there is the usual seasonal rhythm, too, that one expects of Malamud). She appears in the first chapter when Dubin is just beginning his life of D. H. Lawrence, whose theme is "passion," signifying both the sexual (erotic) and the sacrificial (thanatic) for Dubin. She disappears after her assignation with Dubin in Venice, though she remains an absent presence through the insistence of the letters she exchanges with Dubin. She reappears, in the structural center of the novel (chapter five), at a time when Dubin is very troubled, having serious doubts about his marriage, suffering reminders of Fanny through his daughter Maud (who, unwittingly, recites to him Keats's "To Fanny"), and worrying about what Lacan calls "aphanisis," the fading of sexual desire (again, Maud exacerbates the problem by reciting a poem: Lawrence's "Desire may be dead" [171]). Fanny disappears again (at the end of chapter seven) when Dubin, who to himself constantly claims to need change, is unable to leave Kitty for Fanny. Fanny reappears for the final time (at the end of chapter eight) just at the right moment to save Dubin from a potential death (Real) and a threat of death (Symbolic) that haunts him obsessively: the image of his alter ego's — Lawrence's — dying (323). In the novel's final chapter (nine), Fanny sets up housekeeping on a farm across the woods from Kitty and Dubin, and, with help from Dubin, begins to prepare for a career in law.[17]

Fanny's transformations as a subject — a *moi* or self — at least as inferred from her actions and speech, are very directly tied into Dubin's deepest fantasy — to create and to resurrect lives, but also to live life more fully. That fantasy is expressed, inevitably, in his choice of a career; he notes, for example, "Everybody's life is mine unlived. One writes lives he can't live. To live forever is a human hunger" (11). Dubin is aware that he projects this hunger into the lives he writes. The aim for Dubin is that which he attributes to Lawrence: "He lived in a vast consciousness of life. At his best he wants man to risk himself for a plenitude of life through love" (303). Thus, Dubin's risk — with each new biography, but also with a new relationship such as he has with Fanny — is a reenactment of the theme of Oedipus. Specifically, in Dubin's own life, his hunger for plenitude through love is deeply rooted in the ambiguously significant scene in which Dubin violates the Oedipal Law, risks castration, and creates the need for absolution that can be realized for him only in displacing both father and mother. The scene, of course, is the ambiguous enfiguration of Dubin's maternal possession — his saving the life of his mother, at the same time he transgresses against his father. Dubin's language for this scene is generously adrogynous, for the enfiguration of Phallic plenitude it carries is both Paternal and Maternal. The full passage must be read here:

> Yes, she whispered, yes, yes. She drank from the bottle as though famished, as though she had wanted all her life to drink the miraculous potion he served her. It would make her sane again, healthy, young — would restore her chance to have everything she hadn't had in her life. She drank her own everlasting hunger. (68)

As enfigured here, Dubin plays the role of the phallic hero of myth, bringing the boon or token of life; but, at the same time, he also plays the role of the maternal source of life, the bottle he gives her representing the breast as he (no doubt) holds her in his arms. Thus, ever after, Dubin carries with him an ambivalent image of his role, and his profession as biographer allows him to fulfill that role in both its maternal and paternal visages. He can at once create lives (as the mother) and resurrect them (as the paternal savior), and through those lives he can extend his own life into a limitless future. This multiple signification, acknowledging the Lacanian primal signifiers — birth, love, procreation, and death — may finally be the profoundest theme of *Dubin's Lives*. And that may well be what a reading through a Lacanian poetics will always reveal about literary works: that they represent (to paraphrase Robert Frost) a human hunger for a momentary stay against the confusions of the subliminal signifiers of the Symbolic ordinarily revealed only in the fissions of the Imaginary.

Notes

1. Among those who have regarded *Dubin's Lives* as essentially realistic are reviewer Robert Towers, *New York Times Book Review* 18 (February 1979):1, 30–31, and Jason Epstein, "Malamud in Decline," *Commentary* 74, no. 4 (October 1982):49–52. Malamud himself has said that he wanted to write a novel with the "richness" of such nineteenth-century novelists as George Eliot and Thomas Hardy, but one that also used "twentieth-century techniques." Moreover, he says he chose to make Dubin a biographer of D. H. Lawrence "because Lawrence's theories about the relationship of sexual experiences to the deeper sources of life and beyond into a kind of mystical universe gave Dubin things he could think about more than mere experience itself": Ralph Tyler, "A Talk with the Novelist," *New York Times Book Review*, 18 February 1979, 1, 32–34. Though the critical response to *Dubin's Lives* has been less positive than it deserves, a body of criticism is emerging: see, for example, James John Beyer, "*Dubin's Lives* and Bernard Malamud's Earlier Works: The Uses of Repetition," *DAI* 43, no. 8 (February 1983):2665A; Chiara Briganti, "Mirrors, Windows and Peeping Toms: Women as the Object of Voyeuristic Scrutiny in Bernard Malamud's *A New Life* and *Dubin's Lives*" (reprinted in this volume); Rafael Cancel-Ortiz, "The Passion of William Dubin: D. H. Lawrence's Themes in Bernard Malamud's *Dubin's Lives*," *D. H. Lawrence Review* 16, no. 1 (Spring 1983):83–97; Rita Gollin, "Malamud's Dubin and the Morality of Desire," *Papers on Language and Literature* 18, no. 2 (Spring 1982):198–207; Jeffrey Helterman, *Understanding Bernard Malamud* (Columbia, S.C.: University of South Carolina Press, 1985):92–106; Saul Maloff, "Loveliest Breakdown in Contemporary Fiction," *Commonweal* 27 (April 1979):244–46; and Mary Beth Pringle, "(Auto)biography: Bernard Malamud's *Dubin's Lives*," *International Fiction Review* 9, no. 2 (Summer 1982):138–41.

2. Lacan's work, much of which exists only in notes taken by others at his famed *Séminaires*, is only now being translated into English on a large scale; the most important translations are *Écrits: A Selection*, trans. Alan Sheridan (New York: Norton, 1977); *The Four Fundamental Concepts of Psycho-Analysis*, ed. Jacques-Alain Miller, trans. Alan Sheridan (New York: Norton, 1978); and *Speech and Language in Psychoanalysis*, trans., with notes and commentary, by Anthony Wilden (Baltimore, Md.: Johns Hopkins University Press, 1981). Critiques of Lacan are becoming rather numerous; one "authorized" by Lacan is Anika Lemaire, *Jacques Lacan*, trans. David Macey (London: Routledge and Kegan Paul, 1977); for a very lucid brief account of the main premises, see Kaja Silverman, *The Subject of Semiotics* (New York: Oxford University Press, 1983): 149–93. The most comprehensive synthesis of

Lacan is Ellie Ragland-Sullivan, *Jacques Lacan and the Philosophy of Psychoanalysis* (Urbana, Ill.: University of Illinois Press, 1985); her "The Magnetism Between Reader and Text: Prolegomena to a Lacanian Poetics," *Poetics* 13 (1984):381–406, however, is more central to my reading of *Dubin's Lives*. A diverse collection of essays very important in the transmission of Lacan's ideas is *Interpreting Lacan*, ed. Joseph H. Smith and William Kerrigan, *Psychiatry and the Humanities*, vol. 6 (New Haven, Conn.: Yale University Press, 1983). Lacanian interpretation of literature may be found in two books edited by Robert Con Davis: *The Fictional Father: Lacanian Readings of the Text* (Amherst, Mass.: University of Massachusetts Press, 1981) and *Lacan and Narration: The Psychoanalytic Difference in Narrative Theory* (Baltimore, Md.: Johns Hopkins University Press, 1983), which includes a bibliography of works by Lacan and one of works on Lacan and narrative. See also my "*Something Happened*: The Imaginary, the Symbolic, and the Discourse of the Family," in *Critical Essays on Joseph Heller*, ed. James Nagel (Boston: G. K. Hall, 1984):138–55; to be reprinted, slightly revised, in my *Doing Tropology: Analysis of Narrative Discourse* (Urbana,asy Ill.: University of Illinois Press, forthcoming).

3. *Poetics* 13 (1984):382.

4. See "The Mirror Stage as Formative of the Function of the I," in *Écrits: A Selection*, 1–7. For the purposes of this essay, it is not really necessary to go into the intricacies of this stage or phase.

5. Ragland-Sullivan, *Jacques Lacan and the Philosophy of Psychoanalysis*, 111.

6. See Julia Kristeva, "Within the Microcosm of 'The Talking Cure,' " in Smith and Kerrigan, *Intrepreting Lacan*; speaking of her assessment of negation and denial or "(de)negation," death and desire, Kristeva says: "Such an analysis of the position of thought and language, which is coextensive with thought, reveals the perverse economy by which they are sustained" (38–39). Her remark is significant because she attributes to thought and language generally what others might associate only with the unconscious or with art. See also Kristeva's *Revolution in Poetic Language*, trans. Margaret Waller, with an introduction by Leon S. Roudiez (New York: Columbia University Press, 1984).

7. *Poetics* 13 (1984):387.

8. Ibid., 392.

9. *Dubin's Lives* (New York: Farrar Straus Giroux, 1979), 68. Subsequent page references to the novel will be given parenthetically in the text.

10. Perhaps the most important text by Lacan for literary analysis is one in which he plays with the many meanings of "letter"; see his "The Seminar on 'The Purloined Letter,' " trans. Jeffrey Mehlman, *Yale French Studies* 48 (1972):39–72.

11. For an excellent analysis of the discourse of the family, see Silverman's *The Subject of Semiotics*; for its application in a work of fiction, see Christine van Boheemen-Saaf, " 'The Universe Makes an Indifferent Parent': *Bleak House* and the Victorian Family Romance," in Smith and Kerrigan, *Interpreting Lacan*, 275–57.

12. *Jacques Lacan: The Death of an Intellectual Hero* (Cambridge, Mass.: Harvard University Press, 1983), 57.

13. *Poetics* 13 (1984):387.

14. Ibid., 388.

15. Ibid.

16. Ibid.

17. One should point out that Malamud further displaces Dubin's guilt about Fanny by also mediating her into a figure of Kitty herself. Malamud does that through the old woman, Myra Wilson, a neighbor across the woods; when Myra dies, Malamud makes it clear that she is identified with Kitty, and so when Fanny Bick purchases Myra's farm, the two most prominent women in Dubin's life are figuratively doubled in the Imaginary. Thus, when at the novel's very end, Fanny offers to share Dubin with Kitty, it is not merely her

magnanimity, but also the symmetry of the Imaginary doubling that makes the offer seem a perverse economy. Nonetheless, in the economy of the Oedipal structure, Roger Foster will finally displace Dubin in Fanny's life. By the novel's end, Dubin has a completed life of Lawrence, Greenfeld's absolution, Gerald's recognition of him as father, and Fanny's maturation into a responsible human being. Dubin, thus, could let her go, and any incestuous desire he retains *could* have been displaced into the life he and daughter Maud create — the biography of Anna Freud. But Malamud — perhaps unfortunately — stops short of these resolutions.

Malamud's Quarrel with God   Sidney Richman*

I believe in God, I fear Him, yet I cannot love Him — with my whole heart and soul as the Torah commands nor with the *amor Dei intellectualis* that Spinoza demands. Nor can I deny God as the materialists do. All I can do is to the best of my limits treat people and animals in a way I consider proper.
— Isaac Bashevis Singer, *A Little Boy in Search of God*

When a person creates himself, ceases to be a mere species man, and becomes a man of God, then he has fulfilled that commandment which was implicit in the principle of providence. . . . The . . . man of faith transcends the frontiers of the reasonable and enters into the realm of the unreasonable, the intellect is left behind. . . . The man of faith . . . is able to reach the point at which not only his logic of the mind but even his logic of the heart and of the will, everything — even his own "I" awareness — has to give in to an "absurd" commitment. The man of faith is "insanely" committed to . . . God.
— Rabbi J. Soloveitchik, *Halakhic Man* and "The Lonely Man of Faith".

Bernard Malamud's latest novel, *God's Grace*, is at once the most elaborate of his attempts at the fable and unquestionably his most ambiguous. In the chilling nullity of its conclusion, it is quite the most terrible as well. The story it tells is of the extermination of the last man on earth, one Calvin Cohn, himself the sole human survivor of a nuclear holocaust and a subsequent flood. Despite his adaptive skills and moral rectitude (he is a son and grandson of rabbis), Cohn finds himself at the novel's end, his throat slit and his white beard bespattered with blood, awaiting consignment to the ritual flames by a chimpanzee-Abraham named Buz. And all the while a mysterious and apparently insatiably vindictive God looks on impassively — or does not look. Thus even that final outpost of value one finds in so many of Malamud's despairing earlier heroes, the ennobling if

*This essay was specifically written for this volume and is published here for the first time by permission of the author.

sometimes maddening endurance of a Frank Alpine or a Yakov Bok, is in *God's Grace* given to the torch along with the last shreds of human flesh. Man, at least in corporeal terms, is doomed, and that apparently is the message of Malamud's splendid if appalling commentary on the fragility and limitations of human nature and civilization.

As if to match the high and no doubt chancy seriousness of its subject, *God's Grace* also exhibits a narrative audacity matched, if at all, only by Malamud's first and quirkiest novel, where the life of a baseball prodigy is organized on the principles of the Grail Quest. Throughout *God's Grace*, most of which transpires on a nearly deserted island, there are various echoes of *Robinson Crusoe* and *Lord of the Flies*, of *Gulliver's Travels* and *Animal Farm*, perhaps even of *Planet of the Apes*—both upon and under. But the basic narrative is a flexible retelling of *Genesis*, and the six-part structure, perhaps a reflection of the first six days of Creation, runs from the Flood, with Cohn as second Noah, to the sacrifice on Mount Moriah in which he serves as anxious stand-in for Isaac. The parallels are far from exact, and on occasion they may only be the wistful products of Cohn's own inflated desire to give coherence and significance to his experiences; but in the main they are there—often hilariously and usually with point. Indeed, much of the ingenuity of the tale, as well as its deeper implications, lies in Malamud's reworking of the sacred text in order to demonstrate what Cohn sees as "the combinations, transformations, possibilities of a new future."[1]

Malamud's comic use of the Old Testament may shock the reader for a time, but in the end it should remind him that the patterns of Jewish history and consciousness, particularly when centered on issues of transgression against fathers or on suffering and atonement, turn the plots of most of the earlier novels and stories, no matter how humorous. Nor will the yoking together of animals and Jewish identity and rituals, a gorilla in a yarmulke or a group of chimps gathered to the Seder table, cause any consternation in the light of such exemplary fables as "The Jewbird" or "The Talking Horse." Malamud's notion of "Jewishness" is sufficiently wide to include, and not just in a parabolic way, both human and animal reality.

But where *God's Grace* should disconcert the reader is in the very severity of its final judgment. It is surely Malamud's darkest prophecy— the decisive product to date in what now appears to be his increasing focus on the futility of humanistic values in the face of history and man's own disordered nature. It is an assessment to which Malamud himself, though always diffident about matters autobiographical, has supplied direct authority. As he told Helen Benedict in response to her questions about the novel, "Yes, I am more pessimistic than I used to be . . . I feel that the more the world stays the same the worse it seems likely to become."[2] And Benedict herself adds that in *God's Grace* "Malamud's conclusion is the bleakest of all—utter destruction."[3]

It would therefore seem that *God's Grace* reflects something of a crisis of faith on the writer's part, and that it tests as never before the resources of the redemptive spirit one finds at work in most of his earlier fictions. Now to be sure, the affirmations in Malamud's previous works were rarely if ever unequivocal, and it was often as difficult to discriminate his notion of success from that of failure, as was surely the case with, say, Frank Alpine's inspired pain or S. Levin's woebegone submission to the mandates of his foolish heart. But compared to *God's Grace*, or at least to its harrowing conclusion, such earlier enactments must seem happiness enough and more than enough. For the only alternative is to somehow believe that a 500-pound gorilla reciting a "long kaddish" can be construed as consolation for the utter destruction of man and his civilization, as well as an unconditional mark of God's own mercy. Are we intended to believe *that?*

Improbable as it must sound, the answer is *yes*, a precise if not quite ringing yes. But to make any sense of this, no easy matter, demands a good deal of analysis and not a little of plot.

The latter at least may be quickly accomplished. Calvin Cohn is a Jewish paleologist in his late thirties who survives the day of nuclear incineration and its attendant flood while undersea in a submersible craft. The mother vessel, the *Rebekah Q*, also pulls through and serves as a second ark, but one empty of all life save Cohn's and that of a young chimpanzee raised by Dr. Walther Bünder, a famous scientist now gone the way of most other flesh. That Cohn himself lives beyond the "Day of Devastation" turns out to be less a miracle than a simple oversight on the part of the Almighty, who tells the terrified survivor that He had decided to give man death for being "engrossed in evil." Cohn begs to live but God replies: "That cannot be my intent, Mr. Cohn . . . I must slay you; it is just. Yet because of my error, I will grant you time to compose yourself, make your peace. Therefore live quickly — a few deep breaths and go your way."[4]

But God's sense of duration is not Cohn's. After a long float on a dead gray sea, the last man and his simian companion (who, we discover, has not only been given the gift of speech by Dr. Bünder but has also been — to Cohn's manifest discomfort — partially Christianized and named "Gott-lob") come ashore on a tropical island — part Ararat, part Paradise. Along with the chimp, whom he renames Buz after one of Abraham's nephews, Cohn salvages what goods he can from the reef stricken vessel, including a wind-up phonograph and a dozen records of Jewish liturgical music sung by his father, a cantor before he was a rabbi. Cohn establishes a sanctuary in a cave (Buz, who prefers the trees, sleeps there only occasionally), and in time introduces the pastoral arts to the island in order to augment the natural bounty — mostly in fruits and exotic flowers which bloom without benefit of natural pollinators.

There soon appears on the island, their origin an endless puzzle to

Cohn, other members of the primate family. The first is a solitary male gorilla Cohn names "George" (after the father of his dead wife, a dentist and a "good" man), and who early on nurses the semi-conscious human through a prolonged bout with radiation poisoning. The second consists of a heterogenous cluster of chimps, the most noteworthy of whom is a prepubescent female named "Mary Madlyn" by Buz, and an oversized and brutish male Cohn titles "Esau" after the hunter-wanderer son of Isaac who renounced his birthright and the Torah.

Although Cohn feels uneasy about the chimps, apprehension is washed away when Buz manages to teach them English. Behind the swelling population, Cohn suddenly sniffs a "breath of settled purpose in the world," and he decides on the spot to organize a Seder in order to bring "together the island company, and at the same time politely thanking . . . someone for favors received. Nothing wrong with a little sincere gratitude for every amelioration of an unforgivable condition caused by the Creator."[5] By such refined psychic adjustments does Cohn measure his relationship to his incomprehensible God. But in the days that follow, the hope of a new future for the world, one free from error and sin, swells his irrepressible heart. To facilitate the process, he establishes "The School Tree," where for six days a week (he "skipped the Seventh Day to show his respect and good will") Cohn imparts to the apes a knowledge of good and evil, stressing also the obligations required for a constitutional and a truly moral state. The lessons are copiously laced with illustrations drawn from man's transgressions against his own humanity, all pointing out how they "had failed each other in obligations and responsibilities — failed to achieve brotherhood, lost their lovely world, not to mention living lives."[6] And despite occasional grumbling, mostly from Esau, at times from Buz, the messages seem to take. The chimps begin to give over their chimpy ways and Cohn entertains notions of a golden crack in what had seemed a uniformly black future.

But hope quickly collapses. To extend Cohn's outrageous pun, for chimps as well as for men "love is only finger deep." When the one available female chimp on the island, Mary Madlyn, comes into heat, she unnaturally refuses to present her rear either to the slavering Esau or any of the other males, including the now sexually mature Buz. Mary has been humanized, in fact, by Cohn's lectures on freedom and dignity (as well as the text of *Romeo and Juliet*), and entertains a wholly novel concept of what love and sex should be. Not only does she resist her animal instincts, but she discovers in the person of Calvin Cohn the centerpiece for all her romantic fantasies. To him alone will she surrender her virginity. And so for the frustrated male chimps, the immemorial rebellion of the sons against the cave-dwelling father and his sexual prerequisites begins anew. And the unhappy conclusion becomes inevitable when Cohn, despite the admonitions in Leviticus and Deuteronomy, finds his affection for Mary increasing, fed by what he sees as the possibility of establishing with her, if the seed take, a whole new race of beings. They copulate, Mary becomes pregnant, and a bewildered but joyous Cohn wonders "What God was doing in her womb?"

Paralleling the arrival of a hairy white baby girl with human eyes ("Rebecca," Cohn insists) there appears on the island eight soiled baboons, again from no one knows whence; and with their arrival chimp resentment and sexual repression take on new and devastating forms. Unable or unwilling to extend welcome beyond their species (Cohn they consider a sort of "honorary chimp"), the primates see the baboons as "Goddamn strangers" who ought to "go back where you came from." Acquired humanity vanishes and the chimps descend to bestiality. In company with two young males, Esau captures one of the young female baboons, smashes her head, and then devours her—beginning with the brains and only stopping when a few indigestable scraps remain for his brethren. The carnivorous transgression on hospitality (in Cohn's eyes "cannibalism") precipitates a thundering denunciation by Cohn, who banishes the three from the community.

But things go from bad to worse. While Buz looks on with detachment, Cohn is half-throttled by Esau who vows to "break every Jewbone in your head" and survives only because Mary comes to his aid with a hammer. Soon after the chimps kill and devour a second baboon; and one night they enter the cave with Buz's connivance and steal and later destroy Rebecca—and with her, ostensibly, all hope for the *homo ethicalis* Cohn had dreamed of. In a brief coda, the chimps, including Mary, lose their capacity for speech along with any vestige of human restraint. Now led by Buz, the "Alpha ape," they break into the cave, destroy Cohn's treasured remnants of human civilization, and lead the bound and bloody human to the ritual slaughter.

And so ends Malamud's somber fable of mankind's triumphs and failures; not only the most melancholy of his works but perhaps—as Anthony Burgess put it in an insightful review—the very consummation of that postwar wave of fables of despair "of which the two most notable exemplars were *Animal Farm* and . . . *Lord of the Flies.*" The true lesson of *God's Grace*, Burgess assures us, "is that Man is hopeless" and any attempt to "raise the brute creation to man's level is to serve not creative but destructive evolution."[7]

Given man's final extermination in the novel it is not possible to quibble really with the assertion of his basic hopelessness. But it should be stressed that Burgess's second assertion, that the humanizing of brutish nature serves the forces of destruction (a commonplace in the critical response to the novel), is quite another matter. The true failure of the chimps in *God's Grace*—and of mankind generally—is not that they have acquired human character but that they have not acquired a sufficiency of it. Indeed the sudden turn to baboon-eating, the basis of Burgess's contention in this matter, can hardly be construed as the result of Cohn's humanization of the primates. As Jane Goodall has shown, real chimpanzees in real forests kill and devour baboons, and they also savor their victims' brains above all the other parts. Malamud, who cites Goodall as the chief authority for his divagations into primate behavior,[8] clearly recognized that the meat eating was for the chimps a "return to type" and a signal that they, like the humans they replace, had simply failed in their struggle to tame the beast within.

In this respect at least, and for all its remarkably dark intensities, *God's Grace* does deliver man's fate from pure fortuity, and in the process highlights Malamud's often ambiguous attitudes toward questions of morality and the priorities of the "natural." In many of the earlier fictions, the desires of his protagonists to act in accordance with their biological promptings or, relatedly, in the clear light of self-interest, repeatedly collided with those mysterious counters, often enough identified with "Jewishness," which are seen as the manifestations of an unacknowledged self or appear as the still more mysterious sensation of having been "chosen" against one's own will. The riven protagonist of *A New Life*, S. Levin, probably enacts these dichotomous pressures most clearly, but rare is the Malamud hero who escapes the dilemma. (The reader may find in the triangular relationship of Buz, Esau, and Cohn more than a small reminder of the pressures uniting Morris Bober, Frank Alpine, and Ward Minogue.)

Perhaps the most noteworthy difference between the chimps and Malamud's primary protagonists lies in the fact that the former come upon the scene "undivided," pure in their instinctive identities; but with the acquisition of language they move toward selfhood and, relatedly, toward moral commitment. Not all desire it, however. Esau, for one, seems to serve as the novel's primary apologist for the priorities of the natural. As he quite correctly shrieks at Cohn when lectured on the evils of baboon consumption: "You busybody horseass, you stole my natural food out of my mouth."[9] And when Buz is informed by Cohn that Mary will not copulate randomly, as is prescribed by chimp nature, Buz cannot understand it. "She['s] . . . resisting her instincts," Cohn tells him, and Buz replies that he "thought she was mad."[10]

The urge to rise above one's animal nature obtrudes, as it always does with Malamud, on the vexing question of freedom from biological or psychological determination. The desire to change or to hold steady against the promptings of flesh or a too needy heart has been a major one for most of his central characters, while the primary experience of failure is usually accompanied by a sense of guilty regression, circularity, surrender to old drives and habits. The issue is especially strong in *God's Grace*, however, for the failure of man stems from just this fact. "I made man to be free," the Lord tells Cohn, "but his freedom, badly used, destroyed him."[11] And in the same interview in which he told Helen Benedict of his growing pessimism, Malamud stressed that the issue of freedom was central to *God's Grace*, that the novel embodied his own belief that "there's a vast sense of failure that has clouded his [man's] best efforts to produce a greater freedom than he was born with."[12]

The issue is dramatized by Cohn's labors to inspire in the chimps a sense of deliverance from the "necessities" of their primate identity and by his charges' own proclivity to flee from freedom — a tendency symbolized by Buz's fondness for the cage he occupied when in the care of Dr. Bünder, and reemphasized by his conception of the purpose of life as merely "fun."

Malamud's insistence on the moral priorities involved in a difficult freedom are perhaps intrinsic to the sense of "Jewish drama" one finds in his tales — the reflection of a tradition in which distrust of nature was always strong, and — more important still — of "Covenantal theology" itself which tends to view "The unique ontological status of the human being as one who can transcend natural necessity and act within a context of freedom."[13] It is precisely this quest for self transcendence that underlies the struggles of a Frank Alpine or a Yakov Bok; in fact, that binds all of Malamud's protagonists together as sufferers for "the way." Consciously or unconsciously, they understand that freedom can only be achieved in terms of moral commitment, by acts which involve surrender to others. For it is also a truism of "covenantal man" that "one may not commune with the God of the covenant if one is not responsive to the . . . needs of human beings."[14] As Cohn tells the chimps, "freedom depends on mutual obligation." For answer, he heard only a "petrified silence."[15]

The chimps' negative reaction no doubt expresses the same realization of loss that attends S. Levin's surrender to neurotic Pauline. True freedom demands moral purpose, Malamud seems to argue, else it is misused and in the end one is returned to the prison of animal identity. The nearest statement in *God's Grace* of that purpose is probably Cohn's response to Buz's inquiry: "Whot is humon, Dod?" Cohn replies that "he thought to be human was to be responsive to and protective of life and civilization. Buz said he would rather be a chimp."[16]

Cohn's lectures in The School-Tree are designed to hasten the day of proper choice by pointing out man's mistakes as well as his triumphs. A related object is to diminish the egocentricity of his charges by disquisitions on the enormity of space and time — the latter illustrated by specimens of fossil bones he has discovered on the island. Despite his own doubts as to the nature of the Creator, Cohn wishes also to impress upon his students an awareness of a spiritual potentiality moving in the universe and, relatedly, a belief in the sanctity of other life forms.

Cohn pins his hopes on language. "Only if one knows the word," he insists, "can he spread the word."[17] And Cohn does indeed spread it, more thickly and more earnestly than any other of Malamud's protagonists, although several of them also possess a highly developed penchant for the sermonizing and the moral mode. But even if his homilies occasionally bore the chimps (at such times they "shake branches and throw nuts at him"[18]), often enough the words strike fertile ground. Asked by Cohn why she is unwilling to mate with chimps, Mary Madlyn tells him it is in part his fault: "You wanted us to wearn your language. Now that I have, I am different than I used to be. If I hadn't wearned to speak and understand human speech, I would have already presented mysewf to every mawe on the island."[19]

Mary's somewhat precious lambdacism ought not to obscure the soul-ordering powers Malamud attributes to language. It is the gift of gifts; it is the means by which, as Cohn says, a "man becomes more finely and subtly man — a sensitive, principled, civilized human being."[20] Cohn is even willing, somewhat shakily, to accept the notion that it is a direct creation of God; and on yet another occasion he "remembered: God was Torah. He was made of words."[21]

The concept of language in *God's Grace* clearly goes far beyond such obvious matters as transmitting knowledge of the past or the communication of experience. God is made of words, and the idea underscores the sacral aura clinging to the gift of speech. In a remarkable passage, before Cohn has learned that Buz can speak, Cohn decides to tell stories to the chimp:

> How else educate someone who couldn't read? Cohn hoped to alter and raise his experiential level — deepen, humanize this sentient, intelligent creature, even though he did not "speak" beyond a variety of hoots and grunts and make a few pantomined signals.

And in what seems to be a passing reflection:

> . . . if I talk to him and he listens, no matter how much or little he comprehends, I hear my own voice and know I am present. And if I am, because I speak to him, maybe one of these days he will reply so that he can be present in my presence.[22]

Both passages suggest that for Malamud language is a part of God's covenant with man and the primary ground out of which a truer humanity is possible — not alone because language makes for consciousness, but because it opens man to the sense, or burden, of his own life and that of his fellows. In Malamud's fictional universe, it is generally the case that the sign of grace, whether real or metaphorical, attends those dialogic tests in which the protagonist is called upon to destroy the barriers between his own ego and the full and often radiant reality of an Other (Roy Hobbs and Iris Lemon, Frank Alpine and Morris Bober, and so forth). But as Cohn tells Buz, it is primarily "through language that a man . . . opens himself to other men."[23] Indeed the theme of language as sanctified is so central to *God's Grace* that speech seems to exist not just as the product of cerebration and the proper physical organs but as a moral power in the very structure of reality. At the final destruction of the cave, when the now speechless chimps destroy Cohn's possessions and bind him for sacrifice, it is to the accompaniment of a voice without any perceivable source:

> As they tightly tied him up — his arms behind his back, his legs, on Gottlob's insistence, trussed together — they laughed, screamed, barked, hooted, filling the echoing cave with impossible noise. But in the place where the wrecked phonograph stood, a rabbinic voice recited the law. [24]

Mysterious as the passage must be (the artist's own testament to the resources of his medium? the intimation of moral grace over the wreckage of all morality?) the sanctification of language in *God's Grace* casts a fascinating light over the resources of that gnarled diction that is both Malamud's primary "signature" and, I suspect, the basis for most of those small miracles that illuminate his often forbidding fictional universe. One thinks of Frank Alpine's fractured tongue — half poetry, half grunt — or the fugal duet that blends Iris Lemon's discourses on heroism with Roy Hobbs's tuneless responses. But mostly one repairs to that strange and frustratingly unanalyzable blend of Yiddish fabulist, cynical realist, and fantasist of despair that is the voice of Malamud and only his: a miraculous verbal acrobat who can persuade us of the hopelessness of hope at the very same time he whispers, confidentially, that here too is redemption.

For chimps too? Perhaps — but not in the clear light of day; for language does not, in the end, save Cohn's apes from their own bestiality. And so when Cohn cuts the wires that made speech possible for Buz, he does so with the understanding that the chimp, in his betrayal of the father, had in fact failed language itself — or rather the moral force that is hidden within it. Or perhaps it is the case that the language Buz spoke was one of several and that not all can satisfy the transcendental longings of the evolving heart. Despite all his talk of Christianity, Buz in fact is primarily concerned with the language of power and rationality. From his first father, Dr. Bünder, he has inherited a "rectilinear" view of reality. Significantly, he willingly accepts the teachings of Cohn the scientist but rejects the homilies of the former rabbinical student. In this area it is George the gorilla who is Cohn's true disciple; and this is the reason why Buz attempts to incorporate those teachings by literally devouring the pages of scientific texts and dictionaries, while George attempts to eat the record of Cohn's father singing the "Kol Nidre."

The theme of "incorporation" is a peculiar and a large one in the novel, and it seems to be based on an ecological ethic that sounds like an updated version of Old Testamental dietary strictures. Cohn is a fructivor, as is George; Buz, who dislikes the taste of matzo — "the bread of affliction" — hungers for cans of sardines and tuna. Needless to say, cannibalism (or at the least the consumption of a closely related species) is tantamount to the complete rejection of the other, and so it has close connections with the chimps' incapacity to meet the moral demands implicit in language. But the truth is that the apes are not only unable to extend recognition or acceptance to baboons or gorillas; they are also sadly deficient in even the rudiments of biofilial affection. They waste fruit, denude trees, feel nothing at all for the flowers that grace their island. The same egocentrism that was once a symbol of man's unworthiness and eventual self-slaughter is also theirs, made crystal clear in the final pages when Buz, replacing Cohn as the island's prophet, harangues his fellows with the bellicose chant of "Blessed are the chimpanzees . . . for they hov inherited the whole earth."[25]

Buz's martial cry of ape supremacy (a dismal hint of the bloody future awaiting primate evolution) will recall the reader to the historical or mythological parallels that form the background of *God's Grace*, and that eventuate in the Akedah of Isaac, the true climax of the novel. Early on in the novel, the story of Abraham's sacrifice was shown to be Buz's favorite; even as a child he demanded that Cohn relate it over and over again (which prompts Cohn at one point to remark that "the story one heard most probably became the one he would live out"[26] — a prophecy that does its bit to endow events with a sure sense of fatality).

The free retelling of the Akedah, however, is only the major piece in an oblique rendition of the central events of *Genesis* — so skewed a rendition that at times it may seem to be a travesty of the original: Noah's rainbow, for instance, appears to Cohn with a "wedge-shaped section of its arch . . . broken off, as though a triangular mouth had taken a colorful bite."[27] At another point, a sound of whirring wings is heard above the drifting ship, but when the jubilant Cohn looks up, either to behold a bird or "a resplendent angel," he sees instead "a piece of torn blue sky shaped like a hand."[28] And so it goes — tokens of celestial intervention undercut, even as they appear, by anarchic or satiric counters.

But is there really a purpose at work? An answer at this point would be premature, but it is probably wise to state at once that the answer will never be clear. "Yes, no, or maybe" are the possibilities Cohn finds in Buz's last communication, a ringing "poong" from the severed ends of his artificial larynx,[29] which is not a bad rendering of the reader's own puzzled reaction to the novel's final intent. Yet the signs of at least a potential and assuredly mysterious design are certainly present. If no angel or ram appears to save Cohn-Isaac from the knife or the flames, there is still an unaccountable beggar with *seven* fingers who holds up the march to the sacrificial altar long enough to request a blessing *from* the victim. Heaven sent? Pure delirium? It is not possible to say with any conviction. Yet in conjunction with the beggar's grotesque hand, one might recall (along with the shrunken hand sign at the novel's beginning) the seven-branched menorah signifying the completion of the Days of Creation. Cohn's first night on the island, we should remember, is spent in the crook of a candelabrum tree. And why forget the evening when George the gorilla, suffering a cold, sneezed seven times and earned from

Cohn a single blessing? Far-fetched, to be sure; and equally far-fetched are those occasional appearances of the Lord, usually in his "Justice Seat," with now and then an angelic messenger thrown in, who offers Cohn commentaries — usually unclear, rarely reassuring — on the proceedings. (God stops speaking directly to Cohn after the institution of the Laws or Commandments — perhaps a parallel to the Talmudic notion that the Age of the Prophets, when God and man spoke "face to face," ended with Moses.) Or there are signs, typically susceptible of multiple interpretations, which serve to leaven Cohn's doubts even as they raise clashing perspectives on the possible nature of God: sometimes a cruel figure "in a butcher's cap," sometimes a rather "absent-minded" muddler, at other times a "breaker of covenants," and sometimes a pure and transcendent mystery.

To some large degree, any reader must emerge from this welter of possibilities (as did the critics) wondering if they had encountered an exercise in radical despair or been privy to a message of hope out of darkest history. In some respects, of course, the confusions engendered by *God's Grace* are reminiscent of the controversy that attended the publication of *A New Life* and certainly of *The Tenants*. A troubling conclusion and a troubling faith, intact, has always seemed a distinctive aspect of Malamud's manner — a quality of mind probably like that of those Chassidic sages described by Martin Buber, figures who live in a permanent state of "holy insecurity," accepting that "faith must encompass not expunge doubt."[30] Theodore Solotaroff long ago recognized that such a sensibility really accounted for the special authority of Malamud's affirmations. "It is Malamud's pessimism," Solotaroff wrote, "that allows him to make convincing the main idea that a man is not necessarily bound within his limits."[31] But having said as much, it must be added that in no other of his novels has the test of faith been so excrutiatingly problematical as it is in *God's Grace*; and perhaps it is only fitting that Malamud, his own belief flagging, should resort to a retelling of the Akedah, an act which is both "the highest symbol of faith in Judaism"[32] and one which has stretched the credulity of many believers to the breaking point.

But has his faith survived it? On a superficial level, it would seem that at least his character's faith has. In the final paragraphs, the despondent Cohn turns from the ambiguities of Buz's "poong" ("yes, no, or maybe") to discover, by the light of the flames that will eat him, his long white beard. Moreover, he realizes that God, despite His earlier injunction to "live quickly — a few deep breaths and go your way," had fulfilled at least one portion of the covenant He had made with the original Abraham: "You will be buried in a good old age." "Merciful God," cries the grateful Cohn. "I am an old man. The Lord has let me live my life out."[33]

It is small pickings of course on which to base the reclamation of the skeptic — the exchange of a white beard for the loss of humanity and, as dessert, an act of patricide upon the lone survivor. But Cohn's final enthusiasm may include other possibilities. There were, for instance, further promises made by the Lord to Abraham: one, that he would "go to his fathers in peace"; another (oh promise of promises!) that he would himself "be the father of a multitude of nations" and that there would be a "covenant between me and you and your descendents." And these pledges, albeit with noteworthy ambiguity, may be kept.

So it is here, in the opaque but always — for Malamud — revelatory drama of errant sons and suffering fathers that one must finally turn to seek out the nature of Malamud's faith. For that is actually the central and the compelling subject of *God's Grace*, the faith of the father visited upon the prodigal son — the same faith from which mankind, in an act of collective suicide, abandoned. To a remarkable degree, it has been one of the central, perhaps *the* central issue in Malamud's fiction; at times obvious, as in the use of the Fisher-King myth in *The Natural* or the Telemachian structure that underlies *The Assistant*; at other times implicitly, as in *A New Life* and *The Fixer* and *Dubin's Lives*. But in his latest novel Malamud has pulled out all the stops. The very form his stumbling faith in man has taken, the outrageous retelling of the relevant books of the *Bible*, with the sacrifice of the father as the climax, testifies as much as anything can to the particular resonance the metaphor possesses for the writer and how central it is to his quest for redemption.[34]

The major figures in this dark drama are of course Cohn the father and Buz the son. But it must be remembered that Cohn is also a rebel, from God and so from the faith of his own father, a pious rabbi and a good man, who was himself the son of a good and pious rabbi. In his younger years, Cohn had studied for the rabbinate, only to discover he had lost all interest in religion if not in God's nature or the secrets of Creation. In search of both from another perspective, by intellect if not by faith, Cohn had turned to paleology and become "proficient in reading . . . microfossilized cores" although he "could barely read the visible stars."[35]

But paleologist or not, Cohn is really far less the scientist than he is one of Malamud's "unbelieving believers," a manic-depressive *luftmensch* who, like the unforgettable Leo Finkle of "The Magic Barrel," cannot come to God in love and so cannot come to God ("He feared God more than he loved Him"[36]). For the larger part of the novel, Cohn's relationship with the Almighty is a mixed bag of rage and fear and trembling; yet the longing for the way of love and piety, the way of his father and grandfather, is always strong in him: if "not moved by his calling — he was by his father's calling."[37]

The course of Cohn's dismal adventuring as the last man on earth will in time lead him, or so the last page would indicate, back to faith and to the conviction that God had moved from his "Justice seat" and was now firmly ensconced in the "seat of Mercy." But in the process of that change, Malamud employs Cohn's pivotal relationship with Buz to sound a remarkably wide spectrum of issues, psychological, spiritual, and metaphysical. On the immediate level, the two are involved in a complex balancing act in which Cohn's yearning for a son through whom he can save the future by passing on his moral heritage collides with Buz's own mixed feelings of dependency and suppression. The collision is intensified by Cohn's jealous competition with the dead Dr. Bünder (who also craved a son) for the soul of the chimp, an issue which recapitulates the curiously "familial" tension between Judaism and Christianity. Buz's predilection for Christ, his periodic rejection of "Buz" for "Gottlob," inspires a measure of "Jewish" anxiety in Cohn, who fears that a Jewish-Christian schism on the island can bode no good.

And of course it does not. Buz persists in proclaiming the superiority of Jesus to the God of the Old Testament while Cohn grows increasingly nervous. When Cohn illustrates the nature of metaphor, for instance, by citing the concept of "God the father," Buz immediately asks, "What about God the son?" Cohn says it too is a metaphor, but Buz insists it "was the one he liked the best."[38] A related issue has to do with their dispute over the Abraham-Isaac story. For reasons Cohn cannot fully understand, Buz repeatedly requests the tale of the father who cut the throat of his son. Cohn knows that such an interpretation was commonplace in the Midrash, but his "rational" sense of God's nature and of morality prevents his accepting it: "God would not allow it," he argues, and then theorizes that "the resurrection was probably related to the resurrection of Isaac. The New Testament scribes always set the Christian unfolding carefully in the Judaic past." But to this Buz takes instant exception: "Jesus was the first," he cries.[39]

Buz's insistence on Christ's temporal priority is clearly related to the theme of rebellion, or at the least to the son's desire not only to slay the father but to appropriate his rights. The issue is not at all unlike John Irwin's discoveries in his study of Faulkner's Quentin Compson, data which led him to conclude that the younger Compson's primary drive was to become his own grandfather and thus slay the father-as-son who had in turn slain his own son.[40] Fanciful as it may sound, some such permutation seems very likely to work in Malamud's curious retelling of the Akedah, with Buz-the-son in the role of his father and Cohn reduced to a "mere" son.

At any rate, it is with the slaying of Cohn by a turbaned and sandled Buz[41] that the struggle for authority on the island is concluded — a struggle that began with their initial landing and that was symbolized in a variety of ways: from hat wearing (Buz persists in wearing Cohn's hats, albeit not his yarmulke) to such rights of primogeniture as naming. Nor has Cohn himself been without guilt in the struggle, at times displaying an unseemly and occasionally mean-spirited pride in his "special privileges." Indeed his uneasiness over Buz's Christianity often resulted in an emotional if not an "official" repression of his young charge.

But whatever Cohn's failings, and they are remarkably few, given his situation and opportunities, they are certainly undeserving of so much suffering and so ignominious an end; or, rather, undeserved if Cohn's suffering *is* gratuitous and his death ignominious. And with this, blessedly, it is surely time for the critic to declare himself and to insist that the murder which concludes *God's Grace*, as terrible as it must seem and as ambiguous as it surely is, is *not* a punishment nor a manifestation of universal indifference; not is it, as some have said, an act of pure meaninglessness. It is, instead, a ritual of immolation and so intended; not a murder but the first step in that process of atonement and self-creation which is, as Malamud clearly recognized, central to the biblical depiction of human history and rebirth. There also seems little doubt that he had in mind Freud's conception of a prehistoric revolt by the sons against the father, an action which in time became the basis of all morality and civilization.[42] In short, the sacrifice of Cohn-Isaac-Abraham has powerful affirmative sanctions, and in keeping with that fact there are several touches of a Divine presence in the scene, not the least of which is that God, or His emissary, refuses to lay the full weight of responsibility on the chimpanzee. Buz certainly aimed at Cohn's throat with his stone knife, but to the astonishment of both "Blood . . . spurted forth an instant before the knife touched Cohn's flesh."[43]

But in having said as much, it must be added that Malamud has complicated the matter inordinately by undercutting the traditional basis (although not Freud's) for viewing the Akedah from a standpoint of reasonable hope; instead he has denied the biblical version of the story in favor of a medieval one, for the dreadful rendition (it is Buz's, after all) that Isaac was not spared by God. In doing so, and yet in retaining a structure of affirmation, it must be clear that Malamud, his faith in Western values never so low, has rejected as well the possibility of a humanistic perspective. For it is surely only from a perspective of "total faith" that such an interpretation *can* be accepted: a perspective which discovers the abnegation of rationality in God's command to slay the beloved son, and yet makes possible total submission through a state in which "all men's values are cancelled and cast aside for reverence and love of God."[44] It is the same perspective which Kierkegaard arrived at in his study of the Abraham-Isaac story (surely a further influence),[45] and it seems to speak directly to the state of being animating Cohn's own acceptance of his final fate. In the end he goes to his death with none of the rational or humanistic arguments he had laid before God through most of the novel. Like Abraham himself, he could quarrel with God over his announced intention to destroy Sodom, and yet a few chapters later march without pause toward the slaughtering stone on Mount Moriah. Cohn's behavior also suggests that the God of the Covenant, the God in whose likeness man is made, has His other side as well. He embodies a transcendental Mystery, a Force which may even appear demonic, break the covenant at will, and plunge the world into immitigable woe. In the presence of such a Mystery man can only surrender in silence.

Both versions of the Divine appear to Calvin Cohn. On the one hand, there is the Covenantal God who speaks to our hero in a comradely voice that teeters toward a Yiddish accent and rights itself on stilts: "That you went on living, Mr. Cohn, I regret to say, was no more than a marginal error. Such things may happen."[46] It is to this God that Cohn addresses admonitions in the grand manner of those Hebrew prophets, saints and sages who were never loath to point out to the Source Itself His palpable errors: "After Your first Holocaust You promised no further Floods. 'Never again shall there be a Flood to destroy the earth.' That was Your Covenant with Noah and all living creatures. Instead, You turned the water on again. Everyone who wasn't consumed in fire is drowned in a bitter water, and a Second Flood covers the earth."[47] Cohn's squabbles with the Almighty are perhaps the most charming element in the novel, speaking at once for man's legitimate grievance with the scheme of things and suggesting at the same time that curious closeness to God so central to Jewish experience over the millennia — an intimacy Malamud has on several occasions in the past shown a particular knack for dramatizing. But the God here addressed and reprimanded, the omnipotent but now and then erring Father writ large, is hardly the entire picture. The dialogue between Cohn and God bears in truth a heavy freight of anxiety, as if the same God who limits Himself in order to be present for Cohn's apprehension (and to allow man to participate in his own creation) is also prepared to withdraw into His own transcendent and incomprehensible nature. This is The Lord, and He too speaks, but only to warn Cohn not to "presume on Me a visible face . . . I am not that kind."[48] Indeed, the anthropomorphic God, the one-time "tribal God" willing to debate the rightness of His acts with a human being, gives way finally to an utterly different and perhaps a "newer" God (the One who told Moses to announce His presence to the Israelites as "I will be has sent me"?). In a final appearance, it is just this manifestation of the Divine who thunders at the argumentative Cohn, "Who are you / to understand / the Lord's intention? / How can I explain / my mystery / to your mind? / Can a cripple ascend / a flaming of stars?"[49] And it is to this Force that Cohn submits, going to his sacrifice without murmur and with tears of gratitude springing from his eyes.

But it is probably also the case that the two manifestations are really not mutually exclusive, or not fully so, and that their occasionally coordinate reality is deeply involved in the Judaic spirit itself. As David Hartman put it in his fascinating study of that spirit:

> . . . the biblical and rabbinic traditions contain two contrasting themes; one that emphasizes the dignity of human responsibility, intellectual adequacy, self-confidence, and covenantal mutuality with

God, and another that demands utter silence and resignation before the inscrutable transcendent will of God. The rabbinic tradition does not attempt any higher unity or integration of these opposing religious moods. It posits both and does not explain whether they complement each other. The respective weight that a Jew gives to either of them is not prescribed in advance. Which of the two elements will play a dominant role in one's spiritual appreciation of Judaism is not dictated by the texts themselves. Selection and emphasis remain the responsibility of the reader.[50]

Cohn selects submission to the "inscrutable" God, yet he goes to his death confident of the reality of God's grace. It is a confidence which the reader can share, as he can also share in the certainty that the spiritual values symbolized by Judaism — and they are for Malamud always a *particular* form of the truth of the heart and not a unique one — will remain. But beyond that, it is also the case that both the values and God's own grace as well must be seen in a new light, that the very logic of the novel demands that acceptance be accompanied by an end to anthropomorphism. The values live but man is gone, and this must be a reflection either of Malamud's comprehension of a spiritual dynamic operating in the universe which has no exclusive relationship to man as man, or that the novel is indeed pure fable or "hairy" allegory. But to read the work from this narrow latter perspective is a mistake. *God's Grace* is inhabited not just by apes but by a God beyond the limits of a purely human covenant, and in being so it is also a tribute to a spiritually evolving universe calling forth a theocentric rather than an anthropocentric impulse.

And that is why, finally, the last paragraph exists and that the death of Cohn is attended by a new but not a human voice that still can lift above the scene of devastation a benediction fashioned from a mingling of English — "the Lord Our God is One" — and the language of the original Covenant — "Sh'ma, Yisroel." The speaker is of course George the gorilla, "sporting a mud-stained white yarmulke he had one day found in the wood," and who from his perch in a tall tree "began a long Kaddish for Calvin Cohn."[51]

Fanciful as he no doubt is, George is not unprecedented in the canon. Along with the angel Levine, a woebegone crow, an idiot child, he too testifies to the nature of a God who in ways surpassingly problematical spreads His mercy over the suffering world and now and then drops a seed of His essence into the unlikeliest breast. (And he certainly can take his place in a tradition which finds a place for "Holy Idiots" and enduring fools.) Where George does surprise is in the enormity of his shape and substance (and his "reality" as well) — but his appearance is designed to demonstrate the possibilities of a unique creation and a continuity of spirit that can transcend species or biology. The yarmulke he wears is either Cohn's father's magically restored, or else it is Cohn's long lost black yarmulke turned white by God's own hand (a symbolic transformation that had also governed Cohn's unrealized dreams for his chimp community).

From his first appearance, George had served both Cohn and Buz — later the other chimps — as an ongoing and ambiguous test. Like Roy Hobbs in his reaction to Iris Lemon, or Cronin to his prostitute-student, George (who smells of a mingling of sweat and mint, garlic and bay leaves) attracts and terrifies Cohn and simply terrifies Buz who is, in terms of Malamud's moral logic, myopic. But Cohn can and does extend "recognition," suspecting from the beginning a significant core of feeling in the immense isolato, seeing hints of a "true gentleman" and even going so far as to offer him the Elijah seat at the Seder. He further notes that George's reaction to his lectures betoken a level of responsiveness deeper than that of his chimp schoolmates; that, in fact, there was a mysterious and as yet "unformed essence" at work in George: "He looked like himself plus something else he might be."[52] But I suspect that the deeper possibilities Malamud sees in George — or at least those that set him apart from the chimps — have to do with the fact that gorillas *can* cry and chimps cannot and that, further, gorilla fathers are caring fathers and chimps are not.[53]

It is this latter fact, in any case, which finally spells the difference between the gorilla and Buz. The true influence shaping George is not alone Calvin Cohn but Calvin's father — or at least those records of his father chanting his dirges and lamentations and pieties above the fruit laden tree-tops. From the first night the phonograph sounded, the Cantor's voice would bring George arunning as surely as Fay Wray's screams brought Kong; and there by the cave mouth he would crouch, rapt and breathless as the elder Cohn, "a lamentor indeed . . . sang from the pit of his belly, but with respect . . . noisely bray[ing] his passion for God, pity for the world, compassion for mankind."[54] At the end, in a direct counter to Buz's crime, Cohn and *his* father and *his* find their immortality as George finds his tongue . . . and so the message of piety and redemption is passed down without scar or break. More important still, there is now present in the dark and surely darker world to come, a voice ready to praise or to lament and a large ear open to the Voice of Law sounding above the mindless buzz of matter.

Notes

1. Bernard Malamud, *God's Grace* (New York: Avon Books, 1983), 62.

2. Helen Benedict, "Bernard Malamud: Morals and Surprises," *Antioch Review* 41 (Winter 1983):36.

3. Ibid.

4. Malamud, *God's Grace*, 6.

5. Ibid., 122–23.

6. Ibid., 147.

7. Anthony Burgess, "Saying Kaddish for Man," *Inquiry Magazine* 6 (January 1983):36–37.

8. Malamud, *God's Grace*, ii.

9. Ibid., 231.

10. Ibid., 174.

11. Ibid., 11.

12. Benedict, "Morals and Surprises," 29.

13. David Hartman, *A Living Covenant: The Innovative Spirit in Traditional Judaism* (New York: Free Press; London: Collier, Macmillan, 1985), 23.

14. Ibid., 31.

15. Malamud, *God's Grace*, 114–15.

16. Ibid., 80.

17. Ibid., 113.

18. Ibid., 148.

19. Ibid., 176.

20. Ibid., 79–80.

21. Ibid., 104.

22. Ibid., 63.

23. Ibid., 79–80.

24. Ibid., 251.

25. Ibid., 236.

26. Ibid., 98.

27. Ibid., 9.

28. Ibid., 14.

29. Ibid., 258.

30. Malcolm Diamond, *Martin Buber: Jewish Existentialist* (New York: Oxford University Press, 1960), 89.

31. Theodore Solotaroff, "Bernard Malamud's Fiction: The Old Life and the New," *Commentary* III (March 1962):198.

32. Hartman, *Living Covenant*, 115.

33. Malamud, *God's Grace*, 258.

34. As early as 1958 Malamud had suggested, in the context of an interview, that the history of Judaism might be reduced to the tale of an errant people turning from the way of their fathers and after much tribulation, seeking a final return. As he put it, ". . . first, the prophet's 'way of gentleness'; the Sins of the People, Punishment, Exile and Return . . . the primal problem of man seeking to escape the tragedy of the past" (See Joseph Wershba, "Not Horror but 'Sadness,' " New York *Post*, 14 September 1958, M2).

35. Malamud, *God's Grace*, 14.

36. Ibid., 144.

37. Ibid., 64.

38. Ibid., 79.

39. Ibid., 87.

40. John T. Irwin, *Doubling and Incest/Repetition and Revenge* (Baltimore: Johns Hopkins University Press, 1975).

41. The conception of the final scene seems to be based on an ancient illustration of the Akedah which serves as frontispiece to Shalom Spiegel's *The Last Trial*.

42. Sigmund Freud, *Totem and Taboo* (New York: Random House, 1946).

43. Malamud, *God's Grace*, 257.

44. Hartman, *Living Covenant*, 115.

45. Søren Kierkegaard, *Fear and Trembling*, trans. Walter Lowrie (Princeton: Princeton University Press), 1954.

46. Malamud, *God's Grace*, 6.

47. Ibid., 5.

48. Ibid., 4.

49. Ibid., 156–57.

50. Hartman, *Living Covenant*, 60.

51. Malamud, *God's Grace*, 258.

52. Ibid., 150.

53. Jane van Lawick-Goodall, *In The Shadow of Man* (Boston: Houghton-Mifflin, 1971), notes that aside from conception, the male chimpanzee "plays no further part in [the child's] development," and that this is "one of the major differences between human and chimpanzee societies. . . ." Dian Fossey, *Gorillas in the Mist* (Boston: Houghton-Mifflin; London: Hodder and Stoughton, 1983), 64, observes, however, that Gorilla fathers seem to have a real relationship with their offspring.

54. Malamud, *God's Grace*, 65–66.

INDEX

À rebours (Huysmans), 173
Academic satire (*A New Life*), 33–37
Adventures of Augie March, The (Bellow), 73
Aleichem, Sholom, 76, 118
Alpine, Frank (*The Assistant*), 27–28
"Altar of the Dead" (James), 161
Alter, Iska, 5, 11, 14, 75–98
Alter, Robert, 7, 14, 64, 76, 111, 113, 117, 120
American, The (James), 151
American Dream, An (Mailer), 100
"American Schlemiel Abroad: Malamud's Italian Stories and the End of American Innocence, The" (Wegelin), 139–51
American reality, 33
Animal Farm (Orwell), 207
Anna Karenina (Tolstoy), 35
Anti-Semite and Jew (Sartre), 130
Arnold, Matthew, 71
Art and Idea in the Novels of Bernard Malamud (Ducharme), 75
Art versus experience in James, 55
As I Lay Dying (Faulkner), 114
Assistant, The. See Malamud, Bernard, Works
Astro, Richard, 5
Auschwitz, 74, 117, 118, 120, 122
Austen, Jane, 109

Babel, Isaac, 70
Barthes, Ronald, 177
"Baseball à la Wagner: The Nibelung in the Polo Grounds" (Swados), 23–25
Baumbach, Jonathan, 8
Beiliss Case, 117
Bell, Daniel, 94
Bell, Pearl K., 12, 13
Bellman, Samuel, 9

Bellow, Saul, 58, 61, 70, 73, 74, 75, 98, 99, 100, 101, 102, 106, 113, 114, 126; compared with Malamud, 47; Bellow's black in *Mr. Sammler's Planet*, 55–56
Benedict, Helen, 208
Benjamin, Walter, 152
Benson, Jackson J., 5
Bergelson, David, 76
Berkman, Alexander, 44
Bernard Malamud (Hershinow), 5
Bernard Malamud (Richman), 5
"Bernard Malamud and the Jewish Movement" (Solotaroff), 7
Bernard Malamud and the Trial by Love (Cohen), 5
Bersani, Leo, 161
Bettelheim, Bruno, 131
Bicycle Thief, The (De Sica), 159
"Biographer in *Dubin's Lives*, The" (Edel), 61–64
Black Hundreds, 44, 119
Bloom, Harold, 109, 113
Bluefarb, Sam, 5, 7
Bober, Morris (*The Assistant*), 25–29
Bok, Yakov (*The Fixer*), 41–46
Bowen, Robert, 6
Briganti, Chiara, 14, 174–86
Brooks, Van Wyck, 63
Brown, Michael, 11, 120, 121, 122, 124
Broyard, Anatole, 12
Buber, Martin, 8, 213
Burgess, Anthony, 207
Burrows, David, 9

Cahan, Abraham, 74
Campbell, Joseph, 5
Camus, Albert, 116
Cancel-Ortiz, Rafael, 14
Carlyle, Thomas, 168

Cassirer, Ernst, 187
Catch 22 (Heller), 39
Chayefsky, Paddy, 40
Chagall, Marc, 26, 71
Cohen, Sandy, 5
Cohn, Calvin (*God's Grace*), 64–68
Coleridge, Samuel Taylor, 168
Confessions of Nat Turner, The (Styron), 132, 133
Conrad, Joseph, 114
Coover, Robert, 48
Crèvecoeur, J. Hector St. John, 139
"Crime as an American Way of Life" (Bell), 94
Crime and Punishment (Dostoevski), 9
Culler, Jonathan, 108

da Vinci, Leonardo, 63
Daisy Miller (James), 153
Darkness at Noon (Koestler), 44
Dangling Man, The (Bellow), 108n1
David Copperfield (Dickens), 61
de Sade, Marquis, 101, 106
de Saussure, Ferdinand, 187
Deemer, Charles, 13
Deer Park, The (Mailer), 100
Dickstein, Morris, 10, 51–57
Dostoevski, Feodor M., 9, 95, 114, 115, 118
Doubling and Incest/Repetition and Revenge (Irwin), 214
Dubin, William (*Dubin's Lives*), 61–64
Dublin's Lives. See Malamud, Bernard, Works
Ducharme, Robert, 5, 12
Dupee, F. W., 37–41

"Ecco la chiave! Malamud's Italy as the Land of Copies" (Fink), 151–65
Edel, Leon, 13, 61–64
Eliot, T. S., 59
Elizabeth and Essex (Strachey), 64
Elliott, George P., 6, 41–46
Emerson, Ralph Waldo, 113

Fabe, Marilyn Michele, 2, 9
"Fantasist of the Ordinary" (Kazin), 25–29
"Fantasy and Reality" (Goodheart), 33–37
Faulkner, William, 126, 215
Fellini, Federico, 155
Fictionalized biography, 2
Fidelman, Arthur (*Pictures of Fidelman*), 47–51
Fiedler, Leslie, 6, 29, 38, 76, 153

Field, Joyce, 4
Field, Leslie, 4, 5
Fields, James T., 59
Fink, Guido, 9, 151–65
Fitzgerald, F. Scott, 25, 140
Fixer, The. See Malamud, Bernard, Works
Flaubert, Gustave, 109
Foff, Arthur, 6, 29–33
Foregrounding, 168
Formlessness of American Heroes, 158
Frank, Katherine, 13
Freud, Sigmund, 63, 186, 187
Friedman, Melvin J., 14
Fuchs, Daniel, 3

Gide, André, 12, 74
Gilman, Richards, 13
Go Down, Moses (Faulkner), 127
God's Grace. See Malamud, Bernard, Works
Gold, Herbert, 6
Golden Bowl, The (James), 38
Golding, William, 137
Golin, Rita K., 14
Good Man's Dilemma, The: Social Criticism in the Fiction of Bernard Malamud (Alter), 5
"Good Man's Dilemma, The: *The Natural, The Assistant,* and American Materialism" (Alter), 75–98
Goodall, Jane. *See* van Lawick-Goodall
Goodbye, Columbus (Roth), 106
Goodheart, Eugene, 33–37
Gothic in American Fiction, 38
Graw, Joseph, 4
Great Depression, 23, 38, 39
Grebstein, Norman, 7
Greenfeld, Josh, 12
Gross, Evelyn Avery, 11
Gulliver's Travels (Swift), 204
Gunn, Giles B., 7

Habich, Robert D., 4
Halakhic Man (Soloveitchik), 203
Handy, W. J., 5, 10
Hartenfels, James, 44
Hartman, David, 216–17
Hassan, Ihab, 5
Hawthorne, Nathaniel, 31, 140, 152; response to Rome, 142
Hays, Peter L., 5
Hegel, G. W. F., 126
Heidegger, Martin, 126
Heller, Joseph, 75

Hemingway, Ernest, 114, 140
Henderson the Rain King (Bellow), 113
Hentoff, Nat, 2, 9
Hergt, Tobias, 11
Hershinow, Sheldon, 5
Herzog (Bellow), 61
Hicks, Granville, 29
Hill, Douglas, 13
Historical atrocity, 121
Hobbs, Roy (*The Natural*), 23–25, 75–98
Holocaust experience, influence of 11, 115–25
Howe, Irving, 106
Howells, William Dean, 140
Hoyt, Thomas Alva, 8
Huysmans, Joris Karl, 171, 173
Hyman, Stanley Edgar, 76

Idiots First. See Malamud, Bernard, Works
Innocents Abroad (Twain), 151, 160
International novel, 139, 146
International stories, 139
Irwin, John, 215
Italian stories, 9, 153, 155, 156
Italy, myth and reality of, 154

Jackson, Katherine Gaus, 12
James, Henry, 9, 38, 41, 139, 140, 141, 148, 151, 152, 153, 161; compared with Malamud, 141
Japanese translations of Malamud's work, 74
Jewish anti-Semitism, 112
Jewish humor, 115n5
Jewish imagination in American literature, 29, 51
Jewishness as suffering, 26, 162
Jewishness in Malamud's work, 29, 42, 45, 46
Job, 115
"Journey of the Magi, The" (T. S. Eliot), 59
Joyce, James, 2, 12

Kafka, Franz, 2, 12
Kalki (Vidal), 68
Kazin, Alfred, 6, 25–29, 30, 70–71, 75, 166
Kegan, Robert, 8
Kellman, Steven, G., 10, 165–75
Kennedy, J. Gerald, 9, 108
Kierkegaard, Søren, 10, 126, 216
King Lear (Shakespeare), 168
Klein, Marcus, 75

Knopp, Josephine Zadovsky, 76, 90
Koestler, Arthur, 118
Korg, Jacob, 12
Kosinski, Jerzy, 98, 99
Kosofsky, Rita, 4
Kristeva, Julia, 188, 202n6
Kubla Khan (Coleridge), 168
Kumar, Shiv, P., 7

La Dolce Vita (Fellini), 155
Lacan, Jaques, 10, 186–203, 201n2
"Lamed Vov" legend, 8
Landress, Tom, 13
Langer, Lawrence L., 11, 115–25
Lardner, Ring, 5
Lawrence, D. H., 179; on voyeurism, 180, 183, 184, 200
Lawrence, T. E., 168
Lazarus (Hartenfels), 44
Lear, Norman, 9
Lehmann-Haupt, Christopher, 13–14
Lesser, Harry (*The Tenants*), 51–57
Lie Down in Darkness (Styron), 114
Literary exorcism, 109
Literary tragedy, 121
Little Boy in Search of God, A (Singer, I. B.), 203
Living Covenant, A (Hartman), 220
Lolita (Nabokov), 114
Long Work, Short Life (Malamud), 3
Look Homeward Angel (Wolfe), 114
Lord of the Flies (Golding), 125, 204, 207
Love and Death in the American Novel (Fiedler), 37
Lukács, George, 125, 126, 130, 131, 134
Luria, Isaac, 8

McCarthy, Mary, 33
Madonna of the Future, The (James), 9, 152, 158
Magic Barrel, The. See Malamud, Bernard, Works
Mahler, Alma, 2, 12
Mailer, Norman, 75, 99, 106
Malamud, Bernard
    BIBLIOGRAPHIES ON:
    Bernard Malamud: An Annotated Checklist (Kosofsky), 4; *Bernard Malamud: A Bibliographical Survey* (Habich), 4; *Bernard Malamud: A Reference Guide* (Salzberg), 14; "A Comprehensive Checklist of Malamud Criticism" (Risty), 4
    BIOGRAPHICAL SOURCES: 3, 4, 17n18

ESSAY COLLECTIONS ON:
Bernard Malamud: A Collection of Critical Essays (Field), 4; *Bernard Malamud and His Critics* (Field), 4; *Fiction of Bernard Malamud, The* (Astro and Benson), 4

TOPICS AND THEMES:
aggression in works, 14, 63; Akedah story, 8, 212, 216, 220n41; American dream, 11, 76, 82; American romance tradition, 8; archetypal patterns, 76; Chasidic manner of work, 213; Chasidic vision, 8; conflict between art and life, 2, 4; Emersonian self-reliance, 9; eternal feminine in works, 159; existential approach to work, 9; existentialism, 17; fate and freedom, 2; folk figures, 7; grail and vegetation myths, 8; Hebraism and Hellinism, 7; Hebraism of "Strictness of Conscience," 71; Holocaust experience, influence of, 11, 115–25; intertextual approaches, 9; imagination of disaster, 70; Italian stories, 9, 153, 155, 156; international theme, 9; Jamesian motifs, 141; Jewish-American writer, 76; Jewish and Christian motifs, 7, 14; Jewish and Gentile stereotypes, 9, 28, 98; Jewish characters, 4, 32; Jewishness of work, 4, 42; Jungian archetypes, 8; Kafkaesque elements, 10; "Lamed Vov" legend, 8; lyrical realism, 75; Marxian assumptions in work, 8; *mentshlekhkayt*, 76; moral ambiguity, 52; moral and religious sensibility, 7; moral realism, 31; mourning, 1; myth and archetype, 7; names, 164n35, pastoral mode, 8; philosphy of composition, 4; psychological and oneiric approaches to, 7, 9; quarrel with God, 2; rebirth and renewal theme, 56; redemption and transformation, 2; self-creation of characters, 174; self-referential, 15; snow as symbol in works, 136; social criticism, 75–98; symbolic Jews, 6; symbolically entombed heroes, 157; suffering, 115–25; treatment of characters, 17n5; vocation and identity, 178–79; Whitmanesque vision, 8; women as antagonists, 174; Women, treatment of, 14; Yiddish-English idiom, 7, 60; *see also* WORKS–NOVELS

WORKS–COLLECTIONS
Idiots First, 9, 37–41, 52
Magic Barrel, The, 1, 2, 6, 29–33, 39, 71
Rembrandt's Hat, 7, 56–61
Stories of Bernard Malamud, The, 68–74

WORKS–NOVELS
The Assistant, 1, 5, 8, 54, 71, 75–98, 98–99, 100, 101, 102, 105, 107, 119, 120; American dream, 86, 90; anti-Semitism, 121; Bober family as moral repository, 86; double theme, 9; fantasy, 36; Frank Alpine's redemption, 100; Jewish and Italian self-immolation, 73; as morality story, 26; Morris Bober as imaginary Jew, 106; Morris Bober's ethical beliefs, 90–91; redemption, 99; snow as symbol, 136, 137
Dubin's Lives, 2, 5, 113, 162, 174–86, 186–203; androgynous language, 200; biographer as voyeur, 179; D. H. Lawrence on voyeurism, 180; Dubin as narcissist, 182; images of voyeurism, 179; imcompleteness of the biographer, 62; Lawrentian themes, 14; Oedipal fantasy, 192–93; Oedipal structure, 186–203; parable of the biographer's dilemma, 64; past, 181–82
Fixer, The, 1, 7, 8, 41–46, 48, 52, 76, 101, 103, 105, 117, 118, 119, 120, 121, 125–39; anti-Semitism, 46; Jewish "blood ritual," 129; Jewish humor, 45
God's Grace, 2, 8, 162, 203–21; Akedah of Isaac, 212, 215; allegory and animal fable, 14; binding of Isaac, 65, 66; Cohn as second Noah, 204; comic use of Old Testament, 204; covenantal God, 127; fantasy, 66; "incorporation" as theme, 211; language, 210; Malamud's faith, 14, 214; nature of God, 66; postapocalyptic fantasy, 64–68; sacrifice of Isaac (Christian tradition), 66; seven admonitions, 67
Natural, The, 1, 5, 8, 23–25, 64–65, 71, 75–98; American Dream, 78; baseball folklore and mythology, 23, 25; Black Sox scandal, 78; epic and tragedy, 5, 24; Horatio Alger archtype, 77; rags-

to-riches mythology, 79; style, 24
New Life, A, 8, 9, 33–37, 48, 61,
  174–86, 212; academic satire, 33–37;
  pastoral romance, 35; photography as
  voyeuristic aggression, 178; schlemiel
  figure, 35; voyeur, 35, 176
Pictures of Fidelman; An Exhibition, 1,
  5, 47–51, 53, 73, 102, 141; allegory
  of the artistic and moral life, 49;
  artist manqué, 142; "Glass-Blower of
  Venice," 50, 146, 159; hero as homosexual, 103–4; Hogarthian element,
  49; "Last Mohican, The," 102–3, 142,
  153, 157; literary references as game,
  161; as masochistic comedy, 52–53;
  "Naked Nude," 50, 144, 145, 160;
  "Pictures of the Artist" 102, 148;
  "Pimp's Revenge, A," 50, 145, 147,
  152, 158; psychological action, 147;
  salvation, 50–51; stealing as a motif,
  144; stealing as an artistic norm, 160;
  "Still Life," 9, 47, 103, 143, 144, 147
Tenants, The, 8, 68, 76, 162, 165–73,
  212; art versus experience, 55; compared with *Rabbit Redux* (Updike),
  166; Harry Lesser compared to Des
  Esseintes (*À rebours*), 173; Flaubertian influence, 170; Levenspiel as
  reality principle, 171; literary allusions, 167; meditation on time, 56;
  metaliterature, 169; rebirth, 170;
  review of, 51–57; ruined manuscript
  device, 55; self-reflexive novel, 10;
  Willie Spearmint as writer, 169
Tribe, The (unfinished), 2

WORKS—STORIES
"Alma Redeemed," 2, 12
"Angel Levine," 32, 66
"Behold the Key," 141, 152–54, 156
"Black Is My Favorite Color," 40
"Death of Me, The," 41, 69
"German Refugee, The," 41, 69
"Girl of My Dreams," 71
"God's Wrath," 71
"Idiots First," 2, 66, 69
"In Kew Gardens," 2, 12
"Jewbird, The," 108–15, 204
"Lady of the Lake, The," 36, 71, 122,
  141, 151, 156
"Last Mohican, The," 54, 55, 123, 128,
  142, 153, 154, 157
"Life is Better Than Death," 161
"Loan, The," 69, 122

"Lost Grave, A," 2
"Magic Barrel, The," 54, 67, 71, 73, 76
"Man in the Drawer," 59, 69, 70
"Mourners, The," 32, 71, 73, 136
"My Son the Murderer," 60, 61
"Naked Nude," 50, 144, 145, 160
"Notes from a Lady at a Dinner Party,"
  59
"Rembrandt's Hat," 57–61
"Silver, Crown, The," 57, 58
"Still Life," 9, 47, 103, 143, 144
"Take Pity," 2, 69, 72
"Talking Horse," 2, 58, 204
Uncollected stories, 15

"Malamud Hero, The: A Quest for Exist-
  ence" (Handy), 10
"Malamud's Jews and the Holocaust Expe-
  rience" (Langer), 115–25
"Malamud's Novels: Four Versions of Pasto-
  ral" (Mellard), 8
"Malamud's Quarrel with God" (Rich-
  man), 8, 203–21
Mann, Thomas, 2, 158
Manske, Eva, 11
Marble Fawn, The (Hawthorne), 152, 153,
  156
Matter of Britain, 29
Meeter, Glen, 7
Mellard, James M., 8, 10, 186–203
Melville, Herman, 78
Menschlichkeit. See Mentshlekhkayt
Mentshlekhkayt, 16n3, 76, 90–91, 121
Meras, Phyliss, 11
"Metaphor for Holocaust and Holocaust
  for Metaphor" (Brown), 120
Michaels, Leonard, 7, 57–61
Milton, John, 117
"Mirrors, Windows and Peeping Toms:
  Women as the Object of Voyeuristic
  Scrutiny in Bernard Malamud's *A New
  Life* and *Dubin's Lives*" (Briganti),
  174–86
Mr. Sammler's Planet (Bellow), 101
Mock biographies, 61
Mondello Prize, 163n14
Month of Sundays, A (Updike), 114
Moyker-Sforim, Mendele, 7
Mukařovsky, Jan, 168

Nabokov, Vladimir, 114
Naked Lunch (Burroughs), 39
National Book Award, 6, 116, 149
Natural, The. See Malamud, Bernard,

Works
"*Natural, The*: Malamud's World Ceres" (Wasserman), 8
New Life, A. See Malamud, Bernard, Works.
New York, as setting, 54
New York East Side stories, 157
Nietzsche, Friederick Wilhelm, 161
1984 (Orwell), 44
Northanger Abbey (Austen), 109

Old Man and the Sea, The (Hemingway), 114
"Old System, The" (Bellow), 108n1
Orlando (Woolf), 12, 61
Orwell, George, 44
O'Shaughnessy, Sergius, 106
Ozick, Cynthia, 10

Painted Bird, The (Kosinski), 98
Parody, 108
"Parody as Exorcism: 'The Raven' and 'The Jewbird'" (Kennedy), 108–15
Peretz, I. L., 7, 76
"Perverse Economy of Malamud's Art: A Lacanian Reading of *Dubin's Lives*" (Mellard), 186–203
Pictures of Fidelman: An Exhibition. See Malamud, Bernard, Works
Pinsker, Sanford, 7
Plague, The, (Camus), 116
Planet of the Apes (Boulle), 204
Podhoretz, Norman, 5, 6, 39, 41, 106
Poe, Edgar Allan, 108–15
Portage to San Cristobal of A. H., The (Steiner), 118
Portnoy's Complaint (Roth), 105, 106, 107
Postapocalyptic fantasy (*God's Grace*), 64–68
"Portrait of Artist as 'Escape-Goat'" (Scholes), 47–51
"Power of Positive Sex, The" (Dupee), 37–41
Powers, J. F., 39
Prague School, 168
Prison literature, 118
Prison Memoirs of an Anarchist (Berkman), 44
Proteus as modern hero, 161
"Protocols of the Elders of Zion, The," 43
Proust, Marcel, 109, 113, 114, 153, 166

Quart, Barbara Koenig, 14

Ragland-Sullivan, Ellie, 194, 202n2
"Raven, The" (Poe), 108–15
Rebels and Victims: The Fiction of Richard Wright and Bernard Malamud (Avery), 11
Rembrandt's Hat. See Malamud, Bernard, Works
Richard II (Shakespeare), 168
Richler, Mordecai, 12
Richman Sidney, 5, 8, 14, 156, 203–21
Rise of David Levinsky, The (Cahan), 74
Risty, Donald, 4
Robbe-Grillet, Alain, 12
Robinson Crusoe (Defoe), 204
Rockefeller grant, 154
Rogers, W. G., 29
Roman Spring of Mrs. Stone, The (Williams), 153
Rosenfeld, Isaac, 74
Roth, Philip, 2, 6, 9, 10, 11, 33, 70, 75, 98–108, 166, 169; compared with Malamud, 47
Rovit, Earl, 7
Ruotolo, Lucio P., 10, 125–39
Russell and Volkening, 3

"Sad Music" (Schechner), 68–74
Saint Francis, 123, 137, 143, 157
Sale, Roger, 12, 14
Salzberg, Joel, 4, 17
Samuels, Charles Thomas, 11
Sartre, Jean Paul, 107, 129, 130
Saul Bellow: Vision and Revision (Fuchs), 3
Scarlet Letter, The (Hawthorne), 114, 180
Scholes, Robert, 12, 47–51
Schneiderman, Stuart, 191
Schulz, Max F., 8
Second Stone, The (Fiedler), 153, 158
Seldes, Timothy, 3
Self-reflexive novel, 10
Shamela (Fielding), 109
Shaw, Peter, 106
Shear, Walter, 81
Shechner, Mark, 68–74
Sheres, Ita, 8
Shlemiel character, 7, 35, 52, 141, 152, 159, 160, 163n5
Shticker, Mayer, 75, 76
Siegel, Ben, 5
Singer, I. B., 71, 203; anachronism of, 52
"Sliding into English" (Michaels), 57–61
Smith, Bessie, 168
Solotaroff, Theodore, 175, 213

Soloveitchik, Rabbi Joseph B., 203
Solzhenitsyn, Aleksandr, 118
Sophie's Choice (Styron), 119
Sound and the Fury, The (Faulkner), 114
Spinoza, Baruch, 119, 132, 133, 134
Steiner, George, 118, 137
Stern, Daniel, 4
Stories of Bernard Malamud. See Malamud, Bernard, Works
Story of O, 101
Strachey, Lytton, 61, 64
"Strangers amid Ruins" (Foff), 29–33
Structuralism, 187
Styron, William, 114, 119, 131, 133, 140
Sundquist, Eric, 178, 180
Swados, Harvey, 5, 6, 23–25
Syrkin, Marie, 106, 107
Syrkin, Nahman, 107
Systematic Theology (Tillich), 125

Tanner, Tony, 12, 75, 114, 158, 164n25, 168
Tenants, The. See Malamud, Bernard, Works
"*Tenants* in the House of Fiction, The" (Kellman), 165–73
"Theological Fantasy, A" (Alter), 64–68
Thoreau, Henry David, 9, 63, 113
Time Magazine, 10
Tillich, Paul, 125, 126, 127
Tod im Venedig, Der (Mann), 158
Tolstoy, Leo, 33, 115
Torrents of Spring, The (Hemingway), 109
Tristram Shandy (Sterne), 61
Tucker, Martin, 12
Twain, Mark, 63, 113, 151, 168

Underground man, Malamud character as, 69
Universal Baseball Association (Coover), 49
Updike, John, 70, 114

Van Lawick-Goodall, Jane, 208, 221n53
Victim, The (Bellow), 107, 108n1
Vidal, Gore, 68
Vishniac, Roman, 71
Vonnegut, Jr., Kurt, compared with Malamud, 47

Wasserman, Earl, 8, 76
Wegelin, Christof, 9, 139–51
Wershba, Joseph, 4, 220n34
Weston, Jesse, 5
Wharton, Edith, 140
Whistler, James Abbot McNeill, artistic credo, 172
"White Negro, The" (Mailer), 99
Why Are We in Viet Nam? (Mailer), 166
Wiesel, Elie, 11
Williams, Tennessee, 153
Wilson, Edmund, 31
Wisse, Ruth, 7
Wolfe, Thomas, 114
Woolf, Virginia, 2, 12, 17n11, 61, 179
Wordsworth, William, 58
"Writer as Moral Activist, The" (Hershinow), 5

"Yakov Bok" (Ruotolo), 125–39
"Yakov's Ordeal" (Elliott), 41–46
Yeats, William Butler, 142